This book comes with access to more content online.
Quiz yourself, track your progress,
and score high on test day!

Register your book or ebook at
www.dummies.com/go/getaccess.

Select your product, and then follow the prompts
to validate your purchase.

You'll receive an email with your PIN and instructions.

GED® Test Prep 2025/2026

by Tim Collins, PhD

A Wiley Brand

GED® Test Prep 2025/2026 For Dummies®

Published by: **John Wiley & Sons, Inc.**, 111 River Street, Hoboken, NJ 07030-5774, www.wiley.com

For general information on our other products and services, please contact our Customer Care Department within the U.S. at 877-762-2974, outside the U.S. at 317-572-3993, or fax 317-572-4002. For technical support, please visit https://hub.wiley.com/community/support/dummies.

Wiley publishes in a variety of print and electronic formats and by print-on-demand. Some material included with standard print versions of this book may not be included in e-books or in print-on-demand. If this book refers to media that is not included in the version you purchased, you may download this material at http://booksupport.wiley.com. For more information about Wiley products, visit www.wiley.com.

Library of Congress Control Number: 2024949324

ISBN 978-1-394-28743-7 (pbk); ISBN 978-1-394-28745-1 (ebk); ISBN 978-1-394-28744-4 (ebk)

SKY10090204_110724

Contents at a Glance

Table of Contents

Introduction

Perhaps you've applied for a job and have been turned down because you don't have a high school diploma or a GED. Or maybe you were up for a promotion at work, but when your boss found out that you didn't finish high school, they said you weren't eligible for the new job. Maybe you've always wanted to go to college but couldn't even apply because the college of your choice requires a high school diploma or GED for admission. Or perhaps your kids are just about to graduate from high school and you're motivated to finish, too. Perhaps you just want to set a good example for them.

Whatever your reasons for wanting to earn a high school diploma — whether I've mentioned them here or not — this book is for you. It helps you to prepare for the computer-based GED test, which, if you pass, offers you the equivalent of a high school diploma without attending all the classes.

About This Book

If you want a high school diploma, you can always go back and finish high school the old-fashioned way. Of course, it may take you a few years, and you may have to quit your job to do it. Plus, you'd have to sit in a class with teenagers for six or so hours a day (and probably be treated like one, too). You could also try night school, but at one or two courses a year, that could take forever.

For most people, that situation doesn't sound too appealing. *GED Test Prep 2025/2026 For Dummies* presents a different solution: Earn a high school diploma and do so in the shortest time possible, without ever having to share a classroom with other people. If you don't mind preparing yourself for a series of challenging test sections that determine whether you've mastered key skills, you can get a GED diploma that's the equivalent of a high school education — and you can do so in much less than four years.

If taking the GED test to earn your diploma sounds like a great idea to you, this book is a necessary study tool. It's a fun-filled and friendly instruction manual for succeeding on the all-computerized GED test. Use this book as your first stop. It isn't a subject-matter preparation book — that is, it doesn't take you through the basics of math and then progress into algebra, geometry, and so on. It does, however, prepare you for the GED test by giving you detailed information about each section, two full-length practice tests for each section, a complete online test, and plenty of easy-to-understand answers and explanations for the test questions.

Just as important, I walk you through how to take and pass the test using a computer. Although people needing special accommodations may still have access to the old paper-and-pencil test format, for most, it's now offered only on a computer. Having basic computer knowledge is very important. Some of the question formats have changed as well, so knowing how to use the computer mouse and keyboard to answer them is also important.

A Few Assumptions

When I wrote this book, I made a few assumptions about you, dear reader. Here's who I think you are:

>> You're serious about earning your GED as quickly as you can.

>> You've made earning a GED a priority in your life because you want to advance in the workplace or move on to college.

>> You're willing to give up some activities so that you have the time to prepare, always keeping in mind your other responsibilities, too.

>> You meet your state's requirements regarding age, residency, and the length of time since leaving school that make you eligible to take the GED test. (You can find these on the GED Testing Service's website, ged.com.)

>> You have sufficient English language skills to handle the test (or sufficient Spanish language skills if you take the test in Spanish).

>> You want a fun and friendly guide that helps you achieve your goal.

If any of these descriptions sound like you, welcome aboard. I've prepared an enjoyable tour of the GED test.

Icons Used in This Book

Icons — little pictures you see in the margins of this book — highlight bits of text that you want to pay special attention to. Here's what each icon means:

TIP

Whenever I want to tell you a special trick or technique that can help you succeed on the GED test, I mark it with this icon. Keep an eye out for this guy.

REMEMBER

This icon points out information you want to burn into your brain. Think of the text with this icon as the sort of stuff you'd tear out and put on a bulletin board or your refrigerator.

TECHNICAL STUFF

This icon marks information of a highly technical nature that you can normally skip over.

WARNING

Take this icon seriously! Although the world won't end if you don't heed the advice next to this icon, the warnings are important to your success in preparing to take the GED test.

EXAMPLE

I use this icon to flag example questions that are much like what you can expect on the actual GED test. So if you just want to get familiar with the types of questions on the test, this icon is your guide.

Beyond the Book

For some helpful advice to prepare for and succeed on the GED, check out the online Cheat Sheet. Just go to www.dummies.com and type in "GED® Test Prep 2025/2026 For Dummies Cheat Sheet" in the search box.

In addition to all of the tips, study aids, and practice that this book provides, you can go online and work through three full-length practice tests. All you have to do is register by following these simple steps:

1. **Register your book or ebook at Dummies.com to get your PIN. Go to** www.dummies.com/go/getaccess.

2. **Select your product from the drop-down list on that page.**

3. **Follow the prompts to validate your product, and then check your email for a confirmation message that includes your PIN and instructions for logging in.**

If you do not receive this email within two hours, please check your spam folder before contacting us through our Technical Support website at http://support.wiley.com or by phone at 877-762-2974.

Now you're ready to go! You can come back to the practice material as often as you want. Simply log on with the username and password you created during your initial login. No need to enter the access code a second time.

Your registration is good for one year from the day you activate your PIN.

Where to Go from Here

You're ready to dive in, but where do you start? I recommend that every test-taker start with Chapters 1 to 4. These chapters will give you a complete overview of the task at hand. Then, in Chapter 4, I provide two charts that will help you figure out the fastest and most efficient way to use this book to prepare for each test. The first chart helps you evaluate your confidence level for each section of the GED and figure out the best order for you to take the tests. The second chart helps you figure out the exact sections of the book you should study for each test. For some sections of the GED, you may only need to take a couple of practice tests to know you're ready. For others, you may need all the resources in this book.

The chapters in Parts 2, 3, 4, and 5 go into detail about each of the test sections, starting with Reasoning through Language Arts, then Social Studies, Science, and finally Mathematical Reasoning. In each of those parts, you can find an introduction to the specific test section, along with question types and solving strategies, and some practice questions. When you're ready to dive into full-length practice tests that mimic the real GED test, check out Parts 6 and 7 and then check your answers with the detailed answer explanations I provide for each test section. (Just be sure to wait until *after* you take the practice test to look at the answers!) Finally, a third, complete, online-only test lets you test your knowledge under the exact same conditions as the real GED test. I have your bases covered!

1

Getting Started with the GED Test

IN THIS PART . . .

Discover how the GED test and its various sections are organized and what to expect on the test.

Get familiar with each test section's specific focus and manner of dealing with the content.

Explore the format of the online GED test, including how the questions appear on the screen and how you're expected to answer them.

Prepare for the actual test day, and find out what you should or shouldn't do on the day(s) before, the day of, and during the exam.

Chapter **1**

A Quick Glance at the GED Test

The GED test offers people without a high school diploma the opportunity to earn the equivalent of an American high school diploma without the need for full-time attendance in either day or night school. The GED test is a recognized standard that makes securing a job or starting college easier.

The GED test meets current Grade 12 standards in the United States and meets the College and Career Readiness Standards for Adult Education.

The GED test measures whether you understand what high school seniors across the country have studied before they graduate. Employers seek better-educated employees. Colleges want to make sure students are qualified. When you pass the GED test, you earn a high school equivalency diploma that can open many doors for you — perhaps doors that you don't even know exist at this point.

You may wonder why you should even bother taking the GED test and getting your GED diploma. One reason is that people with high school diplomas earn more and spend less time unemployed than people without diplomas. In a recent year, unemployment for people without a high school diploma was 5.6 percent. That dropped to 3.9 percent for individuals with a diploma or a GED certificate. Incomes were almost 25 percent higher for high school or GED graduates than for people without diplomas. On average, GED graduates earn $9,000 per year more than people without this credential. In addition, your GED can qualify you for even more education. Don't underestimate yourself! College may seem like a distant dream, but over 45 percent of my GED graduates go on to college within three years of getting their credential. Earnings increase and unemployment decreases at each level of education from associate's degree on up. Even with just some college, you can earn more, on average.

Ready to get started? This chapter gives you the basics of the GED test: How the test is administered, what the test sections look like, how to schedule the test (and whether you're eligible), and what constitutes a passing score (so you know what you need to pass).

What to Expect: The Testing Format

There are two options for taking the GED. You can take the GED at a testing center or online at home (or at another location). Either way, a computer administers the GED test. That means that all the questions appear on a computer screen, and you enter all your answers into a computer. You read, calculate, evaluate, analyze, and write everything on the computer, including making rough math calculations or outlining your essay. Instead of paper, the test centers provide you with an erasable tablet, or you can use an on-screen whiteboard.

If you know how to use a computer and are comfortable with a keyboard and a mouse, you're ahead of the game. If not, practice your keyboarding. Also, practice reading from a computer screen because reading from a screen is very different from reading printed materials. At the very least, you need to get more comfortable with computers, even if that means taking a short course at a local learning emporium. In the case of the GED test, the more familiar you are with computers, the more comfortable you'll feel taking the test.

If you have a special need, you are also covered. The GED offers accommodations so that all test-takers have a fair chance. You can indicate that you need accommodations when you open your account on ged.com, or later by updating your profile. See the sidebar, "Are Special Accommodations Available?" later in this chapter.

TIP

Throughout this book, you see references to the GED Testing Service's website, ged.com. It's a great repository of information, learning aids, and online practice tests. It's also where you sign up to take the test. If you don't have an account there, now is a good time to open one. Just go to ged.com, select Sign Up, and follow the prompts. The GED Testing Service's official app, GED & Me, offers similar features as well as a number of study aids that are available only on the app.

The GED test provides speedy, detailed feedback on your performance. When you pass (yes, I said *when* and not *if*, because I believe in you), the GED Testing Service provides both a diploma and a detailed transcript of your scores, similar to what high school graduates receive. These are now available in your online account at ged.com or on the GED & Me mobile app, generally within a day of completing the test. You then can send your transcript and diploma to an employer or college. Doing so allows employers and colleges access to a detailed outline of your scores, achievement, and demonstrated skills and abilities. This outline is also a useful tool for you to review your progress. It highlights those areas where you did well and areas where you need further work. If you have to retake the test, your score report will provide a detailed guide to what you should work on to improve your scores. Requests for additional copies of transcripts are handled online and are also available within a day.

Reviewing the Test Sections

The GED test includes the following four sections (also referred to as tests), each of which you can take separately:

>> Reasoning through Language Arts

>> Social Studies

>> Science

>> Mathematical Reasoning

You can take each of the four test sections separately, at different times, and in any order you want. You can also take some of them online at home and others at a testing center. This flexibility is one of the benefits of doing the test by computer. Because everyone is working individually on the various test sections rather than as a group, the computer-based test eliminates the need for the whole group of test-takers to work in tandem. For example, you may be working on the Mathematical Reasoning test, while your neighbor is working on the Social Studies test. Just don't look around at all your neighbors to verify this because proctors may think you're doing more than satisfying your curiosity.

The following sections offer a closer look into what the test sections cover and what you can expect.

Because the GED tests are always evolving, be sure to check out the latest and greatest about the GED program at ged.com.

Reasoning through Language Arts test

The Reasoning through Language Arts (RLA) test is one long test that covers all the literacy components of the GED test. You have 150 minutes overall. However, the test is divided into three sections: First, you have 35 minutes of reading comprehension questions, then 45 minutes for the Extended Response (essay), followed by a 10-minute break, and then another 60 minutes for grammar and language questions. Remember that the time for the Extended Response can't be used to work on the other questions in the test, nor can you use leftover time from the other sections on the Extended Response.

Here's what you can expect on the RLA test:

>> The reading component asks you to demonstrate a critical understanding of various passages.

>> The Extended Response item, also known as "the essay," examines your skills in organizing your thoughts and writing clearly. Your response will be based on one or two source text selections, drawing key elements from that material to prepare your essay.

The essay is evaluated on both your interpretation of the source texts and the quality of your writing. You type on the computer, using a tool that resembles a word processor. It has neither a spell-checker nor a grammar-checker. How well you use spelling and grammar as you write is also part of your evaluation. You'll have an erasable tablet and/or an on-screen whiteboard on which to write notes or an outline before writing your essay on the computer.

>> The grammar and language component asks you to correct errors in various kinds of texts. This includes demonstrating a command of proper grammar, punctuation, and spelling.

>> The scores from all three components will be combined into one single score for the RLA test.

The question-and-answer part of this test consists mainly of various types of multiple-choice questions and drop-down menu questions with four answer choices. You'll also see drag-and-drop questions. For details on the different question types, see Chapters 2 and 3.

The questions are based on source texts, which are materials presented to you for your response. Some of this source material is nonfiction, from science and social studies content as well as from the workplace. Only 25 percent is based on literature. Here's a breakdown of the materials:

>> **Workplace and community materials:** These include work-related letters, memos, and instructions that you may see on the job. They also include letters and documents from companies and community organizations, such as banks, hospitals, libraries, credit unions, and local governments.

- » **U.S. founding documents and documents that present part of the Great American Conversation:** These may include extracts from the Bill of Rights, the Constitution, and other historical documents. They also may include opinion pieces on relevant issues in American history and civics.

- » **Informational works:** These include documents that present information (often dry and boring information), such as the instructional manual that tells you how to set the clock on your DVD player. They also include materials that you may find in history, social studies, or science books.

- » **Literature:** These include extracts from novels and short stories.

TIP

See Chapter 5 for a more detailed overview of the RLA test. Chapters 6 and 7 give the lowdown on both the reading comprehension questions and the grammar and language questions. I devote two whole chapters (Chapters 8 and 9) to helping you with the essay. For practice, see Chapters 19 and 27 for two complete Reasoning through Language Arts tests, with answers and explanations in Chapters 20 and 28. I also provide a third, complete online-only test. Check out Chapter 2 for the format of the questions as they appear on the computer.

Social Studies test

The Social Studies test is scheduled for 70 minutes for the 50 questions. On this test, you will see standard multiple-choice questions, as well as fill-in-the-blank questions, drag-and-drop questions, and drop-down menu questions. A few questions may ask you to calculate an answer. In this case, a calculator icon will appear on your test screen, or you can bring your TI-30XS MultiView calculator if you take the test at a test center. In Chapter 3, you can see examples of these questions.

The questions are based on various kinds of source texts. About half of the questions are based on one source text, such as a graph or short reading, with one question. Other questions have a single source text as the basis for several questions. In either case, you'll need to analyze and evaluate the content presented to you as part of the question. A few questions may ask you to compare and contrast information from two different sources. The test questions evaluate your ability to use reasoning and analysis skills. The information for the source materials comes from primary and secondary sources, both text and visual. That means you need to be able to "read" and interpret tables, maps, and graphs as well as standard text materials.

The content of the Social Studies test is drawn from the following four basic areas:

- » **Civics and government:** The largest part (about 50 percent of the test) focuses on civics and government. The civics and government questions examine the development of democracy from ancient times to present day. Other topics include how civilizations change over time and respond to crises.

- » **American history:** American history makes up 20 percent of the test. It covers all topics from the pilgrims and early settlement to the Revolution, the Civil War, World Wars I and II, the Vietnam War, and current history — all of which involve the United States in one way or another.

- » **Economics:** Economics makes up about 15 percent of the test. The economics portion examines basic theories, such as supply and demand, the role of government policies in the economy, and macro- and microeconomic theory.

- » **Geography and the world:** This area also makes up 15 percent of the test. The areas with which you need to become familiar are very topical: sustainability and environmental issues, population issues, and rural and urban settlement. Other topics include cultural diversity and migration.

A good way to prepare for this test is to read as much as possible. As you prepare for the test, read articles about civics, history, economics, and geography from reliable online sources. Even reading solid news coverage can help you develop the strong reading skills you need. See Chapters 10, 11, and 12 for detailed coverage on how to prepare for the Social Studies test. Chapters 21 and 29 give you two complete Social Studies tests, with complete answers and explanations in Chapters 22 and 30. I also provide a third, complete online-only test. See Chapter 2 for the format of the questions as they appear on the computer.

Science test

The Science test is scheduled for 90 minutes. My advice for the Science test is the same as for the Reasoning through Language Arts test: Read as much as you can, especially science material. Whenever you don't understand a word or concept, look it up in a dictionary or online. The questions in the Science test assume a high school level of science vocabulary.

You don't have to be a nuclear physicist to answer the questions, but you should be familiar with the vocabulary normally understood by someone completing high school. If you work at improving your scientific vocabulary, you should have little trouble with the Science test. (*Note:* That same advice applies to all the GED test sections. Improve your vocabulary in each subject and you'll perform better.)

The Science test concentrates on two main themes:

>> Human health and living systems

>> Energy and related systems

In addition, the content of the test focuses on the following areas:

>> **Physical science:** About 40 percent of the test focuses on physics and chemistry, including topics such as conservation, transformation, and flow of energy; work, motion, and forces; and chemical properties and reactions related to living systems.

>> **Life science:** Another 40 percent of the Science test deals with life science, including biology and, more specifically, human body and health, the relationship between life functions and energy intake, ecosystems, structure and function of life, and the molecular basis for heredity and evolution.

>> **Earth and space science:** This area makes up the remaining 20 percent of this test and covers the Earth and its components, interactions between Earth's systems and living things, and astronomy (the structure and organization of the cosmos).

Go ahead and type one of the three areas of content into your favorite search engine to find material to read. You'll find links to articles and material from all different levels. Filter your choices by the level you want and need — for example, use keywords such as "scientific theories," "scientific discoveries," "scientific method," "human health," "living systems," "energy," "the universe," "organisms," and "geochemical systems" — and don't get discouraged if you can't understand technical material that one scientist wrote that only about three other scientists in the world can understand.

The questions on the Science test are in multiple-choice, fill-in-the-blank, drag-and-drop, and drop-down menu formats. As on the Social Studies test, you will read passages and interpret graphs, tables, and other visual materials. A few questions may ask you to calculate an answer. For these questions, a calculator icon will appear on your test screen, or you can use your own TI-30XS MultiView calculator if you test at a test center.

See Chapters 13, 14, and 15 for detailed coverage on how to prepare for the Science test. Chapters 23 and 31 give you two complete Science tests, with complete answers and explanations in Chapters 24 and 32. I also provide a third, complete online-only test. See Chapter 2 for the format of the questions as they appear on the computer.

Mathematical Reasoning test

The Mathematical Reasoning (Math) test checks that you have the same knowledge and understanding of mathematics as a typical high school graduate. Because the GED is designed to prepare you for both postsecondary education and employment, it has an emphasis on both workplace-related mathematics and academic mathematics. About 45 percent of the test is about quantitative problem solving, and the rest is about algebra.

The Math test consists of different question formats to be completed in 115 minutes. Because the GED test is administered on the computer, the questions take advantage of the power of the computer. Some questions will simply pose a problem for you to solve. Other questions will refer to various kinds of stimulus materials, including graphs, tables, menus, price lists, and much more. Check out Chapters 2 and 3 for more information and a sneak peek at what the questions look like on-screen.

The following are the types of questions that you'll encounter in the Math test:

>> **Multiple-choice:** Most of the questions in the Math test are multiple-choice with four answer choices.

>> **Drop-down:** This type of question is a form of multiple-choice in that you get a series of possible answers, one of which is correct. The only difference is that you see all the options at once within the text where it's to be used. For examples, see Chapters 2 and 3.

>> **Drag-and-drop:** This question type asks you to arrange information in a certain way by clicking and dragging it on your screen. For example, you may be asked to order a list of positive and negative fractions, decimals, and numbers in order from lowest to highest.

>> **Fill-in-the-blank:** In these questions, you have to provide an answer. The fill-in-the-blank questions are straightforward: You're asked for a very specific answer, such as a number or one or two words, and you type the answer into the space provided.

Some questions may be stand-alone with only one question for each stimulus. Others may have multiple questions based on a single stimulus. Each stimulus, no matter how many questions are based on it, may include text, graphs, tables, or some other representation of numeric, geometrical, or algebraic materials. Practice reading mathematical materials and become familiar with the vocabulary of mathematics. As on the Social Studies and Science tests, you will have available an on-screen calculator, or you can bring your own TI-30XS MultiView calculator. On the Math test, you are allowed to use your calculator on all but the first five questions. However, some questions can be answered more quickly using mental math or simple calculations on the whiteboard.

See Chapters 16, 17, and 18 for detailed coverage of the Math test. Chapters 25 and 33 give you two complete Math tests, with complete answers and explanations in Chapters 26 and 34. I also provide a third, complete online-only test. See Chapter 2 for the format of the questions as they appear on the computer.

It's a Date: Scheduling the Test

You book your appointment through the GED Testing Service's website, ged.com, based on available testing dates. Because a computer administers the test, you will schedule an individual appointment. Your test starts when you start and ends when the allotted time ends. If you sign up to take the test online at home, your computer and your home (or other location where you take the test) have to meet special requirements outlined when you sign up. The ged.com website will walk you through these requirements. If you sign up to take the test at a testing center, you will take the test in a computer lab, often containing no more than 15 seats; testing facilities may be located in many communities in your state.

At the time of publication of this latest edition of *GED Test Prep For Dummies,* two states — Iowa and Maine — don't offer the test. And as of this writing, six states do not allow online testing: Florida, Hawaii, Massachusetts, New York, West Virginia, and Wyoming. You can take the test in a neighboring state that allows online or nonresident testing. Just select the state you'd like to test in when you set up your online account. This information changes periodically, so be sure to check ged.com/about_test/price-and-rules for the latest information. And remember: Nearly all employers and higher education institutions nationally will accept your GED credential.

The following sections answer some questions you may have before you schedule your test date, including whether you're eligible to take the test, when you can take the test, and how to sign up to take the test.

Determining whether you're eligible

Before you schedule your test date, make sure that you meet the requirements to take the GED test. You're eligible to apply to take the GED test only if

>> **You're not currently enrolled in a high school.** If you're currently enrolled in a high school, you're expected to complete your diploma there. The purpose of the GED test is to give people who aren't in high school a chance to get an equivalent high school diploma.

>> **You're not a high school graduate.** If you're a high school graduate, you should have a diploma, which means you don't need to take the GED test.

>> **You meet state requirements regarding age, residency, and the length of time since leaving high school.** When you open your online account at ged.com, the software will screen you to ensure that you meet your state's requirements.

Knowing when you can take the test

You can take the GED test when you're eligible and prepared. You can then apply to take the GED test as soon as you want. Pick a day (or days) that works for you. If you want to take the test online at home, you must pass the GED Ready practice test before you can sign up. Even if you are taking the test at a test center, this short online test can help you determine whether you are likely to be successful. This can help you avoid wasting time and money on retests. And if you don't pass, the detailed feedback will help you find your strengths and areas for improvement.

REMEMBER

Taking all four sections of the GED test together takes about seven hours. However, the test is designed so that you can take each section when you're ready. In fact, you can take the test sections one at a time, in evenings or on weekends, depending on the individual testing center. You can also take some of the tests at a testing center and others at home. If you pass one test section, that section of the GED test is considered done, no matter how you do on the other sections. If you fail one section, you can retake that section of the test. At the time of the publication of this book, there are limits on the frequency at which you can retake the test online at home. That's why the GED Ready practice test is required — if you pass it, you will likely pass the real test.

Because the test starts when you're ready and finishes when you have used up the allocated time, you can take it alone and don't have to depend on other people. This offers great flexibility in scheduling the test, especially when testing online at home. When you sign up for the test, you can search for times and locations that suit you.

If you need special arrangements to accommodate your situation, the GED Testing Service will help arrange the test for you at a convenient time and location.

ARE SPECIAL ACCOMMODATIONS AVAILABLE?

The GED Testing Service makes every effort to ensure that all qualified people have access to the tests. If you have a special need, it can be accommodated. You shouldn't feel bad about requesting an accommodation, either. Many people do, and the most common accommodations are for vision-related issues. Remember, though, that if you request an accommodation, you will need to provide acceptable documentation.

Some of the most common vision-related issues can be solved by adjusting the size of the text or the colors on the screen when you take the test. Complete instructions are available on the Accommodations page on the GED website. If you require another kind of accommodation, you need to make your request in advance of testing. Here's what you need to do:

- Review the information and instructions at https://ged.com/about_test/accommodations/.

- At least a month before you want to take the test, go to ged.com and open an online account, or log into an existing account.

- Follow the instructions to request an accommodation. The software will walk you through the steps to request an accommodation and submit the proper documentation.

- You will need documentation of your special need from an appropriate professional. The software will give the exact requirements and instructions you can show the professional so they can provide the correct documentation.

- Complete all the proper forms, and submit them with the required documentation.

The GED Testing Service defines specific disabilities, such as the following, for which it may make special accommodations:

- Learning and cognitive disorders (LCD)

- Attention deficit/hyperactivity disorder (ADHD)

- Psychological and psychiatric disorders (EPP)

- Physical disabilities and chronic health conditions (PCH)

Taking the GED Test When English Is Your Second Language

The good news is that English doesn't have to be your first language for you to take the GED test. In the United States, the GED test is offered in English and Spanish.

TIP

If English (or Spanish) isn't your first language, you must decide whether you can read and write English or Spanish as well as or better than 40 percent of high school graduates. If so, then you can prepare for and take the test without additional language preparation. If you don't read or write English or Spanish well enough to pass, then you need to take additional classes to improve your language skills until you think you're ready. Your local community college or adult education center is the best place to get started. Your account at ged.com can also help you find local programs that will suit your needs.

Knowing What You Have to Score to Pass the GED Test

To pass, you need to score a minimum of 145 on each section of the test, and you must pass each section of the test to earn your GED diploma. If you achieve a passing score, congratulate yourself: You've scored better than at least 40 percent of today's high school graduates, and you're now a graduate of the largest virtual school in the country. And if your scores range between 165 and 174, you've reached the GED College Ready level. This means you may be able to start your college studies right away without any additional college-readiness classes. This can save you time and money. If your scores are even higher, between 175 and 200, you've reached the lofty GED College Ready + Credit level. Depending on the policies of your institution, you can qualify for college credit in each of the GED subject areas.

TIP

If you score at the College Ready or College Ready + Credit level, shop around at various colleges and universities. Some institutions may be more willing than others to waive requirements or grant credit. For example, you can start at a community college that grants credit. Then those credits will be on your transcript if you later go on to a four-year college.

There is more good news. Scores from the computer-based and online tests do not expire, so if you passed some sections years ago, you do not need to take them again. And if you took a test between 2014 and 2016 and scored below 150 but above 145, you will now get credit for passing that section of the test. (The passing score was lowered from 150 to 145 at that time.) Your transcript should have been adjusted automatically, so check your transcript at ged.com; there may be good news waiting for you.

If you discover that your score is less than 145 on any test section, start planning to retake the test(s) — and make sure you leave plenty of time for additional studying and preparing.

TIP

As soon as possible after seeing your results, check out the rules for retaking that section of the test at ged.com. Remember, you need to retake only those sections of the test that you didn't pass. Any sections you pass are completed and count toward your diploma. Furthermore, the detailed feedback you receive on your results will help you discover areas that need more work before retaking a section of the test. That information can help you determine the sections of this book to review or whether you want to sign up for a class. You can find nearby adult education centers on ged.com.

No matter what score you receive on your first round of the section, don't be afraid to retake any section that you didn't pass. After you've taken it once, you know what you need to work on, and you know exactly what to expect on test day. Just take a deep breath and get ready to prepare some more before you take your next test.

Chapter **2**

The Ins and Outs of the Computerized GED Test

The GED test is offered only on a computer, either at a testing center or online at home. Either way, the test format looks quite different from the old paper tests you may have taken. No longer do you have to fill in little circles or use a pencil or scratchpad. Now everything is paperless; even the scratchpad of previous years has been upgraded to an erasable tablet or online whiteboard. Now you enter all your answers into the computer. You use the keyboard to type your essay or the mouse to select your answer choices.

This chapter provides what you need to know for using the computer to take the GED test and explains the different formats of questions on the GED test. I even throw in a few sample questions to ensure that you understand this important information. Demonstrating how to take a test on a computer with a printed book isn't easy, but this chapter includes several screenshots of question formats and other images you need to understand to be successful. All you have to do is read and digest it. I can't promise you a banquet of information, but this chapter is at least a satisfying meal to help you prepare for the next big step on your road to the future.

Familiarizing Yourself with the Computer

When taking the computerized GED test, you have two important tools to use to answer questions: the keyboard and the mouse. The following sections examine each of them in greater depth and explain exactly how you use them to complete the GED test. Make sure that you understand the mechanics and use of the keyboard and mouse beforehand so you don't end up wasting valuable time trying to figure all of this stuff out on test day.

REMEMBER

Because bundling the book with a computer would make it very expensive, I developed a different way for you to interact with the GED test questions in this book. I present questions in a format somewhat similar to the computer screen for that type of question's format, and you mark your choice directly in the book or on an answer sheet. Then, you get to check your answer and read the answer explanation.

Typing on the keyboard

You need to have at least some familiarity with a computer keyboard. If you constantly make typing errors or aren't familiar with the keyboard, you may be in trouble. The good news is that you don't have to be a keyboarding whiz. In fact, the behind-the-scenes GED people have shown through their research that even people with minimal keyboarding skills still have adequate time to complete the test.

On the GED test, you'll use the keyboard to type your answers in the essay (Extended Response) segment in the Reasoning through Language Arts test and in the fill-in-the-blank questions on the other three tests. These answers can include words, phrases, and numbers. Although you may be familiar with typing by using one or two fingers on your smartphone or tablet, with the screen often predicting and suggesting (correctly spelled) words that you need, the word processor on the GED test for the Extended Response has a bare minimum of features. It accepts keyboard entries, cuts, pastes, and copies and lets you redo and undo changes, but no more. It doesn't have a grammar-checker or a spell-checker, so be careful with your keyboarding because spelling and grammatical errors are just that — errors.

TIP

The GED test uses the standard English keyboard (see Figure 2-1), so if you're not familiar with it, take time to acquaint yourself with it before you take the GED test. If you're used to other language keyboards, you will find that the English keyboard has some letters and punctuation that appear in different places. Before test day, practice using the English keyboard so that the differences in the keyboard don't throw you off the day of the test. You won't have time to figure out the keyboard while the clock is ticking.

FIGURE 2-1: An example of a standard English keyboard.

© John Wiley & Sons, Inc.

EXAMPLE

To complete the test in the required time, you should have

(A) comfortable running shoes.

(B) minimal keyboarding skills.

(C) really strong thumbs.

(D) lots of coffee at your desk.

Choice (B) is the correct answer. In preliminary testing, the GED test-makers and bigwigs found that test-takers with minimal keyboarding skills were able to complete the test in the time allotted. That doesn't mean that working on your keyboarding skills is a waste of time. The better these skills are, the faster you can type in answers, and the more time you'll have for the difficult questions.

You may want to wear comfortable running shoes, as Choice (A) suggests, but that in itself won't help you finish the test in the allotted time, although it may make you more comfortable sitting for all those hours. Choice (C) would be useful if you submitted your answers by texting, but on the computerized GED test, you have to use a traditional keyboard, which requires the use of your fingers and knowing which keys are where. Choice (D) may present you with a new set of problems. Computers and liquids don't go well together, and in most cases, the test centers don't let you take liquids into the test room. If you test online at home, you are only allowed to have a glass of water on your desk — in a clear glass. No iced tea is allowed!

REMEMBER

You don't need to become a perfect typist, but you should at least be comfortable pecking away with a couple of fingers. If you want to improve your typing skills, search online in your favorite search engine using the keywords "free typing tutor." Any number of free programs can teach you basic typing skills. (Just know that some software may be free to try for a short period of time or may be loaded with ads.)

EXAMPLE

When looking at the keyboard, you have to remember that

(A) all keyboards are the same.

(B) keyboards from different countries have some letters in different locations.

(C) you should always use the space bar with your little finger.

(D) touch typists don't have to worry about where the keys are located.

Choice (B) is correct. Keyboards from different countries have letters and punctuation in different locations and could present problems to touch typists who have memorized the location of each letter so they don't have to look at the keyboard. Choices (A), (C), and (D) are wrong.

Clicking and dragging with the mouse

Most questions on the GED test require no more than the ability to use the mouse to move the cursor on your screen to point to a selection for your answer and then click on that selection, which is very basic. If you're unfamiliar with computers, take time to become familiar with the mouse, including the clickable buttons and the scroll wheel. If the mouse has a scroll wheel, you can use it to move up or down through text or images. When you hold down the left button on the mouse, it highlights text as you drag the cursor across the screen, or you can "drag and drop" questions on the screen. If you test online at home using a laptop, that computer may have a trackpad mouse (a small panel at the bottom of the screen that you touch with one or more fingers to move the pointer on-screen and click in the left or right corner). Use the instructions that come with your laptop to get familiar with a trackpad mouse. To get familiar with a traditional mouse, you can buy a wired or wireless one for a few dollars online. Make sure that it's compatible with your specific laptop.

On the GED test, you'll use the mouse to answer the four main question types: multiple-choice, fill-in-the-blank, drop-down menu, and drag-and-drop. You'll use both the mouse and the keyboard to answer the Extended Response item on the RLA test. Refer to Chapter 1 for more basics about these types of questions. Here, I simply explain how to use your computer to answer them.

EXAMPLE

On the GED tests, you indicate your choice of answer by

(A) using a pencil.

(B) tapping the screen.

(C) clicking the mouse.

(D) yelling it out.

The correct answer is Choice (C). For most questions, the mouse is your best friend because you use it to indicate the correct answer. The GED's computers don't have touch-screens. Tapping on the screen will only leave fingerprints, so Choice (B) is wrong. If you're going to use a pencil to indicate your answer (Choice A), you're taking the wrong version of the GED test, or you'll look silly trying to mark on the computer screen with a pencil. If you chose Choice (D), at a minimum, you'll be ejected from the test site for being a nuisance and a possible cheater.

Fill-in-the-blanks are another type of question you'll encounter on the GED test. They're simply statements with a blank box in the text somewhere. To answer the question, you need to enter the word(s), name, or number. The statement will be preceded by directions setting up the text, so you'll know what is expected. Here's an example.

Type the appropriate word in the box.

EXAMPLE

The fill-in-the-blank question simply consists of a statement and a sentence with a [   ] into which you type the appropriate text.

The correct answer is *box*.

REMEMBER

You must type the precise word or number required. Spelling mistakes, misplaced decimals, and even wrong capitalization count as errors.

GETTING MORE HELP WITH YOUR COMPUTER SKILLS

Some websites offer free training on basic computer skills, but you need a computer to use them. Your local library should have free computer access if you don't have your own computer. Many libraries and community agencies offer free computer classes that are worth checking out. If you're a bit computer savvy, type "basic computer skills training + free" into a search engine and follow the links until you find one that suits you. Be aware that free or limited-time trial software can be full of advertising.

Take your time at home or in the library developing your computer skills and working through the practice tests. Test day isn't the time to figure out how to use the computer. (For more information on computer skills, see the Appendix.)

Try this question: A good place to get help using a computer is

(A) your local school.
(B) the internet.
(C) libraries.
(D) all of the above.

The correct answer is Choice (D). Any place that offers instruction in using a computer is a good place to go for help.

Recognizing What the Questions Look Like on the Computer Screen

As you take the computerized GED test, you'll encounter four main types of questions to answer: multiple-choice, fill-in-the-blank, drop-down menu, and drag-and-drop.

The following sections show you what the different questions look like on the screen in the different test sections and explain how to answer these questions.

Reasoning through Language Arts test

The Reasoning through Language Arts (RLA) test puts several skills to work, including reading and comprehension, grammar and spelling, and writing skills. Most of the content for answering reading comprehension questions is in the source text itself, but for grammar and spelling, you need to know the answers from your studying.

Multiple-choice questions

Like in all the four test sections, the multiple-choice question is the most common. The basic multiple-choice question, shown in Figure 2-2, looks very similar to what you may expect. It's presented in split-screen form, with the source text on the left and the question and answer choices on the right. If the source text extends beyond one screen, you use the scroll bar on the right side of the left screen. When you're ready to answer, use the mouse to click on the appropriate answer, and then click on Next to continue.

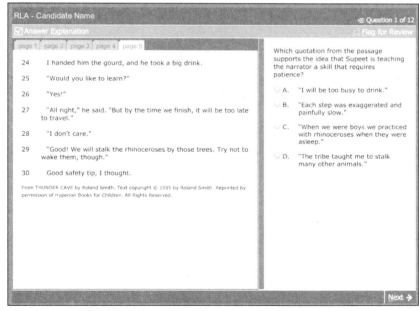

FIGURE 2-2:
An example of a standard multiple-choice question.

If a scroll bar accompanies the source text on the left side of the screen, some of the text isn't visible unless you scroll down. If that scroll bar is on the answer side, some of the answer choices may not be visible without scrolling. This is important to remember because you may miss some important text when trying to answer the question. To use the scroll bar, click on it with your cursor and then move your mouse up or down. When the text you want is visible, release the button.

EXAMPLE

The scroll bar in some questions will help you

(A) find scrolls.

(B) see the on-screen whiteboard.

(C) go on to the next question.

(D) view more text above or below what is currently on the screen.

Choice (D) is correct. The scroll bar tells you more text is available and helps you view it. It doesn't help you do anything else — not see the on-screen whiteboard, go to the next question, or find scrolls.

Sometimes the source text consists of several screen pages (see Figure 2-3). The tabs at the top of the page are your clue. They actually look like tabs on file folders. Each one opens a different page in the source text when you click on the tab. Remember that you must read all the text to be able to answer the question. Notice, too, that the question side of the screen doesn't change as you go through the tabs. Otherwise, it works the same way: read, decide on an answer, click on the matching choice, and then click on Next to continue.

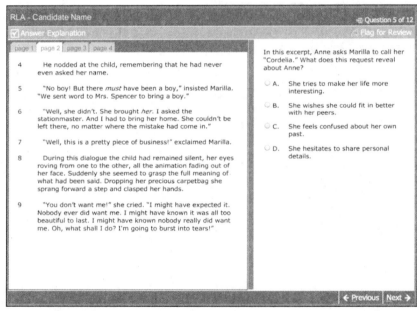

FIGURE 2-3:
An example
of a
multiple-
choice
question
with tabs.

© 2014 GED Testing Service LLC

EXAMPLE

Tabs are a very important part of the passages on the test because

(A) they give you something to do while you think about your answer.

(B) they allow you to advance to the next page of text.

(C) they allow you to move down the page of text.

(D) it's the brand name of a diet cola from yesteryear.

Choice (B) is the correct answer. If you have to advance through a passage, the tabs give you the mechanism to do so. If you choose not to use the tabs, you'll be able to read only one page of the passage. Because the answer to the question is dependent on all the material, it puts you at a major disadvantage.

Most of the questions on the test will be some form of multiple-choice, presented in the same manner as the preceding two examples.

Drag-and-drop questions

The RLA test also uses other question formats suited to computer testing. The drag-and-drop question (see Figure 2-4) is one variation. The source text, an excerpt from *Anne of Green Gables,* is on the left side of the screen.

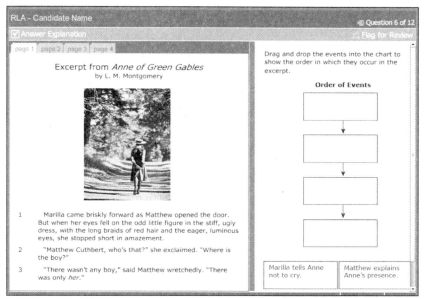

FIGURE 2-4: An example of a drag-and-drop question using boxes.

© 2014 GED Testing Service LLC

This source text covers more than one page, accessible via the tabs at the top of the screen. On the answer side, the scroll bar indicates that the content continues on, and you must scroll down to see it all (see Figure 2-5). When you scroll down, you can see the content you missed on the initial screen.

After you finish reading the content under all four tabs, drag the choices on the right into the boxes. You click on the answer choice, and without letting go of the mouse button, you drag the choice to the correct box. Let go of the mouse button, and the choice drops into the box. If you've moved it properly, it will stay where you dropped it.

Figure 2-6 shows another sample drag-and-drop question. This question uses the same four-page source text and asks you to select characteristics that apply to Anne. The key is that you can select only three of the five listed words. That isn't stated in the question but is obvious from the drag-and-drop targets, which include only three oval spaces. You have to read the text carefully to find the correct choices. When you decide which words apply, drag each word to one of the ovals and leave it there. Click on Next to continue.

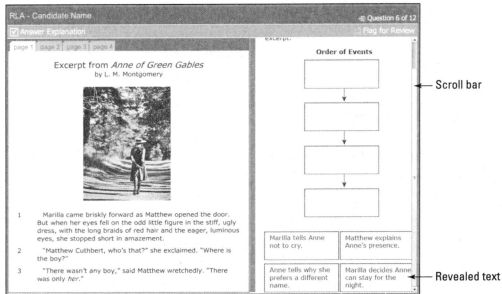

FIGURE 2-5:
Use the
scroll bar to
scroll down.

© 2014 GED Testing Service LLC

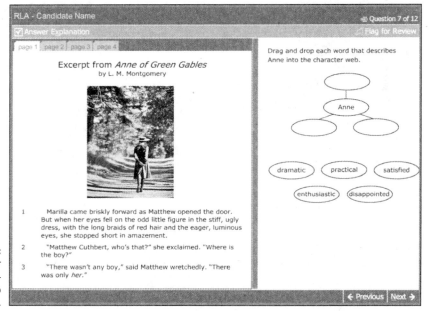

FIGURE 2-6:
Another
drag-and-
drop
example.

© 2014 GED Testing Service LLC

In this book, you clearly can't drag and drop on the practice tests, so for questions in this format, you indicate your answer by writing letters. Here is an example.

EXAMPLE

Answering a drag-and-drop question on the computer requires you to [   ] (choose three letters)

(A) use your mouse.

(B) type directly into a box.

(C) click on and move an answer choice.

(D) select more than one answer choice.

Choices (A), (C), and (D) are correct. Choice (B) is incorrect because you type an answer into a box in a fill-in-the-blank question.

Drop-down menu questions

You'll also encounter other more technologically enhanced questions. Grammar and language questions ask you to choose the answer to complete a sentence correctly. In Figure 2-7, the source text contains drop-down menus. In one line of the text, you see a blank space and the word *Select. . .* with an arrow next to it. When you click on that line, a number of variations appear. You pick the best choice as your answer. Figure 2-8 shows what you see when you click on the Select line.

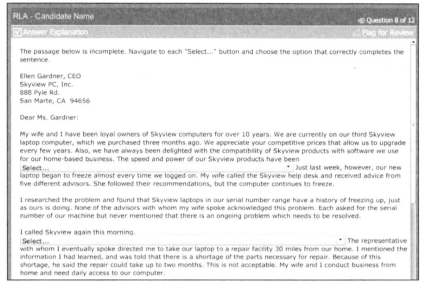

FIGURE 2-7:
An example
of a drop-
down menu
question.

© 2014 GED Testing Service LLC

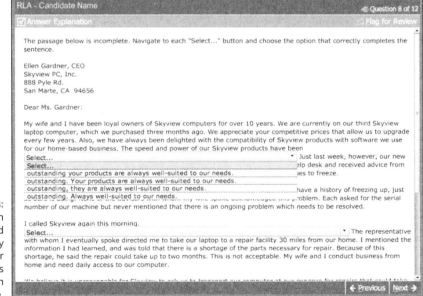

FIGURE 2-8:
Click on
Select, and
a variety
of answer
choices
appear in
that line.

© 2014 GED Testing Service LLC

From the context of the letter, you have to select the sentence that fits best and shows both correct grammar and spelling. Move the mouse to the proper choice and let go. The selected wording will appear in the space. You can now read the entire text to review and decide whether you indeed selected the appropriate choice. Figure 2-9 is a close-up of one question where the drop-down menu asks you to choose only a single correct word.

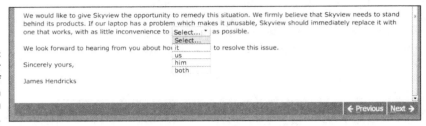

FIGURE 2-9:
Another example of a drop-down menu question.

TIP

For the purposes of this book, the drop-down menu questions look a lot like multiple-choice questions. I include a list of answer choices for you to choose from, labeled with A, B, C, and D. Just know that on the GED test, you'll have to click on Select to view the answer choices.

The Extended Response

In the Extended Response of the RLA test, you get 45 minutes to write an essay. Figure 2-10 shows an example. Note that the source material is longer than one screen. The tabs on the top of the left side indicate that this text is spread out over four pages. Be sure to read all four pages. If you test at home or at a test center, you'll have an online whiteboard for taking notes and organizing your ideas. If you test at a test center, you'll also have an erasable tablet and dry-erase pen for taking notes and organizing your ideas. Either way, nothing you write on the boards will be seen by anyone but you. Only the answer that you enter in the answer window counts.

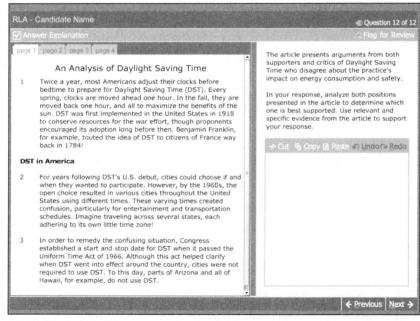

FIGURE 2-10:
A sample Reasoning through Language Arts Extended Response.

The answer window is a very limited mini word processor. In Figure 2-10, you can see that it allows you only to cut, paste, copy, redo, and undo. Since this is a writing test, it doesn't have either a grammar-checker or a spell-checker. Your brain, with its experience and knowledge, supplies those. To copy, cut, paste, or save, you move the mouse cursor to the area of the screen with the symbols for performing these tasks, and then you click on a mouse button to activate the feature (or you can use the standard keyboard shortcuts for copy, cut, and paste). You use these features if you want to quote something in your essay, to delete unwanted words or phrases, or to move something to another part of your essay.

TIP

Take a stab at writing a full-length essay in Chapter 9, in the practice tests in Chapters 19 and 27, and the included online-only test on your computer. Want to make the experience more realistic? Turn off the spell-checker and the grammar-checker in your computer's settings or use the built-in mini word processor in the included online versions of the practice tests. Time the test so you're taking it under the same conditions as the real GED test. By the time you get to the third, online-only test, you should be a whiz at writing a good essay in 45 minutes!

Social Studies test

In the Social Studies test, you encounter types of multiple-choice questions similar to those in the Reasoning through Language Arts test. The following sections give you a brief guide to the kinds of questions to expect.

Multiple-choice questions

Most questions on the Social Studies test are a variation of multiple-choice questions. You're probably most familiar with this simplest version (see Figure 2-11).

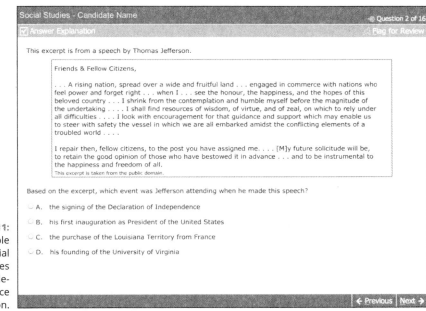

FIGURE 2-11: An example of a Social Studies multiple-choice question.

© 2014 GED Testing Service LLC

To answer this question, you click on the correct choice and then click on Next to continue. (To answer this type of question in the book, you simply mark your choice of answer on an answer sheet.)

You'll also find the multiple-choice and other questions presented as a split-screen, as in Figure 2-12. In this example, the text exceeds one page but only by a little. A scroll bar on the text side lets you scroll down to see the rest.

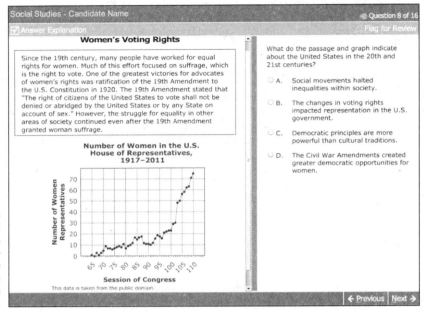

FIGURE 2-12:
A Social
Studies
multiple-
choice
question
with a
scroll bar.

© 2014 GED Testing Service LLC

Other types of Social Studies questions

The other questions on the Social Studies test are just like the ones I discuss earlier in this chapter. They include questions with source text (the materials you need to read to answer the question) spread over several pages (as in Figure 2-13). The tabs on the top left of the screen indicate more pages of text. Each page is one tab.

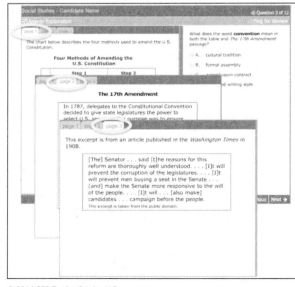

FIGURE 2-13:
An example
of a
multipage
Social
Studies
question
with source
text.

© 2014 GED Testing Service LLC

You'll also encounter fill-in-the-blank questions (as in Figure 2-14). On this type of question, you use the material presented in the passage to fill in the box. As in other subject areas, you need a specific word or number for the blank. You must be accurate; spelling mistakes are scored as an error. In this book, you write the answer on the answer sheet.

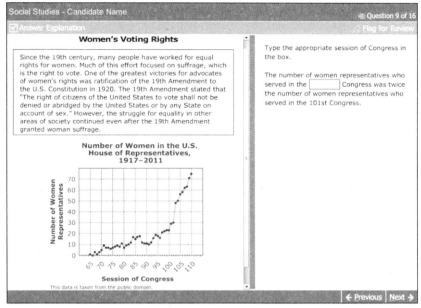

FIGURE 2-14:
A fill-in-the-blank example question.

The Social Studies test also includes drop-down menu questions and drag-and-drop questions. You answer these the same way as on the Reasoning through Language Arts test (refer to the earlier sections, "Drag-and-drop questions" and "Drop-down menu questions," for more information). Figure 2-15 is an example of a Social Studies drag-and-drop question.

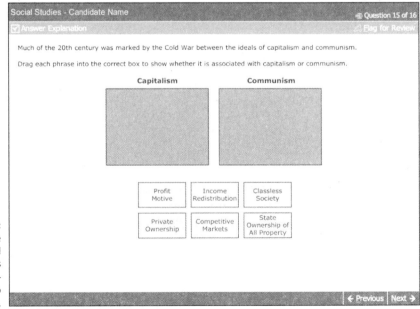

FIGURE 2-15:
An example of a Social Studies drag-and-drop question.

Science test

When you take the Science test, you have to answer a variety of the same types of questions as in the other tests. The following sections focus on the slight differences you may see on the computer screen in the different types of questions.

Multiple-choice questions

Figure 2-16 shows an example of a multiple-choice Science question. Notice that the passage is longer than one page on the computer screen. Tabs on the side can move the text up and down. Moving it down reveals the other possible answers. Always be aware of the screen size limitation, and advance pages or scroll up or down to ensure that you have all the information you need to answer the questions.

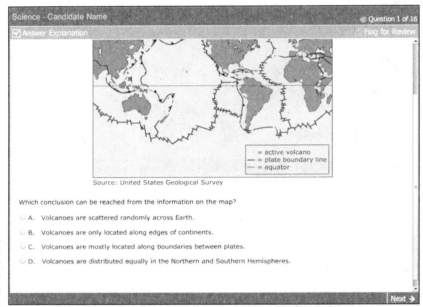

FIGURE 2-16: A sample Science multiple-choice question.

© 2014 GED Testing Service LLC

Fill-in-the-blank questions

Figure 2-17 shows an example of a fill-in-the-blank question. You see a statement or question followed by a box. You're expected to type the appropriate word(s) or number(s) into that box. In the example in Figure 2-17, the percent sign after each box indicates that you need to enter a number.

Drop-down menu questions

Questions involving a drop-down menu (see Figure 2-18) are similar to drop-down menu questions in the other sections of the GED test. They're just a variation of the multiple-choice questions. You use the mouse to expand the choices and then again to select the correct one. (In this book, you mark your answer on the answer sheet.)

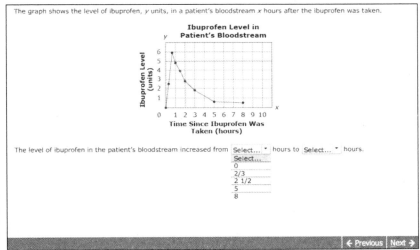

Type your answers in the boxes

A breeder of rabbits is examining the genetics of rabbit coat color. Research shows that black (C) is dominant to all other colors. Chinchilla (c^c) is dominant to Himalayan and albino. Himalayan (c^h) is dominant to albino. Albino (c) is recessive.

A homozygous black rabbit mates with a homozygous chinchilla rabbit. What is the likelihood that each offspring will be a certain color?

black [ ] %

chinchilla [ ] %

Himalayan [ ] %

albino [ ] %

FIGURE 2-17:
A sample Science fill-in-the-blank question.

© 2014 GED Testing Service LLC

The graph shows the level of ibuprofen, *y* units, in a patient's bloodstream *x* hours after the ibuprofen was taken.

Ibuprofen Level in Patient's Bloodstream

The level of ibuprofen in the patient's bloodstream increased from [Select... ▼] hours to [Select... ▼] hours.

Select...
0
2/3
2 1/2
5
8

FIGURE 2-18:
An example of a drop-down menu question.

© 2014 GED Testing Service LLC

Drag-and-drop questions

The general format of these types of questions is similar throughout all the sections of the GED test (refer to Figures 2-4 and 2-15 for examples of this question type). On the computer, you'll see spaces and a list of possible answers to use in filling the spaces. Using the mouse, you can drag the word, numbers, or phrases to their appropriate location to create an answer. (In this book, write the answers on the answer sheet provided. Always check your answers after completing each test section to make sure that you understand the material.)

Mathematical Reasoning test

Here are some of the specific test formats you'll encounter in the Mathematical Reasoning (Math) test.

Calculator

The Math test provides an on-screen calculator for you to use on all but the first five questions of the test. (If you don't see the calculator tab on the screen, then you have to do the math in your head or on the whiteboard.) When you need the calculator, simply click on the Calculator link and the calculator appears (see Figure 2-19). If you test at a testing center, you can bring your own TI-30XS MultiView calculator. The GED Testing Service's website, ged.com, has a number of resources, including a reference sheet that shows you all the features you need to know and an actual on-screen calculator you can practice with.

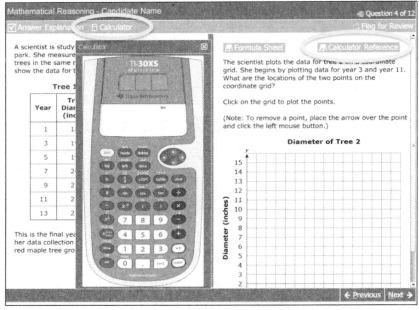

FIGURE 2-19:
The computerized GED Math test has a calculator that you can use on-screen.

© 2014 GED Testing Service LLC

Multiple-choice questions

Most of the questions in the Math test are multiple-choice. The question presents you with four possible answer choices, only one of which is correct, although the other answer choices may be close or incorporate common errors. Carefully read the question and answer choices. Answer the question using the information provided. The only exception is the list of formulas given when you click on the Formula button. You can use any of these formulas where appropriate. Figure 2-20 shows a basic example of a multiple-choice question.

On the computer, you use the mouse to select the answer. (In practice tests in this book, you mark your answer on an answer sheet. Always check your answer with the explanation.)

Sometimes multiple-choice questions appear in a split-screen with the question on the left-hand side and the possible answers on the right-hand side (see Figure 2-21). In either case, after you decide on the correct answer, you click on the appropriate answer choice with your mouse.

This particular question has some interesting buttons integrated into the format: a button to call up the calculator, one to open the formula sheet, and one for the calculator reference sheet.

FIGURE 2-20:
An example of a Math multiple-choice question.

© 2014 GED Testing Service LLC

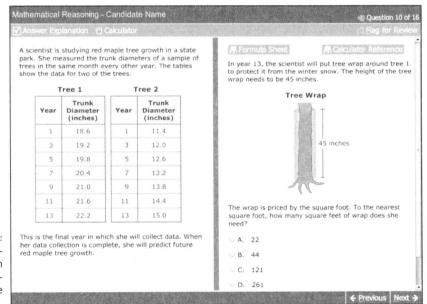

FIGURE 2-21:
A split-screen multiple-choice question.

© 2014 GED Testing Service LLC

REMEMBER

Getting familiar with the calculator reference sheet before the test can save you time during the test. But if you forget something, you can use the online calculator reference sheet to refresh your memory. Good to know if you get nervous and start to fumble with the calculator!

Fill-in-the-blank questions

These questions require that you type a numeric answer or an equation in a box provided, using the keyboard. Check out Figure 2-22. You may have to use the symbols on the keyboard or click on the Æ Symbol tab for additional symbols that you may need (see Figure 2-23).

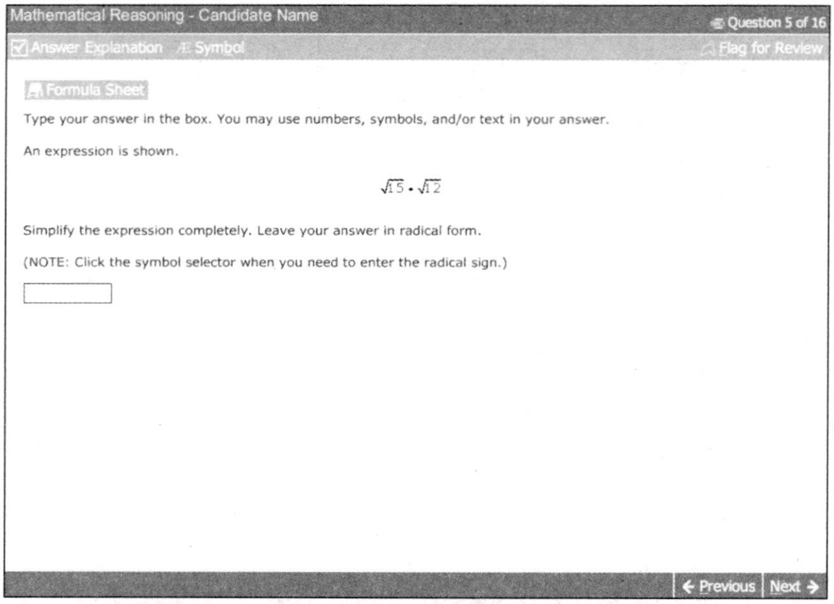

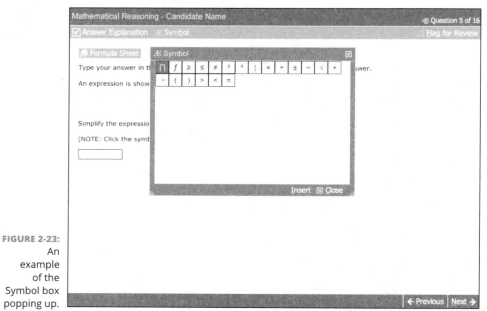

Mathematical Reasoning - Candidate Name
Question 5 of 16
Answer Explanation
Æ Symbol
Flag for Review
Formula Sheet
Type your answer in the box. You may use numbers, symbols, and/or text in your answer.
An expression is shown.
$\sqrt{15} \cdot \sqrt{12}$
Simplify the expression completely. Leave your answer in radical form.
(NOTE: Click the symbol selector when you need to enter the radical sign.)
Previous
Next

FIGURE 2-22: An example of a fill-in-the-blank question on the Math test.

© 2014 GED Testing Service LLC

Mathematical Reasoning - Candidate Name
Question 5 of 16
Answer Explanation
Æ Symbol
Flag for Review
Formula Sheet
Æ Symbol
Insert
Close
Previous
Next

FIGURE 2-23: An example of the Symbol box popping up.

© 2014 GED Testing Service LLC

After reading the question carefully, you use the keyboard and the Symbol box to type your answer in the box. To insert a symbol, place your cursor in the correct place in the answer box. Then click on the Æ Symbol tab. The Symbol box will open. In the Symbol box, click on the symbol you want and then click the Insert button in the lower-right corner of the Symbol box. The symbol will appear next to your cursor. To make the Symbol box go away, press the Close button in the lower-right corner.

Other types of questions

The Mathematical Reasoning test also has drop-down menu and drag-and-drop questions just like the other three sections of the test.

Flag for Review button

The Flag for Review button is a very useful feature on all four tests. This button allows you to mark questions for review later. You can select an answer and then press Flag for Review, or simply press Flag for Review without selecting an answer. At the end of the test, or at any time, you can go to the Review screen, which shows all the questions that are flagged or skipped. This way, you can return to these questions quickly at any time. When you complete the test, you will also be taken to this screen (as long as there is time remaining). You can continue to check your answers or complete unanswered questions until time runs out.

TIP

There is not any extra penalty for guessing on the GED, so do not leave any questions unanswered. Throughout this book, you will learn several strategies for improving your odds when guessing. But if you simply don't know or are running out of time, you have nothing to lose by selecting an answer at random for every unanswered question. Use the Review screen to help you find and answer all unanswered questions in the last few minutes of the test.

Chapter **3**

The GED Test's Four Sections and You

I t's time to start your preparation for the GED test with a look at what to expect on the four sections that comprise the GED exam — Reasoning through Language Arts, Social Studies, Science, and Mathematical Reasoning. You can take them all at once in one really long and tough day or individually whenever you feel sufficiently prepared. *Remember:* You don't have to do all the test sections on the same day. And after you pass a test section, you're finished with that section forever. You'll earn your GED diploma whenever you've completed and passed all four test sections.

In this chapter, I break down what you can expect on each section and help you prepare for answering the different question types. See Chapter 2 for examples of all the different question types and how they appear both on the actual GED test and in the practice tests in this book.

Examining the Reasoning through Language Arts Test

The Reasoning through Language Arts (RLA) test consists of a reading comprehension test, the Extended Response section (the essay), a break, and a grammar and language section.

In this section, I offer some example questions for each part of the RLA test, which show you how the questions work and what's expected of you to answer them. You'll first answer a series of reading comprehension questions, mainly multiple-choice (35 minutes). However, you'll also see questions in the form of fill-in-the-blanks, drag-and-drop questions, and drop-down menu questions. In each case, you will need to look for the answer in the text presented to you. To find the answer, you may simply have to refer to the text, or you may have to draw conclusions from what you've read and choose the best answer from the choices presented or from your understanding of the passage. After that, you will have 45 minutes to complete the Extended Response, followed by a 10-minute break. And, finally, you'll have the 60-minute grammar and language section, which consists entirely of drop-down menu questions. The total time is 150 minutes.

The reading section

On this part of the RLA test, you're given text to read, followed by a set of questions about that text, which are designed to test your ability to read and comprehend. Some questions will simply ask about content; other questions will require analysis. The information you need to answer will be right in the text you read. Some questions will ask you to draw conclusions based on the information in the text, which are the "why" or "how do you know" questions.

TIP

Here are two bits of collective wisdom: First, before taking the RLA test, read, read, and read some more. And, secondly, when taking the RLA test, read carefully; the answer is in the text. The best guarantee that you'll do well on this section is to become a fluent and analytical reader. Read editorials, analyze how the writers make their points, and provide supportive evidence of their points. Read newspaper stories to extract the bare-bones key points that make the story. Read and think about how the writer creates a mood, image, or point of view. Although you don't have to master any specific content before taking the reading portion of the RLA test, the more you read, the better equipped you'll be to deal with this.

I go into detail about the types of questions to expect on the RLA test and how to answer them in the following sections.

Multiple-choice questions

Most of the questions on the RLA test are some form of multiple-choice question, where you choose from four answers. (See Chapter 2 for how multiple-choice questions appear in this test section on the computer screen when you're taking the actual GED test.)

Multiple-choice questions give you the correct answer but make it harder by adding three wrong answer choices. For this reason, it's helpful to read the questions and answer choices first and then the text, looking for related material. Go back to the answer choices and eliminate the obviously wrong ones as you progress. Eventually, you'll be left with one or two choices from which to pick your answer.

REMEMBER

Pick the most correct, most complete answer from the choices offered. You may find, based on your previous knowledge, that none of the choices are complete. However, you need to go with the materials in the text, so use the answer choice closest to what's in the text. The best advice for completing the reading portion of the RLA test is to

(A) read, read, and read some more.

(B) memorize every poem ever written by Shakespeare.

(C) read the short versions of any famous books you can find.

(D) relax, because reading is easy.

The correct answer is Choice (A). You don't have to know any specific content for this test, but you need to be able to read quickly and accurately and understand what you've read. The only way to do that is to practice and practice and practice some more.

Here are a couple of examples of multiple-choice questions like those you'll see on the GED test.

People have a natural metabolic "set point" that is predetermined at birth and influences just how slim or heavy they will be. That is why it is difficult for the obese to lose weight beyond a particular point and for the slim to gain and retain weight for long. Some studies now suggest that the chemicals in clothing and upholstery flame-retardants interfere with that set point when they are absorbed into the body. This may affect a child in the womb and even after birth, which is one reason some jurisdictions are banning flame retardants from children's clothing. California is even considering banning them from upholstery, another common application.

Why are chemicals in upholstery potentially harmful?

(A) They can cause a disability.

(B) They interfere with the natural metabolic set point.

(C) California is considering banning them.

(D) They are ineffective in preventing fires.

The correct answer is Choice (B), which is clearly stated in the text. Choice (A) may be true, but it isn't supported by the text. Choice (C) is irrelevant to the question, and Choice (D) is wrong. Other reasons to place a ban on flame retardants should be considered, but you're not asked about them, so stick with the options offered.

Why is anyone concerned about the metabolic set point?

(A) The set point determines how much people will weigh. Anything that interferes with that is dangerous.

(B) Most people want to be slim.

(C) People don't want chemicals in their bodies.

(D) People are against the misuse of chemicals in the environment.

The correct answer is Choice (A). The text states that these chemicals interfere with the set point, and that is dangerous, causing obesity or drastic underweight. Choices (B), (C), and (D) are all possibly true but aren't supported by the text.

Drag-and-drop questions

The RLA test also uses the drag-and-drop question type. This type of question requires you to drag and drop information from one location on the screen to another. Usually, the purpose is for you to reorder something from least important to most, to place events into a sequence, or simply to select a series of answer choices that answer the question. For example, you may be asked to pick two or three words that describe a person or event in the text from a choice of four or five options. Doing so is relatively simple: You just click on the answer choice you want to move with your mouse, and then, while holding down the mouse button, you drag the answer choice to the new location. When you reach the new location, let go of the mouse button and drop the answer choice. If you've moved it properly, it will stay where you dropped it. Check out Chapter 2 to see how a drag-and-drop question looks on the actual GED test. Answering a drag-and-drop question requires you to

(A) do some heavy lifting.

(B) type an answer into a box.

(C) click on and move an answer choice.

(D) play a lot of computer games.

Choice (C) is correct. Choice (A) refers more to a job in the real world and not taking a test. Choice (B) applies to fill-in-the-blank or Extended Response questions. Choice (D) is one way to waste time that could be better spent preparing for the test. Although playing games on your computer is a good way to practice using the mouse, this answer choice doesn't answer the specific question based on the material in this section.

Here are a couple of types of drag-and-drop questions that you may encounter on the GED test.

> Bradley was determined to get the job. Although he wanted to go to the movies with Keesha, he also needed to work, and the job interview looked promising. He loved his job at the mill, but it was not enough to provide him with the income he needed. Of course, the hours were great, but the hourly rate was not. He could have left early, grabbed some lunch, gone to the interview, and still had his date with Keesha, but that would have created problems with his boss at the mill. Bradley made the only choice he could. He finished his day at the mill and then went to the job interview. Keesha waited by the phone but never heard from him.

EXAMPLE

Put the names and phrases in order of their importance to Bradley in the boxes with the most important on top and the least important at the bottom.

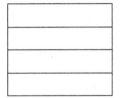

(A) Keesha

(B) job at the mill

(C) job interview

(D) lunch

Based on the text, the best order is Choice (B), *job at the mill*; Choice (C), *job interview*; Choice (A), *Keesha*; and then Choice (D), *lunch*.

EXAMPLE

Which two of these terms best apply to Bradley? Indicate your answers in the box.

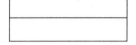

(A) friendly

(B) a good boyfriend

(C) hardworking

(D) determined

You know you need to choose two answers because the instructions state this and because there are two boxes to fill. The correct answers are *hardworking* and *determined.* The text states that "Bradley was determined to get the job." He is also hardworking. He didn't leave his current job early to go to the interview. He left his girlfriend in the lurch, not even calling her about the change in plans, so he is certainly not the best of boyfriends. He may be friendly, but that idea is not developed in the text, and so is not the answer.

In the RLA practice tests in Chapters 19 and 27, when you see a question in this format, you see the content of the boxes as words or phrases preceded by capital letters. You then can enter the letters into boxes on the answer sheet to indicate your choices.

Fill-in-the-blank questions

You're likely familiar with the fill-in-the-blank question type. It requires you to find a word, phrase, or number in the source text that answers a question and then type that text or number in a space. On the GED test, the blank that you need to fill in looks like an empty box. Just click in that box and type in your answer. For the fill-in-the-blank questions in this book, you can write your answer directly in the box or on the answer sheet for the practice tests. Refer to the source text in the previous section to answer this question.

Bradley's girlfriend is named [   ].

There is nothing fancy about fill-in-the-blank questions; they simply require good reading skills.

The grammar and language section

The grammar and language section of the RLA test evaluates your ability to use correct spelling and grammar to write clearly and succinctly. It tests your ability in various ways. Some questions ask you to select the correct alternative to a misspelled or grammatically incorrect sentence. Others ask you to provide a better wording for a sentence. The text will vary from business letters to extracts from textbooks. They can be based on instruction manuals for a phone, a newspaper story, an email, or a contract.

To study and prepare for these types of questions, try the following tips:

>> Review your spelling and grammar skills.

>> Use the local library to find high school grammar texts or look for free grammar and spelling quizzes online. Some online quizzes correct your answers immediately, giving you excellent feedback on what you know and what needs improvement. For a good review of grammar, check out www.grammar-monster.com.

>> After you take the practice tests in Chapters 19 and 27, you may see some areas where you need to improve. Fortunately, the *For Dummies* series has just the thing for you: *English Grammar For Dummies,* 3rd Edition, by Geraldine Woods (Wiley). As you work on your grammar and writing skills, periodically redo the practice tests to see how much you have improved.

Question types

All the questions in the grammar and language section use the same format: the drop-down menu question. In these questions, you select the correct answer from a number of choices. Like multiple-choice, the drop-down menu includes four answer choices.

Drop-down menu questions consist of a sentence with a box on the line containing a down arrow and the word *Select.* When you click on Select, several choices appear. You click on the best choice, and the sentence appears with your selection. *Note:* In this book, you won't see a drop-down menu but just a list of answer choices. See Chapter 2 for details on how this question format appears on-screen in the actual test.

EXAMPLE

When we got there, we discovered [Select... ▼] car was missing.

(A) their

(B) they're

(C) there

(D) they are

The correct answer is Choice (A), *their.* The words in Choices (A), (B), and (C) are *homonyms* — words that sound alike but have different meanings. Choice (A), *their,* shows possession, as in "their book"; Choice (B), *they're,* is a contraction of *they are;* and Choice (C), *there,* is a location. Choice (D) is the full form of *they're,* and so is also incorrect.

EXAMPLE

We [Select... ▼] like to thank you for your kind words.

(A) wood

(B) would

(C) would have

(D) would have had

The correct answer is Choice (B). The auxiliary verb *would* is used here to indicate politeness. Choice (A) is another example of a homonym. There is no reason to use the forms in Choices (C) and (D).

The Extended Response

After you finish the first part of the RLA test (the 35-minute Reading Comprehension question-and-answer section), you start on the Extended Response — where you write an essay by analyzing arguments presented in two pieces of sample text. You get 45 minutes to work through this part of the RLA test, and you can't tack on extra time from the previous section. So if you find that you have time left on the first part, go back and review some of the questions where you had difficulties before starting the Extended Response. And remember, after the Extended Response, you have a ten-minute break and then an hour of grammar and language questions.

For the Extended Response section, you must write an essay with a clear thesis statement, an introductory paragraph, two or three paragraphs of supporting arguments, and a concluding paragraph. You'll have an erasable tablet or an on-screen whiteboard on which to make notes and organize your ideas. You won't use or have access to paper, pencils, or dictionaries. When you are ready to write, you can type your essay into a window on the computer that functions like a basic word processor. The word processor doesn't have a grammar-checker or spell-checker. You're expected to know how to write properly.

The topic you're given to write on is based on given source material: two documents with different or opposing opinions. You're expected to analyze the source material and write an appropriate analytical response. You must show that you can read and understand the source material, do a critical analysis, and prepare a reasoned response based on content drawn from the source texts.

In your essay, you analyze both positions and then give your opinion or explain your viewpoint on which position is better supported by the evidence. Remember to back up your points with specific facts from the source material. When you write this essay, make sure it's a series of interconnected paragraphs on a single topic. Not only should the entire essay begin with an introduction and end with a conclusion, but each paragraph should also have an introductory sentence and a concluding sentence.

WARNING

Write only on the assigned topic. To make sure you understand what the topic is about, read it several times. Essays that are off topic don't receive scores. If you don't get sufficient points on the Extended Response, you likely won't accumulate enough points on the other portions of the RLA test to pass.

Your essay is evaluated on the following criteria:

>> Your argument is based specifically on the source material.

>> You use the evidence from the source material to support your argument.

>> You use valid arguments and separate the supported claims in the material from the unsupported or false claims.

>> Your flow of ideas is logical and well organized.

>> You correctly and appropriately use style, structure, vocabulary, and grammar.

Take a look at these examples of possible Extended Response source materials:

"I will give up my muscle car when the world runs out of oil, not before. . . ."

"We need to find alternatives to gasoline-powered vehicles. Climate change is a real threat, and burning fossil fuels contributes to that problem. . . ."

These two opinions are the beginnings of two arguments, taking obviously different positions.

You start by determining which argument you see as stronger. Then, you make a list of information that may go into your essay to back up your argument. Trim out any information that doesn't pertain to the topic. If one side or the other uses unsubstantiated opinions as evidence, you can use that evidence to argue that it's a weaker argument.

When you start writing your essay, start with a good, strong introductory sentence that will catch a reader's attention. When you're satisfied with your introductory sentence, review your list of information. Follow that introductory sentence with a couple of sentences outlining, without explanation, your key points. Now turn each key point into a paragraph, paying attention to the flow between paragraphs to show that one relates to the previous one. When you have all these paragraphs, it's time for a conclusion. The easiest way to write a good conclusion is to restate your evidence briefly and state that this indeed proves your point. Don't just rewrite your information; summarize it in a memorable way. This may be difficult the first time, but with practice, it can become second nature.

The main criteria used to evaluate your essay are ideas and organization, but spelling, grammar, and punctuation count, too. Still, you don't want to get hung up on these details as you write. Focus on strong ideas and clear logic while writing. Then, when you are finished writing, check your essay for spelling, grammar, and punctuation.

If you have time, you can test how well your essay works and stays on topic. Read the introduction, the first and last sentence of every paragraph, and then the conclusion. They should all have the same basic points and flow together nicely. If something seems out of place, you need to go back and review.

TIP

To prepare for this part of the test, in the months and weeks leading up to your test date read newspapers and news magazines, especially opinion pieces. Analyze how arguments are presented and how the writers try to form and sway your opinion. Examine how well they present their data and how they use relevant and irrelevant data to persuade the reader. Then try your hand with the Extended Response questions in Chapter 9, the two complete GED practice tests in Chapters 19 and 27, and the complete online practice test.

Handling the Social Studies Test

For the Social Studies test, you have 70 minutes to answer 50 questions. The questions use the same formats as the RLA test questions: multiple-choice, fill-in-the-blank, drag-and-drop, and drop-down menu questions (see the earlier sections on Reasoning through Language Arts for details). You may also have some questions that require use of the calculator. (For these questions, the calculator icon appears at the top of the computer screen.) The questions on the Social Studies test deal with the following subject areas:

>> Civics and government (50 percent)

>> American history (20 percent)

>> Economics (15 percent)

>> Geography and the world (15 percent)

The questions in this test are based on written texts (source texts) and visual materials — pictures, tables, graphs, photographs, political cartoons, diagrams, and maps. These textual and visual materials come from a variety of sources, such as government documents, academic texts, work-related documents, and atlases.

You can do only a limited amount of studying for this test. The information to answer each question is in the text or graphic that comes with the question. You need to analyze the material and draw conclusions based on what's presented. However, you can prepare by reading books that offer you a basic outline of American history and by learning about how government functions. Read the newspapers to follow current events and the business section for economics. You don't need to go into great depth or memorize pages of dates and names, but you should have an idea of the general flow of history. You also need to know how government from federal to local works.

A second skill you need to master for this test is reading and extracting information from maps, graphs, and tables. On the Social Studies test, you may see a map with different shadings, and you have to determine what the shadings mean and what the difference is between a light gray and a dark gray area on the map. They're not just decoration. If you look carefully at all the text and boxes with information on the map or chart, you'll see that everything has a meaning. In Chapter 11, I walk you through all the various kinds of graphics that appear on the GED Social Studies test.

You may see the following types of questions on the Social Studies test.

The following question is based on this table.

The Five Longest Rivers in the World

River	*Location*	*Length in Miles*
Nile	Africa	4,160
Amazon	South America	4,083
Yangtze	China	3,915
Mississippi/Missouri/Red Rock	United States	3,741
Huang	China	3,395

EXAMPLE

According to the table, the length of the fourth-longest river in the world is ▢ miles.

(A) 4,160

(B) 4,083

(C) 3,741

(D) 3,395

The correct answer is Choice (C). The table shows that the Mississippi/Missouri/Red Rock River is 3,741 miles long.

The following question is based on this excerpt from the diary of Christopher Columbus.

> Monday, 6 August. The rudder of the caravel *Pinta* became loose, being broken or unshipped. It was believed that this happened by the contrivance of Gomez Rascon and Christopher Quintero, who were on board the caravel, because they disliked the voyage. The Admiral says he had found them in an unfavorable disposition before setting out. He was in much anxiety at not being able to afford any assistance in this case, but says that it somewhat quieted his apprehensions to know that Martín Alonzo Pinzón, Captain of the *Pinta*, was a man of courage and capacity. Made progress, day and night, of twenty-nine leagues.

EXAMPLE

Why would Rascon and Quintero have loosened the rudder?

(A) They were trying to repair the rudder.

(B) The Admiral found them in an unfavorable disposition.

(C) The captain was very competent.

(D) They did not want to be on the voyage.

The correct answer is Choice (D). This answer is the only one supported by the text. The others may be related to statements in the passage, but they don't answer the question.

EXAMPLE

The expedition traveled ▢ leagues that day.

The correct answer is 29. This number is stated directly in the last sentence of the excerpt.

Knowing How to Grapple with the Science Test

Did you know that of all the GED tests, the Science test has the highest initial passing rate? That's good news! When you take the Science test, you have to answer the same variety of question formats, including multiple-choice, fill-in-the-blank, drop-down menu, and drag-and-drop questions, in 90 minutes. The questions deal with the following topics:

>> Life science (40 percent)

>> Physical science, including chemistry and physics (40 percent)

>> Earth and space science (20 percent)

REMEMBER

All of the information you need to answer the questions on the Science test is given to you in the passages and the same sort of graphic material as on the Social Studies test, such as tables, graphs, illustrations, diagrams, and photos. To get a high score, though, you're expected to have picked up a basic knowledge of science. However, even without a lot of background knowledge, you should get a score high enough to pass. As on the Social Studies test, some questions may ask you to calculate a numeric answer. For these questions, the calculator icon will appear.

Although you're not expected to be an expert on the various topics in the Science test, you are expected to understand the vocabulary. To accomplish this, read as widely as you can in science books. If you run across words you don't understand, write them down with a definition or explanation. Doing so will provide a vocabulary list for you to review before the test.

You must read and understand the source material in the Science test to be able to select the best choice for an answer. Practice reading quickly and accurately. Because you have a time limit, practice skimming passages to look for key words. The less time you spend on the passages, the more time you'll have to answer the questions, and the more time you'll have at the end of the test to review your answers and attempt questions that you found difficult the first time you read them. Attempt to answer every question. You may get a point for your answer if you try it, but you can't get a point for a question you've skipped. If you completely run out of time, answer remaining questions with random guesses.

Here are some sample questions similar to those that may be on the Science test.

The following questions are based on this excerpt from a press release.

> A key feature of the Delta 4's operation is the use of a common booster core, or CBC, a rocket stage that measures some 150 feet long and 16 feet wide. By combining one or more CBCs with various upper stages or strap-on solid rocket boosters, the Delta 4 can handle an extreme range of satellite applications for military, civilian, and commercial customers.

EXAMPLE

The CBC in this context is

(A) an upper stage rocket booster.

(B) a common booster core.

(C) a cooperative boosters corps.

(D) a common ballistic cavalier.

The correct answer is Choice (B). After all, it's the only answer choice mentioned in the passage. Skimming the passage for CBC would give you an idea of where to look for a full explanation of the abbreviation.

EXAMPLE

How can the Delta 4 handle a wide range of applications?

(A) developing a Delta 5

(B) continuing research

(C) using the CBC as the base of a rocket ship

(D) creating a common core booster

The correct answer is Choice (C). The passage says that "By combining one or more CBCs with various upper stages or strap-on solid rocket boosters. . ." so Choice (C) comes closest to answering the question.

Conquering the Mathematical Reasoning Test

The Mathematical Reasoning test covers the following four major areas:

>> Algebra, equations, and patterns

>> Data analysis, statistics, and probability

>> Measurement and geometry

>> Number operations

More specifically, about 45 percent of the questions focus on quantitative problem-solving and the other approximately 55 percent focuses on algebraic problem-solving. You have 115 minutes to answer 50 questions.

The Mathematical Reasoning (Math) test has many of the same types of questions as the other sections (multiple-choice, fill-in-the-blank, and so on). Check out Chapter 2 for how these questions look on the computer screen when you take the GED.

Mathematics is mathematics. That may sound simple, but it isn't. To succeed on the Math test, you should have a good grasp of the basic operations: addition, subtraction, multiplication, and division. You should be able to perform these operations quickly and accurately and, in the case of simple numbers, perform them mentally. The more automatic and accurate your responses are, the less time you'll need for each question, and the greater your chances are of finishing the test on time with a few minutes to spare to check any questions you may have skipped or answers you want to double-check.

The other skill you should try to master is reading and solving "story problems." These questions ask you to read a short situation and then figure out how to answer the question. The question may be about how much fabric is needed to make a tablecloth, what food you can order at a fast-food restaurant for under $7, or how many cups of a certain ingredient are needed if you triple the recipe. You need to understand the situation as described and use the information you have to answer the question. These questions also contain extra information, and part of your job is to figure out which information is important and which you can safely ignore as you figure out your answer.

You can use a calculator on all but the first five questions on the GED Math test. If you take the test online at home, you can access the on-screen calculator by clicking the calculator icon in the toolbar. If you test at a testing center, you can use the on-screen calculator or use your own TI-30XS MultiView calculator. You will also have access to a formula sheet with common formulas used on the test. This way, if you forget a common formula, you can look it up by clicking the formula sheet icon on the test screen.

Consider the following questions (one traditional multiple-choice question and two questions that use different formats that you'll encounter on the computer) that are similar to what you may see on the Math test.

A right-angle triangle has a hypotenuse of 5 feet and one side that is 36 inches long. What is the length of the other side in feet?

EXAMPLE

(A) 3 ft.

(B) 48 ft.

(C) 6 ft.

(D) 4 ft.

The correct answer is Choice (D). The tricky part of this question is that you need to know that you have to apply the Pythagorean Theorem to answer this question. Using the Pythagorean Theorem (a formula that's given to you on the formula sheet that is available during the test), you know that $a^2 + b^2 = c^2$, where c is the hypotenuse and a and b are the other two sides. Because you know the hypotenuse and one side, turn the equation around so that it reads $a^2 = c^2 - b^2$.

You can open the formula sheet on the computer when needed. But keep in mind that the less you need to open it, the more time you have to answer questions.

To get c^2, you square the hypotenuse: $(5)(5) = 25$.

The side is given in inches — to convert inches to feet, divide by 12: $36/12 = 3$. To get b^2, square this side: $(3)(3) = 9$.

Now solve the equation for a: $a^2 = 25 - 9$ or $a^2 = 16$. Take the square root of both sides, and you get $a = 4$.

The Math test presents real-life situations in the questions. So if you find yourself answering 37 feet to a question about the height of a room or $3.00 for an annual salary, recheck your answer because you're probably wrong.

The following question asks you to fill in the blank.

Barb is counting the number of boxes in a warehouse. In the first storage area, she finds 24 boxes. The second area contains 30 boxes. The third area contains 28 boxes. If the warehouse has 6 storage areas where it stores boxes and the areas have an average of 28 boxes, the total number of boxes in the last 3 areas is ☐.

The correct answer is 86. If the warehouse has 6 storage areas and it has an average of 28 boxes in each, it has $(6)(28) = 168$ boxes in the warehouse. The first 3 areas have $24 + 30 + 28 = 82$ boxes in them. The last 3 areas must have $168 - 82 = 86$ boxes in them.

A rectangle has one corner on the origin. The base goes from the origin to the point $(3,0)$. The right side goes from $(3,0)$ to $(3,4)$. Where does the missing point go on the graph? ☐

© John Wiley & Sons, Inc.

The correct answer is to $(0,4)$. If you draw the three points given on the graph, you see that a fourth point at $(0,4)$ creates the rectangle. Write that answer in the box.

IN THIS CHAPTER

» Aligning your preparation with your personal strengths and learning style

» Relying on practice tests

» Figuring out what to expect on test day

» Nailing down important test-taking strategies

» Staying calm and relaxed while you take the test

Chapter **4**

Preparing for and Passing the GED Test

Y ou are facing a test that assesses whether you have the same knowledge as a traditional high school graduate. Depending on your prior learning, you may be wondering how to approach this test without feeling daunted. To pass, you also need to know how to perform well on a standardized test, which consists mostly of multiple-choice questions.

The good news is, you've come to the right spot to find out the information you'll need. This chapter offers some important pointers on how to plan and prepare for each section of the test, as well as what to do during the test to be successful. You also discover some important test-taking strategies to help you feel confident.

Creating Your Preparation Plan

A famous author once wrote, "A goal without a plan is just a wish." Luckily, I have planning covered. In this section, you discover a little about your learning style, assess your prior preparation, learn about practice tests and other learning tools, and develop a personal plan for passing the GED.

Matching your preparation to your learning style

You're ready to start serious preparation for the test. You may feel excited or nervous. But before jumping in feet first, take a moment to reflect on when and where you study most effectively. Understanding that can help you shape your preparation to meet your needs. For some people, having a quiet place to study is important. For others, listening to music or sports helps them concentrate. Some like to sit at a table or desk. Others like a comfortable armchair, sofa, or bed. Figure out what suits you. Figure out the time of day that is best for you, too. Some of us are morning larks and others are night owls!

TIP

If you want to know more about your learning style, any number of free websites have more information as well as helpful assessments. Try typing terms such as *learning style assessment* into your favorite search engine, and find a resource that helps you.

No matter where or when you study, it's easier if you keep all of your preparation materials together. If you work at a desk, keep everything there. If you study at the kitchen table after everyone has gone to sleep, then keep your materials in a box or bag. If you go to the library or a cafe to study, you might invest in a small, inexpensive backpack or bag for your materials.

Picking your battles

To succeed on the test, you can't take on all four subject matters at once. And if you try to take all the tests in a single day, you will be testing for over seven hours, with only a few ten-minute breaks. Very few of us can do our best like that!

If you are like most of us, you will want to figure out a strategic way to order your preparation and test-taking. A good way to start is with the test that is easiest for you. This might be the test that was your favorite subject at school. If you use math on your job, math might be the place to start. For most people, the easiest test is usually science — so it might pay to start there. Consider your strengths and prior learning and then use this chart to figure out the best order to test in. First, check the boxes to determine your strengths and concerns. Then use that information to figure out the order in which you want to test, from the easiest to the most challenging. Write numbers from 1 to 4 in the boxes.

Order	Test	Reason or Reasons for this Order
	Language Arts	❏ I liked this subject in school and remember a lot. ❏ I like to read and write. ❏ I write a lot of emails or other documents at work. ❏ This subject has always been hard for me. ❏ Other:
	Social Studies	❏ I liked this subject in school and remember a lot. ❏ I like to read about history, politics, government, and culture. ❏ This subject has always been hard for me. ❏ Other:
	Science	❏ I liked this subject in school and remember a lot. ❏ I like to read about science. ❏ I know a lot about the outdoors and nature. ❏ Science seems to be an easy test, so I'll give it my first shot. ❏ I enjoy science fiction. ❏ This subject has always been hard for me. ❏ Other:
	Math	❏ I liked this subject in school and remember a lot. ❏ I like working with numbers. ❏ I use simple math while shopping. ❏ I use numbers and calculations at work. ❏ This subject has always been hard for me. ❏ Other:

Using practice tests to your advantage

Taking practice GED tests is important for a few reasons, including the following:

>> **They give you an indication of how well you know the material.** Performing well on one or two tests is a strong indication that you are ready to test in that subject. The Answers and Explanations can give you insight on your strengths and areas for improvement.

>> **They confirm whether you know how to use a computer to answer the questions in the time allotted.** Until you try, you simply won't know for sure.

>> **They familiarize you with the test format.** You can read about test questions, but you can't actually understand them until you've worked through several.

>> **They can ease your stress.** A successful run-through on a practice test allows you to feel more comfortable and confident in your own abilities to take the GED test successfully and alleviate your overall anxiety.

TIP

You can find two complete GED practice tests in Parts 6 and 7, as well as a complete online practice test. Practice tests are an important part of any preparation program. To help you, I provide complete answers and explanations for each correct and incorrect response, as well as tips and recommendations. They're the feedback mechanism that you may normally get from a teacher or private tutor. As long as you check your answers after the practice test and read the answer explanations, you will benefit from taking practice tests.

Using the GED Testing Service's resources

The GED Testing Service's website has a wealth of free materials, including test descriptions, sample items, practice tests, and demonstration videos showing how to use key test tools and features (such as the on-screen calculator and whiteboard, and the math formula sheet).

The newest addition is the GED & Me mobile app, which contains practice questions and other learning resources. In key places in this book, I refer you to this website and app. It pays to open an account as soon as you can. That will give you access to more resources as you prepare. It's also where you schedule and pay for your tests, whether you test online or at a testing center.

TIP

Some of the most valuable resources on the GED website are two kinds of practice tests. First, you can find a free quarter-length test for each subject at `https://ged.com/study/free_online_ged_test/`. Second, the GED Testing Service also offers the GED Ready practice test at a low cost, which is your best indicator of whether you are ready to take the test (and is required before you sign up to test at home). Besides telling you how likely you are to pass, it gives you feedback on your areas of strength and suggestions for review and practice.

Focusing on key skills

You don't have to answer every question on the GED in order to pass. On average, you only need to answer about 60 percent of the questions on each test in order to score 145 — which is passing! To improve your chances, I recommend a simple technique. Throughout the practice tests in this book, I give tips on what I call "high-yield" skills — skills that are frequently tested and skills that come up in more than one test. By focusing on these skills, you can make quantum improvements to your preparation.

For example, on the Math test, the Pythagorean Theorem comes up frequently, as do questions about determining the area of various geometric shapes. (If you've never heard of the Pythagorean Theorem, don't worry — I'll explain it later on.) So it pays to focus on these skills. The same goes for science, social studies, and reading. Many of these tests assess the same or similar skills, such as finding the main idea, identifying supporting details, and so on. My tips will give you an edge in finding the most important skills to develop.

Using this book effectively

Every GED test-taker has a different background, skills, and experience. There are as many ways to use this book as there are readers using it! I've designed this book so that there are multiple paths through it depending on your confidence level and previous preparation for each test. No matter what your level of preparation, for your first GED test, you probably need some basic information on how the online test works. After that, for easier subjects, you might just want to take a practice test. For other tests, you may want more practice and preparation. The following charts help you find your best — and shortest — path through this book as you take on each section of the GED. For each subject, choose the chart that applies to your situation and work through the steps. You will soon be testing in record time!

Chart 1: For the subjects that you are most confident about:

❏ 1. Determine if you are ready to test by taking Practice Test 1 (Part 6) in that subject.

❏ 2. If you feel ready, take the GED Ready test at ged.com. If it says you will pass, you are ready! Review Chapter 36 and then take the test!

3. If you need more practice, study these chapters for the test you are working on:
   ❏ Language Arts: Chapters 7 and 9
   ❏ Social Studies: Chapter 12
   ❏ Science: Chapter 15
   ❏ Math: Chapter 18

❏ 4. When you feel ready, take Practice Test 2 (Part 7) in the subject you are working on.

❏ 5. If you still feel good, take the GED Ready test again, and if the results are positive, go for it! Review Chapter 36 and then take the test! If you have concerns, move to step 2 in the next chart.

Chart 2: For subjects where you need preparation:

❏ 1. Take Practice Test 1 to find areas of strength and improvement

2. Prepare for the test: Study these chapters:
   ❏ Language Arts: Chapters 5, 6, 8
   ❏ Social Studies: Chapters 10 and 11
   ❏ Science: Chapters 13 and 14
   ❏ Math: Chapters 16 and 17

❏ 3. Take Practice Test 2 to check your progress. If you feel ready, to on to step 5. If not, continue with step 4.

4. If you need more practice answering GED questions, complete these chapters:
   ❏ Language Arts: Chapters 7 and 9
   ❏ Social Studies: Chapter 12
   ❏ Science: Chapter 15
   ❏ Math: Chapter 18

❏ 5.Once you feel ready, take the GED Ready test at ged.com. If it says, you are ready, you are ready. Review Chapter 36 and then take the test! If not, use the results from GED Ready to determine if you need more practice taking the GED, more study of the test content, or more practice with the computer. Then take the online test and GED Ready again.

> **Chart 3: For subjects where you need the most preparation:**
>
> ☐ 1. Prepare for the test by studying the all the chapters for the test you are working on:
>   ☐ Language Arts: Part 2
>   ☐ Social Studies: Part 3
>   ☐ Science: Part 4
>   ☐ Math: Part 5
>
> ☐ 2. Take GED Practice Test 1.
>
> ☐ 3. Use the results to determine if you need more practice taking the GED, more study of the test content, or more practice with the computer.
>
> ☐ 4. If necessary, do more reading in the subject (especially for science and social studies), find a GED class, or find more practice material.
>
> ☐ 5. Take GED Practice Test 2.
>
> ☐ 6. When you feel ready, take the GED Ready test at ged.com. If it says you are ready, believe it and sign up for the test. Review Chapter 36 and then take the test! If not, use the feedback to structure your preparation.
>
> ☐ 7. Take the online only GED test in this book. Continue reviewing and practicing until you feel ready. Then take the GED Ready test at ged.com again. You're going to make it! With this much preparation, you can do it!

Getting extra support

For some subjects, you may want more preparation. For many test-takers, this is particularly true with Language Arts and Math. Chapter 35 contains a number of suggestions to help you find that support. One of the best suggestions is to find a free GED preparation class near you. The GED website can help you find a convenient class. You can also form a study group, use the online learning tools at ged.com, and use the GED Testing Service's app, GED & Me, which has a wealth of free and inexpensive learning resources. It can also help you identify other materials to help you prepare.

Succeeding on Test Day

You've figured out your strengths, you've reviewed and prepared, and you've gotten familiar with the test format. So what's next? Taking the test, or even the GED Ready practice test, is a serious investment of time and money. Here are some tips to make test day (and practice test day) more effective.

Leading up to test time

Doing well on the GED test involves more than walking into the test site and answering the questions. You need to be prepared for the challenges of the test. To ensure that you're ready to tackle the test head-on, make sure that you do the following leading up to the day of the test:

>> **Get enough sleep.** I'm sorry if I sound like your parents, but it's true — you shouldn't take tests when you're approaching exhaustion. Plan your time so that you can get a good night's sleep for several days before the test, and avoid excess caffeine.

>> **Eat a good breakfast.** A healthy breakfast fuels your mind and body. You have to spend several hours taking the test, and you definitely don't want to falter during that time. Eat some

protein and whole grains and avoid sugars (donuts, jelly, fruit) because they can cause you to tire easily. You don't want your empty stomach fighting with your full brain.

>> **Take some deep breaths.** During your trip to the testing site, prepare yourself mentally for the test. Clear your head of all distractions, practice deep breathing, and imagine yourself acing the test. Don't panic.

>> **Think positive thoughts.** You've studied and prepared. You've read widely. You've practiced using a computer and a mouse. Keep reminding yourself that you've got this!

Over 21 million people have passed the GED test. They did it and so can you!

REMEMBER

>> **Be on time.** Make sure that you know what time the test begins and the exact location of your test site. Arrive early. If necessary, take a practice run to make sure you have enough time to get from your home or workplace to the testing center. You don't need the added pressure of worrying about whether you can make it to the test on time. In fact, this added pressure can create industrial-strength panic in the calmest of people.

If you test online at home, double-check your computer, internet connection, and room arrangement the night before. Make sure that everyone in your house knows that they cannot disturb you during the test. Specifically, they cannot enter the room during the test. If you have children and are using childcare or a babysitter during the test, double-check those arrangements, too.

You can check in for the test as early as 30 minutes before your appointment time if you test online at home, and you can start as soon as a proctor is available. Checking in early can help you finish on time if you have other activities planned after the test.

Deciding what to take to the GED test

Passing the GED can bring you many benefits, so you need to treat it seriously and come prepared. Make sure you bring the following items with you on test day:

>> **You:** The most important thing to bring to the GED test is obviously you. If you enroll to take the test, you have to show up; otherwise, you'll receive a big fat zero and lose your testing fee. If something unfortunate happens after you enroll, go to your online account and see if you can reschedule. You may need to call the GED Testing Service or use their online chat to reschedule.

>> **Correct identification:** Before you can start the test, the test proctors — online and in person — want to make sure that you're really you. Bring a government-issued photo ID — a driver's license, a state ID card, a passport, or a *matrícula consular* are all fine. And, when asked to identify yourself, don't pull out a mirror and say, "Yep, that's me."

>> **Registration confirmation:** The registration confirmation is your proof that you registered. Have it handy in case there is an issue with your registration.

>> **Other miscellaneous items:** In the instructions you receive after you register for the test, you get a list of what you need to bring with you. Besides yourself and the items I listed previously, other items you want to bring or wear include the following:

  • **Comfortable clothes and shoes.** When you're taking the test, you want to be as relaxed as possible. Uncomfortable clothes and shoes may distract you from doing your best. You're taking the GED test, not modeling the most recent fashions.

  • **A bottle of water and a healthy snack.** Check whether you can bring these with you into the room at the testing center. If you test online at home, you are only allowed to have some water, in a clear glass, on the desk with you. But you can eat a quick snack in the ten-minute break between tests if you take more than one test.

- **Reading glasses.** If you need glasses to read a computer monitor, don't forget to bring them to the test. You can't do the test if you can't read the screen.

The rules about what enters the testing room are strict. Don't take any chances. If something isn't on the list of acceptable items and isn't normal clothing, leave it at home. Laptops, cellphones, and other electronic devices are banned from the testing area. However, you may bring a hand-held Texas Instruments TI-30XS MultiView calculator to the testing center, which you may use whenever the calculator icon appears on the screen. But you aren't required to BYOC (bring your own calculator). A calculator icon appears on the screen whenever one is necessary to answer a question. All you have to do is click on the calculator icon, and you have a fully functioning calculator on-screen. However, for many people, a real calculator saves time on the test.

Leave other electronics at home, locked in your car, or in a locker at the testing center. The last place on earth to discuss whether you can bring something into the test site is at the door on test day.

WARNING

Whatever you do, be sure not to bring any books, notes, scratch paper, small electronics (mobile phones, tablets, smart watches), or anything else of value into the testing room at the GED testing center. If you do, you'll have to leave those items outside the room. If you're testing at home, make sure they're out of reach (or out of the room).

Making sure you're comfortable before the test begins

At a test center, you usually take the GED test in an examination room with at least one official (sometimes called a *proctor* or *examiner*) who's in charge of the test. At home, you take the online test in a room that meets the GED Testing Service's requirements under the observation of an online proctor using a webcam. In either case, the test is the same.

TIP

As soon as you sit down to take the GED test, take a few moments before the test starts to relax and get comfortable. You're going to be in that chair for quite some time, so hunker down and keep these few tips in mind before you begin:

>> **Make sure that your chair is comfortable and in good working order.** You are going to be sitting for a long time, so it's important that you are comfortable. If necessary, adjust your chair to a height that suits you.

>> **Adjust your computer, keyboard, and mouse.** Unlike a pencil-and-paper test, you'll be working with a monitor, keyboard, and mouse. Although you can shift the keyboard around and maybe change the angle of the monitor, generally you're stuck in that position for the duration of the test. If you need to make any adjustments, make them before you start. You want to feel as physically comfortable as possible. Make sure that the screen is at a comfortable height and angle. If you are left-handed, you may need to rearrange the keyboard and mouse. After the test starts, you can also adjust the size of the font (the type) on-screen. Choosing the right size for you can make reading easier.

>> **Use the bathroom before you start.** This may sound like a silly suggestion, but it all goes to being comfortable. You don't need distractions. Even if bathroom breaks are permitted during the test, you don't want to take away time from the test. Remember, you cannot leave the room for any reason if you test online at home.

Using important test-taking strategies

You can increase your score by mastering a few smart test-taking strategies. To help you do so, I give you some tips in these sections on

>> Using your time wisely

>> Addressing and answering questions

>> Using intelligent guessing

>> Leaving time for review

Watching the clock: Using your time wisely

When you start the GED test, you may feel pressed for time and have the urge to rush through the questions. I strongly advise that you don't. You have sufficient time to do the test at a reasonable pace. You have only a certain amount of time for each section of the GED exam, so time management is an important part of succeeding on the test. So, plan ahead and use your time wisely.

REMEMBER

You must complete each section in one sitting, except for the Reasoning through Language Arts test. There, you get a ten-minute break after the Extended Response (also known as the essay).

During the test, the computer keeps you constantly aware of the time with a clock in the upper-right corner. Pay attention to the clock. When the test begins, check that time, and be sure to monitor how much time you have left as you work your way through the test. Table 4-1 shows you how much time you have for each test section.

TABLE 4-1 ## Time for Each GED Test Section

Test Section	Time Limit (in Minutes)
Reasoning through Language Arts	95 (split into two sections, 35 and 60)
Reasoning through Language Arts, Extended Response	45
Social Studies	70
Science	90
Mathematical Reasoning	115

TIP

As you start, the opening screen will tell you the number of questions you have to answer. Quickly divide the time by the number of questions. Doing so can give you a rough idea of how much time to spend on each question. For example, on the Mathematical Reasoning test, suppose that you have 50 questions to answer. You have 115 minutes to complete the test. Divide the time by the number of questions to find out how much time you have for each one: 115/50 = 2.3 minutes or 2 minutes and 18 seconds per question. As you progress, repeat the calculation to see how you're doing.

Remember that you can answer the questions in any order, except for the RLA Extended Response. Do the easiest questions first. If you come to a question that will take a long time to answer (such as a complicated math question), skip it. If you get stuck on a question, leave it and come back to it later if you have time. If you are unsure of an answer, use the Flag for Review button to mark it so that you can return to it later if you have time. The Review screen will help you quickly find and return to flagged and skipped questions later in the test. In the meantime, you can keep to that schedule and answer as many questions as possible.

As you can see from Table 4-1, if you don't monitor the time for each question, you won't have time to answer all the questions on the test. Keep in mind the following general time-management tips to help you complete each exam on time:

>> **Measure the time you have to answer each question without spending more time on timing than answering.** Group questions together; for example, use the information in Table 4-1 to calculate how much time you have for each question on each test. Multiply the answer by 5 to give you a time slot for any five test questions. Then try to make sure that you answer each group of five questions within the time you've calculated. Doing so helps you complete all the questions and leaves you several minutes for review.

>> **Keep calm and don't panic.** The time you spend panicking could be better spent answering questions.

When time is up, immediately stop and breathe a sigh of relief. When the test ends, the examiner will give you a log-off procedure. Listen for instructions on what to do or where to go next.

Addressing and answering questions

When you start the test, you want to have a game plan in place for how to answer the questions. Keep the following tips in mind to help you address each question:

>> **Whenever you read a question, ask yourself, "What am I being asked?"** Doing so helps you stay focused on what you need to find out to answer the question. Then try to answer it.

>> **Don't overthink.** Because all the questions are straightforward, don't look for trick questions. The questions ask for an answer based on the information given.

>> **Find the best answer and quickly verify that it answers the question.** If it does, click on that choice and move on. If it doesn't, leave it and come back to it after you answer all the other questions, if you have time. *Remember:* You need to pick the *most* correct answer from the choices offered. It may not be the perfect answer, but it is what is required.

Guess for success: Using intelligent guessing

The multiple-choice questions, regardless of the on-screen format, provide you with four possible answers. You get points for every correct answer. Nothing is subtracted for incorrect answers. That means you can guess on the questions you don't know for sure without fear that you'll lose points. Make educated guesses by eliminating as many obviously wrong choices as possible and then choosing from just one or two remaining choices.

When the question gives you four possible answers and you randomly choose one, you have a 25 percent chance of guessing the correct answer without even reading the question. If you know that one of the answers is definitely wrong, you now have just three answers to choose from, giving you a 33 percent (1 in 3) chance of choosing the correct answer. If you know that two of the answers are wrong, you leave yourself only two possible answers to choose from, giving you a 50 percent (1 in 2) chance of guessing right — much better than 25 percent!

Try to spot the wrong choices by following these tips:

>> **Make sure that the answer choice really answers the question.** Wrong choices usually don't answer the question — that is, they may sound good, but they answer a different question than the one the test asks.

- » **When two answer choices seem very close, consider both of them carefully because they both can't be right — but they both _can_ be wrong.** Some answer choices may be very close, and all seem correct, but there's a fine line between completely correct and nearly correct. Be careful. These answer choices are sometimes given to see whether you really understand the material.

- » **Look for opposite answers in the hopes that you can eliminate one.** If two answers contradict each other, both can't be right but both can be wrong.

- » **Trust your instincts.** Some wrong choices may just strike you as wrong when you first read them. If you spend time preparing for the test, you probably know more than you think.

Leaving time for review

Having a few minutes at the end of a test to check your work is a great way to set your mind at ease. As soon as you answer the last question, the test will take you to the Review screen, which will show you a list of all the questions and whether you skipped or flagged any questions. This way, you can quickly review any questions that may be troubling and go back and answer any ones you skipped earlier. Keep the following tips in mind as you review your answers:

- » **Figure out how much time you have per remaining question, and try to answer each question in a little less than that time.** The extra seconds you don't use the first time through the test add up to time at the end of the test for review. Some questions require more thought and decision-making than others. Use your extra seconds to answer those questions.

- » **Don't change a lot of answers at the last minute.** Second-guessing yourself can lead to trouble. Often, second-guessing leads you to changing correct answers to incorrect ones. Numerous studies show that when a test-taker changes an answer selection, the new selection is usually incorrect. If you have prepared well and worked numerous sample questions, then you're likely to get the correct answers the first time. Ignoring all your preparation and knowledge to play a hunch isn't a good idea, either at the racetrack or on a test.

- » **If you cannot answer all the questions in the time remaining, answer them randomly.** There is no guessing penalty on the GED, so don't leave any questions unanswered. The one or two points you pick up from answering all the questions may be the points you need to pass.

- » **On the Extended Response section, use any remaining time to reread and review your final essay.** You may have written a good essay, but you always need to check for typos and grammar mistakes. The essay is evaluated for style, content, and proper English. That includes spelling and grammar.

Keeping your head in the game

To succeed in taking the GED test, you need to be prepared. In addition to studying the content and skills needed for the four test sections, you also want to be mentally prepared. Although you may be nervous, you can't let your nerves get the best of you. Stay calm and take a deep breath. Here are a few pointers to help you stay focused on the task at hand:

- » **Take time to relax.** Passing the GED test is an important milestone in life. Make sure you leave a bit of time to relax, both while you prepare for the test sections and just before you take them. Relaxing has a place in preparing as long as it doesn't become your main activity.

- » **Make sure that you know the rules of the room before you begin.** If you have questions about using the bathroom during the test or what to do if you finish early, ask the proctor before you begin. If you don't want to ask these questions in public, call the GED office in your area before test day, and ask your questions over the telephone. For general GED questions, call 877-392-6433 or check out ged.com. This site has many pages, but the FAQ page is always a good place to start.

>> **Keep your eyes on your monitor.** Everybody knows not to look at other people's work during the test, but to be on the safe side, don't stretch, roll your eyes, or do anything else that may be mistaken for looking at another test. At a test center, most of the tests will be different on the various computers, so looking around is futile and doing so can get you into a lot of trouble. You should also keep your eyes on the screen if you test online at home. Everything you need to take the test is on the screen in front of you. Looking around the room or looking away from the screen repeatedly could be considered suspicious behavior.

>> **Stay calm.** Your nerves can use up a lot of energy needed for the test. Concentrate on the job at hand. You can always be nervous or panicky some other time.

Because taking standardized tests probably isn't a usual situation for you, you may feel nervous. This is perfectly normal. Just try to focus on answering one question at a time and push any other thoughts to the back of your mind. Sometimes taking a few deep breaths can clear your mind.

Minding Your Ps and Qs: The Reasoning through Language Arts Test

2

IN THIS PART . . .

Find out everything you ever wanted to know about the Reasoning through Language Arts test.

Understand the types of materials you're expected to read and answer questions about.

Recognize how the test and questions are formatted and what the Extended Response item is like.

Discover some strategies to help you do your best on this test and put them into practice on some sample test questions.

Chapter **5**

Preparing for the Reasoning through Language Arts Test

The Reasoning through Language Arts (RLA) test evaluates your ability to do the following:

>> Apply skills in reading comprehension.

>> Apply concepts in grammar and language to correct errors in writing. *Grammar* is the basic structure of language — you know: subjects, verbs, sentences, fragments, and all that. *Language* includes vocabulary, usage, punctuation, capitalization, and other features of written English.

>> Apply writing skills to create a logical and effective extended response (essay).

Most of what you're tested on in the RLA test is stuff that you've picked up over the years, either in school or just by speaking, reading, and observing. However, to help you prepare better for this test, I give you some more skill-building tips in this chapter.

The RLA test is divided into three sections. You start off with a 35-minute question-and-answer Reading Comprehension section. You then spend 45 minutes writing the Extended Response (the essay). After a 10-minute break, you finish with Grammar and Language, a 60-minute question-and-answer section. The overall time is 150 minutes for all three components, including the 10-minute break.

In this chapter, I provide all you need to know to prepare for the Reading Comprehension and Grammar and Language components. From reading everything you can, to improving your grammar and spelling, to increasing your reading speed and comprehension, this chapter equips you with what you need so you can sit down at the computer the day of the test, ready to ace those components. Then, in Chapter 6, I walk you through the various question types you'll find in the Reading and Language Arts components and provide solid tips and strategies for answering each one. In Chapter 7, you can work through some practice questions on each section and compare your answers to the complete answers and explanations I provide.

In Chapters 8 and 9, I turn to one of the most feared parts of the test, the Extended Response item — sometimes called "the essay." It's a four- to seven-paragraph essay that you write in 45 minutes. Not to worry: I have you covered! In Chapter 8, I give you a complete overview of this part of the RLA test. In Chapter 9, I walk you through the steps on writing a passing essay, show you how to evaluate your writing, and give you concrete tips on how to raise your score. Then, in the three practice tests, I give you plenty of writing practice, including ideas on how to evaluate and improve your writing. After all that, you may not be Shakespeare, but you will be able to write a passing essay!

Grasping What's on the Grammar and Language Component

To pass this component of the RLA test, you need to demonstrate that you have a command of the conventions of standard English. You need to know the appropriate vocabulary to use and avoid slang. You need to be able to spell, identify incorrect grammar, and eliminate basic errors, including such common errors as run-on sentences and sentence fragments.

To help you succeed, I provide insightful information in the following sections about what skills this part of the test covers, what you can do to brush up on those skills, and the general question format for this component. With this information in hand, you can be confident in your ability to tackle any type of grammar and language question on test day.

Looking at the skills the Grammar and Language component covers

The Grammar and Language component of the RLA test evaluates you on the following types of skills. Note that unlike the other GED test sections, this component of the RLA test expects that you *know* or at least *are familiar with* the rules of grammar. Just looking at the passages provided won't do you much good if you don't understand the basics of these rules already.

>> **Mechanics:** You don't have to become a professional writer to pass this test, but you should know or review basic mechanics. Check out *English Grammar For Dummies*, 3rd Edition, by Geraldine Woods (Wiley), to review what you should know or may have forgotten. The mechanics of writing include the following:

- **Capitalization:** You have to recognize which words start with a capital letter and which words don't. All sentences start with a capital letter, but so do titles, like *Miss, President,* and *Senator,* when they're followed by a person's name. Names of cities, states, and countries are also capitalized.

- **Punctuation:** This area of writing mechanics includes everyone's personal favorite: commas. (Actually, most people hate commas because they aren't sure how to use them, but the basic rules are simple.) The more you read, the better you get at punctuation.

If you're reading and don't understand why punctuation is or isn't used, check with your grammar guidebook or the internet.

The comma is the most misused punctuation mark in English. Always think carefully before you add or remove a comma.

- **Spelling:** You don't have to spot a lot of misspelled words, but you do have to know how to spell contractions and possessives and understand the different spellings of *homonyms* — words that sound the same but have different spellings and meanings, like *their* and *there.*

- **Contractions:** This area of writing mechanics has nothing to do with those painful moments before childbirth! Instead, *contractions* are formed when the English language shortens and combines two words by leaving out one or more letters. For example, when you say or write *can't,* you're using a shortened form of *cannot.*

The important thing to remember about contractions is that the *apostrophe* (that's a single quotation mark) takes the place of the letter or letters that are left out. That's why you write *can't.* The apostrophe takes the place of *n* and *o.*

- **Possessives:** Do you know people who are possessive? They're all about ownership, right? So is the grammar form of possessives. *Possessives* are words that show ownership or possession, usually by adding an apostrophe and an *s* to a person's or object's name. If Marcia owns a car, that car is *Marcia's* car. The word *Marcia's* is a possessive. Make sure you know the difference between singular and plural possessives. For example: "The girl**'s** coat is torn." (*Girl* is singular, so the apostrophe goes before the *s.*) "The girls**'** coats are torn." (*Girls* is plural, so the apostrophe goes after the *s.*) When working with plural possessives, form the plural first and then add the apostrophe.

Some plural nouns, such as *women,* do not end in *s,* so the plural possessive is formed with *'s:* "The women**'s** coats are torn."

» **Grammar:** Grammar focuses on the basic rules for forming correct sentences. As with mechanics, *English Grammar For Dummies* can help you with commonly tested items such as the following:

- **Complete and incomplete sentences:** These include run-on sentences, sentence fragments, and improperly joined sentences. For example, "The quick red fox jumped over the lazy brown dog the dog kept on sleeping," runs two sentences together. Fix the error with a comma and *but:* "The quick red fox jumped over the lazy brown dog, **but** the dog kept on sleeping."

- **Proper agreement:** In written English, the subject and the verb of a sentence should agree. For example, "Matilda and her sister is watching TV and knitting" is incorrect. To correct this sentence, change *is* to *are* to agree with the subject of the sentence, *Matilda and her sister,* which is plural.

- **Correct word order:** Words should be in the correct order. For example, "She bought some orange, ugly, fake flowers," should be changed to, "She bought some ugly, fake, orange flowers."

Extensive reading before the test can give you a good idea of how good sentences are structured and put together. The advice here is to read, read, and read some more.

» **Usage:** This broad category covers a lot of topics. English has a wide variety of rules, and these questions test your knowledge and understanding of those rules. Verbs have tenses that must be consistent. Pronouns must refer back to nouns properly. If the last two sentences sound like Greek to you, make sure that you review usage rules. They also cover vocabulary and acceptable standard English usage. People have become very comfortable with short forms used in texting, but "LOL" or "C U L8R" aren't acceptable in standard writing.

Having a firm grasp of these writing conventions can help you get a more accurate picture of the types of questions you'll encounter on this part of the test.

Understanding the format of the Grammar and Language component

The Grammar and Language component consists of passages accompanied by a set of drop-down menu questions. (For more information on this question type, see Chapter 2. You can find more examples in Chapter 6 and plenty of practice questions in Chapter 7.) Your task is to read, revise, and edit documents that may include how-to information, informational texts, and workplace materials. Don't worry — since all the questions use the drop-down menu format, you don't have to come up with the answers all on your own. You just have to find each answer among the four answer choices. And the best part: Preparing for this component helps you build the grammar and other language skills needed for the Extended Response.

TIP

To do your best on the Grammar and Language part of the RLA test, read the passage completely before you answer the questions.

Rocking the Reading Comprehension Component

The ability to comprehend, analyze, and apply something you've read is one of the strongest predictors of career and college readiness and is also an important life skill. In the following sections, you explore the four aspects of good reading skills: comprehension, analysis, command of evidence, and synthesis.

Looking at the skills the Reading component covers

The questions on the Reading component of the test focus on the following skills, which you're expected to be able to use as you read both fiction and nonfiction passages:

>> **Comprehension:** Questions that test your *comprehension* skills assess your ability to do close reading — that is, to read a source of information thoughtfully so that you have a precise understanding of what you've read and can restate the information in your own words. Items may also ask you to show understanding by ordering events in a passage or to rephrase what you read without losing the meaning of the passage. In addition, items can ask you to show how the details support the main idea. Other items ask you to determine the meaning of specific words in context and grasp how a writer's use of a particular word or phrase affects the meaning of a sentence, a paragraph, or the entire passage.

>> **Analysis:** Questions that test your *analysis* skills assess your ability to draw conclusions, understand consequences, and make inferences about the passage. To answer these questions, make sure your answers are based only on the information in the passage and not on outside knowledge or the online article you read last week. Items may ask you to explain how parts of the passage (such as paragraphs, sentences, and examples) work together to accomplish the writer's purpose. Other items may ask you to show how transitional words and phrases (such as *however* and *for example)* signal relationships among ideas in the passage.

Other items may ask you to analyze the writer's purposes in writing the passage — to convince, to share knowledge with the reader, or even to amuse the reader!

>> **Command of evidence:** These questions assess your ability to identify and evaluate evidence. You need to understand the passage writer's point of view in order to assess the strength and weakness of their position. Some questions will ask you to identify the evidence that the author uses for support. Other times, you will have to identify among the options additional supporting evidence. Other questions will ask you whether the author's evidence offers valid support for a position, or merely an opinion or belief unsupported by reasons, examples, or facts.

>> **Synthesis:** Questions that test your *synthesis* skills assess your ability to take information in one form and in one location and put it together with information in another context. Here, you get a chance to make connections between two related passages and compare and contrast them. You may be asked to compare and contrast the tone, point of view, style, effectiveness, or purposes of the passages — and saying that the purpose of a passage is to confuse and confound test-takers isn't the answer!

REMEMBER

Some reading questions may ask you to use information in the source text passages combined with information presented in the questions. So make sure you use all the information that you have available. And don't forget to use the tabs and scroll bars to reveal the complete passage and question — you never know where an answer may come from. For complete information on the tabs and scroll bars, check Chapter 2.

Understanding the format of the Reading component

The RLA Reading component measures your ability to understand and interpret fiction and non-fiction passages. It's plain and simple — no tricks involved. You don't have to do any math to figure out the answers to the questions. You just have to read, understand, and use the material presented to you to answer the corresponding questions.

The passages in this test are similar to the works a high school student would come across in English class. To help you feel more comfortable with the RLA Reading component, I'm here to give you a better idea of what this test looks like on paper.

The reading passages are presented on the left side of a split screen with the question on the right. Each passage will be between 450 and 900 words. The passages in this test may come from workplace (on-the-job) materials or from academic reading materials. Seventy-five percent of the source texts will be from informational texts — nonfiction documents. The remaining 25 percent will be drawn from literary texts, generally short stories and novels. With each source text, you have to answer four to eight questions. Some items will present you with two passages. These items will ask you to compare and contrast, integrate information, and draw conclusions.

TIP

Text passages are text passages. Although the next section describes what types of passages appear on the RLA test to help you prepare, don't worry so much about what type of passage you're reading. Instead, focus on understanding the information that the passage presents to you.

Identifying the types of passages and how to prepare for them

To help you get comfortable with answering the questions on the Reading portion of the RLA test, you need to have an idea of the kinds of passages that appear on the test. The good news is that in this section, I focus on the two main types of passages you'll see: nonfiction and literary. I also give you some practical advice that you can use as you prepare for this portion of the test.

REMEMBER

Most of the passages (75 percent of them) come from nonfiction or informational texts. This means the more informational reading you do every day — newspapers, magazine articles, workplace reports, manuals, reviews, webpages, instructions, recipes — the better prepared you are for the RLA Reading test.

Nonfiction passages

Nonfiction passages may come from many different sources. Here's a list of some of the kinds of passages you may see on the test.

>> **Nonfiction prose:** *Nonfiction prose* is prose that covers a lot of ground — and all the ground is real. Nonfiction prose is material that the author doesn't create in their own mind — it's based on fact or reality. In fact, this book is classified as nonfiction prose, and so are the newspaper articles you read every day. The next time you read a textbook, a newspaper, or a magazine, tell yourself, "I'm reading nonfiction prose." Just don't say it out loud in a coffee shop or in your break room at work — or people may start to look at you in strange ways!

>> **Workplace and community documents:** You run across these types of passages in job- and community-related areas of life. The following are some examples:

  • **Workplace statements:** Companies and organizations issue rules for employee behavior, goals for the organization, and even standards for environmental protection. These tell the world the company's goals and basic rules of behavior. The goal statement for your study group may be as follows: "We're all going to pass the GED test on our first attempt."

  • **Historic documents, legal documents, and letters:** Historic documents can include extracts from the Constitution, Declaration of Independence, or other government documents. These documents are obviously older materials, with a somewhat different writing style from what you may see in a modern document. Legal documents and letters may include leases, purchase contracts, and notices from your bank. If you aren't familiar with these kinds of documents, collect some examples from banks or libraries and review them. If you can explain these types of documents to a friend, then you understand them.

  • **Manuals:** Every time you invest in a major purchase, you get a user's manual that tells you how to use the item. Some manuals are short and straightforward; others are long and complicated. Some manuals may be printed, but often they are only available online.

  • **Textbook selections:** Passages may be drawn from social studies or science textbooks, in order to assess your ability to read and understand academic content. But don't worry — this content is no different from what is covered in other parts of the GED test!

TIP

The Reading component can seem daunting, but it can have a big payoff on other parts of the GED. Because both the Science and Social Studies tests involve reading nonfiction prose, your preparation for the Reading component can help you with those tests.

Literary passages

The RLA Reading component includes passages from various kinds of prose fiction. *Prose fiction* refers to novels and short stories. As you may already know, *fiction* is writing that comes straight from the mind of the author (in other words, it's made up; it's not about something that really happened). The only way to become familiar with prose fiction is to read as much fiction as you can. After you read a book or a story, try to talk about it with other people who have read it.

REMEMBER

Regardless of what types of passages the questions in the Reading component are based on, your challenge is the same: reading comprehension. You need to answer the questions using the skills outlined in the earlier section, "Looking at the skills the Reading component covers": comprehension, analysis, command of evidence, and synthesis.

Preparing for the RLA Test with Tactics That Work

The RLA test requires a number of skills from knowing proper spelling, usage, and punctuation to reading quickly and accurately, and familiarizing yourself with the format of the test. You can master all of these skills with practice. The following sections give some advice on how to do that.

Developing skills to read well

To succeed on the RLA test, you can prepare in advance by improving your reading skills. Here are some of the best ways you can prepare:

>> **Read as often as you can.** This strategy is the best one and is by far the simplest, because reading exposes you to correct grammar. What you read makes a difference. Reading catalogs may increase your product knowledge and improve your research skills, but reading literature is preferable because it introduces you to so many rules of grammar. Reading fiction exposes you to interesting words and sentences. It shows you how paragraphs tie into one another and how each paragraph has a topic and generally sticks to it. Reading historical fiction can give you some insight into what led up to today and can also help you with the Social Studies test (see Chapters 10 11, and 12 for more on the Social Studies test).

Reading nonfiction — from instructions to business letters, from press releases to history books and historical documents — is also extremely important. Nonfiction generally uses a formal style, the kind expected of you when you write an essay for the Extended Response item. Older documents can be a special problem because the writing style is very different from what's common today. Getting familiar with such documents will help you get better results and even help with your Social Studies test.

TIP

Read everything you can get your hands on — even cereal boxes — and identify what kind of reading you're doing. Read about topics that interest you, which can include subjects as varied as new cars, sports reporting, healthcare news, or money-saving tips. Reading aloud to your children at bedtime also counts, and so does reading on your phone while you are on the bus or waiting to see your doctor. Ask yourself questions about your reading and see how much of it you can remember.

>> **Develop your reading speed.** Reading is wonderful, but reading quickly is even better — it gets you through the test with time to spare. Check out *Speed Reading For Dummies,* by Richard Sutz with Peter Weverka (Wiley), or do a quick internet search to find plenty of material that can help you read faster. Whatever method you use, try to improve your reading rate without hurting your overall reading comprehension.

>> **Read carefully.** When you read, read carefully and think about what you're reading. This is called *active reading:* Your brain is working as hard as your eyes are. If reading novels, stories, or historical documents is unfamiliar to you, read these items even more carefully and thoughtfully. The more carefully you read any material, the easier it'll be for you to get the right answers on the test.

>> **Ask questions.** Ask yourself questions about what you just read. Could you take a newspaper article and reduce the content to four bulleted points and still summarize the article accurately? Do you understand the main ideas well enough to explain them to a stranger? (Note that I don't advise going up to strangers to explain things to them in person. Pretend you're going to explain it to a stranger and do all the talking in your head. If you want to explain what you read to someone in person, ask your friends and family to lend you an ear — or two.)

Ask for help if you don't understand something that you read. You may want to form a study group and work with other people. If you're taking a test-preparation course, ask the instructor for help when you need it. If you have family, friends, or coworkers who can help, ask them.

>> **Use a dictionary.** Not many people understand every word they read, so use a dictionary. There are many good free or inexpensive dictionary apps for your computer or smartphone. Looking up unfamiliar words increases your vocabulary, which, in turn, makes passages on the Reasoning through Language Arts test easier to understand. When you find a new word, first try to figure out its meaning using the *context* — the other words around it. Then check your understanding by looking up the word. You can also keep track of new words and their meanings by starting a vocabulary section in your notebook. After you look up the word, write it down together with its meaning. If you have a thesaurus, use it, too. Often, knowing a synonym for the word you don't know is helpful. Plus, it improves your Scrabble game!

>> **Use new words.** A new word doesn't usually become part of your vocabulary until you put it to use in your everyday language. When you come across a new word, make sure you know its meaning and try to use it in a sentence. Then try to work it into conversation for a day or two. After a while, this challenge can make each day more exciting. If you don't feel comfortable using new words in conversation, write a sentence using the word in your notebook. Do this every day, and you'll be surprised at how many new words you pick up in just a few weeks.

REMEMBER

All the information you need to answer the reading questions is given in the passages or in the text of the questions that accompany the passages. You're not expected to recognize a passage and answer questions about what comes before it or what comes after it in the context of the entire work. The passages are complete in themselves, so just focus on what you read.

Improving your mastery of grammar and language skills

To prepare yourself for the Grammar and Language section, you can get a leg up by reviewing rules of grammar, punctuation, and spelling. Here are some ways to get started:

>> **Master the rules of basic grammar.** On this test, you don't have to define a gerund and give an example of one, but you do have to know about verb tenses, subject-verb agreement, pronoun-antecedent agreement, possessives, and the like. As your knowledge of grammar and punctuation improves, have a bit of fun by correcting what you read on low-budget websites and in cheap paperback novels — both often have poor editing.

>> **Practice grammar and proper English in everyday speaking and writing.** As you review the rules of grammar, practice them every day as you talk to your friends, family, and coworkers, write on the job, or send emails. Although correct grammar usually "sounds" right to your ears, sometimes it doesn't because you and the people you talk to have become used to using incorrect grammar. If you see a rule that seems different from the way you usually speak or write, put it on a flashcard and practice it as you go through your day. Before long, you'll train your ears so that correct grammar sounds right.

TIP

Correcting other people's grammar out loud or in writing doesn't make you popular, but correcting it in your head can help you succeed on this test. Also, listen for and avoid slang or regional expressions. *Y'all* may be a great favorite in the South, but it wouldn't work well on your GED essay.

>> **Understand punctuation.** Know how to use commas, semicolons, colons, and other forms of punctuation. To find out more about punctuation and when and why to use its different forms, check out a grammatical reference book like *English Grammar For Dummies,* 3rd Edition, by Geraldine Woods (Wiley).

>> **Practice writing.** Write as much and as often as you can and then review your writing for errors. Look for and correct mistakes in punctuation, grammar, and spelling. If you can't find any, ask someone who knows grammar and punctuation for help.

>> **Keep a journal or blog.** Journals and blogs are just notebooks (physical or virtual) in which you write a bit about your life every day. They both provide good practice for personal writing. Blogging or responding to blogs gives you practice in public writing because others see what you write. Whether you use a personal journal or a public blog, though, keep in mind that the writing is the important part. If public writing encourages you to write more and more often, do it. If not, consider privately writing in a journal or diary.

>> **Improve your spelling.** As you practice writing, keep a good dictionary at hand. If you're not sure of the spelling of any word, look it up. I hear you. How do you look up the spelling of a word if you can't spell it? Try sounding out the word phonetically and look in an online dictionary or dictionary app on your phone. Type in the word and select the word that looks familiar and correct. If that doesn't work, ask someone for help. Add the word to a spelling list and practice spelling those words. In addition, get a list of common *homonyms* — words that sound the same but are spelled differently and have different meanings — and review them every day. (You need to know, for example, the difference between *their, there,* and *they're* and *to, two,* and *too.*) Many dictionaries contain a list of homonyms, or you can search for a list of common homonyms online.

>> **Keep in mind that these questions all use the drop-down menu format.** Among the various answer choices, the test questions give you the correct answer. Of course, they also tell you three other answers that are incorrect, but all you have to do is find the correct one! As you practice for the test, tune your ears so the correct answer sounds right, which, believe it or not, makes finding the correct answer easier on the test.

Finding out about the format and content of each test section

Get as much experience as you can with the test content and format. Here are some ways to do that:

>> **Practice and prepare.** In addition to this chapter, you can read Chapters 6 and 7 for more information and preliminary practice for the Reading Comprehension and Language and Grammar components. And don't forget the Extended Response! Complete coverage and some preliminary practice are in Chapters 8 and 9. You can find a test overview and free practice questions on the GED website (ged.com). The free GED & Me mobile app also offers free practice questions.

>> **Take practice tests.** When you feel ready, take the Reasoning through Language Arts Practice Tests in Chapters 19 and 27. Do the questions and check your answers. Look at the detailed answer explanations that I provide in Chapters 20 and 28. Don't move on to the next answer until you understand the preceding one. Then take the online test that comes with this book.

It will give you the best indication of whether you are ready for the actual test. You can also find a free quarter-length practice test at https://app.ged.com/portal/study/preview (log-in required).

TIP

When you feel you are ready to take the real test, take the GED Ready RLA test (available on the ged.com website). You must receive a Green GED Ready score in order to take the online GED test at home. A Green score also means you are ready for the in-person test, but this score is not required to test at a test center. If you don't score high enough, you can use the detailed feedback you get to focus your review.

As you take practice tests, remember to keep it real! Stick to the time limits, and match the testing situation as much as possible. When you take online practice tests, set your work area up as described in Chapter 4. When you go online or to the test center for the real test, you'll feel more at ease because you prepared in a realistic setting.

Language component

» Discovering some test-taking tricks for surviving the RLA Reading Comprehension component

Chapter 6

RLA Question Types and Solving Strategies

he 150-minute Reasoning through Language Arts (RLA) test evaluates your ability to write clear and effective English and to read, analyze, and accurately assess and respond to the content of written passages. I go into detail about the RLA test particulars in Chapter 5. In this chapter, I help you navigate through the different question types on the Reading Comprehension and Grammar and Language components and how to answer them. In Chapter 7, I provide plenty of practice questions, along with complete answers and explanations so you can check your work. And you can find a complete treatment of the Extended Response (essay) component in Chapters 8 and 9. You really have your bases covered!

Tackling Grammar and Language Questions

All the questions on the Grammar and Language component use the drop-down menu format, which makes it easier. You just have to the find the answer from four choices!

On the actual GED test, you click the drop-down arrow in the on-screen button and select the best choice for a word, phrase, or sentence from the options provided to complete the sentence correctly; that choice then appears in the sentence.

The following questions give you examples of the items you will encounter on the actual test. I couldn't simulate the look and feel of the drop-down menu in the print book, so I ask that you use your imagination and check out Chapter 2 for an example of how this question type appears on the actual GED test.

Along with the questions, all based on the following business letter, I give you some advice on the best ways to approach and answer these questions.

BETA Café Equipment, Inc.
700 Millway Avenue, Unit 6
Concord, MA 12345

John Charles
Executive Director
American Specialty Coffee Association
425 Pacific Drive, Suite 301
San Diego, CA 92102

Dear Mr. Charles:

Thank you for [Select... ▼] which serves the rapidly expanding specialty coffee industry. BETA Café Equipment, Inc., [Select... ▼] this year to provide an affordable source of reconditioned Italian espresso/cappuccino machines for new businesses entering the industry.

During our first year of operation, BETA plans to repair and recondition 500 machines for use in restaurants and cafés. This will generate revenue of more than $1,000,000 and create 14 good-paying jobs.

BETA [Select... ▼] will be shipped to our centralized repair and reconditioning depot. After total rebuilding, equipment will be forwarded to regional sales offices to be sold to local restaurants and cafés at a much lower price than comparable new equipment. Entrepreneurs wishing to start new specialty coffee businesses particularly should be interested in our products.

To learn more about BETA, please consult our website or give us a call. Any assistance you can provide in sharing this information with your membership will be very much appreciated.

Yours truly,

Edwin Dale, President

TIP

The drop-down questions on the writing component of the RLA test provide four answer choices, one of which is correct. If you aren't sure which one is correct, guessing is better than skipping the question and leaving it blank. This is because you don't get any points for not answering a question, and wrong answers don't count against you.

EXAMPLE

Thank you for [Select... ▼] which serves the rapidly expanding specialty coffee industry.

(A) your interest in our company,

(B) you're interest in our company,

(C) your interest in our company

(D) yours interest in our company,

This question assesses your understanding of a common comma rule and the homonyms *your* and *you're,* and another related word, *yours.* The possessive *your* — Choice (A) — is the answer. The letter is thanking the reader for their interest in the company. Choice (B) is a contraction for *you are,* which does not make sense in the sentence. Choice (C) tests your knowledge of comma rules. While Choice (C) uses *your* correctly, there is no reason to omit the comma, because a comma is needed to mark this relative clause. Choice (D) has the necessary comma, but a possessive word such as *yours* is not followed by a noun, so this choice is also incorrect.

REMEMBER

An old topic from grammar class can help you with the comma rule here. A relative clause is introduced with *which, that,* or *who.* These clauses give information about another word in the sentence. Here's an example: "The apartment **that I rented** has two bathrooms." The clause **that I rented** adds a necessary piece of information, so it doesn't need commas. Contrast this with, "The landlord, **who is an old friend,** gave me a discount." This time, the clause adds extra information, so it needs commas before and after it.

In the following example question, you're asked to pick the best form of the verb for one part of the sentence.

EXAMPLE

BETA Café Equipment, Inc., ⎡Select... ▼⎤ this year to provide an affordable source of reconditioned Italian espresso/cappuccino machines for new businesses entering the industry.

(A) were formed

(B) had formed

(C) was formed

(D) is formed

Look at the answer choices one by one. Choice (A), *were formed,* is the plural form of the simple past tense. The action happened once in the past, so the simple past tense is correct. However, the subject, BETA Café Equipment, is singular, so the plural verb form *were* is incorrect, making Choice (A) wrong. Choice (B) uses the past perfect tense in the active voice. You don't need to worry about the name, but do remember this: In the active voice, the subject is doing the action; in the passive voice, the action is being done to the subject. Because someone was forming the company (and the company is the subject of the sentence), the voice must be passive. Therefore, Choice (B) is also wrong. Choice (C) uses the singular form of the simple past tense, *was,* which agrees with the singular subject, BETA Café Equipment. You have already determined that the simple past tense is the correct tense, so Choice (C) is correct. However, it always pays to read all the choices. Choice (D) is incorrect because it's in the present tense. The action happened in the past, so using the present tense doesn't work.

TIP

A good way to answer questions like this is to read the sentence and substitute the choices one at a time; you can often pick out the right answer just because it "sounds" right.

The next example shows another technique for finding the answer: the process of elimination.

EXAMPLE

BETA ⎡Select... ▼⎤ will be shipped to our centralized repair and reconditioning depot.

(A) will have purchased used equipment, which

(B) will purchase used equipment, which

(C) had purchased used equipment, which

(D) will purchase used equipment which

This question shows how you can often find the answer by eliminating the obviously incorrect choices. Looking at the answer choices here, Choice (A) simply makes no sense, because it uses the future perfect tense. That implies actions completed in the future, but this event is yet to happen. So, you can eliminate that choice right away. Choice (D) can be eliminated because you must have a comma in front of *which* because it starts a relative clause that adds extra information. (See the note earlier in this chapter about these clauses.) That leaves Choices (B) and (C). Because all the action in the passage is yet to happen, the purchase can't have been completed in the past, so the tense in Choice (C) is wrong. By process of elimination, you have determined that Choice (B) is the answer. Choice (B) is correct because it uses the simple future tense, which is appropriate for an action that will happen.

TIP

Even if you cannot eliminate all the wrong choices, the process of elimination can still help you. In this example, even if you cannot eliminate Choice (C), you have still eliminated two other choices, (A) and (D), effectively improving your odds. Even if you have to guess, your chance of choosing the right answer is fifty-fifty.

Choosing Wisely in the Reading Component

The RLA test Reading Comprehension component consists of excerpts from fiction and nonfiction prose. You're presented with a reading passage (or in some cases, two related reading passages) followed by a series of multiple-choice and drag-and-drop questions. In this section, I give you clues to help you answer each of these.

TIP

When working through the Reading component of the real GED test, read the questions first so you get an idea of what you need to look for in the passage as you read it. Read the questions carefully — they aren't trick questions, but they do require you to be a good reader. Then, read the passage. Remember to keep it simple! Your only task in reading is to find the answers to the questions you just read — nothing more! If you encounter a word that you don't recognize, look at the surrounding text, which can often give you clues about the mystery word's meaning. If you can understand the idea without knowing the word, you can skip the word. That will help you keep moving and save time!

Dealing with multiple-choice Reading questions

Most of the questions on the Reading component are multiple-choice. In this section, I walk you through a few sample questions based on this short newspaper article:

(1) The constitutional mechanism that the United States uses to elect the president and vice president is called the Electoral College. This group of presidential electors forms every four years in order to elect the president and vice president. The number of electors in each state is equal to the number of senators and representatives in its congressional delegation. Holders of federal offices are barred from being electors. There are currently 538 electors, and a majority of 270 or more electoral votes is required to elect the president and vice president. The Constitution has a contingent process if no candidate receives a majority. In that case, the United States House of Representatives holds an election to elect the president, and the United States Senate holds another election to select the vice president.

(2) On election day in November, the states each hold a statewide or districtwide popular vote to choose electors based upon how they have pledged to vote for president and vice president. Every state except two uses a winner-take-all approach to choose electors. Maine and Nebraska choose one elector per congressional district and two electors for the ticket with the highest statewide vote. The electors meet and vote in their state capitals in December, and in January, the votes are counted in a special joint session of Congress. The inauguration takes place in January.

EXAMPLE

How many electors are needed to elect the president and vice president of the United States?

(A) 2

(B) 4

(C) 270

(D) 538

This question is a perfect example of when reading the questions first, before you read the passage, can really benefit you. If you know that you're looking for a specific number, you have the answer as soon as you find it in the passage. On the other hand, if you read the passage first and then have to go back and look for the number, you will lose valuable time. The correct answer in this case is 270, Choice (C), which you can find in the third-to-last sentence of the first paragraph.

EXAMPLE

The president and vice president are typically elected by a majority of electors

(A) in a direct, nationwide popular vote on election day.

(B) at a meeting of the electors in Washington, D.C.

(C) in popular votes held in each state or district on election day.

(D) in the House of Representatives for the president and the Senate for the vice president.

If you read the article carefully, you will see that states choose the electors via a popular vote in each state or district. So Choice (C) is the correct answer. Therefore, Choice (A) is incorrect. Choice (B) is contradicted by the information in the passage: The electors meet in their state capitals. Choice (D) describes a contingency process used only if the Electoral College fails to choose a president and vice president, so it is incorrect.

Dealing with drag-and-drop Reading questions

Some items on the Reading component are called drag-and-drop items. This item type is essentially another multiple-choice question (because you get to select from a list of possible answers and don't have to come up with the answer all on your own). The difference is that you have to sort the choices in a particular order, select which words apply and which ones don't, or show which answers are details that support the main idea. Here's an example of a sorting drag-and-drop question.

EXAMPLE

Look at the following series of events. According to the passage, in which order did they happen? Drag the sentences (or write the letters, in this case) into the boxes in the appropriate order.

(A) The Electoral College votes are counted in a special session of Congress.

(B) Electors meet and make their choices in each state.

(C) States and districts hold popular elections.

(D) The president takes office in a ceremony at the Capitol.

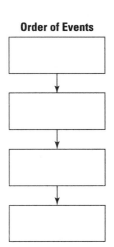

Order of Events

The answer to this question is right in the passage. You just have to sort the events into the order in which they happen every four years. The correct order is Choice (C), (B), (A), and then (D). First, the popular votes are held on election day, Choice (C). Then, the electors meet in their states in December, Choice (B). After that, the Senate and House meet together in a special joint session in early January to count the votes, Choice (A). Finally, the president is inaugurated later in January, Choice (D).

TIP

Answering drag-and-drop questions on test day requires quick and accurate use of the computer mouse. You can get practice with these questions in the online test included in this book and on the GED website.

Dealing with questions with multiple passage sets

Sometimes the GED Reading component will give you two passages related to the same topic. This generally happens with nonfiction prose passages. Your task will be to integrate information in the two passages, compare and contrast information, or evaluate which passage is more logical or has stronger evidence to support it. For example, the passage about the Electoral College might be accompanied by the relevant excerpt from the Constitution, as in this example.

EXAMPLE

Twelfth Amendment to the Constitution of the United States (1804)

(1) The Electors shall meet in their respective states, and vote by ballot for President and Vice-President, one of whom, at least, shall not be an inhabitant of the same state with themselves; they shall name in their ballots the person voted for as President, and in distinct ballots the person voted for as Vice-President, and they shall make distinct lists of all persons voted for as President, and all persons voted for as Vice-President and of the number of votes for each, which lists they shall sign and certify, and transmit sealed to the seat of the government of the United States, directed to the President of the Senate;

(2) The President of the Senate shall, in the presence of the Senate and House of Representatives, open all the certificates and the votes shall then be counted;

(3) The person having the greatest number of votes for President, shall be the President, if such number be a majority of the whole number of Electors appointed; and if no person have such majority, then from the persons having the highest numbers not exceeding three on the list of those voted for as President, the House of Representatives shall choose immediately, by ballot, the President. But in choosing the President, the votes shall be taken by states, the representation from each state having one vote; a quorum for this purpose shall consist of a member or members from two-thirds of the states, and a majority of all the states shall be necessary to a choice.

Which of the following can be concluded by comparing the passage and the excerpt from the Constitution?

(A) The Electoral College gives too much power to states with small populations.

(B) The Electoral College should be replaced with a direct, popular election.

(C) The process for electing the president and vice president changed early in American history.

(D) Few Americans really understand the workings of the Electoral College.

The answer to this question is right in the title of the excerpt. The amendment came into effect in 1804, which is early in the history of the Constitution. Therefore, Choice (C) is correct. By reading the question and the answer choices before reading the excerpt, you would have been able to answer this question as soon as you came to the title of the reading. Option (A) may be true but is not a conclusion you can draw by comparing information in the two passages. Option (B) is an opinion not discussed in either passage and so is incorrect. I hope that Option (D) is not true, but that cannot be concluded from information in the passages.

TIP

Reading two passages can take a lot of time. If you feel pressed for time on test day, you can skip questions based on two passages or flag them for later by pressing the Flag for Review button in the upper-right corner of your screen. That way, you may be able to read and answer more questions. But don't leave any questions unanswered. At the end of the test, use the Review Screen to find and answer all the questions you skipped or flagged — even if you guess. A guess gives you at least a one-in-four chance of getting a point. If you guess on four questions, you will likely get at least one point, and that may be the point you need to get a passing score!

REMEMBER

The GED Reading component will frequently have at least one passage that is based on U.S. history or a fundamental document. So your preparation for the Reading component can help you on the Social Studies test, and vice versa!

Chapter 7

Working through Some Practice RLA Questions

This chapter provides sample Reasoning through Language Arts (RLA) questions for both the Reading Comprehension and Grammar and Language components of the RLA test. A sample Extended Response item is provided in Chapter 9 to help you prepare for taking that component of the GED test.

You can record your answers directly in this book or on a sheet of paper if you think you'll want to try these practice questions again at a later date. Mark only one answer for each question unless otherwise indicated.

At the end of each section, I provide detailed answer explanations for you. Check your answers. Take your time as you move through the explanations. Read them carefully, because they can help you understand why you missed the answers you did and confirm or clarify what you got right.

Remember, this is just preliminary practice. I want you to get used to answering different types of RLA questions. Use the complete practice tests in Chapters 20 and 27 and the included online practice test to time your work and replicate the real test-taking experience. Then use the included online-only practice test as a final check. That way, you will be more than prepared for the GED Ready test on the GED Testing Service's website. Remember, you have to get a rating of Green to take the online GED test at home. It's not required if you test at a testing center, but getting a Green is the best indicator that you are ready to pass. If you do not score high enough, you can use feedback from the test to focus your review.

RLA Grammar and Language Practice Questions

The questions in the Grammar and Language component of the RLA test are doubly important because understanding and using correct grammar adds to your overall score on the RLA test and also counts toward your score on the Extended Response item. One of the important things about proper grammar is that it sounds and reads well. These questions give you an opportunity to develop your ear and eye for proper sentences.

For the questions in this section, pay special attention to the mechanics of writing, spelling, and grammar. Work carefully, but don't spend too much time on any one question. Be sure to answer every question. You can find complete answers and explanations for these items later in this section.

The questions

Questions 1–10 refer to the following executive summary.

Report of the Human Resources Committee of the Metropolitan Dry-Cleaning Industry Association

Executive Summary

Over the past two years, the Human Resources Committee has worked hard to become a cohesive [Select... ▼] on assessing and addressing the human resource implications associated with changes in the fabricare industry. As of August, the Committee has an active membership of [Select... ▼] 15 individuals involved in all aspects of the project. The Committee has taken responsibility for undertaking actions that will benefit this large, highly fragmented [Select... ▼] great difficulty speaking with one voice.

During the initial period that the Committee was in [Select... ▼] work focused on reaching out to and building a relationship with key individuals within the industry. One of its first steps [Select... ▼] was to undertake a Needs Assessment Survey within the industry.

During the first year, the Committee explored ways of meeting the needs identified in the Needs Assessment [Select... ▼] raising the profile of the industry and offering on-site training programs. A great deal of feasibility work [Select... ▼] yet each possible training solution proved to be extremely difficult and costly to implement.

As the Committee moved into its second [Select... ▼] officially established a joint project with the National Fabricare Association to achieve goals in three priority areas: mentorship, training, and profile building.

During this [Select... ▼] effort and vision has gone into achieving the goals established by the Human Resources Committee and the Association. The new priority areas have provided an opportunity for the industry to take these [Select... ▼]

- Introduce technology
- Build capacity and knowledge
- Enhance skills
- Build partnerships and networks

1. Over the past two years, the Human Resources Committee has worked hard to become a cohesive [Select... ▼] on assessing and addressing the human resource implications associated with changes in the fabricare industry.

    (A) group and one which has focused

    (B) group. One which has focused

    (C) group, and one which has focused

    (D) group focused

2. As of August, the Committee has an active membership of [Select... ▼] 15 individuals involved in all aspects of the project.

    (A) most over

    (B) moreover

    (C) over than

    (D) more than

3. The Committee has taken responsibility for undertaking actions that will benefit this large, highly fragmented [Select... ▼] great difficulty speaking with one voice.

    (A) industry which has

    (B) industry, which have

    (C) industry, who has

    (D) industry, which has

4. During the initial period that the Committee was in [Select... ▼] work focused on reaching out to and building a relationship with key individuals within the industry.

    (A) existence, it's

    (B) existence, its

    (C) existence its

    (D) existence; its

5. One of its first steps [Select... ▼] to undertake a Needs Assessment Survey within the industry.

    (A) was

    (B) had been

    (C) were

    (D) would have been

6. During the first year, the Committee explored ways of meeting the needs identified in the Needs Assessment [Select... ▼] raising the profile of the industry and offering on-site training programs.

    (A) Survey and they included,

    (B) Survey. These needs included

    (C) Survey, and they included

    (D) Survey they included

7. A great deal of feasibility work [Select... ▼] yet each possible training solution proved to be extremely difficult and costly to implement.

   (A) were undertaken during this phase

   (B) was undertook during this phase

   (C) was undertaken, during this phase

   (D) was undertaken during this phase,

8. As the Committee moved into its second [Select... ▼] officially established a joint project with the National Fabricare Association to achieve goals in three priority areas: mentorship, training, and profile building.

   (A) year: it

   (B) year it

   (C) year; it

   (D) year, it

9. During this [Select... ▼] effort and vision has gone into achieving the goals established by the Human Resources Committee and the Association.

   (A) passed year, many

   (B) past year, much

   (C) past year much

   (D) passed year, much

10. The new priority areas have provided an opportunity for the industry to take these [Select... ▼]

    - Introduce technology
    - Build capacity and knowledge
    - Enhance skills
    - Build partnerships and networks

    (A) actions

    (B) actions;

    (C) actions,

    (D) actions:

Questions 11–20 refer to the following description of an adult education class at a local community college.

Adult Learning 301: Perspectives on Prior Learning

This course is intended for recent GED [Select... ▼] on assessment of prior learning for college credit. [Select... ▼] are guided through the creation of an online portfolio, which can be evaluated by an academic advisor for college credit. This is an opportunity for adults, who have learned in non-formal as well as formal venues, to document and assess [Select... ▼] prior learning. The course is [Select... ▼]. Students need the permission of their academic advisor or success coach to enroll.

[Select... ▼] should be directed to remedial programs before beginning such a rigorous course. [Select... ▼] on any GED test section may be asked to repeat the test to see if they qualify for GED College Ready + Credit. This course is meant for learners who will gain from [Select... ▼] do not require extensive teaching.

This course is designed to help adult learners gain credit for [Select... ▼] prior learning in preparation for post-secondary study. Students will learn methods for documenting prior knowledge, [Select... ▼] reacquainted with educational environments. Through the use of assessment tools and [Select... ▼] will gain a realistic understanding of their levels of competence, personal strengths, weaknesses, and learning styles.

11. This course is intended for recent GED [Select... ▼] on assessment of prior learning for college credit.

   (A) completers, and focuses

   (B) completers and focuses

   (C) completers it focuses

   (D) completers, it focuses

12. [Select... ▼] are guided through the creation of an online portfolio, which can be evaluated by an academic advisor for college credit.

   (A) Candidates

   (B) However, candidates

   (C) Nevertheless, candidates

   (D) In contrast, candidates

13. This is an opportunity for adults, who have learned in non-formal as well as formal venues, to document and assess [Select... ▼] prior learning.

   (A) their

   (B) there

   (C) they're

   (D) themselves

14. The course is [Select... ▼].

   (A) intents and concentrated

   (B) intents and concentrate

   (C) intense and concentrate

   (D) intense and concentrated

15. [Select... ▼] should be directed to remedial programs before beginning such a rigorous course.

   (A) Candidates who score low in the pre-test,

   (B) Candidates, who score low in the pre-test

   (C) Candidates who score low in the pre-test

   (D) Candidates, who score low in the pre-test;

16. [Select... ▼] on any GED test section may be asked to repeat the test to see if they qualify for GED College Ready + Credit.

   (A) Extremely those who score well

   (B) Those who score well extremely

   (C) Those who score extremely well

   (D) Those extremely who score well

17. This course is meant for learners who will gain from [Select... ▼] do not require extensive teaching.

   (A) review and remediation. But

   (B) review, and remediation but

   (C) review, and remediation but,

   (D) review and remediation but

18. This course is designed to help adult learners gain credit for [Select... ▼] prior learning in preparation for post-secondary study.

   (A) their

   (B) his or her

   (C) our

   (D) my

19. Students will learn methods for documenting prior knowledge, [Select... ▼] reacquainted with educational environments.

   (A) will develop academic skills while becoming

   (B) will develop academic skills, and becoming

   (C) will develop academic skills, and will become

   (D) develop academic skills, and will become

20. Through the use of assessment tools and [Select... ▼] will gain a realistic understanding of their levels of competence, personal strengths, weaknesses, and learning styles.

   (A) counseling; students

   (B) counseling. Students

   (C) counseling students

   (D) counseling, students

Questions 21–25 are based on the following business letter.

Pan African Study Tours, Inc.
2500 River Road
Troy, MI 48083

Dr. Dale Worth, Ph.D., Registrar
BEST Institute of Technology
75 Ingram Drive
Concord, MA 01742

Dear Dr. Worth:

Our rapidly changing economic climate has created [Select... ▼] before known. It has been said that only those organizations [Select... ▼] can maintain loyalty and commitment among their employees, members, and customers will continue to survive and prosper in this age of continuous learning and globalization.

Since 1974, Pan African Study Tours, Inc., [Select... ▼] with universities, colleges, school districts, volunteer organizations, and businesses to address the unique learning needs of their staff and clientele. These have included educational travel programs that [Select... ▼] artistic and cultural interests, historic and archeological themes, environmental and wellness experiences, world music and dance experiences, and wildlife safaris. All our tours [Select... ▼] professional development activities that build international understanding and boost creativity.

We would appreciate the opportunity to share our experiences in educational travel from Egypt to South Africa and discuss the ways we may be of service to your organization.

Yours sincerely,

Ronsard Tazi Nkumbu, MA, President
Pan African Study Tours, Inc.

21. Our rapidly changing economic climate has created [Select... ▼] before known.

   (A) both challenges and opportunities never

   (B) both challenges never

   (C) challenges and opportunities both never

   (D) both challenges and opportunities ever

22. It has been said that only those organizations [Select... ▼] can maintain loyalty and commitment among their employees, members, and customers will continue to survive and prosper in this age of continuous learning and globalization.

   (A) who

   (B) whom

   (C) that

   (D) what

23. Since 1974, Pan African Study Tours, Inc., [Select... ▼] with universities, colleges, school districts, volunteer organizations, and businesses to address the unique learning needs of their staff and clientele.

   (A) have been working

   (B) has been working

   (C) will be working

   (D) would be working

24. These have included educational travel programs that [Select... ▼] artistic and cultural interests, historic and archeological themes, environmental and wellness experiences, world music and dance experiences, and wildlife safaris.

   (A) explore,

   (B) explore

   (C) explore:

   (D) explore;

25. All our tours [Select... ▼] professional development activities that build international understanding and boost creativity.

   (A) incorporates

   (B) incorporated

   (C) had incorporated

   (D) incorporate

The answers

1. **D. group focused.** With this choice, you create a concise sentence and avoid the overly wordy and awkward sentence in Choice (A). Choices (B) and (C) introduce new errors.

2. **D. more than.** Choice (D) uses *more than* correctly to refer to quantities. The other choices introduce additional errors.

TIP

Transitional words and phrases come up on both the Reading and Grammar and Language components of the RLA test. Using them well can also raise your score on the essay. So it really pays to understand how they work!

3. **D. industry, which has.** Choice (D) is correct because a comma is needed to indicate that this relative clause contains nonessential information. Therefore, Choice (A) is incorrect. Choice (B) introduces a subject-verb agreement error. *Industry* is the word that *which* refers to, so a singular verb is required. Choice (C) uses an incorrect pronoun; *which* is required because it refers to a thing, *industry,* not a person.

4. **B. existence, its.** Choice (B) is correct because the possessive form of *it, its,* is needed here, not the contraction for *it is: it's* (Choice A). There is no reason to remove the comma (Choice C) or replace it with a semicolon (Choice D).

5. **A. was.** In this sentence, the subject of the verb is the singular subject *One,* so the singular form of the verb, *was,* is needed.

TIP

Are you thinking that I made a mistake in the preceding sentence? Well, I didn't. The noun that is closest to the verb is not always the subject. The prepositional phrase *of its first steps* doesn't determine how the noun and verb agree. *One,* a singular noun, is subject of the sentence and, therefore, needs *was,* not *were.*

6. **B. Survey. These needs included.** This choice creates two concise sentences instead of one long, rambling one, as in the other choices.

TIP

When answering Grammar and Language questions or writing your essay, keep in mind that sentences shouldn't be so long that you have to take multiple breaths just to read them aloud. Short sentences are easier to read and understand and are less likely to need all sorts of pesky punctuation.

7. **D. was undertaken during this phase,** A comma after *phase* is required because this a compound sentence joined by the conjunction *yet.* A compound sentence needs a comma before the conjunction. Therefore, the remaining choices, which omit this punctuation, are incorrect. In addition, there is no reason to use *were* instead of *was* (Choice A) or to change *undertaken* to *undertook* (Choice B). Choice (C) adds an extra comma that is not needed.

TECHNICAL STUFF

A *compound sentence* contains two independent clauses or thoughts. An independent clause has a subject and verb and can stand alone as a sentence. In a compound sentence, two independent clauses are joined by a comma and a conjunction such as *and, but,* or *yet.*

8. **D. year, it.** This choice is correct because a comma is needed to separate the introductory clause starting with *As* from the rest of the sentence. Replacing the comma with another punctuation mark (Choices A and C) or removing it (Choice B) are both incorrect.

9. **B. past year, much.** Choice (B) is correct because it avoids the homonym spelling error (*passed/past*) in Choices (A) and (D). There is no reason to use *many* instead of *much,* which is another reason Choice (A) is incorrect. A comma is needed after *year,* so Choice (C) is incorrect.

Homonyms are two or more words that sound alike or are spelled alike but have different meanings. The word *passed* is a verb and means "went by," as in "she passed the other car," or "completed a test successfully," as in "he passed the GED." The word *past* is a noun and means "in times gone by, in a prior time," as in, "In the past, there were no computers." The GED Grammar and Language component frequently tests your ability to use the correct homonym, so keep an eye out for them. Writing the wrong homonym in your essay can also contribute to a lower score.

10. **D. actions:** The clause needs a colon at the end to introduce the list that follows (Choice D). Therefore, the other choices are incorrect.

11. **B. completers and focuses.** Choice (B) is correct because *and* joins two verbs (*is based* and *focuses*), not two clauses, and so does not need a comma. Therefore, Choice (A) is incorrect. Choice (C) creates a run-on sentence. Choice (D) creates a comma splice.

Two independent clauses should be joined by a comma and a conjunction, such as *and* or *but*. When you join two clauses with just a comma, it's called a *comma splice*. When you join them without a conjunction and a comma, it's called a *run-on sentence*. Look at these examples.

Joins two clauses correctly: This course is intended for recent GED completers, **and** it focuses on assessment of prior learning for college credit.

Run-on: This course is intended for recent GED completers **it** focuses on assessment of prior learning for college credit.

Comma splice: This course is intended for recent GED completers, it focuses on assessment of prior learning for college credit.

12. **A. Candidates.** The transitional phrases in Choices (B), (C), and (D) do not make sense and so are incorrect. Therefore, Choice (A) is correct.

The process of elimination can help you answer this question. Since none of the transitional words in the choices make sense, you can eliminate them and select Choice (A).

13. **A. their.** *Their* is possessive (showing belonging) and is the correct choice in this sentence.

The homonyms *there, their,* and *they're* probably trip up more people than any other homonyms, and these tricky words are frequently tested on the GED Grammar and Language component. Before test day, be sure you know the difference!

14. **D. intense and concentrated.** *Intense* and *concentrated* are synonyms used in this sentence for emphasis, but in Choices (A) and (B), *intense* is replaced with a close homonym, *intents*. *Intents* means "plans or purposes." *Concentrated* is an adjective, so it is used correctly in Choices (A) and (D). There is no reason to use *concentrate*, as in Choices (B) and (C), which is a verb (*to concentrate*) or a noun (as in *orange juice concentrate*). Only Choice (D) uses both correct words.

15. **C. Candidates who score low in the pre-test.** The clause *who score low in the pre-test* is an *essential relative clause,* which means it refers to a specific noun — *candidates,* in this case — and specifies something about the noun that the sentence needs in order to make sense to readers. Essential relative clauses aren't separated by commas because they're an integral part of the sentence.

Contrast the *essential* relative clause with the *nonessential* relative clause, which adds information about the noun that isn't essential to the meaning of the sentence. If you remove a nonessential clause from the sentence, you can still fully understand the meaning of the sentence. Nonessential relative clauses require commas to separate them from the sentence. For example, consider the following sentence: "The teacher, who had bright red hair, reviewed the grammar rule with the class." The information between the commas (who had bright red hair) isn't essential to the meaning of the sentence. Correcting various kinds of relative clauses comes up frequently on the GED, so it pays to know the rules.

16. **C. Those who score extremely well.** *Those who score extremely well* is the best order of the words. *Extremely*, an adverb, is best placed before the word it modifies, which is *well*.

17. **D. review and remediation but.** Commas are not needed in this series of nouns joined by *and* and *but*. Therefore, Choices (B) and (C) are incorrect. Choice (A) creates a sentence fragment.

TECHNICAL STUFF

A *sentence fragment* is a group of words with an initial capital letter and a final period but that is not a complete sentence. A fragment lacks a subject or a verb. You can avoid a fragment by giving it a complete subject or a complete verb or by joining it to another sentence using the correct conjunction (such as *and* or *but*), punctuation, and capitalization. Correcting sentence fragments comes up frequently on the GED, and you should avoid fragments at all costs in your essay!

18. **A. their.** This item assesses your ability to choose pronouns that agree with their *antecedent* — the noun they refer to. In this case, the antecedent is *adult learners*, so *their*, Choice (A), is correct.

19. **C. will develop academic skills, and will become.** Choice (C) puts the three things students will do (learn methods, develop skills, and become reacquainted) in the same grammatical form, verb phrases. This is called *parallel structure.*

TECHNICAL STUFF

Parallel structure makes writing clear and easy to follow because similar ideas are expressed in the same grammatical form. Parallel structure is frequently tested on the GED. Here are some examples of different kinds of parallel structure:

The GED has tests on math, language arts, social studies, and science. (nouns)

They studied academic content, reviewed test-taking skills, and learned computer skills. (verb phrases)

The students studied in the library, the teachers worked in their classrooms, and the administrators sat in their offices. (clauses)

20. **D. counseling, students.** A comma is needed to set off this phrase from the rest of the sentence. Therefore, Choices (A) and (C) are incorrect. Choice (B) creates a sentence fragment.

TIP

Not sure about commas? Check out *English Grammar For Dummies*, 3rd Edition, by Geraldine Woods (Wiley) for the lowdown on this tricky punctuation mark.

21. **A. both challenges and opportunities never.** Choice (A) uses correct parallel structure and so is correct. Choices (B) and (C) use faulty parallel structure. There is no reason to use *ever* in this sentence, so Choice (D) is incorrect.

22. **C. that.** This item tests your ability to use pronouns correctly. An organization is a thing, so it needs the relative pronoun *that*. Therefore, Choice (C) is correct and Choices (A) and (B) are incorrect. This sentence is not a question, so Choice (D) is incorrect.

23. **B. has been working.** Pan African Study Tours is a single entity because it's one company. Therefore, it's a singular noun and needs the singular verb *has*. Thus, Choice (A), which uses the plural verb *have*, is incorrect. There is no reason to use the verb tenses in Choices (C) or (D).

WARNING

People often refer to companies as *them* when in fact a company is always an *it*. Even if a company has a plural noun in its name, such as this one, Pan African Study Tours, it's still singular.

24. **B. explore.** A punctuation mark is not needed before this list of items in parallel structure, so Choice (B) is the only correct choice.

25. **D. incorporate.** The sentence is about the present and the subject, *tours*, is plural, so Choice (D) is correct.

RLA Reading Comprehension Practice

The Reading component of the RLA test consists of excerpts from nonfiction and fiction prose. Multiple-choice and drag-and-drop questions based on the reading material follow each excerpt.

You have two choices for how to approach the items on this part of the test. You can read each excerpt first, read the question to make sure that you understand what's being asked, and then answer the questions (referring to the reading material as often as necessary). Or, you can read the questions first and then look for the answers in the passage as you read. If you can remember the questions, reading the text with the questions in mind is much easier and faster. You save time because you know what's being asked of you. In this section, you can try both ways to see which approach is more effective for you.

For the multiple-choice questions in this section, choose the one best answer to each question. For the drag-and-drop items, write the letters of the answers in the boxes. Work carefully, but don't spend too much time on any one question. Be sure to answer every question. You can find the answers for these questions later in this section.

The questions

Questions 1–8 refer to the following article from the United States Geological Service Newsroom (www.usgs.gov).

(1) USGS scientists and Icelandic partners found avian flu viruses from North America and Europe in migratory birds in Iceland, demonstrating that the North Atlantic is as significant as the North Pacific in being a melting pot for birds and avian flu. A great number of wild birds from Europe and North America congregate and mix in Iceland's wetlands during migration, where infected birds could transmit avian flu viruses to healthy birds from either location.

(2) By crossing the Atlantic Ocean this way, avian flu viruses from Europe could eventually be transported to the United States. This commingling could also lead to the evolution of new influenza viruses. These findings are critical for proper surveillance and monitoring of flu viruses, including the H5N1 avian influenza that can infect humans.

(3) "None of the avian flu viruses found in our study are considered harmful to humans," said Robert Dusek, USGS scientist and lead author of the study. "However, the results suggest that Iceland is an important location for the study of avian flu."

(4) During the spring and autumn of 2010 and autumn of 2011, the USGS researchers and Icelandic partners collected avian influenza viruses from gulls and waterfowl in southwest and west Iceland. By studying the viruses' genomes the researchers found that some viruses came from Eurasia and some originated in North America. They also found viruses with mixed American-Eurasian lineages.

(5) "For the first time, avian influenza viruses from both Eurasia and North America were documented at the same location and time," said Jeffrey Hall, USGS co-author and principal investigator on this study. "Viruses are continually evolving, and this mixing of viral strains sets the stage for new types of avian flu to develop."

1. How dangerous is this new potential source of avian flu to humans?

   (A) very dangerous

   (B) not at all dangerous

   (C) a concern but not particularly dangerous

   (D) serious enough that it requires monitoring

2. Before this discovery, where did scientists believe most birds carrying the avian flu intermingled with North American birds?

   (A) South Pacific

   (B) Central America

   (C) Eurasia

   (D) North Pacific

3. Why was the finding of Eurasian, North American, and mixed virus genomes in the same locale significant?

   (A) It proved avian flu viruses comingle only in the North Pacific.

   (B) It proved that the avian flu is a risk to humans.

   (C) It proved that avian flu viruses had mingled in Iceland.

   (D) It proved that Iceland is the origin of the avian flu.

4. Why is the mixing of avian flu viruses in Iceland an important concern?

   (A) It can lead to a new, dangerous strain of avian flu.

   (B) Cold viruses are constantly evolving.

   (C) It provides lead time to develop new vaccines.

   (D) It suggests tourists avoid that area.

5. Which of these terms best describes the tone of this passage?

   (A) light-hearted

   (B) deeply concerned

   (C) factual and straightforward

   (D) gloomy

6. Which strain of the avian flu virus can infect humans?

   (A) the bird flu

   (B) the H5N1 strain

   (C) the avian H5 flu

   (D) the Eurasian avian flu

7. How does the word *however* in Paragraph 3 function in the passage?

   (A) It indicates that avian flu is not a risk to humans.

   (B) It contrasts the situation in Iceland and the North Pacific.

   (C) It indicates the writer's skepticism about the scientists' claims.

   (D) It shifts the focus from risk to humans to the need for continued monitoring.

8. Which of these statements is essential to a summary of the article? Which are not essential? Write the letters of the statements in the correct boxes.

Essential to a Summary	Not Essential to a Summary

   (A) The scientists studied gulls in southwest Iceland.

   (B) Analysis revealed viruses with mixed Asian and American genomes.

   (C) None of the viruses found to date are harmful to humans.

   (D) The birds congregated in Iceland's wetlands.

Questions 9–16 refer to the following excerpt from Robert Bloch's short story, "This Crowded Earth" (1958).

(1) The telescreen lit up promptly at eight a.m. Smiling Brad came on with his usual greeting. "Good morning — it's a beautiful day in Chicagee!"

(2) Harry Collins rolled over and twitched off the receiver. "This I doubt," he muttered. He sat up and reached into the closet for his clothing. Visitors — particularly feminine ones — were always exclaiming over the advantages of Harry's apartment. "So convenient," they would say. "Everything handy, right within reach. And think of all the extra steps you save!"

(3) Of course most of them were just being polite and trying to cheer Harry up. They knew damned well that he wasn't living in one room through any choice of his own. The Housing Act was something you just couldn't get around; not in Chicagee these days. A bachelor was entitled to one room — no more and no less. And even though Harry was making a speedy buck at the agency, he couldn't hope to beat the regulations.

(4) There was only one way to beat them and that was to get married. Marriage would automatically entitle him to two rooms — *if* he could find them someplace. More than a few of his feminine visitors had hinted at just that, but Harry didn't respond. Marriage was no solution, the way he figured it. He knew that he couldn't hope to locate a two-room apartment any closer than eighty miles away. It was bad enough driving forty miles to and from work every morning and night without doubling the distance. If he did find a bigger place, that would mean a three-hour trip each way on one of the commutrains, and the commutrains were murder. The Black Hole of Calcutta, on wheels. But then, everything was murder, Harry reflected, as he stepped from the toilet to the sink, from the sink to the stove, from the stove to the table.

(5) Powdered eggs for breakfast. That was murder, too. But it was a fast, cheap meal, easy to prepare, and the ingredients didn't waste a lot of storage space. The only trouble was, he hated the way they tasted. Harry wished he had time to eat his breakfasts in a restaurant. He could afford the price, but he couldn't afford to wait in line more than a half-hour or so. His office schedule at the agency started promptly at ten-thirty. And he didn't get out until three-thirty; it was a long, hard five-hour day. Sometimes he wished he worked in the New Philly area, where a four-hour day was the rule. But he supposed that wouldn't mean any real saving in time, because he'd have to live further out. What was the population in New Philly now? Something like 63,000,000, wasn't it? Chicagee was much smaller — only 38,000,000, this year.

(6) *This* year. Harry shook his head and took a gulp of the Instantea. Yes, this year the population was 38,000,000, and the boundaries of the community extended north to what used to be the old Milwaukee and south past Gary. What would it be like *next* year, and the year following?

(7) Lately that question had begun to haunt Harry. He couldn't quite figure out why. After all, it was none of his business, really. He had a good job, security, a nice place just two hours from the Loop. He even drove his own car. What more could he ask?

9. This story is set sometime in the future. Which of the following clues confirms that this story is set in the future?

   (A) the number of rooms in his apartment

   (B) the population of Chicagee

   (C) the affordability of cars

   (D) the affordable price of a restaurant meal

10. This story was published in 1958. What image did Bloch have of the future?

   (A) incredibly crowded

   (B) suffering from food shortages

   (C) well-organized commutes

   (D) long working hours

11. Besides population numbers, how does the author build up the idea of a crowded world?

   (A) descriptions of bad-tasting food

   (B) communication using telescreens

   (C) descriptions of enormous cities

   (D) descriptions of long, hard workdays

12. Why does Harry sometimes wish he worked in the New Philly area?

   (A) shorter commute times

   (B) shorter working hours

   (C) better pay

   (D) better food

13. Why does Harry live in a one-room apartment when he could afford a two-room apartment?

   (A) He likes the efficiency of the small space.

   (B) His lady friends like the convenience of the apartment.

   (C) He is not married.

   (D) He can't afford a larger apartment.

14. What's the population Harry mentions for Chicagee?

   (A) 38 million

   (B) 63 million

   (C) 38 billion

   (D) 63 billion

15. Which of the following statements can be inferred about Harry from Paragraph 7?

  (A) He feels more fortunate than others but still has vague worries.

  (B) He doesn't like Chicagee and feels his life would be better in another city.

  (C) He feels overwhelmed by life's challenges but still feels optimistic.

  (D) He hates his life but feels that marriage will make his life better.

16. Which of the following details support the generalization that Harry believes that life is difficult and unsatisfying? Write the letters in the box. ☐

  (A) travel on commutrains

  (B) the flavor of his breakfast

  (C) the price of meals in restaurants

  (D) the taste of Instantea

Questions 17–22 refer to the following excerpt taken from the Environmental Protection Agency website (www.epa.gov) and the subsequent passage about climate change.

Weather versus Climate

- Weather is a specific event or condition that happens over a period of hours or days. For example, a thunderstorm, a snowstorm, and today's temperature all describe the weather.

- Climate refers to the average weather conditions in a place over many years (usually at least 30 years). For example, the climate in Minneapolis is cold and snowy in the winter, while Miami's climate is hot and humid in the summer. The average climate around the world is called "global climate."

Weather conditions can change from one year to the next. For example, Minneapolis might have a warm winter one year and a much colder winter the next. This kind of change is normal. But when the average pattern over many years changes, it could be a sign of climate change.

The Greenhouse Effect

The greenhouse effect is the process by which certain gases in the atmosphere trap heat and radiate it back to earth. The greenhouse effect is a natural process that is necessary to life on earth. That's because the greenhouse effect traps heat that otherwise would dissipate into outer space. Heat is trapped by greenhouse gases — mainly carbon dioxide, methane, and water vapor — in the atmosphere, which radiate heat in all directions, including back to earth. Without the greenhouse effect, earth would be a cold, cold place.

So what is the relationship between the greenhouse effect and global warming? When there is a normal amount of greenhouse gases in the atmosphere, earth maintains the warm climate that we know. Studies show that earth's climate has been relatively stable for the last 10,000 years — until about 200 years ago, when technology resulted in more greenhouse gases, especially carbon dioxide, being released into the atmosphere. The amount of methane has increased because of other human activities. For example, large quantities of methane can be released from oil wells and landfills used for trash disposal.

This overabundance of greenhouse gases causes more heat to be trapped than before, which results in rising temperatures. This has led to climate change, which has all sorts of negative consequences, from rising ocean temperatures, to increases in tropical storms and rising sea levels. We are already seeing ways in which climate change is affecting the supply of food and water around the world. Scientists say that climate change is linked to human release of greenhouse gases and not to increased energy from the sun, which has remained constant.

17. When scientists consider climate, what length of time is involved, according to "Weather versus Climate"?

   (A) 30 years or more.

   (B) a decade

   (C) probably a few months

   (D) whatever is going on today

18. Which of the following is indicative of climate change, according to "Weather versus Climate"?

   (A) Chicago has two weeks of subzero weather in January.

   (B) A light dusting of snow falls overnight in Tampa, Florida, in December.

   (C) Northern Maine experiences a day or two of 90-degree weather in August every few years.

   (D) The number of Atlantic hurricanes each year has been steadily increasing for decades.

19. According to "The Greenhouse Effect," which of the following is a cause of global warming?

   (A) The amount of heat received from outer space has increased.

   (B) Gases that trap heat in the atmosphere have increased.

   (C) Oceans are releasing more heat into the atmosphere.

   (D) The amount of energy reaching earth from the sun has increased.

20. From "The Greenhouse Effect," which of these actions can you infer would reduce global warming?

   (A) increasing the amount of trash buried in landfills

   (B) reducing the amount of oxygen released into the atmosphere by photosynthesis in plants

   (C) reducing the amount of methane released into the atmosphere by oil pumps

   (D) increasing the amount of water vapor released into the atmosphere by oceans

21. Which of these sentences most accurately describes the relationship between the two passages?

   (A) "Weather versus Climate" defines weather, climate, and climate change, while "The Greenhouse Effect" explains the cause of climate change.

   (B) "Weather versus Climate" gives the cause of climate change, while "The Greenhouse Effect" explains its consequences for life on earth.

   (C) "Weather versus Climate" contrasts weather and climate, while "The Greenhouse Effect" explains that climate change is a natural process we do not need to worry about.

   (D) "Weather versus Climate" says climate change is not a problem, while "The Greenhouse Effect" asserts that climate change is a crisis situation.

22. Which of these conclusions are supported by both passages?

(A) Global warming is a crisis we must address.

(B) Global warming is the cause of climate change.

(C) We do not need to worry about climate change.

(D) Climate change can be observed in long-term changes in climate we are seeing around the world.

Items 23–25 are based on this passage, which includes an excerpt from the U.S. Constitution.

The Bill of Rights is the first ten amendments to the United States Constitution. These amendments were added to the Constitution because some states were leery of ratifying the Constitution without them. They were afraid that the new government would be too powerful. They felt that the Constitution needed to guarantee fundamental liberties and freedoms that they had fought for and believed in. Some of the most important of these rights are in the First Amendment.

Congress shall make no law respecting an establishment of religion, or prohibiting the free exercise thereof; or abridging the freedom of speech, or of the press; or the right of the people peaceably to assemble, and to petition the government for a redress of grievances.

23. Which of these actions are rights or liberties of all Americans, according to the First Amendment?

(A) complaining to their representative in Congress

(B) owning a firearm

(C) voting in elections

(D) having a trial by jury

24. What does the word *leery* mean in this sentence in Paragraph 1?

These amendments were added to the Constitution because some states were leery of ratifying the Constitution without them.

(A) apprehensive

(B) angry

(C) unwary

(D) confident

25. A television news channel wants to report a story that is critical of the government. The government believes the information in the story is untrue. Which of these sentences describes an action permitted under the First Amendment in this situation?

(A) The government can seize the TV news channel to get it to stop reporting lies.

(B) The news channel must postpone the story until it convinces a court that the story is accurate.

(C) The news channel can show the story whenever it wants to.

(D) The government can force the channel to show another story that presents its point of view.

The answers

1. **D. serious enough that it requires monitoring.** The text states that the comingling of the virus strains is serious enough to require monitoring. Now that a new area of possible comingling has been found, the text implies that it, too, should be monitored. Choice (A) isn't supported by the text, and even though Choices (B) and (C) are possible, they're not as clear and important statements as Choice (D).

TIP

Your preparation for the science test can help you with RLA passages and questions like these, and vice versa. That gives you a leg up on both tests!

2. **D. North Pacific.** The text states that this finding shows the North Atlantic is as significant a melting pot for birds and avian flu as the North Pacific. Choice (B) isn't mentioned; and although *Eurasia* is mentioned, it isn't mentioned as a place where birds from Europe and North America mingle.

3. **C. It proved that avian flu viruses had mingled in Iceland.** According to the text, only this statement is true. The other statements are contradicted by information in the text.

4. **A. It can lead to a new, dangerous strain of avian flu.** The text states that the virus evolves readily and that the mingling of North American and Eurasian strains can lead to new varieties that are dangerous to humans. Cold viruses and flu viruses aren't the same, so Choice (B) has nothing to do with the topic of this text. Choices (C) and (D) are not supported by information in the passage.

5. **C. factual and straightforward.** The tone of the passage is very calm, very factual. It isn't *lighthearted, deeply concerned,* or *gloomy.*

6. **B. the H5N1 strain.** The text refers only to the H5N1 strain as a possible human flu. The term *bird flu* refers to the entire category of disease, not just the version dangerous to humans. There's no mention in the text of an *H5 flu,* and *Eurasian avian flu* simply refers to one part of the world where many strains of avian flu originate.

7. **D. It shifts the focus from risk to humans to the need for continued monitoring.** Choice (D) is correct because the paragraph indicates that the situation currently doesn't pose a high risk to humans but should be further monitored. The other answer choices are not supported by information in the paragraph.

8. **Essential: B, C; Not Essential: A, D.** Choice (B) is one of the key findings of the study, and Choice (C) is relevant for public health around the world, so both statements are essential to the summary. The types of birds, the exact locations in Iceland, and the type of land where the birds gathered are less important, so Choices (A) and (D) are not essential to the summary.

TIP

Question 8 is an example of the drag-and-drop format. On the actual GED, you would use your cursor to drag and drop the answer choices onto the correct parts of the graphic.

9. **B. the population of Chicagee.** The urban population listed is well beyond anything existing today. The other details are possible today and so do not indicate that the story is set in the future.

10. **A. incredibly crowded.** The overwhelming view that Bloch sees is a future of incredible overcrowding. There doesn't appear to be a food shortage based on the content of the story, so Choice (B) is wrong. Working hours appear to be shorter, so Choice (D) is also incorrect. And the passage indicates that the commutes are long and hard, so Choice (C) is incorrect.

11. **C. descriptions of enormous cities.** The author says that cities have expanded greatly from their original borders, which is an indication of massive population growth. The other details are mentioned in the passage but do not indicate that the population has grown so large.

12. **B. shorter working hours.** Harry states that he sometimes wishes he worked there because of the shorter working hours but doesn't say anything about better pay. The text also states that the commuting times would be longer there.

13. **C. He is not married.** The text mentions legal restrictions on accommodations. Harry would have to be married to be entitled to a two-room apartment. Harry states that he makes a good income, so money isn't an issue, which means that Choice (D) is incorrect. His lady friends claim to like the convenience, but Harry knows they're just being polite, which rules out Choice (B). He certainly doesn't like the small space, despite its efficiency, so Choice (A) is incorrect.

14. **A. 38 million.** The text states that the population is 38,000,000 people. The population of New Philly is 63,000,000, which makes Choice (B) incorrect. Choices (C) and (D) are too large.

15. **A. He feels more fortunate than others but still has vague worries.** The third and fourth sentences of the paragraph say that Harry feels fortunate for having a good job, security, and a nice home, yet he can't figure out what is haunting him about the future.

16. **A, B. travel on commutrains** and **the flavor of his breakfast.** The passage says that commutrains and powdered eggs are "murder," so Choices (A) and (B) support the generalization. Choice (C) is not possible because he can afford to eat in restaurants. The passage does not give information on the flavor of Instantea, so this answer choice does not support the generalization.

17. **A. 30 years or more.** The text states that climate refers to the average weather conditions over many years.

TIP

These two passages are examples of the kinds of textbook materials that may appear on the Reading component of the GED. In these cases, skills you develop for social studies and science tests can help you.

18. **D. The number of Atlantic hurricanes each year has been steadily increasing for decades.** Of the answer choices, only Choice (D) shows a change over time, so only this answer choice is possible.

TIP

When you come to readings with two passages, the questions will often tell you which passage(s) they refer to. Use that as a clue to help you look for the answer in the right reading.

19. **B. Gases that trap heat in the atmosphere have increased.** Choice (B) is directly stated in the passage as the cause of global warming. The other answer choices are not named as causes or are contradicted by the information in the passage.

20. **C. reducing the amount of methane released into the atmosphere by oil pumps.** According to the passage, methane is a greenhouse gas. Reducing emissions of it would reduce global warming. Therefore, Choice (C) is correct. Choice (A) would likely increase the release of methane gas, since the passage says that this gas is released from landfills. Choice (B) is incorrect because oxygen is not a greenhouse gas. In addition, reducing the amount of oxygen released into the air would likely have other negative consequences. Choice (D) is

incorrect because water vapor is a greenhouse gas, so releasing increased quantities would increase global warming, not reduce it.

21. **A. "Weather versus Climate" defines weather, climate, and climate change, while "The Greenhouse Effect" explains the cause of climate change.** Of the answer choices, only Choice (A) is possible: The first article contains definitions of the terms. The second article explains how the greenhouse effect works. The other answer choices are contradicted by the information in the passages.

22. **D. Climate change can be observed in long-term changes in climate we are seeing around the world.** Of the answer choices, only Choice (D) is supported by both passages. Choice (A) is not stated in either passage. Choice (B) is supported in only the second passage. Choice (C) is contradicted by the second passage.

23. **A. complaining to their representative in Congress.** Only Choice (A) is mentioned in the First Amendment, so it is correct. The other answer choices are mentioned in other parts of the Constitution.

TIP

This passage is also an example of the kinds of textbook materials that may appear on the Reading component of the GED. In these cases, skills you develop for social studies and science tests can help you on the RLA test, and vice versa. Talk about efficiency!

24. **A. apprehensive.** You can figure out that *leery* means "apprehensive" (Choice A) from the sentences that follow it, which indicate that the states were fearful of losing these rights. Choice (B) does not make sense, and Choices (C) and (D) are the opposite of the states' feelings.

TIP

Many GED questions ask you to figure out the meaning of a word as it is used in the passage. A good way to approach these questions is to swap into the sentence each of the answer choices. The answer choice that makes the most sense is likely correct.

25. **C. The news channel can show the story whenever it wants to.** The First Amendment protects freedom of the press. Choice (C) is the only answer choice that reflects this fundamental right. The actions in the remaining answer choices are forbidden by the First Amendment, and so are incorrect.

Chapter **8**

Preparing for the Extended Response Component

The Extended Response item is one of the components of the GED test that test-takers worry about the most. Let's face it, not everyone likes to write, and you may even have bad memories of writing essays in school. I can't make all of that go away, but I can give you some strategies and tips that will help you on test day — and in further education, if you decide to go to college.

In this chapter, I give you an overview of this test plus tips and strategies to help you write a passing GED essay in 45 minutes. And in Chapter 9, I walk you through the entire process, so that you will know exactly what to do on test day. I also explain how your essay will be evaluated and show you ways to raise your score. You can then use the Extended Response items in the practice tests to develop your skills and get some experience. None of us will ever be William Shakespeare, but by test day, you will at least be ready to pass!

Examining the Extended Response Item

Despite its name, the Extended Response doesn't consist of a long research essay so much as a series of four to seven related paragraphs. You aren't expected to produce a book-length opus, complete with documented research. Rather, you're expected to write a coherent series of inter-related paragraphs on a given topic and use the rules of grammar and correct spelling. Part of that essay will be an analysis of two short readings that are presented to you, and part will be prepara-tion of your own logical argument on the topic of the readings. Examiners look for an essay that's well organized, logical, and relevant to the topic given. They also look at how you adhere to stan-dards of English writing, but there is some good news: The focus is largely on complete sentences and overall understandability. You will not be graded down for small errors as long as your overall essay is clear and you use complete sentences.

In the following sections, I will show you what you need to know about the Extended Response and give you some tools for writing a passing essay.

Looking at the skills the Extended Response covers

After you take the real GED, your essay is sent electronically to a trained reader for evaluation. The evaluation of your essay focuses on three major areas. By having a clear understanding of the main skills covered in this part of the test, you can ensure that you will address all of them when writing your essay; that will translate into success in terms of your essay score. The GED Testing Service defines the three essay criteria you need to address as follows:

>> **Creation of an argument and use of evidence.** This criterion refers to how well you answer the topic, including whether the focus of the response shifts as you write. Stay on topic.

>> **Development of ideas and organizational structure.** This criterion refers to whether you show the reader through your essay that you provide clear, well-explained ideas about the topic and that you're able to establish a definable plan for writing the essay. The evaluation expects that you'll present your arguments in a logical sequence and back those arguments with specific supporting evidence from the source texts.

>> **Clarity and command of standard English conventions.** This criterion refers to your ability to appropriately use what might be called "on-demand draft writing" — that is, writing an essay in a single draft in 45 minutes on a topic you didn't choose. That includes the application of the basic rules of grammar, such as sentence structure, mechanics, usage, and so forth. It's also looking for stylistic features, such as transitional phrases, varied sentence structure, and appropriate word choices. But as I said before, you will not be graded down for small errors as long as they don't interfere too much with understandability.

The evaluation grades your essay on a three-point scale. You receive 2, 1, or 0 points, depending on your success in each of these three categories. In Chapter 9, you can find more information on how your essay will be scored, as well as an example of a high-scoring essay.

WARNING

To pass the entire RLA test, you need to score well on all three parts — reading, grammar, and language — and the extended response. If you don't pass the essay, you probably won't accumulate a high enough score on the other sections to pass the RLA test, and that means you'll have to retake the entire test. So use the following information to do your best on the Extended Response.

Understanding the Extended Response format

This 45-minute part of the Reasoning through Language Arts (RLA) test has only one item: a prompt on which you have to write a short essay.

For this part of the test, you're given one topic and a few instructions. The instructions will likely look something like this:

EXAMPLE

TIME: 45 minutes

YOUR ASSIGNMENT: Analyze the arguments presented in the two passages. Then develop an argument in which you explain how one position is better supported than the other. In your response, include relevant and specific evidence from both passages to support your argument.

Your task is to write an essay of four or more paragraphs on that topic. Remember that you can't write about another topic — if you do, you'll receive zero points for your essay.

While you cannot choose the topic of your essay, keep in mind that the test developers look for topics that most adults will know something about and be able to relate to. The topics will avoid areas that are sensitive or controversial. You can be sure that politics, religion, and other areas of personal belief will not come up.

The test presents you with two passages of argumentation. That means each of the writers takes a position on an issue. You must examine the positions, determine which is the stronger and best-defended one, and write an essay explaining why you made that choice. You have to do that regardless of how you feel about the issue. The point is to analyze and show that you understand the strategies used to defend these positions.

As part of that process, you must analyze the arguments for logical consistency, illogical conclusions, and false reasoning. This is where your critical thinking skills come into play. Does Point A from the author really make sense? Is it valid and backed by facts?

Finally, you must write your answer in a clear, concise, and well-organized response. The evaluation focuses mostly on the content and organization of your essay — whether you provide a logical argument in favor of one of two positions and support your argument with well-developed examples. The evaluation also considers whether you follow the conventions of standard English, but this criterion is much less important than content and organization. That's a big relief if spelling and punctuation are not your strongest suits!

For the online-proctored test and in-person testing, you will have an on-screen, erasable whiteboard for rough notes, ideas, and organization. For in-person testing, you will also have an erasable tablet and dry-erase marker for these tasks. On both tests, you can also highlight sections of the reading passages to refer to as you write. Use these tools to help you plan and organize your answer.

For some test-takers, having access to an erasable tablet for writing notes and organizing ideas is very handy. Other test-takers may prefer the onscreen, erasable whiteboard. Try using the on-screen whiteboard. If you feel you need the erasable tablet to do your best work, you may want to take the RLA test at a testing center.

Preparing to succeed on the Extended Response

The Extended Response essay requires some very specific skills, ranging from grammar and proper language usage to comprehension and analysis skills. If you've ever had an argument about who has the best team or which employer is better, you already know how to assess arguments and respond. Now you need to hone those skills. As you prepare for the RLA Extended Response, do the following:

>> **Read, read, and read some more.** Just as for the other parts of the RLA test (and most other tests on the GED), reading is important. Reading exposes you to well-crafted sentences, which can help you improve your own writing. Reading also expands your horizons and provides you with little bits of information that you can work into your essay.

>> **Read argumentative essays.** Since you will be responding to and writing argumentative essays, It pays to prepare by reading a variety of editorials and opinion pieces. You can find these on news websites and many other locations online. As you read, evaluate the writers' reasoning and the strength of the examples.

TIP

As you read, make an outline of the paragraphs or chapters that you read to see how the material ties together. Try rewriting some of the paragraphs from your outline, and compare what you write to the original. Your results may not be ready for prime time, but this little exercise gives you practice in writing organized, cohesive sentences and paragraphs, which can go a long way in this part of the test.

>> **Review how to plan an essay.** Few people can sit down, write a final draft of an essay without planning, and receive a satisfactory grade. Instead, you have to plan what you're going to write. The best way to start is to jot down your ideas about the topic without worrying about the order. From there, you can organize your thoughts into groups. Later in this chapter you will find help on planning your essay.

>> **Practice general writing.** If writing connected paragraphs isn't one of your strengths, practice doing so! Write long emails. Write long letters. Write to your member of Congress. Write to your friends. Write articles for community newspapers. Write short stories. Write anything you want — whatever you do, just keep writing.

>> **Write practice essays.** Check out the practice tests in Chapters 19 and 27 for some essay prompts (in actual test format). Write essays based on the topics given, and then ask a knowledgeable friend or former teacher to grade them for you. You can also read a couple of sample essays based on the same topics you're given in Chapters 20 and 28. You may also want to take a preparation class in which you're assigned practice topics to write about. When you think you're finished practicing, practice some more.

>> **Practice writing on a topic (and not going off topic!).** Your essay must relate to the given topic as closely as possible. If the test asks you to analyze two positions about daylight savings time and you write about how much you love the summertime, you can kiss your good score on this part of the test goodbye.

TIP

To help you practice staying on topic, read the newspaper and write a letter to the editor or a response to a columnist. Because you're responding to a very narrow topic that appeared in a particular newspaper article, you have to do so clearly and concisely — if you ever want to see it in print. (You can also practice staying on topic by picking a newspaper article's title and writing a short essay about it. Then read the actual story and see how yours compares.)

>> **Practice editing your own work.** When you take the test, the only person able to edit your essay is you. If that thought scares you, practice editing your own work now. Take a writing workshop or get help from someone who knows how to edit. Practice writing a lot of essays and don't forget to review and edit them as soon as you're done writing.

>> **Practice keyboarding.** To write an essay in 45 minutes, you need to be ready to type quickly and accurately on a standard computer keyboard. So use a computer as much as possible. To simulate real testing conditions, turn off the spell-checker and grammar-checker. When you finish, turn them back on to get some instant feedback about your work. If you don't own a computer, try to find one at your public library or an adult education center. If the center has classes or tutorials on keyboarding, take advantage of them! You can also find some free or inexpensive keyboarding tutorials online.

Writing the RLA Extended Response

The RLA Extended Response item asks you to write an essay in 45 minutes on an assigned topic. This part of the test assesses your literacy and understanding. Even if you can understand the essay topic, you must now demonstrate that you're thoroughly familiar with the process of writing an essay, that you know how to spell correctly, and that you understand the rules of grammar and language usage. You're asked to read two source texts that present different viewpoints on an issue. You must determine which argument is better supported and write an essay explaining why the position you chose is the better-supported one.

REMEMBER

Keep in mind that writing this essay isn't that different from writing a letter or a blog — except that you must explain and clarify the subject for the reader without rambling on until you run out of space.

In the following sections, I walk you through the four steps to writing an effective Extended Response and provide a few pointers for making sure you ace this part of the RLA test.

Managing your time

You have 45 minutes to finish your essay for the Extended Response on the RLA test, and in that time you have four main tasks:

>> Reading the passages

>> Planning your essay

>> Writing your essay

>> Revising and editing your essay

The following sections take a closer look at these tasks and explain how you can successfully complete each one in the time allotted.

TIP

A good plan of action is to spend 5 minutes reading, 10 minutes planning, 20 minutes writing, and 10 minutes editing and revising. This schedule is a tight one, though, so if your keyboarding is slow, consider allowing more time for writing. And remember, no one but you will see anything but the final version, so don't worry if you make mistakes while you type. Keep moving and correct these mistakes when you edit and revise.

Reading and planning (15 minutes total)

Before you begin writing your essay, read the instructions carefully. Determine the positions of the two source texts and think about what they mean to you. The next step is key: determining which position is stronger. Read the source texts and evaluate the strength of their arguments. One way to do this is to highlight effective examples and ideas as you read. Make your decision based on the strength of each passage — not your feelings or personal view. Consider the logic of the examples in each passage. If you highlighted examples as you read, which passage has the most highlights?

Once you determine your position, you can gather ideas that support it. You can write notes on the erasable tablet or type them into the on-screen whiteboard. You can also continue to highlight ideas in the passages or copy and paste them into the on-screen whiteboard. Don't worry about the order in which you write your ideas. You can sort through all the information in the next phase. Don't worry about correct grammar or spelling either. No one but you will see your notes.

After you write down these points, sit back for a moment to reflect. (Don't reflect too long, though, because you still have an essay to write! Just take a few minutes.) Then, convert your notes to a simple outline or plan for your essay. Look over your points and find an introduction, such as, "The argument that daylight savings time has outlived its usefulness makes the stronger case." Write this sentence above your brainstorming notes. Then look at the points you came up with earlier that strongly back up your position. Number them in the most effective order. Add some ideas from the reading that you think are false or flawed, so you can address them in your essay, too. All these ideas will be the body of your essay.

Now, write a concluding sentence, such as, "The argument against daylight savings time is stronger. Although once useful, the enormous cost, confusion, and lack of clear benefits show that it's an idea past its time." Glancing at your introduction and the essay topic itself, select points that strengthen your conclusion. Some of these points may be the same ones you used in your introduction.

Your plan will likely look something like this:

>> **Introduction.** "The argument that daylight savings time has outlived its usefulness makes the stronger case."

>> **Body.**

- List the appropriate supporting evidence in order of importance.

- List false arguments or flawed arguments made by either side of the discussion.

>> **Conclusion.** "Although daylight savings time was helpful in a bygone day, the changeover twice a year costs Americans billions of dollars in needless expense, lost wages, and inconvenience without any clear benefit to people's lives."

Now reflect again. Can you add any more points to improve the essay? Don't just add points to have more points, though. This isn't a contest for who can come up with the most points. You want to have logically written points that support your argument.

Look over your outline again. Can you combine any parts to make it tighter? Do you want to add an example? Or change the organization? Now's the time!

When you are satisfied with your outline, you're ready to go on to the next step: drafting your essay.

Writing (20 minutes)

During the writing stage, you think in more detail about the points you came up with in the planning stage, and you get your words typed out on-screen. Begin writing and keep going. Don't get bogged down on spelling or grammar. You can fix those issues later. Just write organized paragraphs and logical sentences.

REMEMBER

Each paragraph starts with an *introductory sentence,* which sets up the paragraph content, and ends with a *transition sentence* that leads from the paragraph you're on to the next one. If you put your sentences in a logical order from introduction to transition, you start to see paragraphs — as well as your essay — emerge.

Editing and revising (10 minutes)

Now comes the hard part. You have to be your own editor. Turn off your ego and remember that every word is written on a computer screen, not carved in stone. Make your work better by editing and revising it. Make this the best piece of writing you've ever done — in a 45-minute time block, of course.

When you're ready to edit and revise, scroll through your essay twice: once for content and again for standards of conventional English. First, read it to make sure that you are satisfied with the content of the essay. Does it make sense? Does it use good examples from the passages? Does it follow a logical order? If it doesn't, you may need to revise. Ask yourself whether each paragraph contributes to your argument. If it doesn't, you may need to do more revising. It could be something as simple as changing the order of the paragraphs, deleting something, or adding transitional phrases.

Then reread your essay for standards of conventional English. Look for errors in spelling, capitalization, subject–verb agreement, and punctuation. If you quote directly from one of the articles, make sure that you use quotation marks correctly. Check for these errors last because this area is the least important of the criteria used to score your essay. If your essay has good ideas, is written in sentences and paragraphs, flows logically, and has only a few small errors that do not interfere with understanding, you are 90 percent there!

Putting together a winning essay

Some of the key points in the essay evaluation appear in the following list. If you have all these characteristics in your essay, your chances of receiving a high score are pretty good:

>> You've read and understood the two source texts and selected the position that has the best support.

>> Your essay clearly explains why you made your choice, using proof from the source texts.

>> Your essay is clearly written and well organized.

>> The evidence you present is developed logically and clearly.

>> You use transitions throughout the essay for a smooth flow among ideas.

>> You use appropriate vocabulary, varied sentence structure, and good grammar and spelling.

Here are a few other tips and ground rules to keep in mind as you prepare for the Extended Response:

>> **You have only 45 minutes to write an essay based on a single topic and very specific source text.** Manage your time and keep moving. Stay focused on the topic and the information in the source texts. Don't go off topic or add your own ideas.

>> **You can prepare your essay by highlighting the source material and using the erasable tablet provided at the test center or the on-screen whiteboard.** As you read the source material, you can highlight ideas you want to include. Use the erasable tablet or on-screen whiteboard to gather and organize ideas, By using these tools, your final essay will be well-supported, logical, and organized. No one will look at the tablet or whiteboard, so what you write there is just for you.

>> **You must write about the topic and only about the topic.** You're graded for writing an essay on the topic, so make sure you really do write on the topic you're given. One of the easiest ways to fail this test is to write about something that isn't on topic. The source text presents divergent views. Your job is to analyze, reflect, and respond.

>> **Effective paragraphs use a variety of sentence types: statements, questions, commands, exclamations, and even quotations.** Vary your sentence structure and choice of words to spark the readers' interest. Some sentences may be short, and others may be long to catch the readers' attention. Just make sure that your sentences are complete and well constructed. Avoid fragments and run-ons!

>> **Paragraphs create interest in several ways: by developing details, using illustrations and examples, presenting events in a time or space sequence, providing definitions, classifying persons or objects, comparing and contrasting, and demonstrating reasons and proof.** Organize your paragraphs and sentences in a way that both expresses your ideas and creates interest.

>> **Don't obsess about spelling, capitalization, and mechanics as you write.** Try to get your ideas on the screen. Later, you can go back and fix those small errors.

Chapter 9

Writing an Extended Response Item

In this chapter, I provide an example of an Extended Response prompt with two passages that present arguments in favor of and against daylight savings time. Your task is to practice writing an essay, analyzing both positions presented in the passages to determine which one is best supported. Then, you look at how your essay is scored and analyze an example of a high-scoring essay.

Getting Familiar with the RLA Extended Response

On test day, the Reasoning Through Language Arts (RLA) Extended Response component is presented to you on a single screen with the directions at the top. The reading passages are on the left, and a word processing box is on the right. You can scroll the passages to read everything, and you can use the highlight feature to mark ideas in the passages that you want to use in your essay.

The word processing box is very similar to a regular word processor but does not have grammar- or spell-check or other advanced features. The only features available are cut, copy, paste, undo, and redo. These features are handy if you decide you want to reorder sentences or paragraphs as you write or revise. On test day, you will also have an online whiteboard that you can use to take notes and organize ideas. At test centers only, you will be handed an actual erasable tablet and dry-erase pen for the same purpose. It's big enough for note-taking but not for writing a whole first draft of your essay in order to keyboard later. For now, have a couple of sheets of paper handy for organizing and writing.

TIP

To become accustomed to the real testing conditions, try to write your essay on a computer if possible. On many word processing programs, you can simulate test conditions by turning off the spell-checker, grammar-checker, and auto-correct. (These controls are frequently found under "Preferences.") Then, after you write, you can turn the features back on to get some free, instant feedback on your work. Just remember, mechanics and spelling are not the most important criteria for evaluating your essay!

A Sample Extended Response Prompt

TIME: 45 minutes

YOUR ASSIGNMENT: Analyze the arguments presented in the two passages. Then develop an argument in which you explain how one position is better supported than the other. In your response, include relevant and specific evidence from both passages to support your argument.

Passage One

In the Good Old Summertime!

For most of us, setting our clocks forward one hour in March is a sure sign that spring is coming, followed by summer! After a long, hard winter, particularly in the cold northern states, summer is a welcome time. Kids are out of school, it may be time for a vacation, and we can barbecue, hike, and enjoy the great outdoors. It's time for patios, porches, parks, and backyards!

One of the big advantages of daylight savings time is that it gives us more time to enjoy the great outdoors in summer. Studies show that people are more active on summer evenings if they have an extra hour of daytime to enjoy. And because of the crisis of obesity in America, more exercise is better for everyone, and the country!

Daylight savings time has some other advantages, too. Traffic studies show that accidents go down during daylight savings time because of the longer daylight hours. And daylight savings time helps the economy, too, because longer hours of daylight in the afternoon encourage people to go out and spend. Malls, shopping centers, and downtowns are more likely to be filled when it's light outside.

So daylight savings time is really beneficial! We should definitely keep this longstanding practice so that everyone can reap the benefits.

Passage Two

Spring Forward, Fall Back — Far Back!

Daylight savings time is a relatively new idea that is now past its prime. Daylight savings time was started only during World War I. Its purpose was to reduce the consumption of important supplies, such as fuel and candles, by allowing for an extra hour of daylight each day. Later, it was reimposed to encourage shopping and outdoor activities in summer. However, this practice is now outmoded.

Several recent studies show that daylight savings time does not result in more summertime activities, as in the past. People are increasingly likely to stay in their air-conditioned homes. Other studies show that the transition to daylight savings time costs our country billions as companies, computer systems, and schedules have to be adjusted twice a year on such a massive scale. Medical studies show that disrupted sleep patterns have all sorts of negative consequences. Heart attacks and strokes go up right after the switchover because of the related stress. And everyone's circadian rhythms are disrupted twice a year, which causes symptoms similar to jet lag. This also causes auto accidents to soar in the days after the transitions as groggy drivers get into needless traffic accidents. Workplace accidents increase, too, as sleep-deprived workers make careless mistakes. In addition, studies of workplaces show that productivity goes down in the days after the twice-annual changeovers. Orders are messed up, and work has to be redone as workers recover from disrupted rest patterns.

Daylight savings time has also lost the energy savings that once made it attractive. Because people nowadays run their air conditioners day and night, energy consumption will not be much affected.

Keeping daylight savings time is also bad for international business. Globally, fewer countries than ever before continue to observe daylight savings time. The European Union recently decided to do away with daylight savings time for just the reasons already mentioned. Each year, the U.S. airline industry loses an average of $150 million realigning schedules to those of countries that don't observe daylight savings time. All of the disruption puts the United States at a disadvantage with the rest of the world.

It's time for the United States to align with a growing number of countries around the world and abolish this annual folly. Families, health, and the economy will only benefit.

Evaluating Your Response

After writing your own response to the essay prompt in the previous section (and before you read the sample essay in the next section), evaluate your answer with the criteria the GED Testing Service uses to evaluate GED essays:

>> Creation of an argument and use of evidence

- Do you clearly state which position was stronger and better argued?

- Do you explain why you came to that conclusion? (You don't have to agree with the position.)

- Do you include multiple pieces of evidence from the passages to support your position?

>> Development of ideas and organizational structure

- Does your introduction clearly state your position?

- Is your evidence presented in a logical order to build your case?

- Do you fully explain your examples and evidence?

- Does your conclusion contain an appropriate summary of the evidence and why you took the stand you did?

- Is your essay written in a clear, concise manner?

- Does your essay stay on topic?

>> Clarity and command of Standard English conventions

- Do you write in complete sentences?

- Do you use proper linkages between paragraphs and ideas?

- Do you use varied and clear sentences and sentence structure?

- Do you follow the conventions of Standard English (spelling and grammar)?

Checking Out a Sample Response

Here's an example of a solid RLA Extended Response for the given prompt. Compare it to yours. Then review both against the evaluation criteria in the previous section.

Switching to and from daylight savings time each year has many pros and many cons. While some people may enjoy some benefits from the switchover, the argument that daylight savings time has outlived its usefulness makes the stronger case.

Changing to daylight savings time has a few advantages. People can get outdoors more, and the added daylight is nice for summer fun. But recent studies show that nowadays people are less likely to go out on summer evenings than in the past. As the second article implies, many people just stay inside in cool, air-conditioned comfort.

There are many more negatives to daylight savings time. The changeover has all kinds of costs. It has very bad effects on our health, including a big increase in heart attacks, as reported in some medical studies. Other medical studies show that people get into more car accidents. Accidents and errors go up at work, too, which is costly. Daylight savings time also puts us out of kilter with the rest of the world. Fewer countries observe it now than before, so American businesses have to make a lot of effort to stay in sync. Daylight savings time gets airline schedules out of whack, too, which costs those companies billions of dollars.

As you can see, although daylight savings time was helpful in a bygone day, the changeover twice a year costs Americans billions of dollars in needless expense, lost wages, poor health, and inconvenience, with few clear benefits to people's lives.

Finding Your Way: The Social Studies Test

Find out what skills you need to succeed on the test, which subject areas the test covers, and how the test is laid out.

Take advantage of key test-taking strategies so that you're prepared to deal with any question type and understand any passage or visual material presented to you.

Chapter **10**

A Graph, a Map, and You: Getting Ready for the Social Studies Test

D o you enjoy knowing about how events in the past may help you foretell the future? Do the lives of people in faraway places interest you? Is politics something you care about? If you answered yes to any of these questions, then you're going to like the Social Studies test! After all, social studies helps you discover how humans relate to their environment and to other people.

The GED Social Studies test assesses your skills in understanding and interpreting concepts and principles in civics, history, geography, and economics. Consider this test as a kind of crash course in where you've been, where you are, and how you can continue living there. You can apply the types of skills tested on the Social Studies test to your experience in community, school, and workplace situations as a citizen, a consumer, or an employee.

This test includes questions based on a variety of written passages and visual content taken from academic, community, and workplace materials, including both primary and secondary sources. The materials in this test are like those you see in most online news content. Reading well-written, reliable news sources regularly can help you become familiar with the style and vocabulary of the passages you find on the GED. Pay attention to articles on politics, the government, the Supreme Court, and the economy. For history, any number of websites have articles on U.S. or world history.

The Social Studies test consists of 50 questions on civics and government (about 50 percent of the test), U.S. history (about 20 percent of the test), economics (about 15 percent of the test), and geography and the world (about 15 percent of the test). Most of the questions are multiple-choice. A few are fill-in, drag-and-drop, and other alternate question types. Don't worry! I walk you through all the different question types in Chapter 11 and provide tips on how to answer each one. You have 70 minutes to complete this section. In this chapter, you take a look at the skills required for the Social Studies section of the GED test, the format of the test, and what you can do to prepare.

Looking at the Skills the Social Studies Test Covers

The questions on the Social Studies test evaluate several specific skills, including the ability to read and understand complex text, interpret and relate graphs to text, and relate descriptive text to specific values in graphs. For example, a question could ask about the relationship between a description of unemployment in text and a graph of the unemployment rate over time.

REMEMBER

You don't have to study a lot of new content to pass this test. Everything you need to know is presented to you with the questions. In each case, you see some content, either a passage or a visual; a question or direction to tell you what you're expected to do; and a series of answer choices.

The questions may require you to draw on your previous knowledge of events, ideas, terms, and situations related to social studies. From a big-picture perspective, the questions in this section ask you to

>> Identify information, events, problems, and ideas and interpret their significance or impact.

>> Use the information and ideas in different ways to explore their meanings or solve a problem.

>> Use the information or ideas to do the following:

- Distinguish between facts and opinions

- Summarize major events, problems, solutions, and conflicts

- Arrive at conclusions based on information provided to you

- Influence other people's attitudes

- Find other meanings or mistakes in logic

- Identify causes and their effects

- Recognize how writers may have been influenced by the times in which they lived

- Compare and contrast differing events and people, and their views

- Compare places, opinions, and concepts

- Determine what impact views and opinions may have both at this time and in the future

- Analyze similarities and differences in issues or problems

- Identify examples that illustrate or support ideas and concepts

- Evaluate solutions

>> Make judgments about the material's appropriateness, accuracy, and differences of opinion. Some questions will ask you to interpret the role information and ideas play in influencing current and future decision making. These questions ask you to think about issues and events that affect you every day. That fact alone is interesting and has the potential to make you a more informed citizen. What a bonus for a test!

Many questions test your ability to read and interpret text in a social studies context. That means you'll be tested on the following:

>> Identifying and interpreting information from sources

>> Isolating central ideas or specific information

>> Determining the meaning of words or phrases used in social studies

>> Identifying points of view, differentiating between fact and opinion, and identifying properly supported ideas

Other questions ask you to interpret graphical information and apply mathematical reasoning to social studies. Much of that relates to your ability to do the following:

>> Interpret graphs

>> Use charts and tables as source data and interpret the content

>> Interpret information presented visually

>> Differentiate between correlation and cause and effect

REMEMBER

Don't let this list intimidate you! You don't have to answer every question correctly to pass the GED Social Studies test. In fact, this test has the second-highest passing rate of all the GED test sections. Besides, you probably are good at many of these skills already, based on prior learning and life experience.

On the GED Social Studies test, a calculator icon appears on the top right of the computer screen for questions that involve math. When the calculator icon appears, you may click on the icon to use the online calculator or use your own TI-30XS MultiView calculator (at a test center only).

TIP

Since only a few items on the Social Studies test involve math, you might want to take the test at home if that is more convenient. Going to the test center in order to use a real calculator on only a few items may not be worth the extra trouble.

Other questions deal with applying social studies concepts, including the following:

>> Understanding how specific evidence supports conclusions

>> Comprehending the connections between people, environments, and events

>> Putting historical events into chronological order

>> Analyzing documents to examine how ideas and events develop and interact, especially in a historical context

>> Examining cause-and-effect correlations

>> Identifying bias and evaluating validity of information, in both modern and historical documents

Being aware of what skills the Social Studies test covers can help you get a more accurate picture of the types of questions you'll encounter. The next section focuses more on the specific subject materials you'll face.

Understanding the Social Studies Test Format and Content

You have 70 minutes to complete the 50 questions on the Social Studies test. The questions come in various forms and are of varying difficulty. Most are in the standard multiple-choice-question format that you know from your school days. Other formats include fill-in-the-blank, drag-and-drop, and drop-down menu items. For a general overview of the types of questions on the Social Studies test, check out Chapter 2. For a deeper look, see Chapter 11.

In the following sections, you explore the subject areas the Social Studies test covers, and I give you an overview of the types of passages you can expect to see.

Checking out the subject areas on the test

Most of the information you need to answer these questions will be presented in the text or graphics accompanying the questions, so it's important to read and analyze the materials carefully but quickly. The questions focus on the following subject areas:

>> **Civics and government:** About 50 percent of the Social Studies test includes topics such as rights and responsibilities in democratic governance and the forms of governance. Many of these questions are about fundamental documents, such as the U.S. Constitution, the Declaration of Independence, and other writings. But don't worry — you don't need to memorize these documents. You will always be provided with excerpts to read.

>> **American history:** About 20 percent of the test covers a broad outline of the history of the United States from pre-colonial days to the present, including topics such as the War of Independence, the Civil War, the Great Depression, and the challenges of the 20th and 21st centuries.

>> **Economics:** Economics involves about 15 percent of the test and covers two broad areas — economic theory and basic principles. These include topics such as how various economic systems work, as well as topics related to consumer economics, such as inflation, the minimum wage, and other bread-and-butter subjects you can relate to.

>> **Geography and the world:** In broad terms, the remaining 15 percent covers the relationships between the environment and societal development; the concepts of borders, region, place, and diversity; and, finally, human migration and population issues.

The test materials cover these four subject areas through two broad themes:

>> **Development of modern liberties and democracy:** How did the modern ideas of democracy and human and civil rights develop? What major events have shaped democratic values, and what writings and philosophies are the underpinning to American views and expressions of democracy?

>> **Dynamic systems:** How have institutions, people, and systems responded to events, geographic realities, national policies, and economics?

If you're a little worried about all of these subject areas, relax. You're not expected to have detailed knowledge of all the topics listed. Although it helps if you have a general knowledge of these areas, the test is based on your ability to reason, interpret, and work with the information presented in the reading passages and visual material. Knowing basic concepts, such as checks and balances in a representative democracy, will help, but you don't need to know a detailed history of the United States.

Identifying the types of passages

The passages in the Social Studies test are taken from two types of sources:

>> **Academic material:** This is the type of material you find in a school — textbooks, maps, newspapers, magazines, software, and internet content. This type of passage also includes extracts from speeches or historical documents.

>> **Workplace and community material:** This is the type of material found on the job — manuals, documents, business plans, advertising and marketing materials, company announcements, letters, emails, and so on.

The material may be from primary sources (original documents such as the Declaration of Independence) or secondary sources (material written about an event or person, such as someone's opinions or interpretation of original documents, historic events, or historic figures, sometimes long after the event takes place or the person dies).

Examining Preparation Strategies That Work

To improve your skills and get better results, I suggest that you try the following strategies when preparing for the Social Studies test:

>> **Answer as many practice questions and take as many practice tests as you can get your hands on.** The best way to prepare is to answer all of the sample Social Studies test questions you can find. Work through practice questions (see Chapter 12), the practice tests in this book (see Chapters 21 and 29), and the online test included with this book. You can also try your luck on a free quarter-length Social Studies practice test at ged.com and at https://ged.com/study/free_online_ged_test/. The GED app, GED & Me, also offers free instructional material and practice items for every section of the GED.

Consider taking a preparation class to get your hands on even more sample Social Studies test questions, but remember that your task is to pass the test — not to collect every question ever written.

>> **Use the answers and explanations.** I provide complete answers and explanations for all the practice items in this book for a reason: to help you improve your ability to answer items on the real test. Read all the explanations, whether you answered correctly or not.

>> **Read a variety of different documents.** The documents you need to focus on include historic passages from original sources (such as the Declaration of Independence and the U.S. Constitution), as well as practical information for citizens and consumers (such as voter guides, atlases, budget graphs, political speeches, almanacs, and tax forms). Read about the evolution of democratic forms of government. Read about climate change and migration, about food and population, and about American politics in the post-9/11 world. Read newspapers and news magazines about current issues, especially those related to civics and government and social and economic issues.

>> **Prepare summaries of the passages you read in your own words.** After you read these passages, summarize what you've read. Doing so can help you identify the main points of the passages, which is an important part of succeeding on the Social Studies test. Ask yourself the following two questions when you read a passage or something more visual like a graph:

   • **What's the passage about?** The answer is usually in the first and last paragraphs of the passage. The rest is usually explanation. If you don't see the answer there, you may have to look carefully through the rest of the passage.

- **What's the visual material about?** Look for the answer in the title, labels, captions, and any other information that's included.

After you get an initial grasp of the main idea, determine what to do with it. Some questions ask you to apply information that you gain from one situation in another similar situation. If you know the main idea of the passage, you'll have an easier time applying it to another situation.

» **Discuss questions and answers with friends and family to make sure you've achieved an understanding and proper use of the material.** If your friends and family understand the question, then you know it's a good one. Discussing your questions and answers with others gives you a chance to explain social studies topics and concepts, which is an important skill to have as you get ready to take this test.

» **Don't assume.** Be critical of visual material and read it carefully. You want to be able to read visual material as accurately as you read text material, and doing so takes practice. Don't assume something is true just because it looks that way in a diagram, chart, or map. Visual materials can be precise drawings, with legends and scales, or they can be drawn in such a way that, at first glance, the information appears to be different than it really is. Manipulating the scale for graphs is one way to skew the information and distort its meaning. At first glance, you never know the purpose for which the visual was created. Even visuals can be biased, so "read" them carefully. Verify what you think you see by making sure the information looks correct and realistic. Finally, before coming to any conclusions, check the scale and legend to make sure the graph is really showing what you think it is showing you.

» **Be familiar with the conventions of maps and graphs.** Maps and graphs have conventions. The top of a map is almost always north. A graph's horizontal axis is always the x-axis, and the vertical axis (the y-axis) is dependent on the x-axis. Looking at the horizontal axis first usually makes the information clearer and easier to understand. Practice reading different sorts of maps online or in an atlas. Check out newspaper and other websites for different kinds of graphs and tables. I give detailed information on interpreting maps, graphs, and tables in Chapter 11. Soon you'll be crunching data like a pro!

See Chapter 4 for general test–taking strategies that apply to all the GED test sections.

Chapter **11**

Social Studies Question Types and Solving Strategies

The Social Studies test consists of 50 questions on civics and government (about 50 percent of the test), U.S. history (about 20 percent of the test), economics (about 15 percent of the test), and geography and the world (about 15 percent of the test). You have 70 minutes to complete this section. Having a basic understanding of what's in this section can help you prepare and avoid any surprises when you sit down to take the test.

The Social Studies test requires you to read a passage or study a visual, analyze the information, evaluate its accuracy, and draw conclusions. It doesn't measure your ability to recall information such as dates, facts, or events. In most cases, you select an answer from four choices. So although there's not much you can do to study for this test, you can improve your chances of passing by answering practice questions and reading and writing summaries of what you've read — and by checking out my test-taking strategies in this chapter.

In this chapter, you explore the types of materials and questions that you'll encounter on the Social Studies test, and I offer you advice on how to answer the questions with ease.

Answering Questions about Text and Visual Materials

There are two broad categories of source materials for the questions on the test. These source materials consist of textual materials, something with which you're probably already quite familiar, and visuals like maps, diagrams, graphs, and tables. Each kind of material requires careful reading, even the visuals, because information can be buried anywhere, and you need to extract it. The materials require you to read thoughtfully, make inferences, come to conclusions, and then determine the answer.

Questions about text passages

About half of the questions on the Social Studies test are based on textual passages, followed by a question or a series of questions. Your job is to read the passage and then answer the question or questions about it.

When you're reading these passages on the test (or in any of the practice questions or tests in this book), read between the lines and look at the implications and assumptions in the passages. An *implication* is something you can understand from what's written, even though it isn't directly stated. An *assumption* is something you can accept as the truth, even though proof isn't directly presented in the text.

REMEMBER

Be sure to read each question carefully so you know exactly what it's asking. Read the answer choices and carefully go through the text again. If the question asks for certain facts, you'll be able to find them right in the passage. If it asks for opinions, you may find those opinions stated directly in the passage, or they may simply be implied (and they may not match your own opinions, but you still have to answer with the best choice based on the material presented).

Answer each question using *only* the information given. An answer may be incorrect in your opinion, but according to the passage, it's correct (or vice versa). Go with the information presented and select the best answer choice.

Questions about visual materials

To make sure you don't get bored, many of the questions on the Social Studies test are based on maps, graphs, tables, political cartoons, diagrams, photographs, and artistic works. You need to be prepared to deal with all these types of visual materials. Some questions combine visual material and text.

If you're starting to feel overwhelmed about answering questions based on visual materials, consider the following:

>> **Maps aren't there only to show you the location of places.** They also give you information, and knowing how to decode that information is essential. A map may show you where Charleston is located, but it can also show you how the land around Charleston is used, what the climate in the area is like, or whether the population there is growing or declining. Start by examining the print information with the map, the *legend* (the table explaining the symbols used on the map), title, and key to the colors or symbols on the map. Then look at what the question requires you to find. Now you can find that information quickly by relating the answer choices to what the map shows.

For example, the map in Figure 11-1 shows you the following information:

- The population of the United States for 2020

- The population by state, by size range

Indirectly, the map also shows you much more. It allows you to compare the population of states with a quick glance. For example, you can see that Florida has a larger population than Montana, North Dakota, South Dakota, and Wyoming combined. If you were asked what the relationship is between a state's size and population, you could argue, based on this map, that there isn't much of a relationship. You could also show that the states in the Northeast have a higher population density than the states in the Midwest. This is part of the skill of analyzing maps.

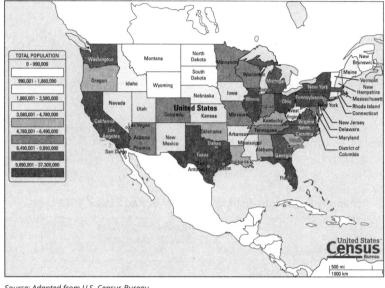

FIGURE 11-1: Population of U.S. states, District of Columbia, and Puerto Rico, 2020 Census Map.

Source: Adapted from U.S. Census Bureau

>> **Every time you turn around, someone in the media is trying to make a point with a graph.** The types of graphs you see in Figure 11-2 are typical examples. The real reason people use graphs to explain themselves so often is that a graph can clearly show trends and relationships between different sets of information. The three graphs in Figure 11-2 are best suited for a particular use. For example, bar graphs are great for comparing items over time, line graphs show changes over time, and pie charts show you proportions. The next time you see a graph, such as the ones in Figure 11-2, study it. Be sure to look carefully at the scale of graphs; even visual information can fool you. A bar graph that appears to show a rapid rise of something may in fact show no such thing. It may only look that way because the bottom of the chart doesn't start with a value of zero. Check carefully to make sure you understand what the information in the graph is telling you.

>> **Tables are everywhere.** If you've ever looked at the nutrition label on a food product, you've read a table. Study any table you can find, whether in a newspaper or on the back of a can of tuna. The population data table in Figure 11-3 is an example of the kinds of data you may see on the test. That table shows you a lot of information, but you can extract quite a bit more information that isn't stated. Some mental math tells you that according to the data in the table, around 236,000 people were serving outside the United States in the armed forces in December 2020. How do you know that? Just subtract the number in the *Resident Population* column from the *Resident Population Plus Armed Forces Overseas* column. You can also calculate the change in the overall population, the rate of increase of the population, and even the size of the armed forces stationed in the United States compared to serving overseas.

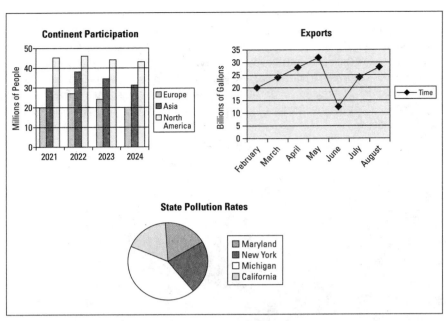

FIGURE 11-2:
Examples
of different
graphs.

© John Wiley & Sons, Inc.

Monthly Population Estimates for the United States, 2024

Month	Resident Population	Resident Population Plus Armed Forces Overseas	Civilian Population
January 1	335,893,089	336,139,132	334,827,918
February 1	336,003,666	336,249,709	334,938,495
March 1	336,115,348	336,361,391	335,050,177
April 1	336,238,570	336,484,613	335,173,399
May 1	336,370,098	336,616,141	335,304,927
June 1	336,512,477	336,758,520	335,447,306
July 1	336,673,595	336,919,638	335,608,424
August 1	336,845,126	337,091,169	335,779,955
September 1	337,032,412	337,278,455	335,967,241
October 1	337,200,318	337,446,361	336,135,147
November 1	337,348,742	337,594,785	336,283,571
December 1	337,497,567	337,743,610	336,432,396

FIGURE 11-3:
Population
data table.

Source: Adapted from U.S. Census Bureau

REMEMBER

Tables are also sometimes called charts, which can be a little confusing, because graphs can also be called charts. Regardless of what they're called, you need to be prepared to extract information even if it isn't stated directly. That's what makes maps and tables and graphs such fun.

>> **Political cartoons appear in the newspapers and online every day.** If you don't read political cartoons in the daily newspaper (usually located in the "Editorial," "Op-Ed," or "Opinion" pages in print or online), give them a try. Some days, they're the best entertainment in the paper. Political cartoons are usually based on an event in the last day or week. They can be mean or funny and are always biased. To get the most out of political cartoons, look for small details, facial expressions, and background clues. The cartoons on the test are obviously older than the ones in daily newspapers, and may include political cartoons from America's past. Then you need to use your knowledge of American history. But don't worry — whether

the cartoon is about war, politics, or the economy, the context will be clear. To become more familiar with past cartoons, search for "political cartoons" online. You can also find websites that build skills for interpreting political cartoons.

>> **You've no doubt seen countless photographs in your day.** Photos are all around you. All you need to do to prepare for the photograph-based questions on the test is to begin getting information from the photographs that you see. Start with the newspapers or magazines, where photos are chosen to provide information that connects directly to a story. See whether you can determine what message the photograph carries with it and how it relates to the story it supports. Use the caption to help you understand the photo. If you don't understand a word or two in the caption, use information from the photo to help you figure it out.

TIP

If you're unsure of how to read a map, go to any search engine and search for "map reading help" or "map reading skills" to find sites that explain how to read a map. If any of the other types of visual materials cause you concern, try similar searches, such as "graph reading skills," "understanding tables," or "interpreting political cartoons." You will get lots of tips and advice, plus plenty of maps, graphs, tables, and political cartoons to look at.

All the visual items you have to review on this test should be familiar to you. Now all you have to do is practice until your skills in reading and understanding them increase. Then you, too, can discuss the latest political cartoon or pontificate about the latest climate change data.

Acing the Social Studies Items

The types of questions that you encounter on the Social Studies test include multiple-choice, fill-in-the-blank, drag-and-drop, and drop-down-menu. In the following sections, I provide strategies for examining information, whether a passage or visual, and for answering sample questions in each of these formats.

Choosing an answer from multiple choices

Multiple-choice questions basically ask you to choose a correct answer from four choices. First, read the questions and the answer choices and then read the passage, looking for the answers.

If you can't decide based on that reading, review the answer choices. You can probably eliminate one or two of them because they're obviously wrong. Then skim the text again, looking for information based on the choices that are left. If that doesn't provide you with an answer, then you may have to guess. If you've eliminated the improbable answer choices, you may have to choose from only two or three choices, which improves the odds of picking the correct one.

In the rest of this section, I walk you through answering some multiple-choice questions based on the following passage.

> Bridging both temperate and tropical regions, Mexico's terrain includes mountains, plains, valleys, jungles, rainforest, lakes and rivers, glaciers, and plateaus. Snow-capped volcanoes slope down to pine forests, deserts experience intense heat, and tourists play in the surf on balmy, tropical beaches. This diverse topography supports a variety of industries, including manufacturing, mining, petroleum, agricultural production, and tourism. A member of the United States-Mexico-Canada Agreement, Mexico has the United States and Canada as its main export partners. In economic terms, Mexico has a GDP (gross domestic product) of

$1.466 trillion ($8,421 per person), which ranks it 12th in the world. Beginning in 1985, Mexico began a process of trade liberalization and privatization. From 1982 to 1992, government-controlled enterprises were reduced from 1,155 to 217.

EXAMPLE

Which of the following is a feature of Mexico's terrain?

(A) volcanoes

(B) inland seas

(C) a polar ice cap

(D) earthquakes

The answer to this question is Choice (A), volcanoes, which is stated directly in the passage. Notice that even if you cannot find this answer quickly, you can eliminate Choice (C), since Mexico is not in a polar region. Inland seas (Choice B) are found in Canada and Europe, but not in Mexico. Mexico experiences earthquakes (Choice D), but they are not a geographic feature and are not mentioned in the passage.

EXAMPLE

Which words or phrases demonstrate that Mexico's climate represents extremes in temperature?

(A) sunny and rainy

(B) dark and misty

(C) plains and valleys

(D) snow-capped and intense heat

Here's an example of answer choices that can be misleading unless you read the question carefully. The question asks for the answer choice that represents extremes in *temperature.* So the only choice that works here is Choice (D) because it's the only one that deals with temperatures. *Snow-capped* volcanoes represent an extremely low temperature, while *intense heat* represents the opposite extreme. The other choices don't refer to temperature. *Sunny* and *rainy* and *dark* and *misty* refer to weather. *Plains* and *valleys* refer to terrain.

EXAMPLE

The phrase *diverse topography* refers to

(A) differences in terrain

(B) uniqueness in manufacturing

(C) differences in agriculture

(D) diversity of tropical beaches

This question shows why understanding subject-appropriate vocabulary is important. *Topography* is another word for "terrain." *Diverse* means "different," so Choice (A) is correct. *Manufacturing* and *agriculture* are types of industries, and *tropical beaches* are just one type of terrain.

EXAMPLE

Which countries are Mexico's top export partners?

(A) the United States and Britain

(B) Spain and Canada

(C) the United States and Canada

(D) Canada and Britain

The answer is Choice (C). The passage states this information directly. Britain and Spain aren't mentioned in the passage. In this question, the answer choices can be misleading unless you read them completely. You could be fooled into selecting any of the incorrect answer choices, which are all partially correct. You need to read all four answer choices and select the one that is the best answer. For this question, that's Choice (C).

EXAMPLE

What happened in Mexico between 1982 and 1992?

(A) Government control of enterprises increased.

(B) The government controlled fewer enterprises.

(C) Mexico achieved the highest GDP in the world.

(D) Mexico's growth rate was less than 6 percent.

The answer is Choice (B). According to the passage, during the decade from 1982 to 1992, Mexico's government reduced its control of enterprises from 1,155 to 217. Therefore, Choice (A) is incorrect. Notice that when two answer choices are opposites, usually one of them is correct. Mexico's GDP ranking (Choice C) is 12th in the world. Mexico's growth rate (Choice D) is not stated in the passage. This question shows how process of elimination can help you if you are unsure about the answer. Since Choice (C), growth rate, is not mentioned in the passage, you can eliminate this answer choice easily. Then, if you have to guess, the odds of guessing correctly are higher.

Coming up with an answer for fill-in-the-blank questions

Fill-in-the-blank questions require you to insert the answer, usually a word, phrase, or number, into a blank. No answer choices are provided, so you have to extract the information carefully from the passage or visual.

For practice, find the information you need in order to answer fill-in-the-blank questions based on the following graph.

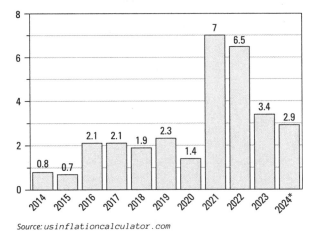

Source: usinflationcalculator.com

EXAMPLE

In what year was the inflation rate the lowest? [   ]

The graph shows the annual inflation rate from 2014 to 2024. You need to identify that the vertical scale on the left refers to the inflation data. Every year is listed on the horizontal axis. To answer this question, you need to find the lowest bar on the graph. That bar is 0.7%. Because the question asks for the year, write the corresponding year, 2015.

What was the difference between the inflation rates in 2022 and 2023? ☐

To answer this item, you need to find two values on the chart and then subtract. Inflation in 2022 was 6.5%. Inflation in 2023 was 3.4%. Subtract to find the difference: 6.5 − 3.4 = 3.1, so write 3.1 in the box. This calculation was easy, and you could do it in your head, but for harder calculations, remember to use your calculator or the on-screen calculator.

The inflation rate in 2021 was ☐ .

To answer this question, find the bar that corresponds to 2021. Then find the inflation rate for that year. The rate is 7%, so write that value in the box.

Dragging and dropping answers where they belong

Drag-and-drop questions require more understanding than basic multiple-choice questions because, in most instances, you need to prioritize, sequence, or sort answer choices, not just pick the answer.

Here's an example of a drag-and-drop item based on the following excerpt from *U.S. History For Dummies*, by Steve Wiegand (Wiley).

> As time passed, however, the country began to side more often with Britain, France, and other countries that were fighting Germany. The sinking of the British passenger ship, *Lusitania,* by a German submarine in 1915, which resulted in the deaths of 128 Americans, inflamed U.S. passions against "the Huns." Propagandistic portrayals of German atrocities in the relatively new medium of motion pictures added to the heat. And finally, when it was revealed that German diplomats had approached Mexico about an alliance against the United States, Wilson felt compelled to ask Congress for a resolution of war against Germany. He got it on April 6, 1917.

Drag (or write, in this case) the list of events into the boxes in chronological order. Write the letters.

Order of Events

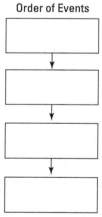

© John Wiley & Sons, Inc.

(A) sinking of the *Lusitania*

(B) declaration of war against Germany

(C) anti-German propaganda in the movies

(D) Germany negotiates with Mexico to attack the United States

The correct sequence of events is Choice (A), (C), (D), and then (B): the sinking of the *Lusitania*, anti-German propaganda in the movies, Germany negotiates with Mexico to attack the United States, and then declaration of war against Germany. The only somewhat tricky part of these choices is the timing for the anti-German propaganda, but the key phrase is in the sentence, "Propagandistic portrayals added to the heat." The word *added* implies that it happened after the sinking of the *Lusitania*, which already generated anti-German "heat."

Choosing from a drop-down menu

A drop-down item is similar to a multiple-choice question because you select your answer from several options by clicking on your choice. Unlike multiple-choice questions, drop-down answer choices are not identified by letters. In this book, I use letters for the answer choices for ease of use.

Drop-down items are frequently used together with graphics. The question usually asks you to complete a caption or a sentence about the graphic.

Try this example about the inflation graph from the previous section.

EXAMPLE

The chart shows the annual _____ of inflation over an 11-year period.

(A) rate

(B) percentage

(C) index

(D) number

The answer is Choice (A). The table is about the rate of inflation. The other choices do not make sense.

Managing Your Time for the Social Studies Test

You have a total of 70 minutes to answer 50 questions. So that means you have 84 seconds for each one. Answering easy questions first should allow you to progress faster, leaving you a little more time per item at the end so that you can come back to work on the harder ones.

To help you keep moving, you can skip questions or flag them for later if you're unsure of your answers. The Flag for Review button, in the upper-left corner of the screen, lets you flag questions that you're not sure about. When you finish the last question, you move to the Review screen, which shows a list of all the questions that are flagged or skipped. You can also go to the Review screen at any time by pressing the Review screen button in the lower-left corner of your screen. This way, you can return to questions you flagged or skipped.

The questions on the Social Studies test are based on both regular textual passages and visual materials, so that when you plan your time for answering the questions, you have to consider the amount of time it takes to read both types of materials. (See the earlier section, "Questions about visual materials," for advice on how you can get more comfortable with questions based on graphs, tables, and the like.)

Each time you come to a new passage or visual, read the questions first and then skim the passage to find the answers. If you still can't answer one or more questions, then read the passage carefully, looking for the answers. This way, you take more time only when necessary.

Because you have such little time to gather all the information you can from visual material and answer questions about it, you can't study the map, graph, or cartoon for long. You have to skim it the way you skim a paragraph. Reading the questions that relate to a particular visual first helps you figure out what you need to look for as you skim the material. The practice tests in Chapters 21 and 29 contain plenty of examples of questions based on visual materials, and so do the sample questions in Chapter 12.

TIP

If you're unsure of how quickly you can answer questions based on visual materials, time yourself on a few and see. If your time comes out to be more than 1.5 minutes, you need more practice.

Realistically, you have about 20 seconds to read the question and the possible answers, 50 seconds to look for the answer, and 10 seconds to select the correct answer. Dividing your time in this way leaves you about 3 minutes for review or for time at the end of the test to spend on difficult items. To finish the Social Studies test completely, you really have to be organized and watch the clock. Check out Chapter 4 for more general time-management tips.

TIP

If you really have no idea, or if you are running out of time, guess! In the last few minutes of the test, use the Review screen to find and answer any unanswered questions. You don't have to answer all the questions correctly to pass the GED, but you shouldn't leave any answers blank. There's no penalty for guessing on the GED, so even if you guess at random on four items, odds are you will get at least one point. That could be the point that puts you over the top!

Chapter 12

Practicing Social Studies Questions

This chapter provides sample Social Studies test questions to help you prepare for taking that section of the GED test.

Record your answers directly in this book or on a sheet of paper if you think you'll want to revisit these practice questions at a later date. Mark only one answer for each item unless otherwise indicated.

At the end of this chapter, I provide detailed answer explanations to help you check your answers. Take your time as you move through the explanations. They can help you understand why you missed the answers you did and confirm or clarify the thought process for the answers you got right.

Remember, this is just preliminary test practice. I want you to get used to answering different types of Social Studies test questions. Use the complete practice tests in Chapters 21 and 29 to time your work and replicate the real test-taking experience. Then take the online test provided with this book — which closely duplicates the experience of taking the real GED.

Social Studies Practice Questions

The official Social Studies test consists mainly of multiple-choice items but also has some technologically enhanced items of the type that I outline in Chapters 3 and 11. They measure general social studies concepts. The items are based on short readings that often include a map, graph, chart, cartoon, or figure. Study the information given and then answer the items following it. Refer to the information as often as necessary in answering. Work carefully but don't spend too much time on any one question. Be sure you answer every question. Remember, on the real test, you can use the on-screen calculator (or your own calculator if you take the test at a testing center).

Questions 1 and 2 refer to the following excerpt from a U.S. government publication.

Democracies fall into two basic categories, direct and representative. In a direct democracy, citizens, without the intermediary of elected or appointed officials, can participate in making public decisions. Such a system is clearly most practical with relatively small numbers of people — in a community organization, tribal council, or the local unit of a labor union, for example — where members can meet in a single room to discuss issues and arrive at decisions by consensus or majority vote.

Some U.S. states, in addition, place "propositions" and "referendums" — mandated changes of law — or possible recall of elected officials on ballots during state elections. These practices are forms of direct democracy, expressing the will of a large population. Many practices may have elements of direct democracy. In Switzerland, many important political decisions on issues, including public health, energy, and employment, are subject to a vote by the country's citizens. And some might argue that the Internet is creating new forms of direct democracy, as it empowers political groups to raise money for their causes by appealing directly to like-minded citizens.

However, today, as in the past, the most common form of democracy, whether for a town of 50,000 or a nation of 50 million, is representative democracy, in which citizens elect officials to make political decisions, formulate laws, and administer programs for the public good.

1. The federal government of the United States is an example of a [   ] (direct *or* representative) democracy.

2. Which of the following is an example of allowing the population as a whole to vote on an issue?

   (A) a vote on issuing library bonds
   (B) the election of a local mayor
   (C) the election of the president
   (D) a school board election

Questions 3 and 4 refer to the following excerpt from a U.S. government publication.

In a democracy, government is only one thread in the social fabric of many and varied public and private institutions, legal forums, political parties, organizations, and associations. This diversity is called pluralism, and it assumes that the many organized groups and institutions in a democratic society do not depend upon government for their existence, legitimacy, or authority. Most democratic societies have thousands of private organizations, some local, some national. Many of them serve a mediating role between individuals and society's complex social and governmental institutions, filling roles not given to the government and offering individuals opportunities to become part of their society without being in government.

In an authoritarian society, virtually all such organizations would be controlled, licensed, watched, or otherwise accountable to the government. In a democracy, the powers of the government are, by law, clearly defined and sharply limited. As a result, private organizations are largely free of government control. In this busy private realm of democratic society, citizens can explore the possibilities of peaceful self-fulfillment and the responsibilities of belonging to a community — free of the potentially heavy hand of the state or the demand that they adhere to views held by those with influence or power, or by the majority.

3. Which of the following is an example of an authoritarian society?

   (A) Canada

   (B) Kingdom of Sweden

   (C) the former USSR

   (D) the Republic of Korea (South Korea)

4. All United States citizens have the right to elect

   (A) their senator.

   (B) Supreme Court justices.

   (C) cabinet secretaries.

   (D) army generals.

Questions 5–9 refer to the following excerpt from U.S. History For Dummies, *by Steve Wiegand (Wiley).*

Partly because of error and partly because of wishful thinking, Columbus estimated the distance to the Indies at approximately 2,500 miles, which was about 7,500 miles short. But after a voyage of about five weeks, he and his crew, totaling 90 men, did find land at around 2:00 a.m. on October 12, 1492. It was an island in the Bahamas, which he called San Salvador. The timing of the discovery was good; it came even as the crews of the *Nina, Pinta,* and *Santa Maria* were muttering about a mutiny.

Columbus next sailed to Cuba, where he found a few spices and little gold. Sailing on to an island he called Hispaniola (today's Dominican Republic and Haiti), the *Santa Maria* hit a reef on Christmas Eve, 1492. Columbus abandoned the ship, set up a trading outpost he called Navidad, left some men to operate it, and sailed back to Spain in his other two ships.

So enthusiastically did people greet the news of his return that on his second voyage to Hispaniola, Columbus had 17 ships and more than 1,200 men. But this time he ran into more than a little disappointment. Natives had wiped out his trading post after his men became too grabby with the local gold and the local women. Worse, most of the men he brought with him had come only for gold and other riches, and they didn't care about setting up a permanent colony. Because of the lack of treasures, they soon wanted to go home. And the natives lost interest in the newcomers after the novelty of the Spanish trinkets wore off.

5. By how much was Columbus in error in guessing the distance to the Indies? Write the answer in the box. ☐

6. On what date did Columbus arrive in the Bahamas?

   (A) October 2, 1492

   (B) October 12, 1492

   (C) December 12, 1493

   (D) Christmas Eve, 1492

7. Why did so many people want to sail with Columbus on his second trip?

   (A) They were eager to settle new lands.

   (B) They wanted adventure.

   (C) They had heard stories about amazing cities.

   (D) They had heard stories of the gold Columbus had found.

8. Why did Columbus cut his first voyage short?

    (A) The *Santa Maria* had hit a reef and sank.

    (B) His men were ready to mutiny.

    (C) He had completed his task by setting up a small colony.

    (D) Disease decimated his crew.

9. Columbus's goal was to sail to the continent of ⬚.

Questions 10 and 11 refer to the following excerpt from U.S. History For Dummies, *by Steve Wiegand (Wiley).*

On his second trip to the Americas in 1493, Columbus stopped by the Canary Islands and picked up some sugar cane cuttings. He planted them on Hispaniola, and they thrived. In 1516, the first sugar grown in the New World was presented to King Carlos I of Spain. By 1531, it was as commercially important to the Spanish colonial economy as gold.

Planters soon discovered a by-product as well. The juice left over after the sugar was pressed out of the cane and crystallized was called *melasas* by the Spanish (and *molasses* by the English). Mixing this juice with water and leaving it out in the sun created a potent and tasty fermented drink. They called it *rum* — perhaps after the word for sugar cane, *Saccharum officinarum*. The stuff was great for long sea voyages because it didn't go bad.

Sugar and rum became so popular that sugar plantations mushroomed all over the Caribbean.

10. What is molasses?

    (A) juice pressed out of sugar cane

    (B) leftover juice after sugar was pressed out of the cane

    (C) sugar cane mixed with water

    (D) *Saccharum officinarum*

11. How many years did it take before the first sugar grown in the New World was presented to the king of Spain?

    (A) 33 years

    (B) 23 years

    (C) 13 years

    (D) 1 year

Questions 12–14 refer to the following table.

Educational Attainment of the Population 25 Years and Over, by Selected Characteristics: 2019
(Numbers in thousands. Civilian noninstitutionalized population.[1])

Both sexes	Total	None - 8th grade	9th - 11th grade	High school graduate	Some college, no degree	Associate's degree	Bachelor's degree	Master's degree	Professional degree	Doctoral degree
Total	2,21,478	8,603	13,372	62,259	34,690	22,738	49,937	22,214	3,136	4,529
Marital Status										
Married, spouse present	1,26,768	4,476	6,069	32,493	18,378	13,410	31,280	15,096	2,240	3,327
Married, spouse absent, not separated	3,633	294	339	1,063	468	293	692	355	39	89
Separated	4,643	342	585	1,618	759	454	617	206	34	28
Widowed	14,852	1,218	1,414	5,459	2,411	1,284	1,960	872	100	134
Divorced	25,235	697	1,645	7,790	4,815	3,038	4,707	1,983	235	327
Never married	46,348	1,576	3,320	13,836	7,858	4,259	10,681	3,704	488	625
Household Relationship										
Family householder	80,502	2,608	4,497	20,288	13,436	8,923	18,642	9,004	1,232	1,872
Married, spouse present	61,073	1,865	2,683	14,226	9,613	6,630	15,539	7,705	1,097	1,714
Other family householder	19,429	742	1,814	6,062	3,823	2,293	3,103	1,299	136	157
Nonfamily householder	41,973	1,494	2,646	11,553	7,323	4,281	9,321	4,045	513	795
Living alone	34,952	1,333	2,284	9,880	6,149	3,552	7,347	3,306	432	668
Living with nonrelatives	7,020	161	362	1,673	1,174	729	1,974	739	82	127
Relative of householder	86,578	3,972	5,399	26,395	12,019	8,459	19,187	8,181	1,266	1,699
Spouse	61,000	2,029	2,897	16,692	8,220	6,379	14,984	7,117	1,102	1,579
Other	25,577	1,943	2,501	9,703	3,799	2,081	4,203	1,064	163	121
Nonrelative	12,426	529	830	4,022	1,912	1,074	2,786	985	125	162
Citizenship, Nativity, and Year of Entry										
Native born	1,81,283	2,767	9,420	52,024	31,198	19,984	41,686	18,120	2,568	3,515
Native parentage[2]	1,63,644	2,382	8,627	47,620	28,126	18,083	37,290	16,212	2,208	3,096
Foreign or mixed parentage[3]	17,639	385	793	4,404	3,072	1,901	4,396	1,907	361	419
Foreign born	40,195	5,836	3,952	10,235	3,492	2,754	8,250	4,095	568	1,014
Naturalized citizen	20,751	1,856	1,427	5,263	2,246	1,794	5,036	2,102	394	634
Not a citizen	19,444	3,980	2,525	4,972	1,245	960	3,214	1,993	174	380
Year of entry										
2010 or later	7,963	766	560	1,845	568	446	2,145	1,329	96	207
2000-2009	10,252	1,636	1,224	2,732	747	620	1,943	929	162	259
1990-1999	9,796	1,413	1,086	2,578	822	771	1,870	876	138	242
1980-1989	6,414	1,064	692	1,597	684	464	1,208	480	82	142
1970-1979	3,446	653	245	807	356	238	672	311	51	112
Before 1970	2,324	303	146	676	314	216	412	168	38	52
Labor Force Status										
Employed	1,37,478	3,597	5,726	34,453	20,731	15,235	35,820	16,050	2,425	3,440
Unemployed	4,531	169	464	1,403	860	450	809	293	45	37
Not in civilian labor force	79,470	4,837	7,182	26,403	13,099	7,053	13,307	5,871	666	1,052
Occupation (Employed Civilians Only)	**1,37,478**	**3,597**	**5,726**	**34,453**	**20,731**	**15,235**	**35,820**	**16,050**	**2,425**	**3,440**
Management, business, and financial occupations	25,465	170	329	3,412	3,315	2,342	10,185	4,848	323	540
Professional and related occupations	34,622	37	117	2,204	2,575	3,677	12,658	8,720	1,914	2,721
Service occupations	20,981	1,191	1,816	7,926	3,913	2,557	2,940	525	61	52
Sales and related occupations	12,598	148	447	3,450	2,388	1,390	3,908	787	36	44
Office and administrative occupations	15,040	95	331	4,586	3,672	2,122	3,385	768	30	51
Farming, forestry, and fishing occupations	929	256	140	314	88	54	62	15	-	-
Construction and extraction occupations	7,283	741	864	3,238	1,016	691	641	69	18	5
Installation, maintenance, and repair occupations	4,132	119	250	1,751	816	783	370	36	6	2
Production occupations	7,705	490	621	3,496	1,422	850	699	105	13	8
Transportation and material moving occupations	8,723	349	811	4,078	1,526	769	972	178	23	17
Industry (Employed Civilians Only)	**1,37,478**	**3,597**	**5,726**	**34,453**	**20,731**	**15,235**	**35,820**	**16,050**	**2,425**	**3,440**
Agricultural, forestry, fishing, and hunting	2,017	297	194	657	254	193	317	80	6	18
Mining	704	14	33	263	115	60	142	65	-	11
Construction	9,849	775	982	3,948	1,458	956	1,384	289	39	17
Manufacturing	14,450	517	746	4,663	2,203	1,608	3,280	1,212	49	172
Wholesale and retail trade	15,893	307	798	5,240	3,155	1,794	3,601	771	81	146
Transportation and utilities	8,009	175	403	2,972	1,676	959	1,447	327	27	25
Information	2,455	11	31	391	385	218	985	390	12	31
Financial activities	9,847	43	120	1,621	1,495	979	4,036	1,312	120	122
Professional and business services	17,821	448	520	3,009	2,183	1,549	6,119	2,689	724	579
Educational and health services	33,060	222	670	5,019	3,756	4,281	9,078	6,895	1,102	2,037
Leisure and hospitality	9,980	503	755	3,299	1,801	928	2,143	500	34	17
Other services	6,590	255	400	2,223	1,018	862	1,171	515	57	90
Public administration	6,802	29	73	1,147	1,232	847	2,117	1,005	176	175

Source: Adapted from U.S. Census Bureau

12. How many foreign-born individuals who entered the United States after 2010 were high school graduates? ☐ Write your answer in thousands.

13. Comparing educational attainment of employed and unemployed individuals, the data shows a ☐ (high *or* low) correlation between education and employment.

14. Which of the following statements can be concluded from the table?

    (A) Men generally achieve higher levels of educational attainment than women.

    (B) People under the age of 25 are likely to complete high school.

    (C) Members of the military tend to have high educational attainment.

    (D) Educational attainment varies greatly depending on personal characteristics.

Questions 15–17 refer to the following excerpt from The Declaration of Independence, 1776.

After a long list of grievances, the Declaration of Independence concludes with these words.

In every stage of these Oppressions We have Petitioned for Redress in the most humble terms: Our repeated Petitions have been answered only by repeated injury. A Prince whose character is thus marked by every act which may define a Tyrant, is unfit to be the ruler of a free people.

Nor have We been wanting in attentions to our British brethren. We have warned them from time to time of attempts by their legislature to extend an unwarrantable jurisdiction over us. We have reminded them of the circumstances of our emigration and settlement here. We have appealed to their native justice and magnanimity, and we have conjured them by the ties of our common kindred to disavow these usurpations, which would inevitably interrupt our connections and correspondence. They too have been deaf to the voice of justice and of consanguinity. We must, therefore, acquiesce in the necessity, which denounces our Separation, and hold them, as we hold the rest of mankind, Enemies in War, in Peace Friends.

We, therefore, the Representatives of the united States of America, in General Congress, Assembled, appealing to the Supreme Judge of the world for the rectitude of our intentions, do, in the Name, and by Authority of the good People of these Colonies, solemnly publish and declare, That these United Colonies are, and of Right ought to be Free and Independent States; that they are Absolved from all Allegiance to the British Crown, and that all political connection between them and the State of Great Britain, is and ought to be totally dissolved; and that as Free and Independent States, they have full Power to levy War, conclude Peace, contract Alliances, establish Commerce, and to do all other Acts and Things which Independent States may of right do. And for the support of this Declaration, with a firm reliance on the protection of divine Providence, we mutually pledge to each other our Lives, our Fortunes and our sacred Honor.

15. Why did the authors of the Declaration of Independence believe the king was a tyrant?

    (A) The king's only answer to their complaints was more repression.

    (B) Appeals to British parliament failed.

    (C) The king had taxed them without representation.

    (D) They rejected the king's authority.

16. How did the authors feel about British parliament making laws for the colonies?

    (A) The laws were usurpations.

    (B) The laws were magnanimous.

    (C) The laws are examples of justice and consanguinity.

    (D) The parliament heeded the authors' concerns.

17. Why is the word *united* in "united States of America" not also capitalized?

    (A) The states viewed themselves as independent entities.

    (B) The representatives saw themselves as belonging to one country.

    (C) This Congress was a meeting of independent states united for action.

    (D) The authors of the Declaration were following old-fashioned rules for writing.

Questions 18–20 refer to the following passage from U.S. History For Dummies, *by Steve Wiegand (Wiley).*

By 1787, it was apparent to many leaders that the Articles of Confederation needed an overhaul, or the union of 13 states would eventually fall apart. So Congress agreed to call a convention of delegates from each state to try to fix things. The first of the delegates (selected by state legislatures) to arrive in Philadelphia in May 1787 was James Madison, a 36-year-old scholar and politician from Virginia who was so frail, he couldn't serve in the army during the Revolution. Madison had so many ideas on how to fix things, he couldn't wait to get started.

Not everyone else was in such a hurry. Although the convention was supposed to begin May 15, it wasn't until May 25 that enough of the delegates chosen by the state legislatures showed up to have a quorum. Rhode Island never did send anyone.

Eventually, 55 delegates took part. Notable by their absence were some of the leading figures of the recent rebellion against England: Thomas Jefferson was in France, Thomas Paine was in England, Sam Adams and John Hancock weren't selected to go, and Patrick Henry refused.

18. What was the name of the original constitution of the United States?

    (A) the Articles of Confederation

    (B) the Constitution of the Confederation

    (C) the Declaration of Independence

    (D) the Declaration of the Rights of Man

19. Why was James Madison especially important to this convention?

    (A) He was eager to get started.

    (B) He represented one of the southern states, which made him very important.

    (C) He had never served in the military.

    (D) He had many ideas on how to fix things.

20. How many states were part of the original Confederation? [＿＿＿＿＿]

Questions 21 and 22 are based on this excerpt from a speech by James Madison on the ratification of the new Constitution of the United States.

What has brought on other nations those immense debts, under the pressure of which many of them labor? Not the expenses of their governments, but war. How is it possible a war could be supported without money or credit? And would it be possible for government to have credit, without having the power of raising money? No, it would be impossible for any government, in such a case, to defend itself. Then, I say, sir, that it is necessary to establish funds for extraordinary exigencies, and give this power to the general government; for the utter inutility of previous requisitions on the States is too well known. Would it be possible for those countries, whose finances and revenues are carried to the highest perfection, to carry on the operations of government on great emergencies, such as the maintenance of a war, without an uncontrolled power of raising money? Has it not been necessary for Great Britain, notwithstanding the facility of the collection of her taxes, to have recourse very often to this and other extraordinary methods of procuring money? Would not her public credit have been ruined, if it was known that her power to raise money was limited? [N]o government can exist unless its powers extend to make provisions for every contingency.

If we were actually attacked by a powerful nation, and our general government had not the power of raising money, but depended solely on requisitions, our condition would be truly deplorable: if the revenues of this commonwealth were to depend on twenty distinct authorities, it would be impossible for it to carry on its operations.

21. According to Madison, what was the major reason for allowing the government to raise revenue?

   (A) to provide a single economic market

   (B) to have the ability to fund extraordinary exigencies

   (C) to limit the power of the states

   (D) to limit the power of the national government

22. What was Madison referring to by "the utter inutility of previous requisitions on the States is too well known"?

   (A) Under the Articles of Confederation, it was easy to convince all the states to contribute money.

   (B) Under the Articles of Confederation, the government had nearly unlimited powers to raise money.

   (C) Under the Articles of Confederation, the states controlled the government.

   (D) Under the Articles of Confederation, the government had only very limited powers to tax.

Questions 23–25 refer to the following passage, excerpted from "A Look Back . . . The Black Dispatches: Intelligence During the Civil War," a CIA Feature Story (www.cia.gov).

William A. Jackson

African-Americans who could serve as agents-in-place were a great asset to the Union. They could provide information about the enemy's plans instead of reporting how the plans were carried out. William A. Jackson was one such agent-in-place who provided valuable intelligence straight from Confederate President Jefferson Davis.

Jackson served as a coachman to Davis. As a servant in Davis' home, Jackson overheard discussions the president had with his military leadership. His first report of Confederate plans and intentions was in May 1862 when he crossed into Union lines. While there are no records of the specific intelligence Jackson reported, it is known that it was important enough to be sent straight to the War Department in Washington.

Harriet Tubman

When it comes to the Civil War and the fight to end slavery, Harriet Tubman is an icon. She was not only a conductor of the Underground Railroad, but also a spy for the Union.

In 1860, she took her last trip on the Underground Railroad, bringing friends and family to freedom safely. After the trip, Tubman decided to contribute to the war effort by caring for and feeding the many slaves who had fled the Union-controlled areas.

A year later, the Union Army asked Tubman to gather a network of spies among the black men in the area. Tubman also was tasked with leading expeditions to gather intelligence.

She reported her information to a Union officer commanding the Second South Carolina Volunteers, a black unit involved in guerrilla warfare activities.

After learning of Tubman's capability as a spy, Gen. David Hunter, commander of all Union forces in the area, requested that Tubman personally guide a raiding party up the Combahee River in South Carolina. Tubman was well prepared for the raid because she had key information about Confederate positions along the shore and had discovered where they placed torpedoes (barrels filled with gunpowder) in the water. On the morning of June 1, 1863, Tubman led Col. James Montgomery and his men in the attack. The expedition hit hard. They set fires and destroyed buildings so they couldn't be used by the Confederate forces. The raiders freed 750 slaves.

The raid along the Combahee River, in addition to her activities with the Underground Railroad, made a significant contribution to the Union cause. When Tubman died in 1913, she was honored with a full military funeral in recognition for work during the war.

23. What made William Jackson an excellent intelligence source?

   (A) He was an African-American.

   (B) He had military experience.

   (C) He worked in the home of Jefferson Davis.

   (D) He was in direct contact with Washington, D.C.

24. What is Harriet Tubman best known for?

   (A) the Underground Railroad

   (B) the drinking gourd song

   (C) being a guerilla leader

   (D) spying on the president of the Confederacy

25. Harriet Tubman led a raid on [_____] in South Carolina.

   (A) the Combahee River

   (B) Montgomery

   (C) Union-controlled areas

   (D) Atlanta

Questions 26 and 27 refer to the following excerpt from U.S. History For Dummies, *by Steve Wiegand (Wiley).*

Despite conflict in war, civilians and soldiers around the world had at least one thing in common in 1918 — a killer flu. Erroneously dubbed "Spanish Influenza" because it was believed to have started in Spain, it more likely started at U.S. Army camps in Kansas and may not have been a flu virus at all. A 2008 study by the National Institute of Allergy and Infectious Diseases suggested bacteria might have caused the pandemic.

Whatever caused it, it was devastating. Unlike normal influenza outbreaks, whose victims are generally the elderly and the young, the Spanish flu often targeted healthy young adults. By early summer, the disease had spread around the world. In New York City alone, 20,000 people died. Western Samoa lost 20 percent of its population, and entire Inuit villages in Alaska were wiped out. By the time it had run its course in 1921, the flu had killed from 25 million to 50 million people around the world. More than 500,000 Americans died, which was a greater total than all the Americans killed in all the wars of the 20th century.

26. Where did the Spanish flu begin?

   (A) Spain

   (B) army camps

   (C) New York City

   (D) Western Samoa

27. How many Americans died of the Spanish flu?

   (A) 20% of its population

   (B) more than 20,000 people

   (C) more than 500,000 people

   (D) 25 to 50 million people

Questions 28–30 are based on the following graphs.

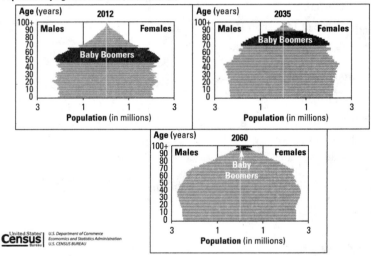

Source: Adapted from U.S. Census Bureau

28. Look at the population pyramid for the year 2012. Notice that the edges appear ragged. Shorter lines mean fewer people in that age group. There are noticeably fewer people in the 30-to-40 age group. In approximately what time period would these people have been born?

   (A) 1960 to 1970

   (B) 1970 to 1980

   (C) 1980 to 1990

   (D) 1990 to 2000

29. Which of the following reasons best explains why there are fewer people in the 30-to-40 age group in the 2012 graph?

   (A) Economic troubles and the Vietnam War were going on at the time of their birth.

   (B) The Korean War was going on at the time of their birth.

   (C) The first Gulf War was going on at the time of their birth.

   (D) The invasion of Grenada was going on at the time of their birth.

30. Look at the tops of the three pyramids. Are there more men or women in the age group of 80+?

Questions 31 and 32 refer to the following passage about the 1920s, excerpted from U.S. History For Dummies, *by Steve Wiegand (Wiley).*

Below the veneer of prosperity, there were indications of trouble. More and more wealth was being concentrated in fewer and fewer hands, and government did far more for the rich than the poor. It was estimated, for example, that federal tax cuts saved the hugely wealthy financier Andrew Mellon (who also happened to be Hoover's treasury secretary) almost as much money as was saved by all the taxpayers in the entire state of Nebraska.

Supreme Court decisions struck down minimum wage laws for women and children and made it easier for big business to swallow up smaller ones and become *de facto* monopolies. And union membership declined as organized labor was unable to compete with the aura of good times.

Probably worst off were American farmers. They had expanded production during World War I to feed the troops, and when demand and prices faded after the war, they were hit hard. Farm income dropped by 50 percent during the 1920s, and more than 3 million farmers left their farms for towns and cities.

31. Which of the following is another example that supports the generalization that, "Below the veneer of prosperity, there were indications of trouble"?

(A) Prohibition outlawed alcohol despite the opposition of many people.

(B) Stock prices soared many times over the underlying value of the companies.

(C) Women gained the right to vote and achieved newfound independence.

(D) Inventions such as the radio and sound motion pictures supplied entertainment to millions.

32. Why did union membership decline in the 1920s?

(A) Unions were illegal.

(B) Unions were no longer necessary.

(C) Growing prosperity made unions seem less relevant.

(D) The government did far more for the rich than for the poor.

Questions 33–35 are based on the following excerpt from The Wealth of Nations, *by Adam Smith (Thrifty Books).*

The increase of revenue and stock is the increase of national wealth. Is this improvement in the circumstances of the lower ranks of the people to be regarded as an advantage or as an inconvenience to the society? The answer seems at first sight abundantly plain. Servants, laborers, and workmen of different kinds, make up the far greater part of every great political society. But what improves the circumstances of the greater part can never be regarded as an inconvenience to the whole. No society can surely be flourishing and happy, of which the far greater part of the members are poor and miserable. It is but equity, besides, that they who feed, clothe, and lodge the whole body of the people, should have such a share of the produce of their own labor as to be themselves tolerably well fed, clothed, and lodged. The liberal reward of labor, as it encourages the propagation, so it increases the industry of the common people. The wages of labor are the encouragement of industry, which, like every other human quality, improves in proportion to the encouragement it receives. A plentiful subsistence increases the bodily strength of the laborer, and the comfortable hope of bettering his condition, and of ending his days perhaps in ease and plenty, animates him to exert that strength to the utmost. Where wages are high, accordingly, we shall always find the workmen more active, diligent, and expeditious than where they are low.

33. What does Smith mean by "what improves the circumstances of the greater part can never be regarded as an inconvenience to the whole"?

    (A) Paying the working class more is an inconvenience to everyone.

    (B) Whatever improves conditions for most people cannot be regarded as bad for society as a whole.

    (C) Only circumstance that helps some improves life for all.

    (D) Company owners don't need to share profits with their employees.

34. According to Adam Smith, how should employers treat the financial well-being of their employees?

    (A) Keep wages as low as possible.

    (B) Reward a laborer liberally.

    (C) Under no circumstances consider changes.

    (D) Avoid the issue.

35. When Henry Ford's Model T car proved to be a success, he doubled his workers' wages, even when all other car manufacturers at the time would not raise wages. Would he and Adam Smith have agreed on this issue?

    (A) Yes. Well-paid workers are more active and diligent.

    (B) No. Paying workers more only encourages sloth.

    (C) Yes. It is only fair.

    (D) No. A business must remain competitive.

Questions 36 and 37 refer to the following passage about the Cuban Missile Crisis, excerpted from U.S. History For Dummies, *by Steve Wiegand (Wiley).*

During the summer of 1962, the Soviets began developing nuclear missile sites in Cuba. That meant they could easily strike targets over much of North and South America. When air reconnaissance photos confirmed the sites' presence on October 14, President John F. Kennedy had to make a tough choice: Destroy the sites and quite possibly trigger World War III, or do nothing, and not only expose the country to nuclear destruction but, in effect, concede first place in the world domination race to the USSR.

Kennedy decided to get tough. On October 22, 1963, he went on national television and announced the U.S. Navy would throw a blockade around Cuba and turn away any ships carrying materials that could be used at the missile sites. He also demanded the sites be dismantled. Then the world waited for the Russian reaction.

On October 26, Soviet leader Nikita Khrushchev sent a message suggesting the missiles would be removed if the United States promised not to invade Cuba and eventually removed some U.S. missiles from Turkey. The crisis — perhaps the closest the world came to nuclear conflict during the Cold War — was over, and the payoffs were ample.

36. Why was the placement of Soviet missiles in Cuba so important to both the Soviet Union and the United States?

   (A) This was the only way missiles of that time could reach into North and South America.

   (B) The Soviets wanted to show their support for Fidel Castro.

   (C) It provided an important trade opportunity.

   (D) The Soviet Union wanted to start a nuclear war.

37. What triggered the Soviet move to put missiles capable of attacking the United States into bases in Cuba?

   (A) The Soviet Union was preparing to attack the United States.

   (B) Fidel Castro demanded them as protection against an American invasion of Cuba.

   (C) The United States had placed its own missiles in Turkey on the border of the Soviet Union.

   (D) The Soviets wanted to divert attention from Vietnam.

Questions 38–40 are based on the following photograph and information.

Source: David Woodbury/Library of Congress/Public domain.

The American Civil War is the first major conflict documented in photos. American photographer Matthew Brady, noted for his photographs of Abraham Lincoln, is often credited with the large number of photos taken during and after key battles of the Civil War. However, while the idea was his, nearly all of the photos were taken by a team of photographers Brady assembled and embedded with the Union army. He sent them with special darkroom wagons and tents, such as the one in the photo, which they used to develop compelling photos of battles and their aftermath. After the photographer developed the photo, the glass plate negative could be easily and swiftly transported to Brady's studio in Washington without risk of being exposed and ruined. The photo shows one of the photographers, David Woodbury, camping with Grant's army, taken after the Battle of Cold Harbor. He's holding a developed glass photographic plate. Exhibitions of the photos became hugely popular, and Brady's studios sold many copies of the images. The photos were later donated to the U.S. government, where they became an invaluable historic record.

38. What does the word "embedded" mean as used in this passage?

    (A) Kept in a safe location far from the action.

    (B) Assigned to fight as a front-line soldier.

    (C) Attached to a military unit involved in the action.

    (D) Assigned to a desk job that supported the troops in the field.

39. How did the wagons help the photographers document the war?

    (A) They had all the tools and equipment needed to take and develop photos.

    (B) They could transmit the photos to Brady by telegraph.

    (C) They had a comfortable place to sleep.

    (D) They could store their undeveloped photos until they got back to Washington.

40. Why is the wagon covered with a dark cloth?

    (A) to camouflage the wagon from the enemy

    (B) to keep the wagon warm

    (C) to match the soldiers' tents

    (D) to block sunlight from entering the darkroom

Questions 41–44 are based on the following tables.

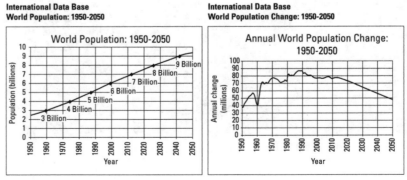

Source: Adapted from U.S. Census Bureau

41. The total population of the world continues to [   ].

42. The number of children born each year has [   ] since 1990.

43. What does the graph titled "Annual World Population Change" actually show?

(A) the change in the world total population over time

(B) the actual net change in world population by year

(C) the actual number of children born each year

(D) the rate of change in births each year

44. Considering the graph shows that the annual world population change is declining, why is the world population continuing to climb?

(A) The graph ignores children who die in the first year of life.

(B) More people means more children, even if individual women have fewer children.

(C) The rate of growth is still climbing.

(D) Families in China are now allowed to have more than one child again.

Question 45–47 are based on the following excerpt from U.S. History For Dummies, *by Steve Wiegand (Wiley).*

While the war on terrorism dominated Bush's presidency, he did attempt to make changes on domestic issues as well. Within a few days of taking office, Bush proposed an ambitious education reform program, called the No Child Left Behind Act. Approved by Congress, the plan reformed federal education funding; increased standards expected of schools, including annual reading and math skills testing; and gave parents more flexibility in choosing schools. The program was variously praised for making schools more accountable and criticized for forcing educators to take cookie-cutter approaches to teaching.

In late 2003, Bush pushed a plan through Congress to reform Medicare, the federal health insurance program for the elderly. The plan gave senior citizens more choice when picking a private insurance plan through which they received medical services, as well as in obtaining prescription drugs.

Bush had far less success in trying to reform Social Security and the U.S. immigration policies. Bush proposed to replace the government-run pension program with a system of private savings accounts. But the plan died in the face of criticism that it would put too much of a burden on individuals and be too expensive in the transition.

Bush also supported a bipartisan plan that would allow an estimated 12 million illegal immigrants to remain in the country on a temporary basis and to apply for citizenship after returning to their own countries and paying a fine. The plan was crushed by the weight of opposition from those who thought it was too draconian and those who thought it was too soft.

45. Why were some people opposed to the No Child Left Behind Act?

(A) Some objected to standardized reading and math tests.

(B) Some felt it would reduce education choices.

(C) It was considered too expensive by some in Congress.

(D) Congress would not approve the plan.

46. Which of Bush's proposals were passed by Congress? Not passed? Write the letter in the correct place. Passed: [   ] Not Passed: [   ]

(A) education reform

(B) Medicare reform

(C) immigration reform

(D) Social Security reform

47. What is one of the reasons Bush's proposal to reform Social Security failed?

(A) It was too costly.

(B) Social Security was unpopular.

(C) Some people thought the proposal was too soft.

(D) It took the burden of saving for retirement off the people.

48. According to the U.S. Trade Representative's office, "U.S. goods and services trade with Canada totaled an estimated $908.9 billion in 2022. Exports were $427.7 billion; imports were $481.2 billion." How much was the U.S. trade deficit with Canada in 2022, in billions of dollars?

[   ]

Questions 49 and 50 refer to the following excerpt from the Australian War Memorial website on the topic of the Australian contribution to the Vietnam War, 1962–1975 (https://www.awm.gov.au/articles/event/vietnam).

[A]lmost 60,000 Australians, including ground troops and air force and navy personnel, served in Vietnam; 521 died as a result of the war and over 3,000 were wounded.

Australian support for South Vietnam in the early 1960s was in keeping with the policies of other nations, particularly the United States, to stem the spread of communism in Europe and Asia.

By early 1965, the U.S. commenced a major escalation of the war. By the end of the year, it had committed 200,000 troops to the conflict. As part of the build-up, the U.S. government requested further support from friendly countries in the region, including Australia. The Australian government dispatched the 1st Battalion, Royal Australian Regiment (1RAR), in June 1965, to serve alongside the U.S. 173rd Airborne Brigade in Bien Hoa province.

By 1969, anti-war protests were gathering momentum in Australia. Opposition to conscription mounted, as more people came to believe the war could not be won. The U.S. government began to implement a policy of "Vietnamisation," the term coined for a gradual withdrawal of U.S. forces that would leave the war in the hands of the South Vietnamese. With the start of the phased withdrawals, the emphasis of the activities of the Australians in Phuoc Tuy province shifted to the provision of training to the South Vietnamese Regional and Popular Forces.

In early 1975, the communists launched a major offensive in the north of South Vietnam, resulting in the fall of Saigon on 30 April. During April, a RAAF detachment of 7–8 Hercules transports flew humanitarian missions to aid civilian refugees displaced by the fighting and carried out the evacuation of Vietnamese orphans (Operation Babylift), before finally taking out embassy staff on 25 April.

49. In what way was the Australian experience in their participation in the Vietnam War similar to that of America?

   (A) They were reluctant to become involved.

   (B) They contributed only humanitarian aid.

   (C) There was strong popular opposition on the home front to participation in this war.

   (D) They supported the spread of communism.

50. Which of the following is an example of humanitarian assistance to the people of Vietnam?

   (A) Australia sent a battalion to Vietnam.

   (B) Australia turned from military engagement to training.

   (C) The Australian government evacuated its embassy.

   (D) Australian forces evacuated orphans.

Answers and Explanations

1. **representative.** In America, citizens elect officials, from state representatives to United States senators, who represent the interests of individual citizens in the administration of the country.

2. **A. a vote on issuing library bonds.** Choices (B), (C), and (D) are all examples of indirect or representative democracy, where someone is elected to *represent* the voter. For example, mayors, who citizens elect directly, are in office to represent them. The voters don't make political decisions; the mayor does. Only in a referendum is the voters' voice directly applied to a decision.

   TIP

   This question is a good example of a common GED question type: finding an example, in this case an example of direct democracy. Answering a question such as this one requires you to show your understanding of a general concept, direct democracy, by finding an example of it.

3. **C. the former USSR.** The former USSR (Choice C), also known as the Soviet Union, was run by a government that allowed elections but with only one political party. The party, not the people, decided who would run for office. Although the form resembled democracy, it didn't allow for pluralism or political choice. The other countries are all pluralist. Canada (Choice A) is a parliamentary democracy with five major political parties. Sweden (Choice B) is also a parliamentary democracy, and like Canada, has a monarch as head of state. It, too, has several political parties contending for office in free elections. South Korea (Choice D) is a republic, run by a legislative assembly and a president elected by popular vote.

4. **A. their senator.** Of the offices in the list, only senators are elected. The others are appointed by the president.

5. **7,500 miles.** Columbus miscalculated by 7,500 miles. He thought the world was considerably smaller than it actually is.

6. **B. October 12, 1492.** The Christmas Eve date refers to his subsequent arrival at the island he called Hispaniola. The other two dates are not mentioned in the text.

7. **D. They had heard stories of the gold Columbus had found.** According to the text, they were all focused on gold. Choice (B) may be partially correct, that they were looking for adventure, but Choices (A) and (C) are not supported by the text.

8. **A. The *Santa Maria* had hit a reef and sank.** Choice (B) is incorrect at this stage of his trip, and although Choices (C) and (D) may be partially correct, they're not the best answers.

9. **Asia.** Columbus wanted to find a shorter route to Asia. He never dreamed that other continents existed.

   TIP

   Questions 7 and 8 are good examples of when reading all the answer choices can help you avoid a mistake. While some of the answer choices are partly correct, only one of the answer choices in each question is the best answer.

10. **B. leftover juice after sugar was pressed out of the cane.** The text states that molasses is "the juice left over after the sugar was pressed out of the cane and crystalized." The juice pressed out of the cane still contains sugar to be extracted, so Choice (A) is incorrect. The cane isn't mixed with water (Choice C), but rather the extracted juices are. And the name *Saccharum officinarum* (Choice D) is simply the Latin name for the sugar cane plant.

WARNING

Don't be confused when the test-makers use a fancy word like *Saccharum officinarum* in the answer choices. You may be tempted to select this answer choice because it stands out from the others. This is another time when reading and evaluating all the answer choices can help you.

11. **B. 23 years.** This problem requires some simple arithmetic. The sugar cane plants arrived in Hispaniola in 1493. The first sugar was presented to the King in 1516. Subtract 1493 from 1516, and you get 23. The answer is 23 years.

TIP

Don't forget that you can use the on-screen calculator on the Social Studies test when math is involved. Although this question involves simple arithmetic, you don't want a small mistake to cost you an easy additional point!

12. **2,642.** To find this number in the table, first find the row on the left that shows foreign-born individuals who entered the United States after 2010. Then find the column at the top that shows high school graduates. The cell in the table where they come together shows that 2,642 thousand is the answer.

REMEMBER

13. **high.** The data in the table consistently shows higher educational attainment in every category for employed individuals.

The data in question 13 shows that your decision to get your GED is the right one. *Keep going!*

14. **D. Educational attainment varies greatly depending on personal characteristics.** Only Choice (D) is supported by the table; the table shows great differences depending on variables such as family status, occupation, and other personal traits. Choice (A) cannot be concluded because the table does not break out data by gender. Choice (B) is incorrect because the table shows data for people ages 25 and older. Choice (C) is incorrect because the table shows data for the civilian population only.

TIP

Don't forget to read the title and other labels on a table or graph! They contain important information, as illustrated by this question, which can be answered by reading just these key bits of information.

15. **A. The king's only answer to their complaints was more repression.** The first line of the text states the answer. Choice (B) has nothing to do with the belief that the king was a tyrant. Choice (C) may be correct but also has nothing to do with the reasons the king was considered a tyrant. Choice (D) does not make sense.

16. **A. The laws were usurpations.** The colonial states felt that the king and British parliament were taking upon themselves powers to which they had no right. They certainly didn't feel that the laws were magnanimous (Choice B), or examples of justice and consanguinity (Choice C), or that the parliament was paying attention to their concerns (Choice D).

17. **A. The states viewed themselves as independent entities.** At this time, the various states considered themselves as having the same rights as independent countries loosely joined in the Confederation. Therefore, the other choices are incorrect.

18. **A. the Articles of Confederation.** The original constitution of the United States was called the *Articles of Confederation* (Choice A), not *the Constitution of the Confederation* (Choice B) or *the Declaration of Independence* (Choice C). Choice (D), *the Declaration of the Rights of Man,* is from France, not the United States.

19. **D. He had many ideas on how to fix things.** The text describes Madison as a man of many ideas about how to fix the Articles of Confederation. Choice (A) is a minor consideration, and Choices (B) and (C) are irrelevant.

20. **13.** This information is stated directly in the passage. The Confederation of 1776 consisted of the original 13 colonies — Connecticut, Delaware, Georgia, Maryland, Massachusetts, New Hampshire, New Jersey, New York, North Carolina, South Carolina, Pennsylvania, Rhode Island, and Virginia. These were the first states in the union. Other states were added at later dates.

21. **B. to have the ability to fund extraordinary exigencies.** Madison had seen that one of the major shortcomings of the Articles of Confederation was that the federal government depended on the states to raise money. It was the need to raise money in the face of extraordinary dangers that was a key element. Therefore, the other answer choices are incorrect.

22. **D. Under the Articles of Confederation, the government had only very limited powers to tax.** This information is stated directly in the passage. Therefore, the other answer choices are incorrect.

23. **C. He worked in the home of Jefferson Davis.** The most important element of the answer choices offered is the fact that William Jackson worked in the home of Jefferson Davis, where he had direct access to all the discussions that took place (Choice C). There's no suggestion that Jackson had any military experience (Choice B), and his direct contact with Washington, D.C., occurred after he crossed Union lines (Choice D). The fact that he was African-American (Choice A) is relevant only to the extent that he was a servant in Davis's home.

24. **A. the Underground Railroad.** Harriet Tubman is best known for her key work in the Underground Railroad. Choice (B) is a song associated with the Underground Railroad but is not mentioned in the passage. Choice (C) is a less well-known accomplishment. Though Harriet Tubman acted as a spy, Choice (D) is an accomplishment of William A. Jackson.

25. **A. the Combahee River.** This information is stated directly in the passage. *Montgomery* (Choice B) refers to the name of a military officer working with Tubman, and in any case, the city of Montgomery is in Alabama, not South Carolina. She was attacking Confederate-controlled areas, not Union areas (Choice C). Atlanta (Choice D) is in Georgia, not South Carolina.

WARNING

Did you select Choice (B)? If so, you fell into a common trap — selecting an answer choice because it was mentioned in the passage in another context. *Montgomery* in this case refers to a person, not a location. Reading the question thoroughly can help you avoid this kind of error.

26. **B. army camps.** This information is stated directly in the passage. Spain (Choice A) was erroneously named as the origin of the epidemic. The places in the other choices are mentioned in the passage as having notably high death counts, not as the disease's place of origin.

27. **C. more than 500,000 people.** This information is stated directly in the passage. The other numbers are for other parts of the world or the entire world.

28. **B. 1970 to 1980.** Subtract 30 and 40 from 2012 to get the high and low end of the range, 1970 to 1980.

29. **A. economic troubles and the Vietnam War were going on at the time of their birth.** The period of 1970 to 1980 was a time of economic difficulty and the winding down of the Vietnam War. With a controversial war, rising inflation, and worries about money, people were less likely to have children at that time. The Korean War (Choice B) had ended many years earlier, and the Gulf War (Choice C) and invasion of Grenada (Choice D) were still to come.

30. **women.** If you look at the tops of the three pyramids, you can see that the right side is wider than the left. The right side reflects the number of females in the population.

31. **B. Stock prices soared many times over the underlying value of the companies.** The rapidly rising prices of stocks covered up the fact that the stocks were trading at many times the true value of the companies. This is an example of a veneer of prosperity covering up an underlying problem. The remaining choices are not related to prosperity.

32. **C. Growing prosperity made unions seem less relevant.** For most people, times appeared to be good. As long as that was the feeling, there seemed to be no real need for labor to organize. Unions were no longer illegal, so Choice (A) is incorrect. Choice (B) is contradicted by the information in the passage; the defeat of minimum wage laws showed that unions still had a role to play. Choice (D) is a reason that made unions relevant, despite people's perception of them at the time, and so is incorrect.

33. **B. Whatever improves conditions for most people cannot be regarded as bad for society as a whole.** Adam Smith proposes that anything that helps those less well-off can only improve society as a whole (Choice B). The other choices are not supported by information in the passage.

34. **B. Reward a laborer liberally.** According to Smith, employers should reward their laborers generously. The other options are contradicted by the text, when Smith states, "no society can surely be flourishing and happy, of which the far greater part of the members are poor and miserable."

35. **A. Yes. Well-paid workers are more active and diligent.** Smith and Ford would have been of one mind on this issue. Ford came under attack by other wealthy industrialists for granting his workers this pay increase, but he argued that paying his workers well allowed them to buy his cars, thereby improving his own business while making the workers happy. Therefore, Choices (B) and (D) are incorrect. Choice (C) is incorrect because Ford was interested in increasing his business, not fairness.

36. **A. This was the only way missiles of that time could reach into North and South America.** At that time, missiles couldn't cross intercontinental distances. As a result, locations close to the intended targets were important. That's why the United States placed missiles in Turkey that could attack the Soviet Union. The USSR was simply responding in kind when it decided to build missile bases in Cuba. The Soviet Union didn't want to start a nuclear war (Choice D); they wanted to be able to counter U.S. missiles in Turkey. There was no trade benefit to the Soviet Union (Choice C), and although the Soviet Union may have wanted to show support for Fidel Castro (Choice B), that wasn't the main reason for deploying the missiles.

37. **C. The United States had placed its own missiles in Turkey on the border of the Soviet Union.** The United States had placed missiles in Turkey that directly threatened the Soviet Union. Soviet actions in Cuba were a direct response. There is no evidence in the passage that the Soviet Union was preparing for an attack (Choice A) or wanted to distract attention from Vietnam (Choice D). Although Castro may have demanded the missiles as protection (Choice B), that wasn't the key element in the Soviets' decision, nor is that argument supported by the text.

38. **C. Attached to a military unit involved in the action.** From the context, you can figure out that this option is correct. The photographers were sent to take photos of the war and its aftermath, so they needed to be close to the action, but not directly participating in the

fighting. In fact, the photo shows the photographer camping with the rest of the army. The other choices do not make sense.

39. **A. They had all the tools and equipment needed to take and develop photos.** The passage makes it clear that they used the "darkroom wagons" to develop photos on the spot, so that the developed plates could be returned quickly and safely to Brady's studio in Washington (Choice A). The other choices do not make sense. Telegraphic transmission of photos was not developed until several years later (Choice B), though many of the photos were converted into wood engravings that appeared in newspapers of the day. The wagon does not look comfortable, so Choice (C) is incorrect. Choice (D) is contradicted by information in the passage and the photo: The photographer is seen holding a developed photographic plate, and the passage states as much.

40. **D. to block sunlight from entering the darkroom.** This answer can be inferred from the photo and the purpose of the wagon. Black absorbs sunlight, whereas light-colored canvas tends to allow light to enter. Therefore, a black covering would block sunlight from entering the darkroom and spoiling the photographs. None of the tents seem to be camouflaged, so Choice (A) does not make sense. Choice (B) is not supported by information in the passage or photo. In addition, the Civil War was fought mostly in the summer in very hot weather, so staying warm would not be a consideration. Choice (C) is contradicted by the color of the other tents in the photograph.

41. **increase.** The line for *World Population* continues to climb upward to the right. Using the scale, that shows an increasing population. The number values on the line confirm that.

42. **declined.** The chart shows the change in the net world population. Because all the numbers on the scale are in the positive domain, the world population is growing. However, the growth peaks around 1990, and declines — unevenly — after that. People are living longer in some parts of the world, and life expectancy in most other parts of the world hasn't changed. So the decline in the growth of the world population must mean that there are fewer children being born.

43. **B. the actual net change in world population by year.** That is, it shows the number of births minus the number of deaths. Choice (A) is partially correct, but Choice (B) is the best option. Choices (C) and (D) are incorrect because they don't take into account both birth and death rates.

44. **B. More people means more children, even if individual women have fewer children.** Although the actual number of children by individual women is declining, the population as a whole is growing. That means there are more women available to have children. So even with fewer children for women, the population continues to grow. Therefore, Choice (B) is correct.

45. **A. Some objected to standardized reading and math tests.** The only option mentioned in the text is Choice (A). According to the text, the act increased parental choice, and the plan was passed by Congress. Although some people in Congress may have considered it too expensive, there's nothing in the text to support that point.

46. **Passed: A, B. Not Passed: C, D.** The success of each policy initiative is stated directly in the passage. While No Child Left Behind and Medicare reform (Choices A and B) were passed, immigration reform and Social Security reform (Choices C and D) were not successful in Congress.

REMEMBER On the actual GED, you will use your mouse and cursor to drag and drop the answer choices into the correct boxes on the screen. For more information on answering this type of question, see Chapter 2.

47. **A. It was too costly.** This information is stated directly in the passage. Choice (B) isn't supported by information in the passage, and in fact is not true: Social Security is one of the most popular government programs. Choice (C) is incorrect because this is a reason Bush's plan for immigration reform failed. Choice (D) is contradicted by the passage. The proposal failed because it put too much responsibility on citizens.

48. **53.5.** To calculate the deficit, subtract exports from imports: $481.2 - 427.7 = 53.5$.

49. **C. There was strong popular opposition on the home front to participation in this war.** According to the text, some people in Australia strongly objected to participation in Vietnam, very much like what happened in the United States. Therefore, Choice (C) is correct. The reluctance to become involved (Choice A) isn't the best choice, there's no evidence that there was a demand to contribute only humanitarian aid (Choice B), and both countries were trying to stop the spread of communism (Choice D).

50. **D. Australian forces evacuated orphans.** Evacuating orphans (Choice D) is an example of humanitarian aid, which helps people. Choices (A) and (B) are examples of military assistance. Choice (C) safeguarded the lives of Australian diplomats assigned to Vietnam. This item is a good example of why it's important to read each answer choice carefully. If you just scan for the word "evacuated," you could select Choice (C) by mistake.

4

Peering at Your Specimen: The Science Test

IN THIS PART . . .

Discover the secrets to the Science test, including what you need to know for the test, how the test is formatted, and some tips for preparing for the different question types and materials.

Put your science knowledge to the test with some strategies for answering the questions.

» Discovering what skills you need
to succeed on the Science test

» Checking out the format and
content of the Science test

» Mastering effective preparation
strategies

Chapter **13**

From Aardvarks to Atoms: Confronting the Science Test

id you know that the passing rate for the GED Science test is 90 percent? That's because the GED Science test doesn't test you on the depth of your knowledge of science. You're not expected to memorize any scientific information to do well on this test. Instead, this test assesses your ability to ferret out information presented in passages or visual materials. However, you should have at least a passing background knowledge of science and scientific vocabulary.

One of the best ways to improve your understanding of science material and scientific vocabulary is to read scientific material, science magazines, websites, and even old textbooks. Look up any words you don't know. Rest easy that you aren't expected to know the scientific difference between terms like *fission* and *fusion* — but just being familiar with them can help you on the test.

And there's more good news! Since the Science test is based on your ability to read and interpret textual material, your preparation for the Reading Comprehension section of the Reading and Language Arts test will help you on the Science test — and vice versa!

The Science test covers material from life science, physical science (chemistry and physics), and earth and space science. Don't panic — you don't need to memorize material from those subjects. You just need to be able to read and understand the material and answer questions correctly. In this chapter, I help you get a feel for the Science test, the skills it requires, and some techniques that you can use to prepare.

Looking at the Skills the Science Test Covers

If you're totally unfamiliar with science and its vocabulary, you'll likely have trouble with the questions on the Science test. You're expected to have some basic knowledge about how the physical world works, how plants and animals live, and how the universe operates. This material tests you on ideas that you observe and develop throughout your life, both in and out of school. You probably know a little about traction, for example, from driving and walking in slippery weather. On the other hand, you may not know a lot about equilibrium aside from what you read in school.

As you prepare to take the Science test, you're expected to understand that science is all about inquiry. In fact, inquiry forms the basis of the *scientific method* — the process every good scientist follows when faced with an unknown. The steps of the scientific method are as follows:

1. **Ask questions.**
2. **Gather information.**
3. **Do experiments.**
4. **Think objectively about what you find.**
5. **Look at other possible explanations.**
6. **Draw one or more possible conclusions.**
7. **Test the conclusion(s).**
8. **Tell others what you found.**

TIP

Look at your studying for the Science test as a scientific problem. The question you're trying to answer is, "How can I increase my scientific knowledge?" Follow the scientific method to come up with a procedure to fix the problem. Your solution should include reading, reading, and more reading! In addition to this book, one or more high school science books can be a great tool to use, or even a course that teaches the basics of high school science. (Go to your local library to get your hands on a copy of one of these books, and check with your local adult education program or community college to find basic science courses that are available in your area.) If several people are preparing for the GED tests at the same time as you are, forming a study group may also be helpful.

Understanding the Test Format and What Topics Are Covered

The Science test contains 50 questions of different formats, which you have 90 minutes to answer. As with the other test sections, the information and questions on the Science test are straightforward — no one is trying to trick you. To answer the questions, you have to read and interpret the passages or other visual materials provided with the questions (and you need a basic understanding of science and the words scientists use when they communicate).

In terms of organization, some of the items are grouped in sets. Some items are stand-alone questions based on one issue or topic. Some questions follow a given passage, chart, diagram, graph, map, or table. Your job is to read or review the material and decide on the best answer for each question based on the given material.

In terms of subject matter, the questions on the Science test check your knowledge in the following areas:

» **Physical science:** About 40 percent of the test is about *physical science,* which is the study of atoms, chemical reactions, forces, and what happens when energy and matter get together. As a basic review, keep the following in mind:

- Everything is composed of atoms, even the paper or computer screen you're reading right now!

- When chemicals get together, they have a reaction — unless they're *inert* (which means they don't react with other chemicals; inert chemicals are sort of like antisocial chemicals).

- You're surrounded by forces and their effects. (If the floor didn't exert a force up on you when you stepped down, you would go through the floor.)

For more information about physical science (which includes basic chemistry and basic physics), read and review a basic science textbook. You can borrow one from your local library. You can also find one on the internet. When reading this material, you may need definitions for some of the words or terms to make understanding the concepts easier. Use a good dictionary, a dictionary phone app, or the internet to find these definitions. (If you use the internet, type any of the topics into a search engine and add "definition" after it. Become amazed at the number of hits produced, but don't spend time reading them all!)

» **Life science:** Another 40 percent of the test covers *life science* — the study of cells, heredity, and other processes that occur in living systems. All life is composed of *cells,* which you can see under a microscope. Don't worry — you aren't expected to have access to a microscope and a set of slides with cells on them. Most life science–related books and websites have photographs of cells that you can study. When someone tells you that you look like your parents or that you remind them of another relative, they're talking about *heredity.* Reading a bit about heredity in biology-related books can help you practice answering some of the questions on the Science test.

Use a biology textbook to help you prepare for this portion of the test. (Get your hands on a copy of one at your local library, a nearby adult education center, or online.)

» **Earth and space science:** The remaining 20 percent of the test covers earth and space science. This area of science looks at the earth and the universe, specifically weather, astronomy, geology, rocks, erosion, and water.

When you look down at the ground as you walk, you're interacting with earth science. When you look up at the stars on a clear night and wonder what's really up there, you're thinking about space science. When you complain about the weather, you're complaining about earth science. In a nutshell, you're surrounded by earth and space sciences, so you shouldn't have a problem finding materials to read on this subject.

The topics on the Science test are focused on two main themes, both of which you probably deal with on some level every day.

>> **Human health and living systems:** Who isn't concerned with being safe and healthy? After all, it's your body and you need it. Most people try to eat nutritious meals, get some exercise, and avoid getting sick. Understanding the human body and other living organisms is an important part of science knowledge.

>> **Energy and related systems:** Energy powers your cars, cooks your food, heats your home, turns on your lights, and keeps the planet going. Understanding how energy flows through organisms and ecosystems can help you navigate your daily life and succeed on the Science test.

REMEMBER

You don't have to memorize everything you read about science before you take the test. All the answers to the test questions are based on information provided in the passages, or on the basic knowledge about science that you've acquired over the years. However, any science reading you do prior to the test not only helps you increase your basic knowledge but also improves your vocabulary. An improved science vocabulary increases your chances of being able to read the passages and answer the related questions on the test quickly.

Examining Preparation Strategies That Work

To get better results from the time and effort you put into preparing for the Science test, I suggest you try the following strategies:

>> **Take practice tests.** Take as many practice tests as you can. You can find two full-length practice tests in this book (in Chapters 23 and 31), as well as a full-length online test. Follow the time limits and check the answers and explanations when you're finished. If you still don't understand why some answers are correct, ask a tutor, take a preparation class, or look up the information in a book or on the internet. Be sure you know why every one of your answers is right or wrong.

>> **Create your own dictionary.** Get a small notebook or create a file on your phone or computer. Then, keep track of all the new words (and their definitions) that you discover as you prepare for the Science test. Make sure that you understand all the science terminology you see or hear. Of course, this goal isn't one you can reach in one night. Take some time to build your vocabulary. You don't need to start talking like a scientist, but you should be able to recognize and understand science-related words when you read them.

>> **Read as many passages as you can.** I may sound like a broken record, but reading is the most important way to prepare for the Science test. After you read a paragraph from any source (textbook, newspaper article, website, and so on), ask yourself some questions about what you read. You can also ask friends and family to ask you questions about what you read.

Check out Chapter 3 for some general test-taking strategies to help you prepare for all the sections of the GED test.

FINDING SCIENCE ON THE INTERNET

The internet can increase your scientific knowledge or simply introduce you to a new area of interest. If you don't have an internet connection at home or through a cellphone, try your local library or community center.

To save yourself time as you begin your online search for additional practice in reading science material, I suggest that you check out the following sites:

- `www.els.net`: Contains tons of information about life sciences.

- `science.nasa.gov/earth/`: Contains lots of intriguing earth- and space-related information.

- `https://www.thoughtco.com/chemistry-4133594`: Contains interesting information related to chemistry. (Note that this is a commercial site, which means you'll see pesky banners and commercial links amid the interesting and helpful information.)

- `https://www.thoughtco.com/physics-4133571`: Contains some interesting physics lessons that are presented in an entertaining and informative manner.

- `ged.com`: The GED Testing Service's site, which contains a great deal of information, both general and specific, regarding the Science test.

To explore on your own, go to your favorite search engine and type the science keywords you're most interested in (*biology, earth science,* and *chemistry,* just to name a few examples). You can also use the same keywords for a YouTube search and find many excellent videos explaining these topics.

Chapter **14**

Science Question Types and Solving Strategies

The Science test is one long 90-minute test. It shares most of the same features and question formats as the other GED test sections. Although the items are mostly in the traditional multiple-choice format, you'll also find fill-in-the-blank, drop-down, and drag-and-drop question formats. The questions are based on scientific text passages or visual images, including diagrams, graphs, maps, and tables. In this chapter, I explore the different question types and strategies for solving them.

Tackling the Science Test Questions

The Science test questions are based on two types of information: textual passages and visual materials. A few questions may be based on both. Having a basic understanding of these two types of information can help you avoid any surprises when you sit down to take the test.

You want to make sure that you read and understand every chart, diagram, graph, map, table, passage, and question that appears on the GED Science test. Information — both relevant and irrelevant — is everywhere, and you never know where you'll find what you need to answer the questions quickly and correctly, especially when dealing with visuals, graphs, tables, and diagrams.

TIP

If a passage and visual information appear together, look at the graphic first, before you read the passage. Visual information is usually easier and faster to process than text. Use the information that you extract from the graphic to help you read and understand the textual information.

Don't skip something because it doesn't immediately look important. And make sure you use the tabs and scroll bars to view all the information. For a review of these important features, see Chapter 2. In this section, I'll show you how to answer questions about textual passages and visual materials.

Questions about text passages

The text passages on this test — and the questions that accompany them — are very similar to those on a reading-comprehension test: You're given textual material and you have to answer questions about it. The passages present everything you need to answer the questions, but you usually have to understand all the words used in those passages to figure out what they're telling you (which is why I recommend that you read as much science information as you can prior to the test).

The difference between the text passages on the Science test and on other reading-comprehension tests is that the terminology and examples are all about science. Thus, the more you read about science, the more science words you'll know, understand, and be comfortable seeing on the test — which, as you may imagine, can greatly improve your chances of success.

TIP

Keep the following tips and tricks in mind when answering questions about text passages:

>> **Read each passage and question carefully.** Some of the questions on the Science test assume that you know a little bit from past experience. For example, you may be expected to know that a rocket is propelled forward by an engine firing backward. (On the other hand, you won't have to know the definition of *nuclear fission* — thank goodness!)

Regardless of whether an item assumes some basic science knowledge or asks for an answer that appears directly in the passage, you need to read each passage and corresponding question carefully. As you read, do the following:

- Try to understand the passage and think about what you already know about the subject.

- If a passage has only one question, read that question extra carefully.

- If the passage or question contains words you don't understand, try to figure out what those words mean from the rest of the sentence, the entire passage, or any graphic or illustration. However, if you still understand the overall main idea without knowing that word, you can skip the word and go on.

>> **Read each answer choice carefully.** Doing so helps you get a clearer picture of your options. If you select an answer without reading all the choices, you may end up picking the wrong one because, although that answer choice may seem right at first, it may be only partially correct. Another answer choice may be more complete or accurate. As you read the answer choices, do the following:

- If one answer choice is right from your reading and experience, select it and go on to the next item.

- If you aren't sure which answer choice is right, exclude the choices that you know are wrong, and then exclude choices that may be wrong.

- If you can exclude all but one answer choice, it's probably correct, so choose it.

- If you can only exclude one or two answer choices, guess and go on to the next item. Use the flag feature in the online interface to mark any items you cannot answer or want to return to if you have more time.

Try out these tips on the sample passages and questions in the later section, "Practicing with Sample Items."

Questions about visual materials

Visual materials are images that contain information that you use to answer the corresponding questions. Visual materials can include tables, graphs, diagrams, photos, and maps. A graphic image can contain as much information as — or more information than — a passage. As the saying goes, "A picture is worth a thousand words." This section (and the practice tests) can help you get the practice you need to get the most out of visual materials.

REMEMBER

Any visual object is like a short paragraph. It has a topic and makes comments or states facts about that topic. When you come across a question based on visual material, the first thing to do is to figure out the content or topic of the material. Usually, visual objects have titles or captions that help you understand their meanings, so read those first. If you don't understand any of the words, use the image to help you figure out the words. After you understand the main idea behind the visual object, ask yourself what information you're being given and what information you need to find out; reading the question can be helpful. After you know these two pieces of information, you're well on your way to answering the question.

The following sections take a more detailed look at the different visual materials that you may find on the Science test. As a bonus, this advice also applies to the Social Studies test. (Check out Chapter 11 for examples of all the visual materials mentioned in the following sections.)

Tables

A *table* is a graphical way of organizing information. This type of visual material allows for easy comparison between two or more sets of data. Some tables use numbers and symbols to represent information; others use words.

TIP

Most tables have titles that tell you what they're about. Always read the titles first so you know right away what information the tables include. If a table gives you an explanation (or *key*) of the symbols, read the explanation carefully, too; doing so helps you understand how to read the table.

Graphs

A *graph* is a picture that shows how different sets of numbers are related. On the Science test, you can find the following three main types of graphs:

>> **Bar or column graphs:** Bar (horizontal) or column (vertical) graphs present and often compare numbers or quantities.

>> **Line graphs:** On line graphs, one or more lines connect points drawn on a grid to show the relationships between data, including changes in data over time.

>> **Pie graphs (also called pie charts or circle graphs):** Arcs of circles (pieces of a pie) show how data relates to a whole. Often, data in pie charts is expressed as a percent of a whole.

All three types of graphs usually share the following common characteristics:

>> **Title:** The title tells you what the graph is about, so always read the title before reviewing the graph.

>> **Horizontal axis and vertical axis:** Bar, column, and line graphs have a horizontal axis and a vertical axis. (Pie graphs don't.) Each axis is a vertical or horizontal reference line that's labeled to give you additional information.

>> **Label:** The labels on the axes of a graph usually contain units, such as feet or dollars. Read all axis labels carefully; they can either help you with the answer or lead you astray (depending on whether you read them correctly). The labels in a pie chart will indicate the unit of measurement and the quantities (often percentage).

>> **Legend:** Graphs usually have a *legend,* or printed material that tells you what each section of the graph is about. They may also contain labels on the individual parts of the graph and explanatory notes about the data used to create the graph, so read carefully.

WARNING

Graphs and tables are both often called *charts,* which can be rather confusing. To help you prepare for problems with graphs, make sure you look at and understand plenty of graphs before the test. Remember that graphs show relationships. If the numbers represented on the horizontal axis are in millions of dollars and you think they're in dollars, your interpretation of the graph will be more than a little incorrect.

Diagrams

A *diagram* is a drawing that helps you understand how something works. Diagrams on the Science test often have the following two components.

>> **Title:** Tells you what the diagram is trying to show you.

>> **Labels:** Indicate the names of the parts of the diagram.

When you come to a question based on a diagram, read the title of the diagram first to get an idea of what the diagram is about. Then carefully read all the labels to find out the main components of the diagram. These two pieces of information can help you understand the diagram well enough to answer questions about it.

Photos

A *photo* may sometimes appear on the GED. You can use these features of photos to help you understand them:

>> **Caption:** The caption tells you the subject of the photo. For example, a photo of the planet Mars may identify the planet and say how the photo was taken: "A space probe took this close-up photo of the planet Mars."

>> **Labels:** Labels may mark or identify people or objects in the photo. For example, a photo of Mars may have its ice cap labeled.

When you come to a question based on a photo, read the caption first. Then carefully read any labels. Then look at the photo. If you don't understand any words in the label, use the photo to figure them out.

Maps

A *map* is a drawing of some section — large or small — of the earth or another planet. People even call images of the solar system or of the stars in the night sky a map. Because the entire world is too large to depict on one piece of paper, maps are drawn to scale.

Most maps give you the following information:

>> **Title:** Tells you what area of the world the map focuses on and what it shows.

>> **Legend:** Gives you general information about the meaning, colors, symbols, or other graphics used on the map.

>> **Compass:** Indicates the map's orientation. In general, north is at the top of a map, but for certain maps, this may not be the case. On many maps, a small compass will show which way is north. (Sometimes this compass may be omitted if the map is very familiar. A map of the United States likely would not have a compass, as most people know the north is at the top.)

>> **Labels:** Indicate what the various points on the map represent.

>> **Scale:** Tells you what the distance on the map represents in real life. (For example, a map with a scale of 1 inch = 100 miles shows a distance of 500 miles on the real earth as a distance of 5 inches on the map.)

Although maps are seldom used in science passages, you may still run across them, so you want to be familiar with them. And you will certainly encounter them on the Social Studies test. The best way to get familiar with maps is to spend some time looking at road maps and world atlases, which you can find in your local library or online.

REMEMBER

The exact meaning of any visual materials may not be obvious or may even be misleading if not examined carefully. You must understand what the legends, scale, labels, and color-coding are telling you. Numbers on a table also may be misleading or even meaningless unless you read the legend and labels carefully. Colors on a map aren't just for decoration; each color has a meaning. Each piece of a visual represents meaning from which you can put together the information you need to determine the answers to test questions.

Practicing with Sample Items

To help increase your odds of doing well on the Science test, you want to be as familiar as you can be with the kinds of questions you'll encounter on the real GED test. The following sections show the different kinds of questions that may appear on the Science test. Not all of the item types here will appear on the test, but you can be sure that there will be plenty of multiple-choice questions and a few fill-in-the-blank questions. Get familiar with each question type. I'll give you some tips and tricks to help you answer each kind.

Multiple-choice questions

Most of the questions on the Science test are in the traditional multiple-choice format, where you get four answer choices. Your job is to pick the best answer that's supported by the passage or visual material. If the material is in the form of a text passage, read the passage quickly to answer the question. If the material is in the form of a visual, read the title and the verbal information so you understand what the visual is all about.

REMEMBER

If one answer must be correct, then three answers must be wrong. If you can exclude the wrong answers, you'll be left with the right one. Read the passage carefully to figure out the right or wrong choices.

The example questions in this section refer to the following passage.

One of the great discoveries in earth science is rocks. Rocks have many useful purposes in science. They can be used as paperweights to keep academic papers from flying away in the wind. Rocks can be used to prop laboratory doors open when the experiments go wrong and horrible smells are produced. Smooth rocks can be rubbed when pressure builds and you just need a mindless activity to get through the day.

EXAMPLE

According to the passage, one of the great discoveries in science is

(A) atomic energy.

(B) static electricity.

(C) rocks.

(D) DNA.

The correct answer is Choice (C). The important words in the question are *According to the passage.* When you see this phrase, you know to look in the passage for the answer. Because none of the choices except rocks is even remotely mentioned, rocks must be the answer.

EXAMPLE

How do rocks help scientists when experiments go horribly wrong and produce terrible odors?

(A) They can be used to smash the windows.

(B) They can hold open the doors.

(C) They can be thrown in anger.

(D) They can be rubbed.

The answer is Choice (B). According to the passage, the rocks can be used to hold open the door of the lab. Rocks can also be used to smash windows and can be thrown in anger, but the passage doesn't specifically mention these uses. The passage mentions rubbing rocks as one of their uses, but it does so in another context.

TIP

Did you notice that the passage used the word *prop* and the answer choice used the word *hold*? The test-makers use synonyms such as these to make sure you are really paying attention. This is an example of another way that having a rich vocabulary will help you on the test.

Fill-in-the-blank questions

For science fill-in-the-blank questions, you have to provide your own answer(s) — a specific calculation, a word, or words — to show that you understand a concept, to complete a definition, or to describe a trend on a graph. This is another example of why you should read as much scientific material as possible. A misspelled word is scored as incorrect. Keeping a vocabulary list as a review method before the test will really help.

The following fill-in-the-blank question is based on this excerpt from a job posting on the Federal Government Jobs website (www.usajobs.gov).

> A career with the Forest Service will challenge you to manage and care for more than 193 million acres of our nation's most magnificent lands, conduct research through a network of forest and range experiment stations and the Forest Products Laboratory, and provide assistance to State and private forestry agencies.
>
> It's an awesome responsibility — but the rewards are as limitless as the views.

EXAMPLE

Based on the information in the passage, what would the person hired for this job do in conjunction with range experiment stations? [＿＿＿＿]

The answer is *conduct research.* The successful applicant would conduct research with the range experiment stations as part of their duties. This is stated explicitly in the passage.

Try another fill-in-the-blank question on for size, based on the following excerpt from the USDA Animal and Plant Health Inspection Service website (www.aphis.usda.gov).

The Lacey Act combats trafficking in "illegal" wildlife, fish, and plants. The 2008 Farm Bill (the Food, Conservation, and Energy Act of 2008), effective May 22, 2008, amended the Lacey Act by expanding its protection to a broader range of plants and plant products. The Lacey Act now, among other things, makes it unlawful to import certain plants and plant products without an import declaration.

The Lacey Act is a piece of government legislation to control the transportation and selling of [ ] plants.

EXAMPLE The passage states that this act was passed to combat the trafficking of illegal wildlife, fish, and plants. So the answer is *illegal.*

Because math is used in science, some items may test math skills. These items are frequently fill-in-the-blank items or multiple-choice items. Here is an example:

To calculate density, you divide mass by volume. A sample of ice at 0°C has a volume of 64 cm³ and a mass of 58.7 g.

What is the density of the sample, rounded to three decimal points? [ ] g/cm³ You may use numbers, a decimal point (.), and/or a negative sign (−) in your answer.

EXAMPLE The information says that to calculate density, you divide mass by volume: 58.7/64 = 0.9171875. Rounded to three decimal places, the answer is 0.917 g/cm³. Because *g/cm³* is already provided, you just need to type 0.917.

TIP A calculator icon appears on the top right of the computer screen for some questions on the Mathematical Reasoning, Science, and Social Studies tests. You may click on the calculator link to help you compute your answers. If you have a hand-held Texas Instruments TI-30XS calculator, you may use it when testing at a test center.

TIP Pay careful attention to the instructions when answering a fill-in-the-blank question with a number. Even small errors, such as not rounding to the number of places specified, can cost you the answer. On the previous item, the test software will also accept .917, but not 0.9172, which has too many decimal places. With math questions, always read and follow the directions!

Drag-and-drop questions

For this question format, you have to drag answer choices from a list to a designated position — whether that's placing labels on a graph or diagram or dropping words or images on a specific location on a chart or other type of visual. This question format requires a bit more than just picking the correct answer. In drag-and-drop questions, you may have to sort and prioritize your selections. Although you're given a list of possible answers, more than one may be correct. Read the passage carefully to either eliminate wrong answers or choose correct ones.

Here's an example of a question in the drag-and-drop format.

EXAMPLE In Ms. Fleming's graduating class, three of her students want to specialize in science:

>> Gilda wants to study physics.

>> Domenic wants to study biology.

>> Freida wants to learn everything she can about NASA's missions.

Drag (or write, in this case) the appropriate name into the column labeled with the general area each student wants to study.

(A) Gilda

(B) Domenic

(C) Freida

Earth and Space Science	Life Science	Physical Science

The correct response here is that Gilda wants to study physical science, Domenic wants to study life science, and Freida wants to study earth and space science. General knowledge from your experience and reading would enable you to fit the specific interests into the general areas.

Drop-down menu questions

The drop-down menu is a type of multiple-choice question, in that you're given a number of answer choices to choose from to complete a sentence so that it reads correctly and accurately. Usually, drop-down menu questions involve more science vocabulary, so your reading in science will help you choose the correct answer. As with most multiple-choice items, the drop-down menu includes correct and incorrect answers.

The following drop-down menu question refers to this excerpt from the Missions page on NASA's website (www.nasa.gov).

> The Post-landing Orion Recovery Tests (PORT) began in late March at the Naval Surface Warfare Center, Carderock Division in Bethesda, MD. This first round took place in a controlled water environment. Testing near Kennedy Space Center in April will be done in the rougher, uncontrolled waters of the Atlantic Ocean. Crews will head out over several days and at varying distances from land to assess the vehicle's performance in open water landing conditions. Recovery teams will gain experience dealing with Orion in water. The tests will also help NASA understand the motions astronauts will experience within the craft. The same boats that have been used to recover the space shuttle's solid rocket boosters will tow the capsule for these tests.

EXAMPLE

The Orion will be tested in open waters in the Atlantic to

(A) ensure that the astronauts can swim.

(B) ensure the safety and security of the astronauts.

(C) assess the Orion's ability to travel far in space.

(D) allow the astronauts to fish to provide them with provisions.

The answer is Choice (B), *ensure the safety and security of the astronauts.* Dropping a sealed capsule into the ocean wouldn't test swimming ability (Choice A), assess the ship's ability to travel far in space (Choice C), or offer fishing possibilities (Choice D).

Drop-down questions are frequently used with visual materials. In these questions, you have to complete a caption for the visual material. For example, the test might present you with a graph of the average global temperature for each year from 1900 to the present, with the graph showing a steadily rising temperature.

EXAMPLE

This graph of average global temperatures since 1900 shows a generally [   ] pattern year over year. (*Note:* Since this is an example of a question type, the graph is not shown).

(A) rising

(B) falling

(C) stable

(D) unpredictable

Choice (A) is correct. According to the description, the graph shows a generally increasing global temperature, so only this choice is possible.

Managing Your Time for the Science Test

The Science test has 50 questions that you must answer in 90 minutes, which means you have on average about 100 seconds (or about a minute and two-thirds) to read each textual or visual passage and its corresponding question(s) and determine the correct answer. If a passage has more than one question, you have slightly more time to answer those questions because you should read the passage only once.

To help you manage your time, check out Chapters 2 and 3 for some general time-management strategies that you can use on all the test sections. For the Science test, specifically, I suggest you focus on these two time-saving strategies:

>> **For questions about passages, read the question first and then scan the material for the answer.** The passage always contains the answer, but your background knowledge in science and your familiarity with scientific terms can help you understand the material more easily and quickly. Reading the question first provides you with a guide to what's being asked and what the passage is about so that you know what to look for as you read it.

>> **For questions about a visual material such as a graph or table, read the question first and then scan the visual material.** Look at the visual material to see the big picture; questions usually don't ask about minute details.

As a general tip, answer the easiest questions first. Use the Flag button (in the upper-right corner of your screen) to mark questions you want to return to. Remember, when you finish all the items, you will be offered the opportunity to see a list of all the questions you answered, skipped, and flagged in the Review screen. You can use that list to return to items you had questions about or skipped earlier. If you run out of time or want to see the list of skipped and flagged items at any time, press Review in the lower-right corner of your screen.

TIP

There's no penalty for guessing on the GED, so don't leave any answers blank. Use the last few minutes of the test to answer any unanswered items, using the Review screen.

And don't panic! Your worst enemy on this or any other test is panic. Panicking takes time and energy, and you don't have a surplus of either one. Use a calming technique (such as inhaling deeply) and then keep moving forward. If you find yourself spending too much time on one question, flag it and keep moving. Return to the question at the end of the test when you know exactly how much time is left.

Chapter **15**

Sampling Some Science Practice Questions

This chapter provides sample Science test questions to help you prepare for taking this section of the GED test.

Record your answers directly in this book or on a sheet of paper if you think you'll want to revisit these practice questions at a later date. Mark only one answer for each item. At the end of the chapter, I provide detailed answer explanations for you to check against your answers.

Remember, this is just preliminary practice. I want you to get used to answering different types of Science test questions. Use the complete practice tests in Chapters 23 and 31 (or online) to time your work and replicate the real test–taking experience. Lastly, use the online-only test I provide for a final check. With all this practice, you'll be ready for test day!

Science Practice Questions

The Science test consists of a series of items intended to measure general concepts in science. The items are based on short readings that may include a graph, chart, or figure. Study the information given and then answer the question(s) following it. Refer to the information as often as necessary in answering the questions. Work carefully, but don't spend too much time on any one question. Be sure to answer every question.

Questions 1 and 2 refer to the following diagram and excerpt adapted from NASA's Glenn Research Center website for Space Flight Systems.

Source: NASA

Many differences exist between the forces acting on a rocket and those acting on an airplane.

- On an airplane, the **lift force** (the aerodynamic force perpendicular to the flight direction) is used to overcome the **weight**. On a rocket, **thrust** is used in opposition to weight. On many rockets, **lift** is used to stabilize and control the direction of flight.

- On an airplane, most of the aerodynamic forces are generated by the wings and the tail surfaces. For a rocket, the aerodynamic forces are generated by the fins, nose cone, and body tube. For both airplane and rocket, the aerodynamic forces act through the center of pressure (the dot with the black center on the figure), while the weight acts through the center of gravity (the solid dot on the figure).

- While most airplanes have a high lift-to-drag ratio, the drag of a rocket is usually much greater than the lift.

- While the magnitude and direction of the forces remain fairly constant for an airplane, the magnitude and direction of the forces acting on a rocket change dramatically during a typical flight.

1. In the diagram, which force must be the greatest for the rocket to leave the earth?

    (A) drag
    (B) lift
    (C) thrust
    (D) weight

2. Which statement most accurately describes lift on airplanes and rockets?

    (A) On airplanes, lift holds the airplane in the air; on some rockets, lift helps steer the rocket.
    (B) On airplanes, lift helps steer the plane; on rockets, lift holds the rocket in the air.
    (C) Rockets and planes both use lift to leave the earth.
    (D) Rockets use lift; planes use thrust.

Questions 3 and 4 refer to the following excerpt adapted from the U.S. Environmental Protection Agency's website on climate change (www.epa.gov/climatechange).

As temperatures increase, the habitat ranges of many North American species are moving northward in latitude and upward in elevation. While this means a range expansion for some species, for others it means a range reduction or a movement into less hospitable habitat or increased competition. Some species have nowhere to go because they are already at the northern or upper limit of their habitat.

For example, boreal forests are invading tundra, reducing habitat for the many unique species that depend on the tundra ecosystem such as caribou, arctic fox, and snowy owl. Other observed changes in the United States include expanding oak-hickory forests, contracting maple-beech forests, and disappearing spruce-fir forests. As rivers and streams warm, warmwater fish are expanding into areas previously inhabited by coldwater species. Coldwater fish, including several trout species valued by many people for their high protein content, are losing their habitats. As waters warm, the area of feasible, cooler habitats to which species can migrate is reduced. Range shifts disturb the current state of the ecosystem and can limit opportunities for fishing and hunting.

3. As temperatures become warmer and ranges move, the new territory may prove to be less
   ☐ for specific species.

4. Which of the following is a consequence of the warming of the habitats of coldwater fish?

   (A) Coldwater fish migrate to new habitats.

   (B) Warmwater fish move into the habitats of coldwater fish.

   (C) Coldwater fish adjust to warmer water.

   (D) Opportunities for fishing increase.

Question 5 refers to the following excerpt from Womenshealth.gov.

"Mirror, Mirror on the wall who's the thinnest one of all?" According to the National Eating Disorders Association, the average American woman is 5 feet 4 inches tall and weighs 140 pounds. The average American model is 5 feet 11 inches tall and weighs 117 pounds. All too often, society associates being "thin" with "hard-working, beautiful, strong and self-disciplined." On the other hand, being "fat" is associated with being "lazy, ugly, weak and lacking will-power." Because of these harsh critiques, rarely are women completely satisfied with their image. As a result, they often feel great anxiety and pressure to achieve and/or maintain an imaginary appearance.

Eating disorders are serious medical problems. Anorexia nervosa, bulimia nervosa, and binge-eating disorder are all types of eating disorders. Eating disorders frequently develop during adolescence or early adulthood but can occur during childhood or later in adulthood. Females are more likely than males to develop an eating disorder.

5. Which of the following would add further support to the passage?

   (A) Images of unusually thin women are pervasive in media.

   (B) Women have trouble losing weight.

   (C) Males are generally taller and weigh more.

   (D) Males are not subject to the same pressure about weight as women.

Question 6 refers to the following statement by the U.S. Surgeon General (www.surgeongeneral.gov).

We must increase our efforts to educate and encourage Americans to take responsibility for their own health. Over the past 20 years, the rates of overweight doubled in children and tripled in adolescents. Today nearly two out of every three American adults and 15 percent of American kids are overweight or obese. That's more than 9 million children — one in every seven kids — who are at increased risk of weight-related chronic diseases. These facts are astounding, but they are just the beginning of a chain reaction of dangerous health problems — many of which were once associated only with adults.

6. The percentage of children who are overweight or obese is estimated at

   (A) 9 percent.
   (B) 15 percent.
   (C) 20 percent.
   (D) 30 percent.

Question 7 refers to the following definition from the U.S. Environmental Protection Agency's climate change glossary (www.epa.gov/climatechange).

Black carbon (BC) is the most strongly light-absorbing component of particulate matter (PM), and is formed by the incomplete combustion of fossil fuels, biofuels, and biomass. It is emitted directly into the atmosphere in the form of fine particles.

7. Based on this information, why would reducing automobile use result in a cleaner environment?

   (A) Traffic would be lighter.
   (B) Most automobiles run on fossil fuel.
   (C) Subways are a more efficient form of moving people.
   (D) Electricity is less expensive than fossil fuels.

Question 8 refers to the following definition from the U.S. Environmental Protection Agency's climate change glossary (www.epa.gov/climatechange).

The greenhouse effect is the trapping and build-up of heat in the atmosphere (troposphere) near the Earth's surface. Some of the heat flowing back toward space from the Earth's surface is absorbed by water vapor, carbon dioxide, ozone, and several other gases in the atmosphere and then reradiated back toward the Earth's surface. If the atmospheric concentrations of these greenhouse gases rise, the average temperature of the lower atmosphere will gradually increase.

8. Heat reradiated from the Earth's surface is absorbed by several ⬚ in the Earth's atmosphere.

Question 9 refers to the following excerpt from NASA's Science website (science.nasa.gov).

Examples of the types of forecasts that may be possible are the outbreak and spread of harmful algal blooms, occurrence and spread of invasive exotic species, and productivity of forest and agricultural systems. This Focus Area also will contribute to the improvement of climate projections for 50–100 years into the future by providing key inputs for climate models. This includes projections of future atmospheric CO_2 and CH_4 concentrations and understanding of key ecosystem and carbon cycle process controls on the climate system.

9. Long-term forecasts of this type are important to people because

   (A) they will help hunters know when their favorite sport will become impossible.
   (B) they will allow scientists to develop research projects that will address the consequences of dramatic climate change.
   (C) people will know what type of winter clothing to buy for their children.
   (D) it will spur research into more efficient subway systems.

Question 10 refers to the following excerpt from NASA's Science website (science.nasa.gov).

Throughout the next decade, research will be needed to advance our understanding of and ability to model human-ecosystems-climate interactions so that an integrated understanding of Earth System function can be applied to our goals. These research activities will yield knowledge of the Earth's ecosystems and carbon cycle, as well as projections of carbon cycle and ecosystem responses to global environmental change.

10. This type of research should lead to advances in our understanding of how the carbon cycle and our ecosystem respond to [   ].

Questions 11 and 12 refer to the following excerpt from NASA's Jet Propulsion Laboratory website (www.jp.nasa.gov).

We live on a restless planet. Earth is continually influenced by the Sun, gravitational forces, processes emanating from deep within the core, and by complex interactions with oceans and atmospheres. At very short time scales we seem to be standing on terra firma, yet many processes sculpt the surface with changes that can be quite dramatic (earthquakes, volcanic eruptions, landslides), sometimes slow (subsidence due to aquifer depletion), seemingly unpredictable, and often leading to loss of life and property damage.

Accurate diagnosis of our restless planet requires an observational capability for precise measurement of surface change, or deformation. Measurement of both the slow and fast deformations of Earth are essential for improving the scientific understanding of the physical processes, for optimizing responses to natural hazards, and for identifying potential risk areas.

11. Although people often talk about standing on solid ground, the truth is that

    (A) the Earth is capable of supporting huge buildings anywhere on its surface.
    (B) the ground is solid and stable.
    (C) the ground is capable of sudden, dramatic movement.
    (D) people should not live near an active volcano.

12. Accurate scientific research into surface change is essential to

    (A) offset the physical processes.
    (B) warn people about volcanoes.
    (C) ensure better responses to natural hazards.
    (D) make more accurate weather forecasts.

Question 13 refers to the following diagram from NASA's Glenn Research Center website (www.grc.nasa.gov).

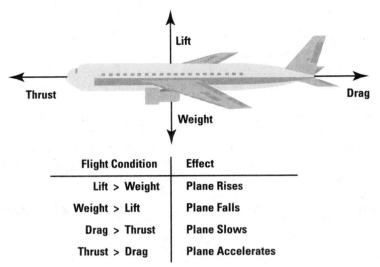

Flight Condition	Effect
Lift > Weight	Plane Rises
Weight > Lift	Plane Falls
Drag > Thrust	Plane Slows
Thrust > Drag	Plane Accelerates

Source: NASA

13. For the plane to take off, [   ] and [   ]. Write the appropriate answers in the boxes.

(A) lift > weight

(B) weight > lift

(C) drag > thrust

(D) thrust > drag

Question 14 refers to the following excerpt from NASA's website (www.nasa.gov).

It would be impractical, in terms of volume and cost, to completely stock the International Space Station (ISS) with oxygen or water for long periods of time. Without a grocery store in space, NASA scientists and engineers have developed innovative solutions to meet astronauts' basic requirements for life. The human body is two-thirds water. It has been estimated that nearly an octillion (1,000,000,000,000,000,000,000,000,000) water molecules flow through our bodies daily. It is therefore necessary for humans to consume a sufficient amount of water, as well as oxygen and food, on a daily basis in order to sustain life. Without water, the average person lives approximately three days. Without air, permanent brain damage can occur within three minutes. Scientists have determined how much water, air, and food a person needs per day per person for life on Earth. Similarly, space scientists know what is needed to sustain life in space.

14. Why is it necessary to recycle air and water on a space ship?

(A) to keep the interior smelling clean

(B) to keep the ISS moving

(C) to keep the astronauts alive

(D) so that the astronauts don't get thirsty between meals

Question 15 refers to the following diagram from NASA's Glenn Research Center website (https://www.nasa.gov/centers/glenn/home/index.html).

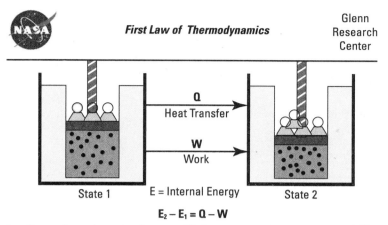

First Law of Thermodynamics

Glenn Research Center

Q
Heat Transfer

W
Work

State 1   E = Internal Energy   State 2

$$E_2 - E_1 = Q - W$$

Any thermodynamic system in an equilibrium state possesses a state variable called the internal energy (E). Between any two equilibrium states, the change in internal energy is equal to the difference of the heat transfer <u>into</u> the system and work done <u>by</u> the system.

Source: NASA

15. Circle the vessel on the diagram with the higher temperature.

Questions 16–18 refer to the following information and graph.

Cobalt (Co) is a metal that is used in the manufacture of lithium-ion batteries used extensively in mobile devices and electric vehicles, as well as in numerous other industrial applications. Your mobile phone will not work without cobalt. The largest known reserves of cobalt are in the Democratic Republic of the Congo, with over 70 percent of known deposits, followed by Indonesia, Russia, and Australia. This chart summarizes global uses of this essential material in a recent year.

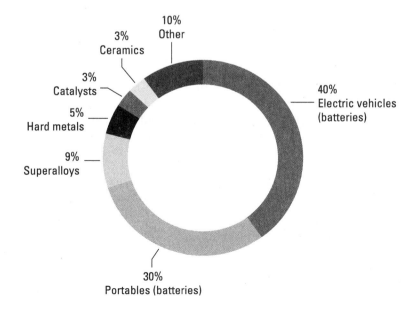

10%
Other

3%
Ceramics

3%
Catalysts

5%
Hard metals

9%
Superalloys

40%
Electric vehicles
(batteries)

30%
Portables (batteries)

16. What are the most important uses of cobalt? Write the letters in order from most important to least important.

[   ]

(A) coloring ceramics

(B) batteries for mobile devices

(C) hardening metals

(D) batteries for electric vehicles

17. Based on the information, the United States is most likely

(A) a net producer of cobalt.

(B) a net consumer of cobalt.

(C) a net exporter of cobalt.

(D) not a user of cobalt.

18. Cobalt is **an element / a compound** (circle one).

Question 19 refers to the following definition adapted from the U.S. Environmental Protection Agency's climate change glossary (www.epa.gov/climate-change).

Weather is an atmospheric condition at any given time or place. It is measured in terms of such things as wind, temperature, humidity, atmospheric pressure, cloudiness, and precipitation. In most places, weather can change from hour-to-hour, day-to-day, and season-to-season. Climate is usually defined as the "average weather," or more rigorously, as the statistical description in terms of the mean and variability of relevant quantities over a period of time ranging from months to thousands or millions of years. The classical period is 30 years, as defined by the World Meteorological Organization (WMO). These quantities are most often surface variables such as temperature, precipitation, and wind. Climate in a wider sense is the state, including a statistical description, of the climate system. A simple way of remembering the difference is that climate is what you expect (e.g., cold winters) and weather is what you get (e.g., a blizzard).

19. If you were sitting around with a group of friends complaining about how the rain forecast for tomorrow was going to ruin your baseball game, you would be complaining about the [   ].

Question 19 refers to the following definition from the U.S. Environmental Protection Agency's climate change glossary (www.epa.gov/climate-change).

Atmospheric lifetime is the average time that a molecule resides in the atmosphere before it is removed by chemical reaction or deposition. This can also be thought of as the time that it takes after the human-caused emission of a gas for the concentrations of that gas in the atmosphere to return to natural levels. Greenhouse gas lifetimes can range from a few years to a few thousand years.

20. Why is it important for humans to become more aware of the pollution they are causing by overuse of fossil fuels?

(A) Gasoline is becoming expensive.

(B) The greenhouse gases can remain in the atmosphere for many years.

(C) Traffic congestion is causing health problems.

(D) Humans are turning the blue sky gray.

Question 21 refers to the following excerpt from NASA's Earth Observatory website (www.earth observatory.nasa.gov).

If Kepler's laws define the motion of the planets, Newton's laws define motion. Thinking on Kepler's laws, Newton realized that all motion, whether it was the orbit of the Moon around the Earth or an apple falling from a tree, followed the same basic principles. "To the same natural effects," he wrote, "we must, as far as possible, assign the same causes." Previous Aristotelian thinking, physicist Stephen Hawking has written, assigned different causes to different types of motion. By unifying all motion, Newton shifted the scientific perspective to a search for large, unifying patterns in nature. Newton outlined his laws in *Philosophiae Naturalis Principia Mathematica* ("Mathematical Principles of Natural Philosophy"), published in 1687.

21. Newton was inspired by

(A) Hawking.

(B) Aristotle.

(C) Kepler.

(D) Einstein.

Question 22 refers to the following information, taken from the U.S. Department of Labor's Occupational Safety & Health Administration website (www.osha.gov).

Unexpected releases of toxic, reactive, or flammable liquids and gases in processes involving highly hazardous chemicals have been reported for many years. Incidents continue to occur in various industries that use highly hazardous chemicals which may be toxic, reactive, flammable, or explosive, or may exhibit a combination of these properties. Regardless of the industry that uses these highly hazardous chemicals, there is a potential for an accidental release any time they are not properly controlled. This, in turn, creates the possibility of disaster.

Recent major disasters include the 1984 Bhopal, India, incident resulting in more than 2,000 deaths; the October 1989 Phillips Petroleum Company, Pasadena, TX, incident resulting in 23 deaths and 132 injuries; the July 1990 BASF, Cincinnati, OH, incident resulting in 2 deaths, and the May 1991 IMC, Sterlington, LA, incident resulting in 8 deaths and 128 injuries.

22. Of the incidents reported in the passage, which one caused the most fatalities?

(A) Bhopal, India

(B) Pasadena, Texas

(C) Cincinnati, Ohio

(D) Sterlington, Louisiana

Question 23 is based on the following excerpt from the National Oceanic and Atmospheric Administration's Office of Response and Restoration website (response.restoration.noaa.gov).

Reactivity is the tendency of substances to undergo chemical change, which can result in hazards — such as heat generation or toxic gas by-products. The CRW (Chemical Reactivity Worksheet) predicts possible hazards from mixing chemicals and is designed to be used by emergency responders and planners, as well as the chemical industry, to help prevent dangerous chemical incidents.

The chemical datasheets in the CRW database contain information about the intrinsic hazards of each chemical and about whether a chemical reacts with air, water, or other materials. It also includes case histories on specific chemical incidents, with references.

23. What is the most important contribution of the CRW to the prevention of hazardous accidents?

    (A) provides information

    (B) enforces the regulations

    (C) creates laws

    (D) closes companies for infractions

Question 24 refers to the following excerpt from the U.S. Environmental Protection Agency's website on climate change (www.epa.gov/climate-change).

Climate change, along with habitat destruction and pollution, is one of the important stressors that can contribute to species extinction. The IPCC estimates that 20–30% of the plant and animal species evaluated so far in climate change studies are at risk of extinction if temperatures reach levels projected to occur by the end of this century. Projected rates of species extinctions are 10 times greater than recently observed global average rates and 10,000 times greater than rates observed in the distant past (as recorded in fossils).

24. One of the great dangers to the earth as a result of climate change is the [   ] of species.

Question 25 refers to the following excerpt from the U.S. Environmental Protection Agency's website on climate change (www.epa.gov/climate-change).

When coral reefs become stressed, they expel microorganisms that live within their tissues and are essential to their health. This is known as coral bleaching. As ocean temperatures warm and the acidity of the ocean increases, bleaching and coral die-offs are likely to become more frequent. Chronically stressed coral reefs are less likely to recover.

25. Coral bleaching refers to

    (A) a chemical reaction between the ocean waters and microorganisms in the coral.

    (B) expulsion of microorganisms from within coral reefs.

    (C) the effect of extremely strong sunlight on coral reefs.

    (D) coral die-offs.

Question 26 refers to the following excerpt from the U.S. Environmental Protection Agency's website on climate change (www.epa.gov/climate-change).

For many species, the climate where they live or spend part of the year influences key stages of their annual life cycle, such as migration, blooming, and mating. As the climate has warmed in recent decades, the timing of these events has changed in some parts of the country. Some examples are

- Warmer springs have led to earlier nesting for 28 migratory bird species on the East Coast of the United States.

- Northeastern birds that winter in the southern United States are returning north in the spring 13 days earlier than they did in the early 20th century.

- In a California study, 16 out of 23 butterfly species shifted their migration timing and arrived earlier.

Changes like these can lead to mismatches in the timing of migration, breeding, and food availability. Growth and survival are reduced when migrants arrive at a location before or after food sources are present.

26. Severe climate changes can lead to extinction of a species through [_____] in aspects of their lives upon which their survival depends.

Question 27 refers to the following excerpt from NASA's Science website (`science.nasa.gov`).

New remote sensing technologies are empowering scientists to measure and understand subtle changes in the Earth's surface and interior that reflect the response of the Earth to both the internal forces that lead to volcanic eruptions, earthquakes, landslides and sea-level change and the climatic forces that sculpt the Earth's surface. For instance, InSAR [interferometric synthetic aperture radar] and LiDAR [light detection and ranging] measurements from satellite and airborne sensors are used to provide images of millimeter scale surface changes that indicate an awakening of volcanic activity long before seismic tremors are felt. Ground based geodetic GPS instruments provide time continuous measurements of this activity though they are often lost during intense volcanic activity. Thermal infrared remote sensing data from NASA satellites signal impending activity by measuring ground temperatures and variations in the composition of lava flows as well as the sulfur dioxide in volcanic plumes. The combination of instruments provides accurate information that can be used for both long term and short hazard assessment. These same LiDAR, InSAR and thermal instruments also provide accurate information on the velocity of ice steams, sub glacial lake activity, glacial rebound of the Earth's crust, and the retreat and advance of mountain glaciers that are related to climatic changes.

27. New remote sensing technologies provide [_____] that may lead to long- and short-term hazard assessment.

Question 28 refers to the following excerpt from the National Science Foundation website (`www.nsf.gov`).

By observing galaxies formed billions of years ago, astronomers have been able to paint an increasingly detailed picture of how the universe evolved. According to the widely accepted Big Bang theory, our universe was born in an explosive moment approximately fifteen billion years ago. All of the universe's matter and energy — even the fabric of space itself — was compressed into an infinitesimally small volume and then began expanding at an incredible rate. Within minutes, the universe had grown to the size of the solar system and cooled enough so that equal numbers of protons, neutrons, and the simplest atomic nuclei had formed.

28. Astronomers believe that the universe evolved about [_____] billion years ago.

Question 29 refers to the following excerpt from NASA's Earth Observatory website (`www.earth observatory.nasa.gov`).

Within a single frame of reference, the laws of classical physics, including Newton's laws, hold true. But Newton's laws can't explain the differences in motion, mass, distance, and time that result when objects are observed from two very different frames of reference. To describe motion in these situations, scientists must rely on Einstein's theory of relativity.

At slow speeds and at large scales, however, the differences in time, length, and mass predicted by relativity are small enough that they appear to be constant, and Newton's laws still work. In general, few things are moving at speeds fast enough for us to notice relativity. For large, slow-moving satellites, Newton's laws still define orbits. We can still use them to launch Earth-observing satellites and predict their motion. We can use them to reach the Moon, Mars, and other places beyond Earth. For this reason, many scientists see Einstein's laws of general and special relativity not as a replacement of Newton's laws of motion and universal gravitation, but as the full culmination of his idea.

29. Einstein's theory provides a frame of reference for explanations of differences in time, length, and mass from

   (A) two very different speeds
   (B) two very different scales
   (C) observations from two very different frames of reference
   (D) two very different perspectives

Question 30 refers to the following excerpt from NASA's Science website (science.nasa.gov).

As basic research leads to prediction of solid Earth processes, so does the need to adapt this research to real societal problem-solving. Knowledge that improves human abilities to prepare and respond to disasters involving the dynamism of the Earth's interior offers the immediate benefit of saving lives and property. The Earth Surface and Interior focus area (ESI) seeks to coordinate the efforts of NASA's Research and Analysis Program in Solid Earth with the Applied Sciences Disaster Management Program to provide a continuum of development from research to applications that will enable first responders, planners, and policy makers to improve decision-making tools through NASA science and technology.

30. ESI provides first responders with [   ] to improve their decision-making in the event of a disaster.

Question 31 refers to the following excerpt from the U.S. Environmental Protection Agency's website on climate change (www.epa.gov/climate-change).

A food web is made up of predators and prey that interact in a habitat or ecosystem. The impact of climate change on a particular species can ripple through a food web and affect a wide range of other organisms . Declines in the duration and extent of sea ice in the Arctic leads to declines in the abundance of ice algae, which thrive in nutrient-rich pockets in the ice. These algae are eaten by zooplankton, which are in turn eaten by Arctic cod, an important food source for many marine mammals, including seals. Seals are eaten by polar bears.

31. The information in the passage implies that a rise in Arctic temperature may result in

   (A) an increase in the nutrient-rich pockets in the ice.
   (B) a decline in the number of polar bears.
   (C) an extension of the sea ice.
   (D) an increase in the species of zooplankton.

Question 32 refers to the following excerpt from the U.S. Environmental Protection Agency's stratospheric ozone glossary (www.epa.gov/ozone-layer-protection).

Consumer aerosol products in the United States have not used ozone-depleting substances (ODS) since the late 1970s because of voluntary switching followed by federal regulation. The Clean Air Act and EPA regulations further restricted the use of ODS for non-consumer products. All consumer products, and most other aerosol products, now use propellants that do not deplete the ozone layer, such as hydrocarbons and compressed gases.

32. The propellants that are currently used in aerosol products are [   ] and [   ].

Question 33 refers to the following definition from the U.S. Environmental Protection Agency's climate change glossary (www.epa.gov/climate-change).

Biofuels are gas or liquid fuels made from plant material (biomass). They include wood, wood waste, wood liquors, peat, railroad ties, wood sludge, spent sulfite liquors, agricultural waste, straw, tires, fish oils, tall oil, sludge waste, waste alcohol, municipal solid waste, landfill gases, other waste, and ethanol blended into motor gasoline.

33. Biofuels are ecologically sound because

(A) they are inexpensive

(B) they do not pollute the Earth

(C) they are made from indestructible materials

(D) they can be used as fuels

Question 34 refers to the following definition from the U.S. Environmental Protection Agency's climate change glossary (www.epa.gov/climate-change).

The carbon cycle is all parts (reservoirs) and fluxes of carbon. The cycle is usually thought of as four main reservoirs of carbon interconnected by pathways of exchange. The reservoirs are the atmosphere, terrestrial biosphere (usually includes freshwater systems), oceans, and sediments (includes fossil fuels). The annual movements of carbon, the carbon exchanges between reservoirs, occur because of various chemical, physical, geological, and biological processes. The ocean contains the largest pool of carbon near the surface of the Earth, but most of that pool is not involved with rapid exchange with the atmosphere.

34. The largest pool of carbon on Earth is the [   ].

Questions 35 and 36 refer to the following definition from the U.S. Environmental Protection Agency's climate change glossary (www.epa.gov/climate-change).

Carbon footprint is the total amount of greenhouse gases that are emitted into the atmosphere each year by a person, family, building, organization, or company. A person's carbon footprint includes greenhouse gas emissions from fuel that an individual burns directly, such as by heating a home or riding in a car. It also includes greenhouse gases that come from producing the goods or services that the individual uses, including emissions from power plants that make electricity, factories that make products, and landfills where trash gets sent.

35. Which of the following would increase people's individual carbon footprint?

(A) walking more and driving less

(B) lowering their thermostats during the cold weather

(C) not barbequing

(D) taking airplanes more frequently

36. People's personal carbon footprints are also affected by processes out of their control, such as

(A) grocery shopping.

(B) recycling depots.

(C) power plants.

(D) driving less.

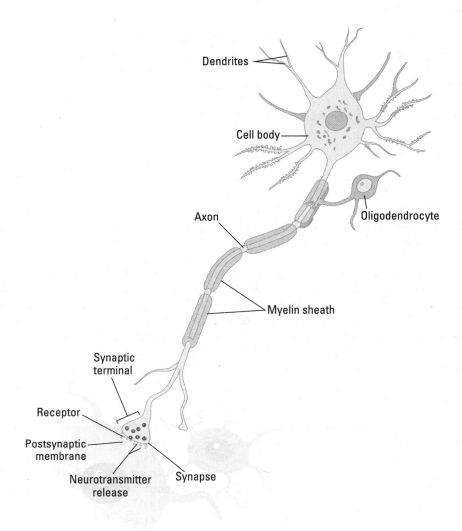

Source: U.S. Department of Health and Human Services

37. The nerve cells in your body carry messages in the form of electrical signals. The signals travel from the cell body along the axon, which is protected by the ⬚.

Question 38 refers to the following excerpt from NASA's website (www.nasa.gov).

Saving lives does not have to be as complex as robotic surgery but can be as simple as providing the life-giving source of clean water. This specifically is of utmost importance to a community in rural Mexico, showing the far-reaching benefits of the water purification component of NASA's Environmental Control and Life Support System (ECLSS). ECLSS provides clean water for drinking, cooking and hygiene aboard the space station. This technology has been adapted on Earth to aid remote locations or places devastated by natural disaster that do not have access to clean drinking water.

In Chiapas, Mexico, many people are at risk of illness from drinking contaminated water from wells, rivers or springs not treated by municipal water systems. Children in Chiapas, previously sickened by parasites and stomach bugs, now have access during school to clean, safe drinking water. This is due to the installation of the ECLSS-derived water purification plant. Renewable solar energy powers the water treatment technology for the community in Chiapas. Results include improved overall health and cost-savings from not having to buy purified water or medication to treat water-borne illnesses.

38. How do innovations by NASA help people in a part of Mexico?

   (A) by setting up space industries

   (B) by providing clean water

   (C) by supplying food

   (D) by ridding the area of parasites

Question 39 refers to the following excerpt from the U.S. Department of Labor's Occupational Safety & Health Administration website (www.osha.gov).

Chemicals have the ability to react when exposed to other chemicals or certain physical conditions. The reactive properties of chemicals vary widely, and they play a vital role in the production of many chemical, material, pharmaceutical, and food products we use daily. When chemical reactions are not properly managed, they can have harmful, or even catastrophic consequences, such as toxic fumes, fires, and explosions. These reactions may result in death and injury to people, damage to physical property, and severe effects on the environment.

39. What is the main idea of this passage?

   (A) Chemicals can poison the food supply.

   (B) Chemicals can have dire consequences if not handled properly.

   (C) Chemicals play a vital role in our lives.

   (D) Chemicals have many advantages, but also pose serious risks.

Question 40 refers to the following chart.

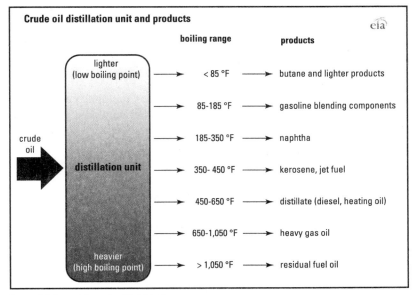

Source: U.S. Energy Information Administration

40. Why is it easier to obtain naphtha from crude oil in a distillation unit than diesel oil?

   (A) It naturally floats to the surface where it can be skimmed off.

   (B) It has a lower boiling point, so it evaporates sooner than diesel oil.

   (C) It has a higher boiling point, so it remains behind as diesel is evaporated.

   (D) Naphtha can be filtered out.

Questions 41 and 42 refer to the following chart.

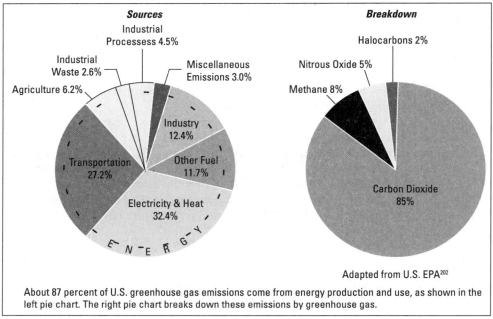

About 87 percent of U.S. greenhouse gas emissions come from energy production and use, as shown in the left pie chart. The right pie chart breaks down these emissions by greenhouse gas.

Source: U.S. Global Change Research Program

41. What is the largest single source of greenhouse gas emissions in the United States?

   (A) electricity and heat

   (B) transportation

   (C) industry

   (D) agriculture

42. According to the Intergovernmental Panel of Climate Change, methane gas has 34 times the effect of carbon dioxide, pound for pound, over a 100-year period. Based on the chart, how does methane compare to carbon dioxide as an issue in climate change?

   (A) It is a bigger problem than carbon dioxide.

   (B) It is approximately equal to carbon dioxide as a problem.

   (C) It is less of a problem than carbon dioxide.

   (D) Cannot be determined from the table.

Questions 43 to 45 refer to the following diagram.

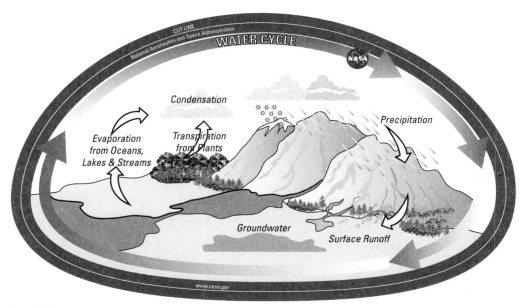

Source: NASA

43. What is the energy source that powers the water cycle?

    (A) wind
    (B) solar energy
    (C) geothermal energy
    (D) hydroelectric power

44. How does surface runoff of water eventually return to the atmosphere?

    (A) It collects in lakes and streams and evaporates.
    (B) It is absorbed into the ground.
    (C) It is used by plants to make food.
    (D) It falls as precipitation.

45. Based on the diagram of the water cycle, the purest water would be found in which of the following?

    (A) the rivers
    (B) the groundwater
    (C) the ocean
    (D) the mountain ice caps

Question 46 refers to the following diagram.

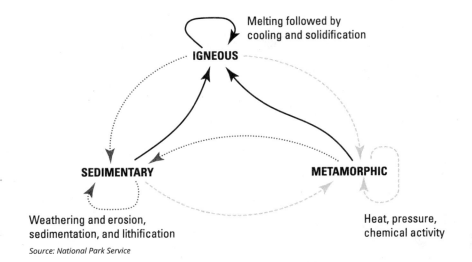

Source: National Park Service

46. According to the diagram, how is igneous rock created?

(A) weathering and erosion

(B) chemical activity

(C) lithification

(D) melting, cooling, and solidification

Questions 47 and 48 refer to the following diagram.

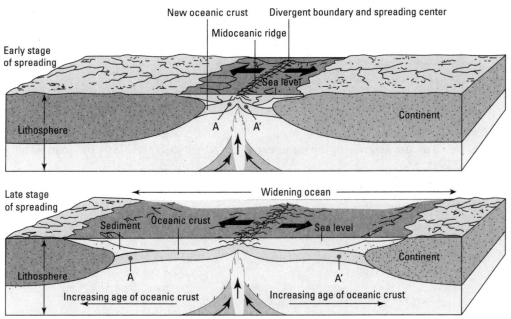

Source: U.S. Geological Survey and National Park Service

47. The diagram shows an area where a "hot spot" in the lithosphere allows magma to work its way through the Earth's crust to the surface. Because this is taking place under the ocean, it has resulted in a ridge that runs most of the way from Antarctica to the arctic down the middle of the North and South Atlantic. Write the letters of the steps in order to describe the process.

   (A) Repeated intrusions of magma widen the gaps, fill them in, and then create new gaps.

   (B) The magma creates gaps in the sea floor, which are filled by fresh magma.

   (C) The magma cools, forming ridges, which break open as new magma pushes its way up.

48. How have scientists been able to confirm that this spreading of the sea floor is actually happening and has gone on for millions of years?

   (A) Core samples of the ocean sediments show evidence of increasing age the farther away the samples were taken from the mid-ocean ridge.

   (B) Scientists have been able to use lasers to measure the distance between continental coasts.

   (C) Satellite observation has shown continuing movement of the Earth's crust.

   (D) Seismic monitors detect movement in the sea floor.

Questions 49 and 50 refer to the following diagram and excerpt from the U.S. Environmental Protection Agency website (www.epa.gov).

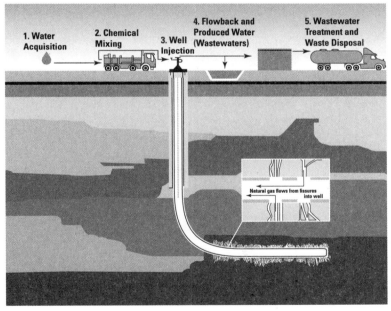

Source: U.S. Environmental Protection Agency

This diagram shows a process for obtaining a natural gas by a method called "fracking" or hydraulic fracturing. In the process, water mixed with chemicals is injected into a well under high pressure. The pressure fractures the earth around the well and allows natural gas to seep into the well. The natural gas, along with waste water, comes to the surface where it is separated, treated, and processed.

49. Which of the following is a way that fracking can contaminate groundwater?

   (A) The process uses a large quantity of both surface and groundwater.

   (B) The natural gas released in the process can accidentally enter aquifers.

   (C) Methane can be released into the atmosphere.

   (D) Fracking can trigger a seismic event.

50. What effect has the hydraulic fracturing process had on the availability of crude oil and natural gas in the United States?

   (A) Fracking has resulted in a large increase in crude oil and natural gas production.

   (B) Fracking has had very little effect to date.

   (C) Fracking has had no effect to date.

   (D) The effect cannot be determined from the information given.

Answers and Explanations

1. **C. thrust.** The thrust of the rocket engines must provide more energy than the weight of the rocket for it to leave the earth. The other forces have an effect, but the thrust lifts it off the ground.

2. **A. On airplanes, lift holds the airplane in the air; on some rockets, lift helps steer the rocket.** This information is stated directly in the passage. Therefore, the other choices are incorrect.

3. **hospitable.** As the passage states, the new territory may be less *hospitable* because of the natural conditions of the territory.

4. **B. Warmwater fish move into the habitats of coldwater fish.** Only Choice (B) is supported by information in the passage. The other choices are either contradicted by the passage or cannot be concluded from it.

5. **A. Images of unusually thin women are pervasive in media.** Choice (A) provides another reason that would make women dissatisfied with their images and so is correct.

    TIP

    Questions of this type, which ask you to identify an additional detail to support a main idea, appear frequently on the GED Science and Social Studies tests. To answer this type of item, identify the main idea in the passage. Then find the answer choice that most effectively supports that main idea.

6. **B. 15 percent.** The passage clearly states, "15 percent of American kids are overweight or obese."

    TIP

    This question is a good example of how reading the question first can help you find the answer. In this case, you can look for the specific number, 15, as you read the passage.

7. **B. Most automobiles run on fossil fuel.** Most automobiles run on gasoline, which is a fossil fuel, the incomplete combustion of which forms black carbon. The other choices may be important from a traffic congestion or economic point of view but aren't mentioned in the passage and do not answer the question.

8. **gases.** The passage states that water vapor, carbon dioxide, ozone, and several other gases are responsible for the reradiation of heat from the Earth's surface.

9. **B. they will allow scientists to develop research projects that will address the consequences of dramatic climate change.** More accurate forecasts will allow scientists to work on experiments to address the changes that may be coming. Choices (A) and (C) may be possibilities but aren't mentioned in the passage. Choice (D) is probably a good general idea but has nothing to do with the passage.

10. **global environmental change.** The passage states this as one of the results of this research.

11. **C. the ground is capable of sudden, dramatic movement.** Some of the examples given to support this choice are volcanic eruptions, earthquakes, and landslides. The other choices aren't supported by any content in the passage, although Choice (D) is probably a good idea.

12. **C. ensure better responses to natural hazards.** The other choices aren't mentioned in the passage.

13. **A. lift > weight; D. thrust > drag.** For a plane to take off, it must accelerate and rise. In order to do that, lift must be greater than weight and thrust must be greater than drag.

14. **C. to keep the astronauts alive.** Without a constant supply of air and water, the astronauts couldn't survive in space, and because carrying a sufficient supply of air and water would be impossible given weight restrictions, they must be recycled.

15. **State 1.** State 1 should be circled because it has the higher temperature. According to the diagram, the heat transfer, Q, would be from State 1 to State 2, indicated by the arrow labeled Q.

16. **D, B, C, A.** This information is given directly in the chart.

TIP

This question is a good example of a drag-and-drop item. On the actual test, you would use your computer's cursor to drag the choices into the correct order.

Did you notice that this doughnut-shaped graph is actually a pie chart? Don't let its slightly different appearance throw you off!

REMEMBER

17. **B. a net consumer of cobalt.** The information shows that cobalt is used in many products and processes in the United States, although the United States is not among the top producers in the world. Therefore, it's likely that the United States is a net consumer of this metal (Choice B).

18. **an element.** The scientific symbol Co shows that cobalt is an element.

On the actual GED, this question would be a drop-down question.

REMEMBER 19. **weather.** *Weather* is current and is a short-term condition. *Climate* is the average weather over a period of time. So *weather* refers to the condition on any given day.

20. **B. The greenhouse gases can remain in the atmosphere for many years.** The passage states that the lifetime of greenhouse gases ranges from a few years to a few thousand years, and these gases are a danger to people's health. Choice (A) is a *truism* (a commonly heard true statement), and Choice (C) may be true but not in the context of the passage. Choice (D) may be a symptom of the increase in pollution but isn't the best choice.

21. **C. Kepler.** The passage is very clear about Kepler's influence on Newton. Hawking and Einstein both lived after Newton's publication, and Aristotle differed from Newton's conclusion.

22. **A. Bhopal, India.** According to the passage, this incident resulted in more than 2,000 fatalities, which is larger than the number of fatalities at the other locations.

TIP

This question is another good example of when reading the question first can help you find the answer quickly. In this case, you can look for the location with the largest number, 2,000, as you read the passage. When you return to the question after reading, you can immediately select Bhopal and move on to the next item.

23. **A. provides information.** The CRW provides information about hazardous materials so that companies can use them safely. The other choices are incorrect according to the passage.

24. **extinction.** The passage states that climate change will cause species to become extinct at an accelerated rate.

25. **B. expulsion of microorganisms from within coral reefs.** Stressed coral reefs expel microorganisms essential to their health. Choice (A) sounds correct if you skim the passage, but it's incorrect. Choice (C) is also wrong because there's no mention of the effect of sunlight on the reefs, and Choice (D) does not make sense.

26. **mismatches.** These mismatches can lead to dramatic changes in the lives of a species, which could lead to eventual extinction.

27. **information.** According to the passage, all the technologies mentioned provide information that may help scientists in assessing the potential for impending hazards.

28. **15.** The Big Bang theory says that this series of occurrences took place about 15 billion years ago.

29. **C. observations from two very different frames of reference.** As the passage states, Einstein's theory is relevant under these circumstances. The other choices are either incomplete or incorrect.

30. **information** (or **knowledge**). ESI provides information to the people and departments in charge of making decisions in the case of a disaster.

31. **B. a decline in the number of polar bears.** The passage explains the ripple effect of a food web: It can be reasonably inferred that a rise in Arctic temperature will cause a decline in the extent of sea ice, which will lead to fewer ice algae. Fewer ice algae will lead to fewer zooplankton, which will lead to fewer cod, which will lead to fewer seals. Without a sufficient diet of seals, polar bear populations will decline.

32. **hydrocarbons; compressed gases.** These two propellants are used because they don't deplete the ozone.

33. **B. they do not pollute the Earth.** Materials made from biomass tend to be made from recycled materials, making them less polluting.

34. **ocean.** Although you may not usually think of water as containing carbon, the ocean is the largest pool of carbon on Earth because the ocean isn't pure water. Oceans contain large amounts of carbon in the form of dissolved carbon dioxide gas.

35. **D. taking airplanes more frequently.** Only this action would increase people's carbon footprint. Walking more and driving your car less, lowering your thermostat during the cold weather, and not barbequing all would reduce people's carbon footprint.

36. **C. power plants.** Power plants may increase or decrease pollution depending on the process used, which tends to affect your carbon footprint positively or negatively.

37. **myelin sheath.** You can see in the diagram that the axon is surrounded by the myelin sheath, a protective coating.

38. **B. by providing clean water.** NASA used a form of its water purification process to provide clean water.

39. **D. Chemicals have many advantages, but also pose serious risks.** The passage gives the advantages and dangers of chemicals, so this choice sums up the passage best. The other choices are either advantages or disadvantages.

40. **B. It has a lower boiling point, so it evaporates sooner than diesel oil.** Naphtha is a component of crude oil. It has a lower boiling point than diesel fuel and thus evaporates at a lower temperature than diesel fuel. This allows it to be separated from the crude oil before diesel fuel.

41. **A. electricity and heat.** The production of energy and heating in the United States produces more greenhouse gases than any other single activity.

42. **D. Cannot be determined from the table.** The key term here is *by weight.* The pie chart doesn't indicate whether the emissions are by weight or by volume. Therefore, it's impossible to calculate a comparative value.

43. **B. solar energy.** The basic source that drives the water cycle on Earth is solar energy. Heat from the Sun causes water to evaporate. Heat from the Sun causes movement of air mass on Earth, thus creating winds and evaporation. Winds carry the evaporated moisture from place to place on Earth. Eventually, the evaporated moisture condenses, forming rain or other forms of precipitation.

44. **A. It collects in lakes and streams and evaporates.** Of the choices, only this one results in water returning to the atmosphere.

45. **D. the mountain ice caps.** The purest water would be found in the ice caps of the mountains because it would be the least contaminated. Water in surface runoff picks up minerals from the soil as it runs down the mountains and flows into groundwater, rivers, and oceans.

46. **D. melting, cooling, and solidification.** The diagram states right beside the word *igneous* that the process consists of melting, cooling, and solidification. The other choices refer to processes involved in creating or changing sedimentary or metamorphic rocks.

TIP

Don't be distracted by Choice (C). You don't need to know the word *lithification* to answer the question but might be attracted to this answer choice and choose it anyway because it's a fancy, "five dollar" word. You can exclude this option because according to the diagram, lithification goes with sedimentary rock, and the question is about igneous rock.

47. **B, C, A.** Sea floor spreading is caused when magma forces its way into faults or thinner or softer areas of the Earth's crust. The thinnest areas are typically located under an ocean. As the magma forces its way to the sea floor, filling cracks in the crust, it forces the crust apart slightly and creates ridges. It cools, solidifies, and then is subjected to pressure from underneath yet again. More cracks are filled with magma, and in the process, ridges are created, the sea floor is forced further and further apart, and the gap is filled with magma. This question is another good example of a drag-and-drop item.

48. **A. Core samples of the ocean sediments show evidence of increasing age the farther away the samples were taken from the mid-ocean ridge.** The question asks for evidence that this process has been going on for millions of years. The only choice that has any evidence over such a time period is Choice (A). The remaining choices offer evidence that the continents are continuing to move in the present time, and you can extrapolate from that information that this process has been going on for a long time. However, there's no proof, because you can't measure historical data in the present. Therefore, core samples of sediments on the ocean floor are the only useful evidence among the choices presented.

49. **B. The natural gas released in the process can accidentally enter aquifers.** According to the EPA, Choices (A), (C), and (D) are all concerns about fracking, but only Choice (B) is related to groundwater contamination.

50. **D. The effect cannot be determined from the information given.** The diagram shows how the process works but offers no information on the volume of natural gas or oil products produced by this process.

5

Counting All the Possible Solutions: The Mathematical Reasoning Test

Dive into the nuances of the Mathematical Reasoning test, how it's formatted, and what types of skills you need before you show up on test day.

Build your confidence with some key strategies and practice questions and get familiar with the formula sheet and the calculator specific to the GED Mathematical Reasoning test.

Chapter **16**

Safety in Numbers: Facing the Mathematical Reasoning Test

Welcome to the dreaded Mathematical Reasoning test (or Math test for short). Although you may have done everything to avoid math in high school, you can't escape this test if you want to pass the GED. To tell you the truth, test-takers really do have nightmares about this test, but don't worry! This chapter helps you prepare, not for nightmares but for taking the test successfully!

Most of the questions on the other GED test sections are about reading comprehension: You're given a passage and are expected to understand it well enough to answer the questions that follow. Although you can prepare for the other tests by doing a lot of reading and taking sample tests, you don't have to come in with a lot of knowledge or great skills in the test areas themselves.

The Mathematical Reasoning test is different. It tests your understanding of mathematical concepts and your ability to apply them to situations you may find in the real world. That means that you have to spend time answering as many math questions as you can and improving your math skills as much as possible before you take this test. This chapter gets you started by introducing the test format and the skills it covers and then providing some tips and tricks for tackling the test.

Looking at the Skills the Math Test Covers

To do well on the Math test, you need to have a general understanding of numbers, their relationships to one another, measurements, geometry, data analysis and statistics, probability, patterns, functions, and algebra. (If you don't know what I mean by these terms, check out the next section, "Understanding the Test Format.") In essence, to be successful on this test, you need to have the mathematical knowledge base that most high school graduates have, and you need to know how to apply it to solve real-life problems.

REMEMBER

The GED Math test provides a formula sheet for you to use during the test. Keep in mind that you may not need all the formulas provided, and you will not need a formula for every question. Part of the fun of math is knowing which formula to use for which problems and figuring out when you don't need one at all. You may want to memorize some of the more common formulas to save time. But when you need a formula, you can look it up. You don't have to memorize them all! That makes preparing easier. You can find the formula sheet in Chapter 25.

The Math test assesses the following four areas:

>> **Basic math:** This area of math covers, you guessed it, the basics! Here's a breakdown of the two topics in this category:

● *Number operations* are the familiar actions you take in math problems and equations, such as addition, subtraction, multiplication, and division. You probably mastered these operations in grade school; now all you have to do is practice them.

● *Number sense* is the ability to understand numbers. You're expected to be able to recognize different kinds of numbers (such as fractions, decimals, percentages, and square roots), know their relative values, and know how to use them (which takes us back to number operations).

>> **Geometry:** Here, you get a chance to play with mathematical shapes and manipulate them in your head — and on the GED's new on-screen whiteboard. You get to use the Pythagorean Theorem to do all sorts of interesting calculations, and you get to use measurements to do things like find the volume of ice cream in a cone or the amount of wall you need to cover with paint. If you relax, you can have fun with these questions and then maybe even use a lot of the knowledge in real life. This category breaks down into two topics:

● *Measurement* involves area, volume, time, and the distance from here to there. Measurement of time is a good thing to know when taking any test because you want to make sure that you run out of questions before you run out of time!

● *Geometry* deals with relationships and properties of points, lines, angles, and shapes (such as squares, circles, and triangles). This branch of math requires you to draw, use, and understand diagrams.

>> **Basic algebra:** Algebra is used to solve problems by using letters to represent unknown numbers, creating equations from the information given, and solving for the unknown numbers — thus, turning them into known numbers. If you ever said something like, "How much more does the $10 scarf cost than the $7.50 one?" you were really solving this equation: $\$7.50 + x = \$10.00$.

>> **Graphs and functions:** Graphs and functions allow you to analyze data. You can learn how to analyze data in graphs, tables, and the coordinate plane.

● *Data analysis* is when you see a graph of the stock market's performance (or lack of performance), calculate or read about baseball statistics, or figure out how many miles per gallon your car gets.

>> *Function*s are part of mathematics. They involve the concept that one number can be determined by its relationship with another. A dozen always consists of 12 units, for example. If you were buying two dozen eggs, you'd be buying $12 \times 2 = 24$ eggs.

● *The coordinate plane* graphically shows the location of points on the plane or a line and helps you to determine such things as the slope, or steepness, of a line.

Make sure you understand how to answer questions involving these four areas of math. (Check out Chapter 17, where I walk you through strategies on solving each type of math question you'll see on the GED test.)

If you already have a firm grasp of these topics, go ahead and take the practice tests in Chapters 25 and 33 and the included online-only practice test. However, if you need more preparation, read the following section and Chapter 17, and then try your hand on the test questions in Chapter 18. You can check your answers and read the explanations when you're done. Then you can take the full practice tests in Chapters 25 and 33 and the included online full practice test. Any time you feel you need more practice or review, try the free practice on the GED & Me app and the GED website. The website offers free practice questions, a free quarter-length practice test, and a number of other learning products. When you feel you are ready to test, take the GED Ready test. If you score green, you are good to go! If not, it will give you tips on areas for review.

Understanding the Test Format

Math isn't scary, and it has yet to appear as the villain in any major Hollywood horror films (at least that I know about). In fact, math can even be fun when you put your mind to it. In any case, the Mathematical Reasoning test assesses your abilities in math, so you have to be ready for it. This is the one GED test subject that requires a special way of thinking and understanding — improving your ability to think mathematically will make passing this test easier.

The Mathematical Reasoning test is 115 minutes long and consists of multiple-choice, drop-down, drag-and-drop, and fill-in-the-blank questions, but it doesn't have any type of essay question. You really have to be thankful for small mercies!

REMEMBER

To get ready for the Math test, you first have to relax and realize that math is your friend — perhaps not a lifetime friend but a friend at least until you finish the test. You also need to consider that you've been using math all your life (and probably didn't even know it). When you tell a friend that you'll be over in 20 minutes, for example, you use math. When you see a sale sign in the store and mentally figure out whether you can afford the sale-priced item, you use math. When you complain about the poor mileage your car gets (and can prove it), you use math. You already know more math than you thought, and I show you the rest in this chapter.

Revealing Some Helpful Prep Pointers

As you prepare for the Mathematical Reasoning test, do the following:

>> **Master arithmetic fundamentals.** About half of the Math test depends on basic arithmetic (addition, subtraction, multiplication, division, decimals, and fractions). The better you know the fundamentals, the better you can do on the test.

>> **Answer practice questions.** To get a handle on how to solve basic mathematical problems, answer a lot of practice questions before the test. Start with the practice questions in Chapter 18. Use the Answers and Explanations to check your work and make sure you understand the answers. Try the practice questions on the GED's new mobile app, GED & Me, too. If you want more practice, borrow or buy a math book or two or find some online and use the questions in them to develop skills. (Be sure to get books that also provide the answers so you can check your work.) Check every answer immediately after you work the question.

If you answered it incorrectly, figure out why. If you still have trouble with that question, ask someone to explain the solution to you. You can also look online for short instructional videos on solving various math questions. YouTube is a particularly good source.

>> **Understand the rules and formulas of math.** Math books are full of rules, theorems, formulas, and so on. Read over as many of these rules as you can, focusing on the formulas in the formula sheet. Try to explain the main ones to a friend. If you can explain a particular rule (the Pythagorean Theorem, for example) to a friend and they understand it, you've mastered the rule. If you can't explain it, ask someone to help you better understand the rule.

>> **Sign up for a math prep class or a math study group.** The loneliest experience is sitting in a room staring at a wrong answer without anyone to ask why it's wrong. If you're having trouble with math, swallow your pride and enroll in a math class or study group where you can get some help and have access to someone who can answer your questions.

>> **Take practice tests and check your answers.** See Chapters 25 and 33 in this book for two full-length practice tests, as well as the included online full practice test. As you take the practice tests, answer every question and adhere to the time limits. If you run out of time, mark where you stopped and then continue answering the remaining items. Be sure to check your answers. Going through the answer explanations can help you figure out which areas you need more work on. Even for questions you answered correctly, reading the explanation can be helpful.

The only part of the test you can't duplicate is the feeling of sitting in the examination room just before you start the test. But the more practice tests you take, the more comfortable you'll be when the test day finally arrives.

>> **Get familiar with the on-screen calculator ahead of time.** You're probably familiar with calculators that add, subtract, multiply, and divide. The calculator used on the GED test is a scientific calculator, the TI-30XS MultiView calculator, which means it does all those operations and a whole lot more, such as calculating fractions, percentages, exponents, and problems involving parentheses. In the test, you access the on-screen calculator by clicking the calculator icon at the top of the screen. Usually, you will see a short film on how to use the calculator before taking the Math test. But for the best results, watch the film online as you prepare, at www.youtube.com/watch?v=VoLZLsRXuKE. It's well worth the time. You can also get hands-on practice with the on-screen calculator using the tutorial on the GED website at https://ged.com/practice-test/en/calculator/. Note that you won't be able to use the calculator on the first five questions of the test, and you won't necessarily use all the keys on the calculator to take the test.

TIP

If you take the GED in person at a testing center, you can use the on-screen calculator or buy and bring your own TI-30XS MultiView calculator with you. If using your own calculator is faster or easier for you, you might consider taking the Math test at a testing center.

Learn to use the GED test's on-screen whiteboard. Sometimes, when solving a math problem, it helps to write down the numbers or draw a diagram. You can use the on-screen whiteboard or the erasable tablet (at a test center only). Get familiar with the whiteboard on the GED Testing Service's website, ged.com. As with the calculator, if the online whiteboard is difficult for you to use, you might consider taking the test in person at a testing center so you can use the erasable tablet.

>> **Become familiar with the formula sheet.** Make sure you know how to find and use the formulas to answer questions.

>> **Learn to use the GED test's Æ Symbol tool.** You use this tool to insert special symbols such as > (greater than) into answers to fill-in-the-blank questions or the online whiteboard. You can see an explanation of the tool on the Mathematics Formula Sheet at the beginning of Chapter 25. You can access the Symbol tool by clicking the Æ icon on the test screen.

>> **Make sure that you understand what you read.** What all the GED test sections have in common is that they all assess, in one way or another, reading comprehension; if you can't read and understand the items, you can't answer them. As I mention time and time again in this book, just reading isn't always enough — you have to stop and ask yourself questions about what you read. A good way to practice this skill is to find an old math textbook. Read through each question and ask yourself: What does this question want me to find? How can I calculate it? What is the answer in general terms?

TIP

If you need more practice reading and understanding math questions, check out one of the following books (all published by Wiley):

>> *Basic Math and Pre-Algebra For Dummies* by Mark Zegarelli

>> *Basic Math and Pre-Algebra Workbook For Dummies* by Mark Zegarelli

>> *Math Word Problems For Dummies* by Mary Jane Sterling

» **Getting familiar with the calculator and formula sheet**

» **Doing a little math to help manage your time on the test**

Chapter **17**

Mathematical Reasoning Question Types and Solving Strategies

he Mathematical Reasoning (Math) test is 115 minutes long. The first five questions are designed to be done without a calculator and must be attempted before you can continue. For the rest of the items, you may or may not need a calculator to complete them. If you see the calculator icon on the screen, you can use the on-screen calculator (or your own if you've brought one to the test center) to solve the problem. You will use a special calculator — more on that later! Getting a basic understanding of the question formats helps you avoid any surprises when you sit down to take the test. The Math test presents you with questions from every area of math. It ranges from arithmetic calculations to basic algebra and more. In this chapter, I explain the question formats that you encounter on this test and offer advice on how to solve them with ease.

Perfecting Your Approach with Sample Questions

This may be your first experience taking a math test on a computer, but don't worry! The test is still about math — the same old math that has been around for several thousand years. The basic operations are still addition, subtraction, multiplication, and division. Practice doesn't make perfect but will increase your chances of getting the correct answer to the question.

TIP

Because you're not penalized for guessing, if you don't know the answer to a question, go ahead and guess. Although you can't get a point for a blank answer, you can get a point for eliminating all but the most possible answer and marking it (if you get it right, of course).

Making the most of multiple-choice questions

Most of the questions on the Math test are a form of multiple-choice. You're given four possible answers, and all you have to do is choose the one best answer.

Answering basic multiple-choice questions

The multiple-choice questions on the Math test are pretty straightforward. You're given some information or a figure and asked to answer based on that information. Here are a couple of examples.

EXAMPLE

Milton wanted to be taller than his father, who was 2 yards tall. Milton was 5 feet 10 inches tall even when he stretched. How much taller would Milton have to grow to be taller than his father by at least an inch?

(A) 1 inch

(B) 2 inches

(C) 3 inches

(D) 4 inches

The first thing you have to do with questions like this one is make sure all measurements are in the same format. Two yards equals 6 feet (1 yard = 3 feet). So Milton is 2 inches shorter than his father. The question asks how much he would have to grow to be at least 1 inch taller than his father. If he were to grow 3 inches, he would have reached that goal. Choice (C) is correct.

EXAMPLE

Samantha was a super salesperson and by far the best salesperson at Industrial Chemicals Inc. She was so good that she knew that she had to work for only three months not only to beat the sales records of her fellow salespeople but also to boost the total sales for the company substantially. The following chart appeared in the company's annual report. In which quarter do you think Samantha made all her sales?

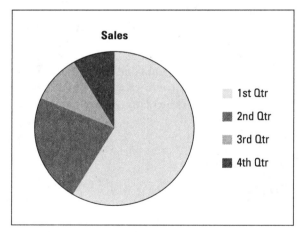

© John Wiley & Sons, Inc.

(A) 1st

(B) 2nd

(C) 3rd

(D) 4th

The graph shows that the majority of sales were made in the first quarter, and if Samantha's boasts were true, she would have made the majority of those sales. In the other nine months of the year, without her sales, overall sales slipped considerably. In a graph such as this one, the area of the segment of the circle represents the data. Thus, the answer is Choice (A).

Extracting the information you need

Some of the questions on the Math test may have extra information that you don't need; in those cases, just ignore it. Of course, you have to make sure that the information you think is extra really is. For example, if the last question in the previous section said that Irving was the poorest salesperson the company had ever employed, that information really would be extra and would make no difference to the rest of the question.

The people who write the test questions include extra information for a reason: Extra information can make guessing more difficult and separate the test-takers who are paying attention from those who aren't. Sometimes, extra information is put in to make the question a bit more realistic: In real life, you figure out the relevant information to solve problems all the time. You don't want to disregard anything essential to solving the problem.

While reading the following question, try to visualize the situation and consider where the plot takes an extreme turn. This is usually the place where the information turns from important to irrelevant or vice versa.

Kenny, Dharma, and Sophie went out for an early lunch. The wall of their favorite burger place had the following menu:

EXAMPLE

Item	Calories (kcal)	Fat (g)	Cost ($)
Hamburger	780	44	4.09
Cheeseburger	793	56	4.09
Vegetable Wrap	450	25	3.69
French Fries	360	17	1.59
Blueberry Muffin	450	15	2.10
Chocolate Chip Cookies	160	7	1.00
Soda	220	0	1.49

Their total bill came to $24.31, and after a long discussion, they decided to tip the server 15%. What was the server's tip?

(A) $2.92

(B) $3.00

(C) $3.65

(D) $4.86

The menu may be interesting, but it's irrelevant for answering this question. The relevant information is the part about the server's tip. The only important information is the amount of the bill and the percentage of the tip. So you multiply the total bill by 15% to get a tip of $24.31 \times 0.15 = \$3.65$, rounded to the nearest penny. Thus, Choice (C) is the answer.

Reading the question first can help you figure out the relevant information you need from the graphic. That way, you can focus on only the information you need.

TIP

In other items, you may have to find and extract the details you need from the information and the item and combine them. Take a look at this example.

EXAMPLE

A hamburger meal combo at the restaurant includes French fries and a soda for $6.49. If you order before 12 p.m., you get a free cookie. How much can Dharma save from the menu prices by ordering the special, not counting tax or tip, at 11:45 a.m.?

(A) $0.68

(B) $1.00

(C) $1.68

(D) $2.68

In this question, you have to use information from the question to figure out what's included in the combo when ordered before noon (hamburger, French fries, soda, and a free cookie). Next, you use the menu to determine the total cost of items and then subtract the cost of the special: $4.09 + 1.59 + 1.49 + 1.00 - 6.49 = \$1.68$. Thus, Choice (C) is the answer.

Providing the answer in fill-in-the-blank items

Fill-in-the-blank items require that you fill in the answer without the benefit of four answer choices to choose from. On the Math test, these questions will always involve some calculation, and the answer is always a number. I walk you through answering two fill-in-the-blank questions in this section.

EXAMPLE

Demitri wanted to buy a new LCD television. His old one had a diagonal measurement of 32 inches, but he wanted to buy a 50-inch diagonal television. The new one would be [   ] inches larger, measured diagonally. You may use numbers, a decimal point (.), and/or a negative sign (−) in your answer.

To answer this question, you have to find the difference between the two televisions. The new one would be $50 - 32 = 18$ inches larger, measured diagonally.

EXAMPLE

Carol found a part-time job to increase her income. She was paid $13.45 an hour and was promised a 15% raise after three months. Business had been very poor during that period, and the owner of the business called Carol in to explain that he could afford only an 11% raise but would reassess the raise in the next quarter, depending on how business was. With this raise, Carol's new hourly rate would be [   ]. You may use numbers, a decimal point (.), and/or a negative sign (−) in your answer.

To calculate the amount of an 11% raise, multiply by 111% ($100\% + 11\% = 111\%$, or 1.11 expressed as a decimal). Carol's new salary would be calculated at the rate of $13.45 times 111%, or $13.45 \times 1.11 = \$14.93$ (rounded to the nearest penny).

Answering other special item types

Some special items will ask you to select an answer from a drop-down menu or drag numbers or words into the correct position using your cursor and mouse. You can see how these questions work on the GED test in Chapter 2. You can try your hand on these items in the practice questions in Chapter 18, the two full-length practice tests in Chapters 25 and 33, and the included full-length online practice test. The GED website also offers free practice items and tutorials that can help you understand these special item types.

Occasionally, items on the GED will ask you to use the cursor to indicate a point on a table or graph. This item format, called hot-spot, is seldom tested and happens mostly with items that use the coordinate plane. I mention it here "just in case." Look at the sample item:

Mark the point (1,1) on the coordinate plane.

EXAMPLE

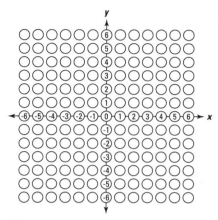

© John Wiley & Sons, Inc.

In this case, use the mouse to place the cursor over the correct point, and click.

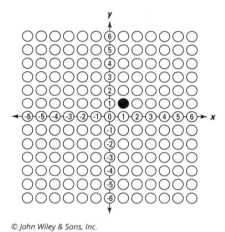

© John Wiley & Sons, Inc.

Using the Mathematical Reasoning Test's Special Features

During the Mathematical Reasoning test, you can use the on-screen (or your own) TI-30XS MultiView calculator for all but the first five questions. Before you start celebrating, remember that the calculator is an instrument that makes calculations easier. It doesn't solve problems or perform other miracles. You still have to solve the problems using the computer between your ears.

The test also has a formula sheet. This feature also isn't a miracle that can work out problems for you. It's just a memory aid if you don't remember the formulas. And as a special treat, the Math test also provides symbols for you to use in the fill-in-the-blank items as needed. I explore all these features in the following sections. You can find a tutorial on these special features on the GED website, at https://app.ged.com/portal/tips. Log in and select "Get to Know the Test."

REMEMBER

One of the most valuable tools for preparing for the GED is an account at ged.com. Besides being the place where you sign up to take the test, this website offers tools and study aids. You have to be logged into your account to access many of the special features I reference in this chapter.

Solving questions with and without a calculator

For all but the first five items in the Math test, you can use a calculator. You have to finish the first five items before you go on to questions that use the calculator. To pull up the calculator on the computerized GED Math test, click the calculator icon. A calculator — a Texas Instruments TI-30XS MultiView calculator to be exact — appears on-screen.

It's a good idea to get familiar with the calculator before taking the GED test. You can either use the one on the GED Testing Service website for practice or find an identical hand-held one. (The computer version of the calculator operates just like the hand-held device.) Then make sure you know how to solve the various types of mathematical problems, and depend on the calculator only to do mechanical operations more quickly and easily.

TIP

Keep the calculator in mind when you decide where to take the Math test. If you test at home, you can only use the on-screen calculator. At a testing center, you can bring your own TI-30XS MultiView calculator. If using a hand-held calculator is easier for you, consider taking the Math test at a testing center, even if it is less convenient for you in other ways. A few points on the Math test can make a big difference! And don't worry about the other tests — you can take any of the tests online or at a test center — it's your choice!

Often, using mental math is faster than using a calculator, especially with multiple-choice questions where you have four answer choices to choose from. And the more questions you answer in your head, the easier it will be. Here are some ways to practice using mental math (without a calculator):

>> When you go shopping, add up the prices as you put items in your cart. Check your total at the cash register.

>> Calculate discounts off items you see or buy when you shop.

>> Be the first at your table in a restaurant to figure out the tip. And for bonus practice, figure out different tip percentages on your bill, such as 15, 18, and 20 percent tips.

TIP

For multiple-choice questions, sometimes estimating the answer to a question is easier and faster. For example, 4.2×8.9 is approximately 4×9, which equals 36. If only one answer choice is close to 36, that choice is probably correct. If you see that two or more answer choices are close to 36, however, you need to spend time calculating the exact answer.

Refreshing your memory with the formula sheet

The GED Math test includes a formula sheet with a list of formulas that you may need for the test. You simply click on the formula icon to make the page of formulas appear. Unfortunately, no genie will appear to tell you which formula to use. Figuring out which formula you need is your job.

To get familiar with the formulas you may need on the GED test, study the formulas in this book (you can find a list of formulas in the practice tests in Chapters 25 and 33) and make sure you know their purpose. For example, if you have a formula for the volume of a rectangular cube and the question asks you how many cubic feet of water a swimming pool contains, you know this formula will enable you to work out the answer. If the question asks you how many tiles it takes to go around the rim of the pool, you need another formula.

Inserting special symbols

When answering fill-in-the-blank items, you sometimes need to insert special symbols, such as add or subtract, greater than or less than, equals, pi (π), and so on. You can see all the symbols at the beginning of Practice Test 1. To make a symbol appear in the fill-in-the-blank box on the test, click the symbols icon at the top of the screen (Æ), and then click the symbol you want to include in the box. You can also use the symbols in the online whiteboard. You can find a tutorial on these special features on the GED website, at `https://app.ged.com/portal/tips`. After you log in, select "Get to Know the Test."

Managing Your Time for the Math Test

Try not to be intimidated by the word *math* or the subject as a whole. A math teacher once said that mathematicians are lazy people — they always use the easiest way to find the right answer. I don't want to insult or irritate any mathematicians by calling them lazy, but finding the easiest way to solve a problem is usually the right way. If your way is too long and complicated, it's probably not right.

The Mathematical Reasoning test allows you 115 minutes to complete 50 questions. That's less than 1½ minutes per question, so you have to keep moving. You must answer the first five items without using the calculator, and then the rest follow after you have answered these five questions.

To help you manage your time for the Math test, check out the following suggestions (see Chapter 3 for some general time-management tips):

>> **Stay on schedule.** Being able to manage your time is the most important indicator of success on the Math test. If you can keep to your schedule of less than 1½ minutes per question, you'll have enough time to go over your answers and make any changes necessary after you finish solving all the questions. If a question is hard for you or involves a lot of time-consuming calculations, click the flag feature in the test. That will mark the item for you to return to later if you have time. Spending all your time trying to solve one problem at the expense of the others isn't a good idea.

REMEMBER

With such a tight schedule for taking the Math test, you have no time to panic. Aside from the fact that panicking distracts you from your overall goal, it also takes time and you have very little time to spare. So relax and just do your best — save the panicking for another day.

>> **Know when to move ahead.** If you don't see what's being asked by a question within a few seconds, reread the question and try again. If it still isn't clear, skip the question or use the Flag feature and go on to the next question. Later you can use the Review screen to return to these questions — even if only to guess!

>> **Keep an eye on the time.** The timer on the computer screen is your only time-management tool. You're not allowed to bring any electronics into the testing area except your calculator, and then only if you test at a testing center.

Chapter 18

Practicing Sample Mathematical Reasoning Problems

The best way to get ready for the Mathematical Reasoning (Math) test is to practice. The questions on this test evaluate your skills in a wide variety of areas, so check out the sample questions in this chapter to help you prepare for all of them. At the end of this chapter, you find detailed answer explanations where you can check your answers.

Record your answers either directly in this book or on a sheet of paper, if you think you might want to try these practice questions again at a later date. The Mathematical Reasoning test doesn't include an Extended Response item, so there's no need for extra sheets of lined paper. (Writing an essay about quadratic equations or the beauty of exponents — now *that* would be painful!) Get out a couple pieces of scratch paper, though, to calculate, write down formulas, or draw simple sketches to help you visualize a question. And remember to use your calculator when you think it can help you work more quickly and accurately. For these questions, you can use any calculator, including the one on your phone, though using a real TI-30XS MultiView calculator is the best preparation for the real test.

Remember, this is just preliminary practice. I want you to get used to answering different types of Mathematical Reasoning questions. Use the complete practice tests in Chapters 25 and 33 and online to time your work and replicate the real test-taking experience.

Mathematical Reasoning Practice Questions

The following math practice questions test your knowledge of mathematical operations and reading skills in math. Read the questions carefully, making sure that you understand what's being asked. You may have to convert some units of measurement to another, but in all cases, they'll make sense. For example, if you see that the measurement for a wall is 120-something high, read the problem carefully because the wall was probably measured in inches and not feet.

1. Vlad is shopping for new shirts because all the stores are having end-of-season sales. Sam's Shirts offers Vlad 20% off all his purchases, while Harry's Haberdashery has a special sale offering five shirts for the price of four. Tim & Tim's Clothes offers buy four, get one free. The regular price for shirts is the same at all three stores. Vlad decides to get 5 shirts. Which is the better deal?

    (A) Tim & Tim's Clothes

    (B) Sam's Shirts

    (C) Harry's Haberdashery

    (D) They are all the same.

2. Olga designed a company logo consisting of an equilateral triangle in a circle. She designed the logo with one vertex of the triangle pointing northeast. The client said she liked the design but preferred that the vertex of the triangle point due south. What rotation would Olga have to perform to satisfy her client?

    (A) 90 degrees to the right

    (B) 110 degrees to the right

    (C) 135 degrees to the left

    (D) 135 degrees to the right

3. Solve the following equation for x:

    $x = 2y + 6z - y^2$, if $y = 6$ and $z = 2$

    (A) 12

    (B) 11

    (C) −11

    (D) −12

Question 4 refers to the following table of prices for new vacuum cleaners.

Make and Model	Price
Hopper Model A1	$249.99
Vacuous Vacuum Company Model ZZ3	$679.99
Clean-R-Up Special Series	$179.00
Electrified Home Upright	$749.99
Super Suction 101	$568.99

4. Nate is looking for a new vacuum cleaner for his apartment. He has been told by his best friend that spending around the average price will get him an adequate unit. Which vacuum cleaner is closest to the average price for vacuum cleaners? [_____]

5. Evaluate the following formula:

$N = a + c - 2ac$, if $a = 5$ and $c = 3$

(A) −22

(B) 22

(C) 28

(D) 38

6. Solve the following equation for x.

$3x + 12 = 24$

(A) 3

(B) 4

(C) 5

(D) 12

7. Rachel and Ronda were planning for their first apartment, and they decided to split the required shopping tasks. Rachel was responsible for finding out how much it would cost to carpet their living room, and Ronda was responsible for finding out how much it would cost to paint the bedroom walls. What formula would each of them need to use to get an answer that would let them figure out the price for each job?

(A) $P = 2(l + w)$

(B) $A = l \times w$

(C) $V = l \times w \times d$

(D) $A = \pi r^2$

8. Lillian is drawing a scale diagram of her apartment to take with her while shopping for rugs. If she has taken all the measurements in the apartment, what mathematical relationship would she use to draw the scale drawing?

(A) decimals

(B) exponents

(C) ratios

(D) addition

9. Sylvia couldn't fall asleep one night and got to wondering how much water her bedroom would hold if she filled it to the ceiling. She had previously measured all the walls and knew all the measurements, including length, width, and height. She should use _____ to calculate how many cubic feet of water would be needed to fill the room.

(A) addition

(B) subtraction

(C) multiplication

(D) division

10. Alvin is drawing a diagram of his room. He has drawn the line representing the floor and is ready to draw the line representing the wall. This line would be _____ to the line representing the floor.

   (A) congruent

   (B) parallel

   (C) similar

   (D) perpendicular

11. Aaron wants to paint the floor of his apartment. His living room/dining room is 19 feet by 16 feet, his bedroom is 12 feet by 14 feet, and his hallways are 6 feet by 8 feet. Bowing to pressure from his friends, he has decided not to paint the floor of the kitchen or the bathroom. How many square feet of floor must he paint?

   (A) 520

   (B) 304

   (C) 250

   (D) 216

Question 12 refers to the following table.

Week	Calories Consumed Per Week	Weight (Pounds)	Height (Feet/Inches)
1	12,250	125	5 ft. 1.5 in.
2	15,375	128	5 ft. 1.5 in.
3	13,485	128	5 ft. 1.5 in.
4	16,580	130	5 ft. 1.5 in.
5	15,285	129	5 ft. 1.5 in.

12. Alan kept track of his caloric intake, his weight, and his height for a period of five weeks. His activity level remained about the same the whole time. What conclusion can you draw from his observations?

   (A) Eating a lot makes you taller.

   (B) Eating more calories will make you gain weight.

   (C) Gaining weight will make you taller.

   (D) There's no correlation between the data presented.

13. On Monday, Mary walked 12 blocks. On Tuesday, she walked 10 blocks, and on Wednesday, she walked 14 blocks. If she wants to walk more than her average trip for those three days on Thursday, at least how many blocks must she walk?

   (A) 9

   (B) 10

   (C) 11

   (D) 13

14. Hassan has developed a new trick to play on his classmates. He asks them to write down their ages and multiply by 4, divide by 2, then subtract 6, and, finally, add 8. When they tell him the resulting number, Hassan can always tell them their age. If one of his friends tells Hassan the resultant number is 52, how old is he?

(A) 24

(B) 25

(C) 33

(D) 52

Question 15 refers to the following table.

a	b	F
1	2	–16
2	1	–3
3	2	–18
2	3	–35
3	4	x

15. Herman developed the following function to amuse himself: $F = 2a + 3b^2 - 2ab$. He kept track of his results in this table.

Using Herman's function, what is the value of x?

(A) −82

(B) 30

(C) 53

(D) 88

16. Calvin and Kelvin, carpenters extraordinaire, are building an attic staircase for their client, Ms. Coleman. The stairway is to bridge a space 10 feet high, and the distance from the front of the bottom step to the back of the top step is 14 feet. What is the slope of the attic staircase to 2 decimal places?

(A) 0.69

(B) 0.70

(C) 0.71

(D) 0.72

Questions 17 and 18 refer to the following information.

April is considering two apartments. They are of equal size except for the bedrooms. Bedroom A is 19 feet by 14 feet, and bedroom B is 17 feet by 16 feet.

17. How many square feet larger is the larger bedroom?

(A) 8

(B) 7

(C) 6

(D) 5

18. April wants an area rug for the larger bedroom that would cover the floor, leaving a space 1 foot from each wall. If the rug had a 1-inch fringe all the way around it, how many feet long would the fringe be?

(A) 85

(B) 58

(C) 55

(D) 29

19. The school nurse made this table, which shows the results he got from asking several students about their heights and birth months.

Month of Birth	Height
March	5 ft. 4 in.
June	5 ft. 6 in.
March	5 ft. 1 in.
January	5 ft. 8 in.
August	5 ft. 5 in.
January	5 ft. 6 in.

In which month was the shortest person born?

(A) January

(B) March

(C) June

(D) August

20. Order these numbers from smallest (1) to largest (4).

$\sqrt{4}$ 0.75   1/3 1^3

21. Susie is shopping for a few groceries. She buys a loaf of bread for $1.29 and a half gallon of milk on sale for $1.47. She sees her favorite cheese on sale for $2.07. If she has $5.00 in her purse, she **can / cannot** (circle one) buy the cheese if there is no tax on food.

Question 22 refers to the following table.

Annual Sales of the Wonderful World of Widgets

Year	Annual Sales (In Million Units)
2023	70
2022	65
2021	43
2020	29
2019	72

22. The general manager of the Wonderful World of Widgets wants to present these figures in a visual, easily understood way to the board of directors to help them understand the effect that the downturn in the economy in 2020 had on the sales of widgets. What would be the best way to present the figures?

    (A) a graph

    (B) a series of tables

    (C) verbal descriptions

    (D) a movie of how widgets are used in America

23. Mark the points $(3,1)$, $(-4,-3)$, and $(-5,5)$ on the graph to draw a geometric figure and identify the figure [_____].

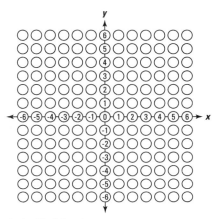

24. Georgio leaned a 25-foot ladder on the side of his house. The bottom of the ladder is 7 feet from the wall. Therefore, the top of the ladder is touching a point [_____] feet above the ground. You may use numbers, a decimal point (.), and/or a negative sign (−) in your answer.

25. Where are all the points with an x-coordinate of −4 located on a graph?

    (A) 4 units above the x-axis

    (B) 4 units below the x-axis

    (C) 4 units to the right of the y-axis

    (D) 4 units to the left of the y-axis

26. In a recent 10-year period, the average age of Americans claiming Social Security went up from 63.6 to 64.7 for men, and from 63.6 to 64.6 for women. How much was the age increase for women claiming Social Security over that period?

    (A) 0 years

    (B) 0.1 year

    (C) 1 year

    (D) 1.1 years

27. The students in a math class are looking at the equation $A = l \times w$. The teacher asks what result doubling the length (l) would have on the area (A). What answer is correct?

   (A) makes it two times larger

   (B) makes it three times larger

   (C) makes it four times larger

   (D) makes it five times larger

28. Herman is going to paint a wall that is 20 feet long and 8 feet high. If all of it is to be covered with one coat of primer, how many square feet of wall have to be covered with primer?

   (A) 28

   (B) 56

   (C) 160

   (D) 610

29. Where on a graph would the point $(-4, -4)$ be?

   (A) four units to the right and four units below the corresponding axis

   (B) four units to the left and four units below the corresponding axis

   (C) four units to the left and four units above the corresponding axis

   (D) four units to the right and four units above the corresponding axis

30. Roger and Ekua went shopping together. Ekua spent twice as much for clothing as Roger did. If their total expenditure for clothing was $90.00, how much did Roger spend for clothing?
   $ [_____]

   Questions 31 and 32 refer to the following table, which shows the median age of marriage for men and women in the United States over several years.

Year	Men	Women
2023	30.2	28.4
2022	30.1	28.2
2021	30.4	28.6
2020	30.5	28.1
2019	29.8	28.0

31. Althea saw this table in her social studies book. According to the table, which of these statements is a logical conclusion?

   (A) Women tend to get married later in life than men.

   (B) Men tend to get married earlier in life than women.

   (C) Women are getting married later in life as time goes by.

   (D) Fewer people are getting married now than in the past.

32. In which year did the median age of marriage for women go down over the previous year?

(A) 2015

(B) 2017

(C) 2021

(D) 2022

33. The reading on the illustrated meter is [   ].

© John Wiley & Sons, Inc.

Question 34 refers to the following table, which shows Sheila's grades in her high school classes.

Subject	Grade (%)
Literature	94
Mathematics	88
Physical Education	86
Science	92
Spanish	90

34. Imagine that Sheila's Spanish grade dropped by 6 percentage points. What would be her average grade after the drop? [   ].

35. Barry earns $1,730 per month after taxes. Each month he spends $900 for rent and $600 for living expenses such as food and utilities. After all his expenses are paid, he has $☐ left over to buy luxuries and spend on entertainment.

Questions 36 and 37 refer to the following table.

Car Manufacturer	Sales — July 2021 (In Thousands)	Sales — July 2020 (In Thousands)	% Change
Commonwealth	90	105	–14
Frisky	175	147	+19
Goodenough	236	304	–22
Horsesgalore	99	64	+55
Silkyride	24	16	+50

36. From the table, which car manufacturer showed the greatest percentage increase in sales?

   (A) Commonwealth
   (B) Frisky
   (C) Goodenough
   (D) Horsesgalore

37. Which car manufacturer had the largest increase in the number of cars sold?

   (A) Frisky
   (B) Goodenough
   (C) Horsesgalore
   (D) Silkyride

Question 38 refers to the following table.

Person	Flavor Preference			
	Chocolate	Vanilla	Strawberry	Rocky Road
Donalda's mother	Yes	Yes	Yes	No
Donalda's father	No	No	Yes	No
Donalda's brother	No	No	No	Yes
Donalda's sister	Yes	Yes	Yes	No

38. Donalda loves all flavors of ice cream, but her other family members are fussier than she is. She wants to buy some ice cream for a family barbecue. She wrote down every family member's preferences in this table. She wants to buy only two flavors. Which two flavors will satisfy everyone in her family?

   (A) Chocolate and vanilla
   (B) Chocolate and strawberry
   (C) Vanilla and rocky road
   (D) Strawberry and rocky road

39. The dimension of a cube is 9 inches on all sides. What is the volume of the cube in square inches?

   (A) 12
   (B) 27
   (C) 81
   (D) 729

40. The fuel gauge on Alesh's car reads 1/4 full. If the fuel tank holds 24 gallons, and gas costs $5.00 per gallon, how much will Alesh pay to fill it? [   ]

Answers and Explanations

1. **D. They are all the same.** In this case, all the offers are for 20% off. They are just expressed differently. "Five shirts for the price of four" and "buy four and get one free" are the same deal expressed differently. Consider buying four shirts for $10 each and getting one more free. Five shirts would cost $40, or an average price of $8 each, which is 20% off the regular price ($10). Keep in mind that the same prices are often stated in different ways.

Questions involving percent come up frequently on the GED, so it pays to understand how percents work. Questions that are about tips, interest, or discounts involve percents.

TIP

2. **D. 135 degrees to the right.** If you visualize the equilateral triangle drawn within the circle with one vertex pointing northeast, you can see that the vertex is 45 degrees above the horizontal, which is due east. Due south would be at the halfway point of the circle or at 180 degrees. Simply subtract 45 degrees (the initial position) from 180 degrees (the final position) to discover that the vertex has traveled 135 degrees to the right. Another way to answer this question is with addition. To go from due east to due south requires a rotation of 90 degrees to the right. The entire rotation would consist of 45 degrees + 90 degrees = 135 degrees to the right.

If reading about this problem is confusing, draw it. Diagrams often make problems easier to visualize.

TIP

3. **D. −12.** You can solve this equation by substituting 6 for y and 2 for z, which produces this equation: $2(6)+6(2)-6^2=-12$.

4. **Super Suction 101.** You can calculate the average price by adding all the prices and dividing the sum by the number of prices. To simplify the calculations, you can round to the nearest dollar. $(\$250+\$680+\$179+\$750+\$569)/5=\$485.60$. The machine that comes closest is the Super Suction 101 because the difference between the price of the Super Suction 101 and the average price is $\$569-\$486=\$83$. The difference between the price of the Hopper Model A1 and the average price is $\$486-\$250=\$236$, leaving the Super Suction 101 the clear selection, using the friend's criteria.

Note that this question is a clear example of the advantage of using rounding to make a question fast and easy to solve. That can help you keep moving from item to item on test day!

TIP

5. **A. −22.** Only this result follows the correct order of operations.

Always remember to follow the correct order of operations, which is Parentheses, Exponents, Multiplication and Division, and Addition and Subtraction. You always work from left to right, and always work multiplication and division together and addition and subtraction together. A good way to remember is with the letters PEMDAS.

TIP

6. **B. 4.** If $3x+12=24$, you can subtract 12 from both sides so that $3x=24-12$, or $3x=12$; then divide both sides by 3 to find x, or $x=4$. Again, remember the cardinal rule of equations: Whatever you do to one side, you must do to the other.

As you prepare for the Mathematical Reasoning section of the GED test, you definitely want to remember this rule about equations: Whatever you do to one side of the equation, you must do to the other side.

REMEMBER

7. **B. $A = l \times w$.** In each case, Rachel and Ronda have to calculate the area of the space they're dealing with to get a price for the carpet and the paint. The formula for area is $A = l \times w$.

Questions about area and perimeter of different geometric shapes come up frequently on the GED. It pays to know and understand the formulas for each geometric shape.

Did you select Choice A? That is the formula for perimeter. Confusing area and perimeter is one of the most common errors on the GED. Knowing your formulas will help you avoid falling into this trap.

8. **C. ratios.** A scale drawing involves representing one dimension with a smaller one, while keeping the shape of the room the same. Lillian may have decided to represent 1 foot in real life by 1 inch on her drawing (a ratio of 1 foot to 1 inch), resulting in a 12-foot wall being represented by a 12-inch line. None of the other three choices are mathematical relationships and would, therefore, have to be excluded immediately.

9. **C. multiplication.** The formula to calculate the volume of a room is to multiply the length by the width by the height. (On the GED test, the formula for calculating volume is listed on the formula sheet.)

10. **D. perpendicular.** The line is perpendicular because walls are perpendicular to floors. (If they weren't perpendicular, the room would probably collapse.)

11. **A. 520.** To find the total area, you must multiply the length by the width for each area. The area of the living room/dining room is $19 \times 16 = 304$ square feet, the area of the bedroom is $12 \times 14 = 168$ square feet, and the area of the hallway is $6 \times 8 = 48$ square feet. The total area is the sum of the room areas or $304 + 168 + 48 = 520$ square feet.

12. **B. Eating more calories will make you gain weight.** The more Alan ate, the heavier he became (which represents a possible causal relationship). The table provides no basis for the other answers.

If two values change in tune with each other, they have a *correlating* relationship. For example, there's a positive correlation between height and age during the teenage years. In other words, you get taller as you get older. If one event leads to another or causes another, the events form a *causal* relationship. For example, eating all the red jellybeans alters the percentage of orange jellybeans in a mixture of equal numbers of different colors because eating a red jellybean removes it from the pool of jellybeans. As a result, the percentage of orange jellybeans (and of every other remaining color) increases.

13. **D. 13.** Mary's average trip for those three days was $(12 + 10 + 14) / 3 = 36 / 3 = 12$ blocks. To beat her average, she has to walk 13 blocks on Thursday. If she walks 12 blocks, she will equal (not beat) her average trip. All the other answers are less than her average.

14. **B. 25.** Hassan knows that multiplication and division are opposite operations, which means that multiplying by 4 and dividing by 2 produces a number twice the original. Addition and subtraction are opposites, too, so subtracting 6 and adding 8 results in a number 2 larger than the original. If the number Hassan's friend tells him is 52, Hassan simply has to subtract 2 from the resultant number (52) and divide by 2, giving him an answer of 25. Or Hassan could start with 52 and then work backward (first subtracting 8, then adding 6, and so on) through the directions to arrive at the correct answer.

15. **B. 30.** Using Herman's function, $x = 2(3) + 3(4)(4) - 2(3)(4) = 6 + 48 - 24 = 30$.

16. **C. 0.71.** To calculate the slope, you have to divide the rise by the run. That is $\frac{10}{14} = 0.7142857$, or 0.71 rounded to 2 decimal places.

The *slope* of a line is rise over run. Thus, the slope of a stairway is equal to the distance above the floor of the last step over the distance from the front of the first step to the back of the top step.

17. **C. 6.** The area of bedroom A is $19 \times 14 = 266$ square feet. The area of bedroom B is $17 \times 16 = 272$ square feet. Bedroom B is larger by $272 - 266 = 6$ square feet.

18. **B. 58.** The measure of the fringe is the perimeter of the rug. Because the rug would cover the floor 1 foot in from each wall, the length of the rug would be $17 - 2 = 15$ feet, and the width would be $16 - 2 = 14$ feet. The reason you have to subtract 2 from each measurement is that the rug would be 1 foot from each wall, resulting in a rug that was 2 feet shorter than the room in each dimension. Perimeter $= 2(l + w)$, where l is the length and w is the width, so the perimeter of the rug is $2(15 + 14) = 2(29) = 58$ feet.

19. **B. March.** The shortest person in the survey is 5 ft. 1 in. tall. That person was born in March.

20. **The correct order is (1) 1/3, (2) 0.75, (3) 1³, and (4) $\sqrt{4}$.** The largest number is $\sqrt{4}$, which is equal to 2. The exponent 1^3 is equal to 1 ($1 \times 1 \times 1 = 1$). And the fraction 1/3 (0.33) is smaller than 0.75.

TIP

Questions that ask you to order numbers expressed in different ways (decimals, fractions, exponents, and square roots) often come up on the GED. The question can be in a drag-and-drop format, as here. Sometimes, the question will ask you to drag and drop the numbers onto a number line.

21. **can.** The simplest way to solve this problem is to add the cost of the bread and milk to get $2.76, and then add the price of the cheese ($2.07) to get a total of $4.83, which is less than $5.00. You can also estimate the result by rounding and adding $1.30 and $1.50 to get $2.80, and then adding $2.10 for the cheese for a total of $4.90, which is less than $5.00. Using rounding can help you answer some questions quickly and move on to the next ones.

22. **A. a graph.** A graph is a visual representation of data; it's easily understood and can be used to compare data visually. You could use some of the other choices to represent the data, but they would all be more complex than a graph.

23. **Because there are only three points on the graph, the figure is a triangle.**

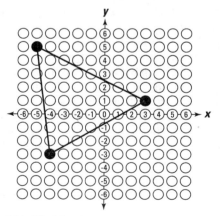

© John Wiley & Sons, Inc.

TIP

Questions where you mark your answer on the quadrant plane come up from time to time on the GED. Good mousing skills are essential to answering these questions correctly.

24. **24.** You can represent the ladder leaning against a house as a right triangle with an hypotenuse of 25 feet and a base of 7 feet. You can use the Pythagorean Theorem to answer this question. The Pythagorean Theorem states that $a^2 + b^2 = c^2$, where c is the measure of the

hypotenuse. You can set up the solution as $25^2 = 7^2 + \text{height}^2$ and solve for the height. You can simplify to $625 - 49 = \text{height}^2$. The answer is $24 = \text{height}$. (The square root of 576 is 24.)

REMEMBER

Pythagoras, a Greek mathematician, is credited with the discovery that the square of the hypotenuse of a right-angled triangle is equal to the sum of the squares of the other two sides. The *hypotenuse* is the side opposite the right angle. You'll find the Pythagorean Theorem on the formula sheet you get with your test.

TIP

The Pythagorean Theorem is frequently tested on the GED, so it pays to understand how to use it.

25. **D. 4 units to the left of the *y*-axis.** All points with *x*-coordinates that are negative are located to the left of the *y*-axis (the vertical axis). Therefore, if a point has an *x*-coordinate of –4, it's located on a line 4 units to the left of the *y*-axis.

26. **C. 1 year.** The average age for women claiming Social Security increased from 63.6 to 64.6 during that period. That's an increase of exactly 1 year, which makes Choice (C) the correct answer. This item shows that it pays to read the information and the question carefully and focus only on the information needed to answer the question. In this case, you only need to pay attention to the information about women. That's why Choice (D) is incorrect. Choice (D) shows the increase for men.

27. **A. makes it two times larger.** In this linear equation, any multiple of one term results in the same multiple of the answer. Multiplying *l* by 2 results in increasing *A* by 2.

28. **C. 160.** You can use the formula for area to calculate the number of square feet Herman has to cover in primer. The dimensions of the wall are 20 feet by 8 feet, which is 160 square feet. If your first choice for the answer was Choice (A), you added the length and height instead of multiplying. If you picked Choice (B), you confused perimeter with area. Remember that *perimeter* is the distance all the way around an object — in this case, $2(20 + 8) = 56$. Choice (D) is the answer with the first two digits reversed. This item is a good illustration of making sure that you use the correct formula (in this case, area of a rectangle, not perimeter) and then apply it correctly. It's also a good reminder to select your answer carefully. Reversing digits under the stress of time limits isn't impossible or unusual.

29. **B. four units to the left and four units below the corresponding axis.** Because both coordinates are negative, the point would have to be the corresponding distance to the left and below the corresponding axis.

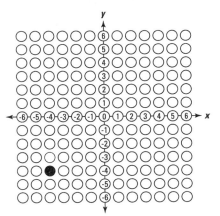

© John Wiley & Sons, Inc.

30. **30.00.** If you use x to represent the amount of money Roger spent, the amount of money that Ekua spent is $2x$. You can represent their total spending by the equation $90 = x + 2x$ or $3x = 90$, in which case $x = 30$. So Roger spent $30.00 for clothing.

31. **C. Women are getting married later in life as time goes by.** The data in the table shows that in most years the average age for marriage for women increased. Choices (A) and (B) are contradicted by the data in the table. Choice (D) cannot be concluded from the data in the table.

TIP

Did you notice that Choices (A) and (B) are essentially the same? When two answer choices are the same, you know that both are incorrect.

32. **D. 2022.** Over the years covered in the table, 2022 is the only year in which the average age for women declined, from 28.6 to 28.2.

33. **1,483.** Read the gauge carefully to find the answer.

34. **88.8.** The average grade, with Sheila's grade in Spanish falling 6 points, would be $\left(94 + 88 + 86 + 92 + 90 - 6\right) / 5 = 88.8$.

35. **230.** Barry spends $900 + $600 = $1,500 for rent and living expenses. He has $1,730 - $1,500 = $230 left over.

36. **D. Horsesgalore.** The greatest percentage increase was experienced by Horsesgalore, with a 55% increase in sales.

37. **C. Horsesgalore.** To find the increase in cars sold in July over those two years, subtract the number sold in 2020 from the number sold in 2021. The biggest increase was for Horsesgalore, with an increase of 35 thousand cars ($99 - 64 = 35$). Note that you don't have to calculate for Goodenough, which had a decline in sales.

38. **D. Strawberry and rocky road.** This combination of flavors is the only one with at least one flavor that everyone in the family likes. For all the other combinations, at least one person in the family doesn't like either flavor.

39. **D. 729.** The volume of a cube is determined by the formula for a rectangular solid: length $\times$ width $\times$ height. For this cube, the formula becomes $9 \times 9 \times 9 = 729$. Choice (A) incorrectly adds $9 + 3$. Choice (B) incorrectly multiplies 9×3. Choice (C) incorrectly calculates the area of a square with a side of 9 inches (9×9) instead of the volume of a cube.

TIP

Remember to use the formula sheet to look up the correct formula, in this case, volume of a regular solid.

40. **$90.** If the gauge reads 1/4 full, it has 24/4 = 6 gallons of fuel left in it. Because it holds 24 gallons, it needs 24 – 6 = 18 gallons to fill it. Since gas costs $5.00 a gallon, Alesh will pay $90 (18 × $5 = $90) to fill it.

6

Putting Your Skills to the Test: GED Practice Test 1

See how your stamina measures up by taking a full-length GED practice test, including the Extended Response prompt for the RLA test.

Score your test quickly with the answer key.

Discover how to improve your performance by reading through the answer explanations for all practice test questions and evaluating your Extended Response.

Chapter 19

Practice Test 1: Reasoning through Language Arts

You're ready to take a crack at a full-blown practice GED Reasoning through Language Arts test. You're feeling good and ready to go! (Well, maybe not, but you're at least smart enough to know that this practice is good for you!)

You have 95 minutes to complete the question-and-answer section and then another 45 minutes to write the Extended Response (a separate item). You get a ten-minute break before starting the Extended Response. Remember, you can't save time from one section to use in the other. Use the timer on your mobile phone to keep track of time. If you run out of time, mark the last item you completed. Then finish the remaining items. This will give you an idea of much how faster you must work to complete all the items on the real test.

The answers and explanations to this test's questions are in Chapter 20. Go through the explanations to all the questions, even for the ones you answered correctly. The explanations are a good review of the techniques I discuss throughout the book.

REMEMBER

Whether you take the online-proctored GED at home or take the test at a testing center, you'll be taking the test on a computer. Instead of marking your answers on an answer sheet, like you do for the practice tests in this book, you'll see clickable ovals, and you'll be able to click with your mouse to answer drop-down and drag-and-drop items where indicated. I formatted these special items in this book to make them appear as similar as possible to the real GED test, but I had to retain A, B, C, and D choices for marking your answers on the answer sheet. Also, to make it simpler for you to time yourself, I present the questions for the Reading Comprehension and Grammar and Language components together in one section rather than separately (as on the real GED), with the Extended Response at the end of the test. If possible, write the essay on a computer to simulate conditions on test day. Have one or two sheets of paper to use to jot down notes and organize your ideas. Otherwise, use the lined paper I provide for you.

Answer Sheet for Practice Test 1, Reasoning through Language Arts

1. _____	18. _____	35. _____
2. _____	19. _____	36. _____
3. _____	20. _____	37. _____
4. _____	21. _____	38. _____
5. _____	22. _____	39. _____
6. _____	23. _____	40. _____
7. _____	24. _____	41. _____
8. _____	25. _____	42. _____
9. _____	26. _____	43. _____
10. _____	27. _____	44. _____
11. _____	28. _____	45. _____
12. _____	29. _____	46. _____
13. _____	30. _____	47. _____
14. _____	31. _____	48. _____
15. _____	32. _____	49. _____
16. _____	33. _____	50. _____
17. _____	34. _____	

TIME: 95 minutes

QUESTIONS: 50

DIRECTIONS: You may answer the questions in this section in any order. Mark your answers on the answer sheet provided.

Questions 1–9 refer to this passage.

(1) A study from Harvard University sheds light on a topic important to all of us: the secret of having happy, fulfilling lives. The study, currently directed by Harvard professor Robert Waldinger, is one of the longest-running studies of what makes people happy. The study began in 1938 by studying a group of 724 Harvard students and a group of 456 residents of Boston, Massachusetts. The Boston residents all came from some of the poorest neighborhoods of Boston. The study followed the participants, year after year, throughout their lives. Over the years, they periodically got medical checkups, took psychological tests, participated in interviews, gave information on their income and finances, and much more. Researchers came to their homes to examine living conditions. The researchers used interviews and questionnaires to assess the participants' sense of happiness and fulfillment in life. And they used medical data to evaluate participants' health and well-being.

(2) When World War II broke out, many of the participants went to war. The participants later went on to all jobs and occupations. Some became doctors or lawyers, while others became construction workers or got jobs in factories. Some of them achieved amazing success in business or government. One even became president of the United States. Others weren't so successful. Some of them suffered from poor health, experienced mental illness, became alcoholics or addicts, or even died.

(3) This method is one of the few ways to gather valid data about how people's life choices and circumstances affect them later in life. Most of the time, we can only ask people to recall how their past decisions affect their current happiness. However, people often forget or even cover up uncomfortable truths. They may misremember or forget. Other studies, called cross-sectional, look at different people at different stages in their lives. But these studies cannot trace long-term effects over a lifetime. The Harvard study, called a longitudinal study, was different because it followed the participants through their lives. This study lasted from 1938 until the present day. At first, it studied only males, but the researchers later began including wives of the participants. The data they examined included questionnaires, reviews of medical records, blood tests, brain scans, and interviews with family members. Because studies like this one are costly and involve long-term commitments from researchers and participants, these studies are highly uncommon. So, this study can provide precious insights into factors that contribute to a happy life.

(4) Waldinger says that the results show that happiness and contentment with life do not correspond to wealth, power, fame, or prestige. Despite these being the goals of many people, the data shows that achieving them does not correspond to feeling content with life. Rather, the study says, the people who had strong, positive relationships with others — family, friends, and community members — were the most likely to be healthy and happy. Those who reported feeling lonely tended to be less happy and to experience health problems sooner than people reporting positive relationships. People who were lonely also reported more aches and pains as they aged. The study also revealed that alcoholism was a major cause of problems. Alcoholism was the principal reason for divorce among the Harvard participants. Alcoholism and tobacco smoking were the main causes of early death among participants. Alcoholism was also associated with development of mental illnesses. A really important finding was that the people who

lived happy and healthy lives into their 80s, were likely to be in long-term relationships with people who they felt they could really depend on. This was true whether or not the couples argued or disagreed from time to time. The most important factor was whether they felt commitment to one another.

1. What was the purpose of the study?

   (A) to show that a Harvard education can lead to a happy life

   (B) to discredit the idea that money can buy happiness

   (C) to find out factors that contribute to people's satisfaction in life

   (D) to find ways for people to avoid common pitfalls in life

2. Which choice puts the sentences in the correct order?

   1. The people in the study participated in World War II.

   2. The researchers gathered data from the people.

   3. The researchers used their data to draw conclusions.

   4. The researchers continued to gather data.

   5. The participants began careers in a variety of fields and workplaces.

   6. The researchers identified people to include in the study.

   (A) 2, 6, 1, 4, 3, 5

   (B) 6, 2, 1, 5, 4, 3

   (C) 5, 4, 3, 6, 2, 1

   (D) 6, 2, 4, 5, 1, 3

3. Which of the following is the most likely reason residents from poor neighborhoods in Boston were included as participants in the study?

   (A) People of this background usually have unhappy lives.

   (B) These participants would help researchers find out factors that make people unhappy.

   (C) Researchers could compare people from a variety of social backgrounds.

   (D) The researchers wouldn't have to pay them much for their participation.

4. What is the purpose of this sentence at the end of Paragraph 3?

   Because studies like this one are costly and involve long-term commitments from researchers and participants, these studies are highly uncommon.

   (A) The author wants to discredit the study.

   (B) The author wants to show that this study is valuable because it is unusual or unique.

   (C) The author wants to show that the study was difficult to carry out.

   (D) The author wants to show that this study is biased because it didn't consider women.

5. Which of these details support the conclusion that loneliness has negative consequences?

   (A) People who are in committed relations tend to live longer than people not in such relationships.

   (B) Community engagement helps people live longer.

   (C) People who are lonely develop health problems earlier in life than people who are not lonely.

   (D) People who argue frequently tend to be unhappy.

6. What is the purpose of Paragraph 3?

   (A) to give the results of the study

   (B) to state the purpose of the experiment

   (C) to explain the research method and its advantages

   (D) to describe the participants of the study

7. What does the word "longitudinal" mean in this sentence from Paragraph 3?

   The Harvard study, called a longitudinal study, was different because it followed the participants through their lives.

   (A) The study is long and uninteresting

   (B) The study examines different people of different ages for short periods of time.

   (C) The study examines the participants over time.

   (D) The study uses questionnaires, medical tests, and interviews.

8. Which of the following people would be more likely to live an unhappy life and suffer poor health, according to the study?

   (A) a husband who lives by himself in an isolated cottage in the country after his beloved spouse died two years ago

   (B) a single mother who is busy raising three teenage kids and has a loving boyfriend

   (C) a married couple who are devoted to each other but often quietly bicker while cooking dinner

   (D) an older widow who often plays cards with her friends and stays busy as a community volunteer

9. According to the passage, which of the following is the greatest cause of divorce?

   (A) tobacco use

   (B) mental illness

   (C) alcoholism

   (D) overwork

Questions 10–17 refer to the following passage and excerpt from the Emancipation Proclamation.

Our Newest Holiday

(1) Juneteenth is the United States' newest federal holiday. In June 2021, the U.S. Congress passed, and President Joe Biden signed, a bill recognizing June 19 as a national holiday. Prior to this, the newest federal holiday was the birthday of Dr. Martin Luther King, which was declared a holiday in 1983. Juneteenth marks a vitally important date in the history of the United States: the end of a terrible institution, slavery, in Texas, and the United States, at the end of the Civil War. Slavery had existed in British colonies since at least 1619, when the first group of kidnapped Africans arrived near what is now Hampton, Virginia. Slavery existed in the colonies and the United States until it was abolished in the Confederacy by the Emancipation Proclamation on January 1, 1863.

(2) However, news of the Emancipation Proclamation didn't arrive in Texas until after the war had ended. On June 18, 1865, the union army entered Galveston, Texas. The very next day, the union army commander, General Gordon Granger, issued General Order Number 3, which announced the end of the Civil War on April 9 of that year and the abolition of slavery in Texas. The order was issued nearly two and a half years after Abraham Lincoln issued the

Emancipation Proclamation, which abolished slavery in the Confederacy. The order read in part, "The people of Texas are informed that, in accordance with a proclamation from the Executive of the United States, all slaves are free. This involves an absolute equality of personal rights and rights of property between former masters and slaves, and the connection heretofore existing between then becomes that between employer and hired labor."

(3) People in Texas began celebrating this great event the very next year with gatherings in churches and communities. By 2021, this proud day was recognized widely throughout the United States and had become an official holiday in many states. For example, it had been an official holiday in Texas since 1980. This important date became a federal holiday on June 17, 2021. The very first official federal holiday took place on the very next workday, June 18, 2021, the Friday before the actual date. At last, all Americans can celebrate this historic event!

Emancipation Proclamation (Issued January 1, 1863)

(4) On the first day of January, in the year of our Lord 1863, all persons held as slaves within any State or designated part of a State, the people whereof shall then be in rebellion against the United States, shall be then, thenceforward, and forever free; and the Executive Government of the United States, including the military and naval authority thereof, will recognize and maintain the freedom of such persons, and will do no act or acts to repress such persons, or any of them, in any efforts they may make for their actual freedom.

10. What event is commemorated by the Juneteenth holiday?

    (A) the issuance of the Emancipation Proclamation
    (B) the arrival of U.S. troops in Texas
    (C) the end of slavery
    (D) the arrival of General Gordon Granger in Texas

11. According to the passage, when was Juneteenth first celebrated as a holiday?

    (A) June 19, 1865
    (B) June 19, 1866
    (C) June 18, 2021
    (D) June 19, 2021

12. Which of the following is mentioned in the Order issued by General Granger?

    (A) The U.S. military can help formerly enslaved people gain their freedom.
    (B) Formerly enslaved people may move to another location to gain their freedom.
    (C) Formerly enslaved people may become employed workers.
    (D) The government will ensure that all enslaved people are freed.

13. Who does the phrase, "the Executive of the United States," refer to in the following sentence from Paragraph 1 of the passage?

    The people of Texas are informed that, in accordance with a proclamation from the Executive of the United States, all slaves are free.

    (A) President Abraham Lincoln
    (B) General Gordon Granger
    (C) President Joe Biden
    (D) Dr. Martin Luther King

14. Which choice puts the sentences in in the correct order?

    1. The first Juneteenth was celebrated.
    2. Juneteenth became an official U.S. federal holiday.
    3. General Granger arrived in Texas.
    4. General Granger issued Order Number 3.
    5. Juneteenth became an official holiday in Texas.

    (A) 4, 3, 1, 5, 2
    (B) 3, 4, 1, 5, 2
    (C) 3, 1, 4, 2, 5
    (D) 4, 5, 1, 3, 2

15. According to the passage, the president signed the bill on June 17, 2021, and the first official federal holiday was the very next day. Based on this information, which of these answer choices is correct?

    (A) News about the new holiday arrived late.
    (B) The Supreme Court needed time to review the bill.
    (C) The government wanted to celebrate the holiday the same year it became a holiday.
    (D) The government is slow and bureaucratic.

16. What is the relationship between the Emancipation Proclamation and Order Number 3?

    (A) The Order freed enslaved people in the Confederacy, and the Emancipation Proclamation ended slavery in Texas.
    (B) The Emancipation Proclamation abolished slavery in the Confederacy, and the Order announced it in Texas.
    (C) The Emancipation Proclamation abolished slavery in the Confederacy, and the Order ended the Civil War.
    (D) The Order corrected some errors in the Emancipation Proclamation.

17. Which of these phrases best sums up the tone of "Our Newest Holiday"?

    (A) unemotional
    (B) proud and happy
    (C) matter-of-fact
    (D) ironic

Questions 18–25 refer to the following excerpt from Jack London's "In a Far Country" (1899).

(1) When the world rang with the tale of Arctic gold, and the lure of the North gripped the heartstrings of men, Carter Weatherbee threw up his snug clerkship, turned the half of his savings over to his wife, and with the remainder bought an outfit. There was no romance in his nature — the bondage of commerce had crushed all that; he was simply tired of the ceaseless grind, and wished to risk great hazards in view of corresponding returns . . . and there, unluckily for his soul's welfare, he allied himself with a party of men.

(2) There was nothing unusual about this party, except its plans. Even its goal, like that of all the other parties, was the Klondike. But the route it had mapped out to attain that goal took away the breath of the hardiest native, born and bred to the vicissitudes of the Northwest. Even Jacques Baptiste, born of a Chippewa woman and a renegade voyageur (having raised his first whimpers in a deerskin lodge north of the sixty-fifth parallel, and had the same hushed by blissful sucks of raw tallow), was surprised. Though he sold his services to them and agreed

to travel even to the never-opening ice, he shook his head ominously whenever his advice was asked.

(3) Percy Cuthfert's evil star must have been in the ascendant, for he, too, joined this company of Argonauts. He was an ordinary man, with a bank account as deep as his culture, which is saying a good deal. He had no reason to embark on such a venture — no reason in the world, save that he suffered from an abnormal development of sentimentality. He mistook this for the true spirit of romance and adventure.

18. Which of the following words or phrases describes Carter Weatherbee?

   (A) romantic

   (B) a hardy native

   (C) willing to take a risk for a good return

   (D) a hero

19. What was meant by "bondage of commerce" in this sentence in Paragraph 1?

   There was no romance in his nature — the bondage of commerce had crushed all that; he was simply tired of the ceaseless grind, and wished to risk great hazards in view of corresponding returns . . . and there, unluckily for his soul's welfare, he allied himself with a party of men.

   (A) the corresponding returns

   (B) the romance of his nature

   (C) the drudgery of life as a clerk

   (D) the risk of great hazards

20. What was the goal of the party?

   (A) to find the old trails

   (B) to reach the Klondike

   (C) to map out a route

   (D) to tell the tale of the Arctic

21. Which word best describes the chosen route to the Klondike?

   (A) blissful

   (B) hardy

   (C) scenic

   (D) ominous

22. Why was Jacques Baptiste important to the party?

   (A) He was born of a Chippewa woman.

   (B) He was a renegade voyager.

   (C) He was born in a deerskin lodge.

   (D) He was a native of the Northwest.

23. According to the passage, what was unusual about the group?

   (A) their proposed route

   (B) their desire to find gold

   (C) their destination

   (D) their use of a local guide

24. Why do you think Percy Cuthfert joined the party?

   (A) to show that he is an ordinary man

   (B) because of his evil nature

   (C) to seek romance and adventure

   (D) to get rich

25. Based on the hints the author gives, how will the story likely end for Carter Weatherbee?

   (A) It will be a triumphant success.

   (B) He will escape with only his life.

   (C) He will die on the journey.

   (D) He will break even and make it home safely.

Questions 26–31 refer to this passage from a website.

Social Security _____ financial protection for our nation's people for over 80 years. Chances are, you either receive Social _____ someone who does. With retirement, disability, and _____ benefits, Social Security is one of the most successful anti-poverty programs in our nation's history.

We are passionate about supporting our customers by delivering financial support, providing superior _____ the safety and security of your information — helping you secure today and tomorrow.

Social Security is committed to helping maintain the basic well-being and protection of the people we serve. We pay benefits to about 64 million people including retirees, children, widows, and widowers. From birth, to marriage, and into _____ are there to provide support throughout life's journey.

One of our priorities is getting you secure access to the information you need when, where, and how you need it. Whether it is in person, on the phone, or through your personal *my* Social Security _____ are committed to providing superior customer service to put you in control.

26. Social Security _____ financial protection for our nation's people for more than 80 years.

   (A) has provided

   (B) provided

   (C) provides

   (D) providing

27. Chances are, you either receive Social _____ someone who does.

   (A) Security or know

   (B) Security, or know

   (C) security or know

   (D) Security or knew

28. With retirement, disability, and _____ benefits, Social Security is one of the most successful anti-poverty programs in our nation's history.

(A) survivors

(B) survivors'

(C) survivor's

(D) survivors's

29. We are passionate about supporting our customers by delivering financial support, providing superior _____ the safety and security of your information — helping you secure today and tomorrow.

(A) customer service. And safeguarding

(B) customer service, and safeguarding

(C) customer, service and safeguarding

(D) customer, service, and safeguarding

30. From birth, to marriage, and into _____ are there to provide support throughout life's journey.

(A) retirement we

(B) retirement, we

(C) retiring, we

(D) retiring we

31. Whether it is in person, on the phone, or through your personal *my* Social Security _____ are committed to providing superior customer service to put you in control.

(A) account, we

(B) account we

(C) account. We

(D) account,

Questions 32–40 refer to this letter.

Dear Customer,

We are writing to provide you with information on some important updates to your Cash Back Advantage credit card account. Effective March 1, we will stop offering _____.
On this date your account _____ to our exciting, new Unlimited Cash Back credit card. Your new card will keep all the _____ card but will have several improvements and new features.

Effective March 1, you will receive unlimited 1% cash back on all purchases _____ you use the card. _____ you received 1% percent cash back at supermarkets and filling stations, and 0.5% everywhere else. Now you can get the same high cash back rate on all your purchases, including purchases made in drug stores, warehouse clubs, and online. _____ you shop!

Effective March 1, our new Warranty Plus plan will double the manufacturer's warranty on all major purchases. If your new computer has a year-long warranty, we will double it to two years. This plan _____ to any purchase over $200 that comes with a warranty. Do you need a new washing machine? A new computer? A new TV? They're all covered! This coverage does not apply to used or second-hand items.

Effective March 1, you will also get free insurance for your mobile phone. We will repair or replace your mobile phone as long as you pay your monthly phone bill _____. Pay your phone bill with your card, and you're covered for that month. It's that easy!

All these benefits are waiting for you. _____ new card will arrive in the mail in the next few weeks.

32. Effective March 1, we will stop offering _____.

   (A) this card

   (B) that

   (C) it to nobody

   (D) them

33. On this date your account _____ to our exciting, new Unlimited Cash Back credit card.

   (A) would transition

   (B) had transitioned

   (C) will transition

   (D) transitioned

34. Your new card will keep all the _____ card but will have several improvements and new features.

   (A) grate features of your old

   (B) great features of your old

   (C) grate feature of your old

   (D) great feature of your old

35. Effective March 1, you will receive unlimited 1% cash back on all purchases _____ you use the card.

   (A) wherever and anywhere

   (B) whenever and anywhere

   (C) whoever

   (D) every time

36. _____ you received 1% percent cash back at supermarkets and filling stations, and 0.5% everywhere else.

   (A) Subsequently,

   (B) Simultaneously,

   (C) Previously,

   (D) Unfortunately,

37. _____ you shop!

   (A) Everywhere

   (B) You get that rate everywhere

   (C) That rate is gotten

   (D) You are being given that rate everywhere

38. This plan _____ to any purchase over $200 that comes with a warranty.

   (A) is applied

   (B) applicable

   (C) was applicable

   (D) applies

39. We will repair or replace your mobile phone as long as you pay your monthly phone bill _____.

   (A) on time using your card

   (B) using your card on time

   (C) on time and using your card

   (D) and on time using your card

40. _____ new card will arrive in the mail in the next few weeks.

   (A) your

   (B) You're

   (C) That

   (D) Your

Questions 41–50 refer to this article.

Energy drinks are a very popular and growing segment of the beverage industry. In a recent year, sales of these invigorating drinks reached $57 billion worldwide. Next to multivitamins, energy drinks are the most _____ consumed nutritional supplement among American teenagers and young adults. _____ health experts warn that these drinks can pose a number of health risks.

First, energy drinks contain large amounts of sugar. Just 8 ounces of an energy drink, on average, _____ around 30 g of sugar. A single 16-ounce can of energy drink exceeds the recommended _____ amount of added sugar in our diet for both men and women. Excessive sugar can cause a number of heart problems. It can also lead to weight gain and diabetes. _____ drinks also promote tooth decay. Sugar-free and zero-calorie energy drinks avoid this sugar but contain artificial sweeteners with risks of their own.

Second, energy drinks usually contain large amounts of caffeine. Caffeine, a stimulant, makes us feel alert and awake. At low levels, caffeine is thought to have a number of health benefits. Most experts agree that caffeine can improve memory, increase alertness, and give us energy. Experts agree that for most people, _____. However, a large can of some energy drinks can contain up to 250 mg of caffeine. In contrast, a cup of coffee contains 100 mg of caffeine or less and a can of cola contains less than 50 mg of caffeine. Excessive amounts of caffeine _____ our nervous systems and hearts. In a single four-year period, emergency room visits associated with energy drinks doubled, with a significant number requiring hospitalization. Some emergency room doctors have noted an association of energy drink consumption with heart attacks. Caffeine can also disrupt our sleep patterns, causing more fatigue in the days after consuming the drinks. In addition, excessive caffeine can make us feel jumpy, nervous, or irritable — the "caffeine jitters" people sometimes talk about. Dehydration is another negative consequence of caffeine intake. _____ the body removes caffeine from the system, water goes with it. _____ from caffeine make these drinks particularly risky when exercising. The drinks are also associated with unsteadiness of the hands, which adds additional risk when weight training. Before, during, and after exercise, the best drink is plain, ordinary water.

Energy drinks may also contain other herbs and supplements, such as guarana, ginseng, taurine, glucuronolactone, and bitter orange. While people have taken most of these substances for centuries, their health benefits are unproven. In addition, some of these exotic ingredients may have unknown or unusual side effects for some people.

Clearly, energy drinks pose a number of health risks. Good, old ordinary water is a much better alternative. And if you need some _____ a healthful snack, such as an apple or banana, a handful of nuts, or some raisins.

41. Next to multivitamins, energy drinks are the most _____ consumed nutritional supplement among American teenagers and young adults.

   (A) frequent
   (B) frequently
   (C) usual
   (D) popular

42. _____ health experts warn that these drinks can pose a number of health risks.

   (A) Instead,
   (B) In addition,
   (C) And
   (D) But

43. Just 8 ounces of an energy drink, on average, _____ around 30 g of sugar.

   (A) contains
   (B) contain
   (C) contained
   (D) had contained

44. A single 16-ounce can of energy drink exceeds the recommended _____ amount of added sugar in our diet for both men and women.

   (A) daily
   (B) day
   (C) daytime
   (D) per day

45. _____ drinks also promote tooth decay.

   (A) Sugar
   (B) Sugars
   (C) Sweet
   (D) Sugary

46. Experts agree that for most people, _____.

    (A) safely consuming up to 400 mg of caffeine per day

    (B) up to 400 mg of caffeine are safe to consume

    (C) it's safe to consume up to 400 mg of caffeine per day

    (D) its safe to consume up to 400 mg of caffeine per day

47. Excessive amounts of caffeine _____ our nervous systems and hearts.

    (A) can effect

    (B) can affect

    (C) effects

    (D) affects

48. _____ the body removes caffeine from the system, water goes with it.

    (A) Because

    (B) During

    (C) As

    (D) Before

49. _____ from caffeine make these drinks particularly risky when exercising.

    (A) Dehydration coupled with increased heart rate and blood pressure

    (B) Dehydration, increased heart rate, and blood pressure

    (C) Dehydration, heart rate, and increased blood pressure

    (D) Dehydration and heart rate and blood pressure

50. And if you need some _____ a healthful snack, such as an apple or banana, a handful of nuts, or some raisins.

    (A) energy, try

    (B) energy try

    (C) energy. Try

    (D) energy; try

At this point, you may take a 10-minute break before beginning the Extended Response.

Extended Response

TIME: 45 minutes

YOUR ASSIGNMENT: The following articles present arguments from both supporters and critics of video games. In your response, analyze both positions presented in the two articles to determine which one is best supported. Use relevant and specific evidence from the articles to support your response. If possible, write your essay on a computer with spell-check, grammar-check, and autocorrect turned off. Otherwise, use the following sheets of lined paper to prepare your response. Spend up to 45 minutes reading the passages and planning, writing, revising, and editing your response.

Article 1 Video Games Are Harmful

While playing video games can be seen as a fun pastime, these games actually are at the root of a number of social problems.

Studies show that violent video games encourage violence and violent behavior. In fact, the high level of violence in these games has even garnered the attention of a U.S. Supreme Court Justice, who was astounded by the deaths, injuries, and weapons depicted in popular games. Many experts note a correlation between increased video game playing and violence in the United States.

Video games also encourage a sedentary lifestyle. With obesity at an all-time high, people should be exercising, playing sports, or working out. They should not be seated at their computer or lying on their couch, playing games for hours on end.

Experts warn that video games can become addictive and also cause injury. It's not uncommon for players to sit for hours, day after day, playing games. Experts believe that playing games to relax or unwind can pull your focus away from important priorities, such as work, school, home, and family. In addition, playing video games for hours on end has resulted in a large increase in repetitive stress injuries, which can be painful and debilitating. One common injury is called "video game thumb," which occurs because players use their thumbs so much to play.

For all these reasons, people are better off cutting back or eliminating video games, and engaging in other, more positive pastimes, such as exercising, listening to music, enjoying hobbies, or spending time with their families and friends.

Article 2 Video Games Score High

While many people are against video games, video games actually provide a lot of benefits to those who play them.

Video games teach important values such as teamwork, competition, and fair play. When you play a video game, you don't just play alone. You play with a friend or friends in the same room, or connected online. This way, players learn valuable skills needed for teamwork, including cooperation and communication. These skills are highly valued in the workplace today. Players also learn the value of competition as they compete against each other to win. And finally, players learn about fair play. Playing a video game involves following the rules. Playing fair, being a gracious winner, and not being a sore loser are all valuable skills players can use in other areas of their lives.

Video games also develop players' imaginations. Video games take place in a variety of interesting and exotic situations. While playing, players become immersed in an imaginative world full of color, action, and adventure. Some video games are so imaginative that they have been made into movies or rides at amusement parks. While people complain about the violence in video games, no reputable scientific study has shown a connection between watching video games and engaging in real-world violence.

Video games also provide a lot of fun, safe entertainment. Playing video games provides hours of fun without having to leave your home. These days, that is an important consideration.

Video games also have a massive economic impact. They generate billions of dollars of revenue and create thousands of jobs. Because these games are popular overseas, they are an important export, too.

Moreover, there is an important question of rights. Who has the right to stop video games or control their content? That's censorship! Video games come with maturity ratings, and families need to monitor their children's use of them. But banning them or banning certain content is not the American way!

Finally, video games are just plain fun. For many people, video games provide moments of entertainment and relaxation. They can forget their problems and enjoy a few minutes of distraction from their everyday problems. What's wrong with that?

For all these reasons, video games are a fun, useful, and important part of our culture. I think that all the people who don't like video games should try one. It might change their minds.

Chapter 20

Answers for Practice Test 1, Reasoning through Language Arts

n this chapter, I provide the answers and explanations to every question in the Reasoning through Language Arts practice test in Chapter 19. If you just want a quick look at the answers, check out the abbreviated answer key at the end of this chapter. However, if you have the time, be sure to read the answer explanations. Doing so will help you understand why some answers were correct and others not, especially when the choices were really close. You can discover just as much from your errors as from the correct answers.

Answers and Explanations

1. **C. to find out factors that contribute to people's satisfaction in life.** Choice (C) is made clear in the first few sentences of the passage. While Choice (B) may be a conclusion drawn from the study, it was not the purpose of the study. Choice (D) is incorrect because the study only examines the effects of the pitfalls on happiness. While the folks at Harvard might want you to believe Choice (A), this choice is not the purpose of the study. In fact, the study contradicts it. The passage stresses that happiness is available to us all.

2. **B. 6, 2, 1, 5, 4, 3.** Only Choice (B) puts the statements in the correct order. A good way to answer items like this is to find the first event in the series, in this case, Sentence (6). That allows you to quickly eliminate Choices (A) and (C). Of the remaining choices, both say that Sentence (2) came next, so you only need to figure out which came third, Sentence (1) or (4). The passage says that the researchers gathered data before and after the war, so Choice (B) is correct.

TIP

Ordering questions, such as this one, can take a long time to answer. These types of questions come up frequently on the Language Arts, Social Studies, and Science tests, so it pays to know how to answer them. Process of elimination, as described previously, can help you answer quickly and keep moving. Another good way to answer ordering questions is to write the answer choices in order on the online or erasable whiteboard you are provided. If you find yourself taking too long, however, flag the question for review later and move on to a question that is easier to answer.

3. **C. Researchers could compare people from a variety of social backgrounds.** Choice (C) makes the most sense because later in the passage results from the two groups are compared. Choices (A) and (B) are incorrect because the researchers avoid foregone conclusions in their studies. Choice (D) is not supported by information in the passage.

4. **B. The author wants to show that this study is valuable because it is unusual or unique.** The next sentence in the passage shows that the author thinks the study is valuable, so Choice (B) is correct. Therefore, Choice (A) is incorrect. Choice (C) is incorrect because the sentence is about more than just the difficulty of carrying out the study. While it is true that the study was biased in this way at first, this sentence does not refer to bias, so Choice (D) is incorrect.

5. **C. People who are lonely develop health problems earlier in life than people who are not lonely.** Only Choice (C) supports the generalization. Choices (A) and (B) do not support the conclusion. Choice (D) is contradicted by information in the passage.

6. **C. to explain the research method and its advantages.** Choice (C) is correct because the first sentence in Paragraph 3 makes clear that the paragraph is about research methods, and the paragraph then goes on to compare different research methods. The other choices are not discussed in the paragraph.

7. **C. The study examines the participants over time.** Choice (C) is correct. This information is implied in the sentence and can be inferred from other sentences in the paragraph. For example, the paragraph says that the study continued from 1938 until the present day. Therefore, Choice (B) is incorrect. Choice (A) contains an opinion not implied in the passage. Choice (D) is about the ways researchers gathered data; it's not about the time frame of the study.

Question 7 asks you to use the context (the surrounding words and sentences) to figure out the meaning of a word. This skill is often tested on the GED. In addition, using it can help you read faster in general.

8. **A. a husband who lives by himself in an isolated cottage in the country after his beloved spouse died two years ago.** Choice (A) is correct because this person is lonely and not engaged with family, friends, or community. The people in the other choices are positively engaged with family, friends, and community and so would likely live long, healthy, and happy lives.

9. **C. alcoholism.** Choice (C) is stated directly in Paragraph 4. Therefore, the other choices are incorrect.

10. **C. the end of slavery.** This answer is stated directly in Paragraph 1. The Emancipation Proclamation was issued earlier in the Civil War, so Choice (A) is incorrect. Choices (B) and (D) took place at around the same time as the holiday but are not the reasons for it.

11. **B. June 19, 1866.** The passage states that the first celebrations took place a year after the issuance of the Order. Therefore, Choice (B) is correct, and Choice (A) is incorrect. Choices (C) and (D) relate to the first federal recognition of the holiday so are incorrect.

12. **C. Formerly enslaved people may become employed workers.** Choice (C) is mentioned only in the Order. Choices (A), (B), and (D) are stated in or implied by the Emancipation Proclamation

13. **A. President Abraham Lincoln.** Choice (A) is correct because it refers to the president who issued the Emancipation Proclamation, Lincoln. General Granger issued the order (Choice B). President Biden signed the bill recognizing Juneteenth as a federal holiday (Choice C). Dr. King (Choice D) was a vital leader of the civil rights movement.

14. **A. 4, 3, 1, 5, 2.** Only Choice (A) puts the statements in the correct order. Analyzing the item and finding the first action can help you narrow the choices. In this question, first figure out which event came first, Sentence (3) or (4), as these are the only events that are ordered first in the answer choices. Because the passage says that General Granger issued the order a day after arriving in Galveston (Sentence 3), you can narrow the selection to Choices (B) and (C). That also tells you that Choice (A) is correct because the celebration (Sentence 1) took place after the order was issued (Sentence 4).

15. **C. The government wanted to celebrate the holiday the same year it became a holiday.** Choice (C) is correct because the short time between signing and celebrating the holiday shows that the government wanted to move quickly and avoid waiting a year for the first celebration. Choice (A) is incorrect because the news of the Emancipation Proclamation, not the bill, arrived late, according to the passage. The Supreme Court is not mentioned in the passage, so Choice (B) is incorrect. Though many people believe that Choice (D) is true, this conclusion is contradicted by the information. If you selected Choice (D), keep in mind that on the GED, you should choose your answers based only on the information in the passage and not on your own beliefs and opinions.

16. **B. The Emancipation Proclamation abolished slavery in the Confederacy, and the Order announced it in Texas.** Choice B is stated directly in the passage in this sentence: "On June 19, 1865, U.S. Army General Gordon Granger entered Galveston, Texas, and issued General Order Number 3, which announced the end of the Civil War on April 9 of that year and the abolition of slavery in Texas." Therefore, the other choices are incorrect.

17. **B. proud and happy.** Choice B is correct because the author states positive feelings about the end of slavery and the celebration of the holiday in several places throughout the article. Therefore, the other choices are incorrect.

18. **C. willing to take a risk for a good return.** Choice (C) is correct because Carter left his job because of the lure of Arctic gold. The passage states that he's willing to take a risk for commensurate return. He isn't a romantic (Choice A) or a hardy native (Choice B), and he's certainly not a hero (Choice D).

19. **C. the drudgery of life as a clerk.** Carter wanted to escape his everyday drudgery in life as a clerk. "Bondage of commerce" refers to his dislike of his daily routine in the business world. Therefore, Choice (C) is correct. His need for returns, or wealth (Choice A), romance (Choice B), and risk-taking (Choice D) are different factors that don't apply to the question.

20. **B. to reach the Klondike.** According to the text, "Even its [the party's] goal . . . was the Klondike." Therefore, Choice (B) is correct, and the other choices are incorrect.

21. **D. ominous.** Choice (D) is correct because the chosen route to the Klondike seems ominous as there is a foreboding of ill-fortune throughout the passage. Words such as *unluckily, ominously,* and *evil star . . . in the ascendant* give the passage a feeling that something bad will happen. The route certainly wasn't blissful (Choice A) or scenic (Choice C), and *hardy* (Choice B) refers to a native of the region, so these choices are incorrect.

22. **D. He was a native of the Northwest.** The fact that Jacques was native-born and raised in the Northwest made him important to the party, so Choice (D) is correct. The facts that he was a renegade voyageur (Choice B), born of a Chippewa woman (Choice A) in a deerskin lodge (Choice C), though mentioned in the passage as true, aren't relevant to his importance to the party.

Did you select Choice A by mistake? Don't be fooled when all of the choices are mentioned in the passage. When this happens, it really pays to take time to read the question and all the answer choices. Only one of the choices will answer the question.

TIP

23. **A. their proposed route.** Choice (A) is stated directly in the second sentence of Paragraph 2. According to Paragraph 1, the search for gold motivated people to go to the Klondike, so Choices (B) and (C) are incorrect. Choice (D) is not described as unusual in the passage, and in any case, hiring a guide would be a likely course of action for a group of inexperienced travelers.

24. **C. to seek romance and adventure.** The passage says that Percy was seeking some romance and adventure in his otherwise mundane life. Choice (A) is mentioned in the passage to describe his personality but is not given as a reason for his joining the group. Choice (B) is incorrect because the passage says that he has an evil star, which means he suffers from bad luck, not that he himself is evil. Though the passage indicates that he is not wealthy, it does not say he seeks to get rich.

25. **C. He will die on the journey.** The passage says, "unluckily for his soul's welfare, he allied himself with a party of men." This statement implies that he will die on the trip. Words such as "ominously" and "evil star" also imply a bad ending to the adventure.

26. **A. has provided.** This choice is correct because the action started in the past and continues to the present. The clue is the phrase, "for over 80 years." For this reason, Choices (B) and (C) are incorrect. Choice (D) is not a complete verb, and so cannot be correct.

27. **A. Security or know.** Choice (A) is correct because Security must be capitalized because it's part of a proper noun, and no comma is needed to join two verbs with *and.* Therefore, Choices (B) and (C) are incorrect. *Knew* (Choice D) results in faulty parallel structure and does not make sense.

28. **B. survivors'.** Choice (B) is correct because *survivors* is plural. The possessive form of a plural noun ending in -*s* is formed by adding an apostrophe after the -*s: survivors'*. Therefore, the remaining choices are incorrect.

29. **B. customer service, and safeguarding.** Choice (B) is correct because commas are used to separate items in a list of three or more words or phrases joined by a word such as *and*. Choice (A) creates a sentence fragment followed by an awkward sentence. Choice (C) omits this comma and adds another, unnecessary comma. Choice (D) adds an unnecessary comma.

REMEMBER

Comma rules are not always clear-cut; some sources (but not the GED) omit the comma after the last item in a series. Luckily, this part of the comma rule is seldom tested, but the rules about other commas in a list or series are often on the test.

30. **B. retirement, we.** Choice (B) is correct because *retirement* results in correct parallel structure, and this choice includes the comma required after the introductory phrases. Choices (A) and (D) omit this comma. Choices (C) and (D) result in faulty parallel structure.

31. **A. account, we.** Choice (A) is correct because *whether* indicates the beginning of a dependent clause. When an independent clause comes after a dependent clause, a comma comes between the two clauses. Therefore, Choice (B) is incorrect. Choice (C) creates a sentence fragment. Choice (D) omits the subject of the independent clause and creates a dependent clause joined by a comma to a sentence fragment.

32. **A. this card.** Choice (A) is correct because, of the four choices, it's the clearest reference to "Cash Back Advantage credit card account." Choice (B) is vague. Choice (C) contains a double negative, *nobody*. Choice (D) is incorrect because "Cash Back Advantage credit card account" is singular and *them* is plural.

33. **C. will transition.** Choice (C) is correct because this sentence occurs with a number of other sentences in the future tense, so the future tense makes sense here. The other choices do not make sense.

34. **B. great features of your old.** Choice (B) is correct because the word *great* ("very good"), not its homonym *grate* ("metal screen"), is needed here, and *feature* should be plural. Therefore, the other choices are incorrect.

35. **D. every time.** Choice (D) is the only adverb that makes sense in the sentence. Choices (A) and (B) have faulty parallel structure. Choice (C) does not make sense.

36. **C. Previously,** Choice (C) is correct because the sentence is about the original credit card's benefits. Only Choice (C) indicates this relationship.

37. **B. You get that rate everywhere.** Choice (B) is the only choice that is a complete sentence and avoids a verb error. Choice (A) results in a sentence fragment. Choices (C) and (D) result in awkward and wordy sentences in the passive voice.

38. **D. applies.** Choice (D) is correct because a simple present tense verb expresses the meaning that the plan is always available. Therefore, Choice (C), which uses the simple past tense, is incorrect. Choice (A) is awkward and wordy. Choice (B) creates a sentence fragment.

39. **A. on time using your card.** Only Choice (A) uses the phrases with the correct meaning. Choice (B) is confusing. Choice (C) is awkward and wordy. There is no reason to add *and*, so Choice (D) is incorrect.

40. **D. Your.** Choice (D) is correct because a possessive word is needed here. Therefore, the homonym *you're* (Choice B) is incorrect. Choice (A) is incorrect because a capital letter is needed at the beginning of every sentence. Choice (C) is possible, but Choice (D) is a more natural, usual sentence in written English.

41. **B. frequently.** Choice (B) is correct because an adverb is needed to modify an adjective such as *consumed.* The other choices are adjectives, so they are incorrect.

42. **D. But.** Choice (D), *But,* indicates the correct relationship between the ideas in the sentence and the one before it — contrast. The sentence does not propose an alternative, so Choice (A) is incorrect. The sentence does not add an idea, so Choices (B) and (C) are incorrect.

43. **B. contain.** Choice (B) is correct because the subject of the sentence is *ounces,* a plural noun. A plural verb, *contain,* is required to agree with its plural subject. If you selected Choice (A), you probably thought that *energy drink,* which is singular, was the subject. The noun that is closest to the verb is not always the subject. This question shows the value of reading all the choices before selecting your answer. Choices (C) and (D) are incorrect because there is no reason to use these past tense forms in this sentence.

44. **A. daily.** Choice (A) is correct because the adjective *daily* is required here to modify the noun *amount.* Therefore, Choice (B) is incorrect. Choices (C) and (D) do not make sense.

45. **D. Sugary.** Choice (D) is correct because an adjective, *sugary,* is needed to describe the noun *drinks.* Therefore, Choices (A) and (B), which are both nouns, are incorrect. Choice (C) is not as good a choice as *sugary* because sweet drinks made without sugar do not cause tooth decay.

46. **C. it's safe to consume up to 400 mg of caffeine per day.** Choice (C) uses the contraction *it's* correctly and avoids the errors in the other choices. Choice (A) creates a sentence fragment. Choice (B) is awkward and wordy. Choice (D) uses the possessive word *its* in place of *it's.*

47. **B. can affect.** Choice (B) is correct because it uses the verb *affect* correctly. Choices (A) and (C) use a homonym of *affect,* the noun *effect,* as a verb, and so are incorrect. Choice (D) uses the correct homonym but has an agreement error. The verb should be plural *(affect)* to agree with the plural subject *amounts.*

A good way to remember the difference between the confusing homonyms *affect* and *effect* is that *affect* is a verb and *effect* is a noun.

REMEMBER

48. **C. As.** Choice (C) is correct because this word best shows the relationship between the two parts of the sentences, which describes two things that happen at the same time. Choice (A) is incorrect because the sentence does not describe a cause–effect relationship. Choice (B) is incorrect because *during* is a preposition and so introduces a phrase not a clause. Choice (D) does not make sense.

49. **A. Dehydration coupled with increased heart rate and blood pressure.** Choice (A) is correct because only this choice has correct parallel structure. Choice (B) is incorrect because a word such as *elevated* is required before *blood pressure.* Choice (C) is missing such a word before *heart rate.* Choice (D) is missing this word entirely.

50. **A. energy, try.** Choice (A) is correct because a comma is needed to join a dependent clause to an independent clause. Therefore, Choice (B) is incorrect. Choices (C) and (D) create sentence fragments.

Sample Extended Response

The following sample essay would receive solid marks. It isn't perfect, but as the GED Testing Service tells you, you're not expected to write the perfect essay. You're expected to write a good, first-draft-quality response. When you prepare your essay, consider using a schedule similar to this: 5 minutes to read and analyze the source passages, 10 minutes to prepare, 20 minutes to write, and the remaining 10 minutes to revise and edit.

Compare the following sample to the response you wrote and then compare your essay to the criteria the GED Testing Service uses to evaluate your writing:

>> Creation of an argument and use of evidence

>> Development and organizational structure

>> Clarity and command of standard English conventions

People continue to disagree as to whether video games are harmful or not. While there is evidence on both sides, the article, "Video Games Score High," presents the stronger argument.

The argument that video games cause violence is not convincing. The first article claims that there is a correlation between violence in the U.S. and increased game playing. However, the second article states that no reputable study has proven there is a link. In addition, people play these games in other countries where violence has not increased. So video games are probably not the cause of violence.

The first article says that video games encourage a sedentary lifestyle. It's true that people sit to play games, but most gamers I know take time for sports and exercise. People just need to manage their time playing.

Video games also seem to provide many benefits. People learn sportsmanship from games, as well as other valuable skills, such as teamwork. In addition, people have fun playing them. There is nothing like coming home from a long, frustrating day at work and playing a fun game with friends online. I often play a video game on study breaks while preparing for the GED. It helps me to relax so I can focus on learning.

For all these reasons, the second article makes a much stronger case. I will continue to play video games knowing that they are not harmful or bad.

Answer Key

1.	C	14.	A	27.	A	40.	D
2.	B	15.	C	28.	B	41.	B
3.	C	16.	B	29.	B	42.	D
4.	B	17.	B	30.	B	43.	B
5.	C	18.	C	31.	A	44.	A
6.	C	19.	C	32.	A	45.	D
7.	C	20.	B	33.	C	46.	C
8.	A	21.	D	34.	B	47.	B
9.	C	22.	D	35.	D	48.	C
10.	C	23.	A	36.	C	49.	A
11.	B	24.	C	37.	B	50.	A
12.	C	25.	C	38.	D		
13.	A	26.	A	39.	A		

Chapter 21

Practice Test 1: Social Studies

The Social Studies test consists of questions that measure general social studies concepts. The questions are based on short readings that often include a map, graph, chart, cartoon, or figure. Study the information given and then answer the question(s) following it. Refer to the information as often as necessary in answering the questions.

The Social Studies test of the GED consists of one section. You have 70 minutes to complete the test. Remember, on the real test you can use the on-screen calculator (or your own TI-30XS MultiView calculator if you take the test at a testing center).

The answers and explanations to this test's questions are in Chapter 22. Go through the explanations to all the questions, even for the ones you answered correctly. The explanations are a good review of the techniques that I discuss throughout the book.

REMEMBER

Unless you require accommodations, you'll be taking the GED test on a computer. Instead of marking your answers on an answer sheet, as you do for the practice tests in this book, you'll see clickable ovals and fill-in-the-blank text boxes, and you'll be able to click with your mouse and drag and drop items where indicated. I formatted the questions and answer choices in this book to make them appear as similar as possible to the real GED test, but I had to retain some A, B, C, D choices for marking your answers, and I provide an answer sheet for you to do so.

Answer Sheet for Practice Test 1, Social Studies

1. _____

2. _____

3. _____

4. _____

5. _____

6. _____

7. _____

8. _____

9. _____

10. _____

11. _____

12. _____

13. _____

14. _____

15. _____

16. _____

17. _____

18. _____

19. _____

20. _____

21. _____

22. _____

23. _____

24. _____

25. _____

26. _____

27. _____

28. _____

29. _____

30. _____

31. _____

32. _____

33. _____

34. _____

35. _____

36. _____

37. _____

38. _____

39. _____

40. _____

41. _____

42. _____

43. _____

44. _____

45. _____

46. _____

47. _____

48. _____

49. _____

50. _____

TIME: 70 minutes

QUESTIONS: 50

DIRECTIONS: Mark your answers on the answer sheet provided.

Questions 1–5 refer to an excerpt from a speech on voting rights for women that Mark Twain gave to an audience of women employed in New York factories and an excerpt from the U.S. Constitution.

Votes for Women (1901)
By Mark Twain

Referring to woman's sphere in life, I'll say that woman is always right. For twenty-five years I've been a woman's rights man. I have always believed, long before my mother died, that, with her gray hairs and admirable intellect, perhaps she knew as much as I did. Perhaps she knew as much about voting as I.

I should like to see the time come when women shall help to make the laws. I should like to see that whiplash, the ballot, in the hands of women. As for this city's government, I don't want to say much, except that it is a shame — a shame; but if I should live twenty-five years longer — and there is no reason why I shouldn't — I think I'll see women handle the ballot. If women had the ballot today, the state of things in this town would not exist.

If all the women in this town had a vote today they would elect a mayor at the next election, and they would rise in their might and change the awful state of things now existing here.

19th Amendment (1920)

The right of citizens of the United States to vote shall not be denied or abridged by the United States or by any State on account of sex. Congress shall have power to enforce this article by appropriate legislation.

1. What was the purpose of Twain's speech?

    (A) He wanted to end corruption in New York.

    (B) He wanted to show support for women's suffrage.

    (C) He wanted to encourage equal access to education.

    (D) He wanted to praise his mother.

2. Which of the following is an opinion?

    (A) Twain supported voting rights for women.

    (B) The 19th Amendment was ratified in 1920.

    (C) Women are better at stopping corruption than men.

    (D) In 1901, people were concerned about corruption in New York government.

3. What does Twain mean when he calls the ballot "a whiplash"?

    (A) Elections are more trouble than they are worth.

    (B) Elections are a way to control government.

    (C) Elections are a good way to control citizens.

    (D) Elections lead to corruption.

4. Which of the following details could Twain add to strengthen his case in favor of extending the vote to women?

   (A) A woman's place is in the home.

   (B) Women did not have the vote in ancient Greek democracies.

   (C) Women lack the same intelligence and skills as men.

   (D) Women in New York worked in unsafe factories, and if given the vote, working women would improve conditions.

5. Which of the following does the 19th Amendment demonstrate?

   (A) When women started to vote, corruption in politics decreased.

   (B) When women were able to vote, they could only vote in federal elections.

   (C) Women received the right to vote sooner than Twain predicted.

   (D) The federal government was unwilling to enforce women's right to vote.

6. In 1973, after 19 years of direct involvement, the United States ended its involvement in the Vietnam War. President Richard Nixon called the treaty that ended the war "peace with honor." By 1975, Vietnam, Cambodia, and Laos all fell under Communist rule. Which of these statements is a conclusion that can be drawn from this information?

   (A) Capitalism is a better system than Communism.

   (B) The Communist forces in Vietnam honored the treaty.

   (C) The U.S.-backed government in South Vietnam was stronger than the Communist regime in the North.

   (D) U.S. involvement in the war was a failure.

Question 7 refers to the following photograph.

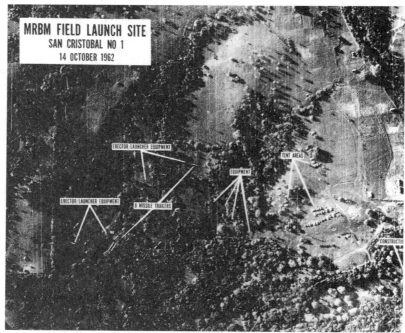

Source: United States Government/Public domain.

7. In 1962, Russia agreed with Cuba to place nuclear weapons on that island to deter a possible U.S. invasion and to counter American missiles in Turkey aimed at Russia. Rumors of the missiles abounded, but proof was lacking. Finally, clear photographic evidence provoked the Cuban Missile Crisis, a standoff between the Soviet Union and the United States.

What is the significance of the photographic evidence?

(A) The photographs showed that the missiles could not counter the American missiles in Turkey.

(B) The photographs proved that the missiles could reach the United States.

(C) The photographs convinced the Soviet Union to remove the missiles.

(D) The photographs provided undisputable proof of the presence of the missiles in Cuba.

8. The Federalist Papers were a series of newspaper articles published anonymously in support of ratifying the U.S. Constitution. The authors were prominent patriots. Federalist Number 10, by James Madison, said, "The instability, injustice, and confusion introduced into the public councils, have, in truth, been the mortal diseases under which popular governments have everywhere perished; as they continue to be the favorite and fruitful topics from which the adversaries to liberty derive their most specious declamations."

Which of the following would Madison most likely believe is a threat to democracy?

(A) a TV news report about controversy in Congress over a new spending bill

(B) a newspaper article about the release of an official U.S. government study of UFOs

(C) a series of social media posts saying that the army is secretly getting ready to take over Washington, D.C.

(D) an Internet news story on ways that diverse Americans exercise their religious freedom

9. After war in Europe broke out in 1914, the United States tried to stay neutral. In January 1917, Germany sent a telegram to the government of Mexico that said, "We intend to begin on the first of February unrestricted submarine warfare. We shall endeavor in spite of this to keep the United States of America neutral. In the event of this not succeeding, we make Mexico a proposal of alliance on the following basis: make war together, make peace together, generous financial support and an understanding on our part that Mexico is to reconquer the lost territory in Texas, New Mexico, and Arizona."

Which of the following statements can be inferred from this message?

(A) Germany was confident it could win the war with additional support.

(B) Germany did not think that unrestricted submarine warfare would widen the conflict.

(C) Germany's willingness to widen the war showed it was becoming increasingly desperate.

(D) Germany felt that the United States was not a serious threat to them.

10. On October 12, 2000, the American naval ship USS *Cole* was attacked by Al-Qaeda suicide bombers while it was refueling in a harbor in Yemen. A large hole was blown in the hull of the ship, and 17 sailors died. The ship's captain later said that the navy's rules prevented it from firing on the attackers as they approached the ship.

Which of the following is an opinion about the attack?

(A) President Clinton's decision not to attack Al-Qaeda directly after the attack was a mistake.

(B) The navy developed new rules for fending off attacks.

(C) The U.S. government developed a new strategy for dealing with terrorist organizations.

(D) Al-Qaeda was disappointed the United States did not respond militarily and changed its strategy.

Executive orders are instructions the president can issue. The Constitution grants the president the right to issue executive orders on how to enforce laws or how to use federal resources. Other times, specific laws give the president latitude on how to implement the law. This table shows the number of executive orders issued by recent U.S. presidents.

Executive Orders Issued by Recent U.S. Presidents

President	Terms	Number of Executive Orders	Average Per Year
William J. Clinton	2	305	38
George W. Bush	2	291	36
Barack H. Obama	2	276	35
Donald J. Trump	1	219	55

Source: Adapted from Federal Register

11. According to the information, what can the president do in an executive order?

    (A) create a new law that Congress is unwilling to pass

    (B) order the State Department to increase scrutiny of visa applications

    (C) declare war against an enemy country

    (D) direct a government official to conduct an illegal action

12. Which of the following statements can be concluded from this information?

    (A) One-term presidents tend to issue more executive orders than two-term presidents.

    (B) President Trump issued more executive orders per year than the other three presidents in the table.

    (C) Presidents tend to issue more executive orders in their first terms than their second terms.

    (D) Executive orders have declined over the years.

13. What is the average number of executive orders issued per year by these four presidents?

    (A) 36

    (B) 41

    (C) 273

    (D) 1,091

14. Which president issued the most executive orders?

    (A) William J. Clinton

    (B) George W. Bush

    (C) Barack H. Obama

    (D) Donald J. Trump

15. Civil rights and political rights are two ways to classify people's rights. Civil rights guarantee people's lives and safety as well as freedoms of religion, speech, and other important rights. Political rights include people's legal rights (such as right to a fair trial) and rights to participate in government (such as the right to vote or to protest the actions of the government). Which of the following people is using their civil rights?

    (A) Mandy distributes flyers in support of a certain school board candidate.

    (B) Seema attends weekly prayers at her local mosque.

    (C) David writes a letter to his representative in Congress to complain about a new proposed law.

    (D) Frank is visiting his daughter in another state, so he votes using an absentee ballot.

16. In 1971, the U.S. Constitution was amended to grant the right to vote to anyone 18 years of age or older. Before then, states set different voting ages. Some states allowed women to vote at age 18, but men had to wait until age 21. This situation resulted in men being drafted into the army before they were old enough to vote. Which of the following beliefs supported this change?

    (A) Discrimination against women should stop.

    (B) Women should have the right to serve in combat roles in the military.

    (C) Members of the military are patriotic.

    (D) Soldiers should have a say in choosing their elected officials.

17. State voting patterns are often discussed in terms of red states or blue states, depending on which party they usually vote for.

    Which statement can be concluded from the map?

Red States and Blue States in Recent Elections

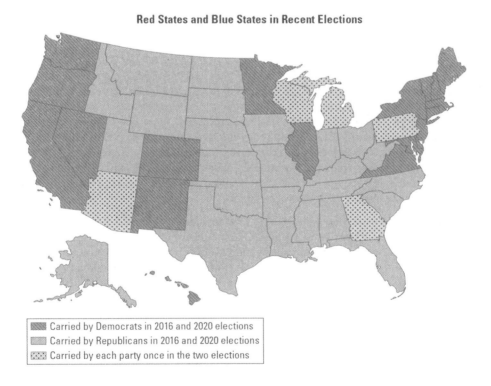

Carried by Democrats in 2016 and 2020 elections
Carried by Republicans in 2016 and 2020 elections
Carried by each party once in the two elections

    (A) American voters are very concerned about the future of the country.

    (B) Democrats are strong in rural and agricultural areas.

    (C) Purple states are disloyal to their parties.

    (D) Voting patterns show that the United States is very divided politically.

18. The Constitution of the United States implements a system of separation of powers among three (1) _____ branches of government. The executive branch (2) _____ the law.

(1A) divided

(1B) equal

(1C) related

(1D) similar

(2A) enforces

(2B) makes

(2C) interprets

(2D) removes

19. Under the U.S. Constitution, the legislative branch (1) _____ laws and the (2) _____ branch interprets the laws.

(1A) enforces

(1B) enacts

(1C) interprets

(1D) removes

(2A) legislative

(2B) judicial

(2C) executive

(2D) military

Questions 20–25 refer to the following letter.

Dear Residents of the Johnson-Earl Apartments:

This is a very important time for you to join the Johnson-Earl Apartments Residents' Association. As you know, our apartment building is facing unprecedented changes because of the new owners. Services have declined while rent has increased. Some of our members have received rent increases of over 10 percent when renewing their leases. When they move out, the management renovates their apartments and converts them into luxury apartments that rent for much more. Management has frequently retained tenants' damage deposits, even though their plan was to completely gut the apartment. Clearly, management's goal is to force all of us out of our long-time homes and keep our damage deposits.

As you know, the Association believes that management's actions violate city and state laws. So far, the association has filed five suits on behalf of individual tenants who are being forced from their homes, in addition to a class-action lawsuit against the building owners on behalf of all residents. You can find all the latest news and updates about the association on our website. The website also contains the names, phone numbers, and email addresses of key government officials in case you want to contact them. You can download our weekly newsletter, which we also place under the door of each apartment.

As you know, affordable housing is scarce in the capital area, so it's essential that we fight for our homes. Former tenants who have moved have been forced into inferior housing in unsafe areas. Don't let this happen to you!

Now is the time to support the association. Membership is only $20 per year. Joining now will help us ensure that our rights as residents are respected. Help us stop management from taking your home. Join today!

Sincerely,

Marta Obredor,

President, Johnson-Earl Residents' Association

20. What issue is the letter primarily concerned about?

(A) The association has filed lawsuits against the building.

(B) Apartments in the building are unsafe and need renovation.

(C) The association is composed of neighbors living in the building.

(D) The association is working to stop the management's illegal actions.

21. Why does the president of the association add information about problems tenants face after they move out?

(A) so tenants will ask the government to build more affordable housing

(B) to add urgency to her message

(C) to make management aware of the association's concerns

(D) to convince management to abandon its plan for the building

22. Which right or freedom in the U.S. Constitution supports the association and its activities?

(A) freedom of religion

(B) the right to bear arms

(C) the right to petition for redress of grievances

(D) the right to a fair and speedy trial

23. Which other Constitutional right supports the association and its work?

(A) freedom of speech and press

(B) freedom from undue search and seizure

(C) the right to a jury trial

(D) the right to avoid self-incrimination

24. Which of the following actions could the association also legally undertake using their Constitutional rights?

(A) set up a picket line on the sidewalk in front of the building

(B) make multiple false reports to the police

(C) refuse to pay their rent

(D) write an article with false information about the building manager

25. Which of these additional ideas could the president of the association add to make her case stronger?

(A) The management already converted two other affordable buildings to luxury apartments.

(B) A top architect designed the new apartments.

(C) All apartments in the building have beautiful views.

(D) Break-ins have increased, so tenants should make sure they lock their doors.

Question 26 refers to this excerpt from an executive order issued by President Joe Biden.

As the nation's largest employer, the federal government must be a model for diversity, equity, inclusion, and accessibility, where all employees are treated with dignity and respect. Accordingly, the federal government must strengthen its ability to recruit, hire, develop, promote, and retain our nation's talent and remove barriers to equal opportunity. It must also provide resources and opportunities to strengthen and advance diversity, equity, inclusion, and accessibility across the federal government. The federal government should have a workforce that reflects the diversity of the American people. A growing body of evidence demonstrates that diverse, equitable, inclusive, and accessible workplaces yield higher-performing organizations.

26. Which of the following is a likely effect of this executive order?

(A) It will become easier for differently abled people to find federal jobs.

(B) Private employers will be required to follow the guidelines in the order.

(C) Waste in the federal government will increase.

(D) Speakers of English as a second language will have trouble getting federal jobs.

27. Everyone knows that if the president dies or resigns, the vice president becomes president. But what happens after that? The line of succession is defined in various parts of the Constitution and laws. After the vice president, the Speaker of the House of Representatives becomes president. If that person is not available or qualified, then the president pro tem of the Senate becomes president. The next person in line is the secretary of state.

Which of these principles is the line of succession based on?

(A) one person, one vote

(B) separation of powers

(C) continuity of government

(D) federalism

28. President George W. Bush welcoming President-Elect Barak Obama to the White House shortly after the 2008 election, on November 10, 2008, part of a fundamental feature of American democracy, _____.

Source: The White House/Wikimedia Commons/Public domain.

(A) an election debate

(B) an inauguration ceremony

(C) a peaceful transition of power

(D) a victory celebration

Questions 29–33 refer to the following information.

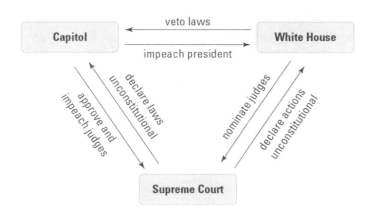

29. The system of _____ and balances is a key part of separation of powers in the U.S. constitutional system.

(A) weights

(B) measures

(C) checks

(D) counterweights

30. Which of these powers is a limitation on the power of the president, according to the diagram?

(A) Congress can pass a law.

(B) The president can veto a law.

(C) Congress can override a veto.

(D) The Supreme Court can declare a law unconstitutional.

31. Which of the following individuals or committees has as a primary role a check over the Executive Branch?

(A) the Speaker of the House, who is the presiding officer of the House

(B) the House Oversight Committee, which reviews presidential actions

(C) the House Minority Leader, who leads the party that is out of power

(D) the House Ethics Committee, which ensures that representatives in the House act appropriately

32. What is the purpose of this system?

(A) to ensure that the president does not become too powerful

(B) to ensure that the budget is balanced

(C) to prevent one part of government from becoming too powerful

(D) to ensure the rule of law

33. What do this system and the Bill of Rights have in common?

(A) They are both in the Declaration of Independence.

(B) They both support freedom of religion.

(C) They both give the government too much power.

(D) They are both limitations on the power of the federal government.

Questions 34 and 35 refer to this drawing, attributed to Benjamin Franklin, which is believed to be the first political cartoon. First used in the French and Indian Wars, it later was used during the Revolutionary War.

Source: The Library of Congress / Wikimedia Commons / Public domain

34. The origin of which of these principles of American government can be seen in this cartoon?

    (A) separation of powers
    (B) federalism
    (C) freedom to bear arms
    (D) rule of law

35. To which of these other sayings from the American Revolution is this cartoon related?

    (A) Don't fire until you see the whites of their eyes.
    (B) We must, indeed, all hang together *or*, most assuredly, we shall all hang separately.
    (C) No taxation without representation.
    (D) Give me liberty or give me death.

Questions 36–38 refer to the following passage and table.

The federal minimum wage law sets the minimum hourly pay for most workers in the United States. Tipped workers receive a lower wage, but the difference must be made up in tips. States may set a higher minimum wage. In 2021, 29 states had minimum wages higher than the federal minimum wage. Here is information about the history of the federal minimum wage.

Recent Increases to the U.S. Minimum Wage

Year of Increase	Minimum Wage
1981	$3.35
1990	$3.80
1991	$4.25
1996	$4.75
1997	$5.15
2007	$5.85
2008	$6.65
2009	$7.25

36. For the years 1981 to 2008, what is the longest number of years the minimum wage has remained the same?

    (A) 5
    (B) 9
    (C) 10
    (D) 12

37. Which year saw the largest increase in the minimum wage?

    (A) 1997
    (B) 2007
    (C) 2008
    (D) 2009

38. The minimum wage in Wyoming is $5.15 per hour, as of 2022. How much should workers in this state earn in 2022?

   (A) $2.10
   (B) $5.15
   (C) $7.25
   (D) $15.00

Questions 39 and 40 refer to the following passage.

The Great Recession was a widespread global economic slowdown that occurred between 2007 and 2009. Economists consider this event to be the second-biggest downturn in history since the Great Depression of the 1930s. The Great Recession was triggered in large part by a collapse of housing prices in the United States. Many mortgages were backed by subprime mortgages issued to less-than-qualified buyers on homes that frequently had an inflated value. When the homeowners were unable to pay, housing prices declined and the value of the bonds backing those mortgages collapsed. The result was a dramatic economic downturn felt especially in North America, Europe, and South America.

39. What is one of the reasons mortgage-backed securities were a problem?

   (A) They provided financing for mortgages.
   (B) They were based on mortgages issued to people with poor credit.
   (C) Their collateral was real estate.
   (D) They were a new kind of investment security.

40. Which of the following would be likely effects of the Great Recession on companies?

   (A) defaulting on home mortgages
   (B) losing cars to repossession
   (C) losing jobs
   (D) declining sales

41. A monopoly is a company that controls a large segment of a particular product or market to the detriment of other companies, consumers, and the economy as a whole. Certain companies, such as utilities, are exempt from laws designed to prevent monopolies.

   Which of the following would be considered an illegal monopoly?

   (A) a water company that provides water to every home and business in a certain city
   (B) an online ad provider that controls most Internet advertising
   (C) the top-rated TV network in the United States
   (D) a publicly operated toll road that is the only practical route linking three states

42. Supply and demand show how free markets determine prices. High demand and low supply lead to high prices, while low demand and large supply lead to low prices.

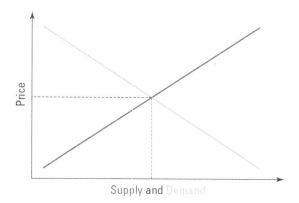

Which of the following is needed for the law of supply and demand to operate correctly?

(A) high supply

(B) a free market

(C) low demand

(D) a strong economy

Questions 43–46 refer to the following excerpt from a speech that former Prime Minister Winston Churchill delivered in Fulton, Missouri, in 1946, shortly after the end of World War II.

A shadow has fallen upon the scenes so lately lighted by the Allied victory. Nobody knows what Soviet Russia and its Communist international organization intends to do in the immediate future or what are the limits if any to their expansive and proselytizing tendencies. I have a strong admiration and regards for the valiant Russian people and for my wartime comrade, Marshal Stalin. There is sympathy and goodwill in Britain — and I doubt not here also — towards the peoples of all the Russia and a resolve to preserve through many differences and rebuffs in establishing lasting friendships. We understand the Russian need to be secure on her western frontiers by the removal of all possibility of German aggression. We welcome Russia to her rightful place among the leading nations of the world. Above all we welcome constant, frequent and growing contacts between the Russian people and our own people on both sides of the Atlantic. It is my duty however, for I am sure you would wish me to state the facts as I see them to you, to place before you certain facts about the present position in Europe.

From Stettin in the Baltic to Trieste in the Adriatic, an "iron curtain" has descended across the continent. Behind that line lie all the capitals of the ancient states of Central and Eastern Europe. Warsaw, Berlin, Prague, Vienna, Budapest, Belgrade, Bucharest and Sofia; all these famous cities and the populations around them lie in what I must call the Soviet sphere, and all are subject in one form or another, not only to Soviet influence but to a very high and, in many cases, increasing measure of control from Moscow. Athens alone — Greece with its immortal glories — is free to decide its future at an election under British, American, and French observation. The Russian-dominated Polish Government has been encouraged to make enormous and wrongful inroads upon Germany, and mass expulsions of millions of Germans on a scale grievous and undreamed-of are now taking place. The Communist parties, which were very small in all these Eastern States of Europe, have been raised to pre-eminence and power far beyond their numbers and are seeking everywhere to obtain totalitarian control. Police governments are prevailing in nearly every case, and so far, except in Czechoslovakia, there is no true democracy.

43. What is Churchill's speech primarily about?

    (A) celebrating the end of World War II

    (B) warning about the expansion of Communism

    (C) celebrating democracy in Greece

    (D) announcing his retirement as prime minister

44. Which choice best describes the relationship between Churchill and Stalin at the time of this speech?

    (A) Churchill respects Stalin as an ally but fears his present intentions.

    (B) Churchill believes Stalin knows the best way forward for Europe.

    (C) Churchill has always distrusted Stalin.

    (D) Churchill believes that the Allies should never have accepted the Soviet Union as a partner in the war.

45. Which of the following countries have already fallen to Communism at the time of the speech, according to Churchill?

    (A) France

    (B) Poland

    (C) Czechoslovakia

    (D) Greece

46. What does Churchill mean when he talks about an "Iron Curtain"?

    (A) Russia built a wall of steel between countries it controlled and the rest of Europe.

    (B) Europe has been divided into one area with democratic governments and another under Communist dictatorships.

    (C) The Soviet Union has incorporated several former countries in Europe into its borders.

    (D) Countries under Communist rule are as free as countries in the rest of Europe.

Questions 47 and 48 refer to the following passage.

The number of refugees in the world is at an all-time high. This decade began with nearly double the number of refugees than just ten years before. Most refugees are fleeing war or violence, but others are seeking food security or water security. The main countries that refugees are fleeing from include Burundi, Eritrea, Central African Republic, Sudan, Democratic Republic of Congo, Somalia, Burma, South Sudan, Afghanistan, and Syria. While governments, international organizations, and NGOs (non-government organizations) work to assist refugees, these migrants often find themselves living in difficult circumstances in their new locations. Many are in large camps living in poor conditions. In addition to these refugees, there are also record numbers of internally displaced people, such as people in Eastern Ukraine fleeing Russia-supported invaders.

47. Of the countries mentioned in the information, which continent are most of them located in?

    (A) Middle East

    (B) Asia

    (C) Europe

    (D) Africa

48. Which of the following statements is true of the refugee crisis?

    (A) The number of refugees worldwide has grown to an all-time high.

    (B) Refugees are primarily seeking food and water security.

    (C) Refugees are well taken care of once they flee.

    (D) Refugees are internally displaced people.

49. Ancient Athens is often considered the origin and inspiration of Western-style democracy. A direct democracy, Athens did not elect representatives. Instead, every adult male could participate personally. Athenian democracy lasted for about 300 years, until Macedonia invaded Greece.

    Why is Athenian democracy significant today?

    (A) It provides an underpinning for Western democracy today.

    (B) It demonstrates the power of representative government.

    (C) It shows that democracy is doomed to fail.

    (D) It shows that democracy is not a usual or common system of government.

50. Kazakhstan, a vast, thinly populated country south of Russia in relatively isolated Central Asia, has a tremendous wealth of natural resources. In addition to fossil fuels, such as coal, gas, and oil, this enormous country has important deposits of iron, copper, tungsten, and uranium. It also has vast resources in rare-earth, highly prized metals found in very small quantities. These substances are key to rechargeable batteries as well as to many common small electronic devices, such as mobile phones and computers. Though fossil fuel reserves will likely be depleted soon, mineral resources will grow in importance.

    Which of the following is likely true of Kazakhstan?

    (A) Its mineral wealth is unusable because of its isolated location.

    (B) Mineral wealth gives this country strategic and economic importance.

    (C) Kazakhstan's wealth will diminish as its fossil fuels are depleted.

    (D) Kazakhstan's population is too small for it to use its resources fully.

Chapter 22

Answers for Practice Test 1, Social Studies

n this chapter, I provide the answers and explanations to every question in the Social Studies practice test in Chapter 21. If you just want a quick look at the answers, check out the abbreviated answer key at the end of this chapter. However, if you have the time, it's more useful for study purposes to read all the answer explanations carefully. Doing so will help you understand why some answers were correct and others not, especially when the choices were really close. It will also point you to areas where you may need to do more review. Remember, you learn as much from your errors as from the correct answers.

Answers and Explanations

1. **B. He wanted to show support for women's suffrage.** In several places throughout the passage, Twain mentions his support for extending voting rights to women, so Choice (B) is correct. He mentions corruption (Choice A) only with regard to women's votes ending it. Choice (C) is not mentioned in the passage. Though he speaks of his mother (Choice D), it's only to support his case that women deserve to vote.

2. **C. Women are better at stopping corruption than men.** While Twain was convinced that women should vote, the idea that women are better than men at stopping corruption is Twain's opinion (Choice C). The other choices are facts expressed in the excerpts.

3. **B. Elections are a way to control government.** Choice (B) is correct. He is suggesting that the punishment of losing an election would reduce corruption. The remaining choices are the opposite of what Twain believes.

4. **D. Women in New York worked in unsafe factories, and if given the vote, working women would improve conditions.** Twain could use the idea that women voters would work to make factories safer to strengthen his argument, so Choice (D) is correct. The other choices would weaken his argument.

5. **C. Women received the right to vote sooner that Twain predicted.** Choice (C) is correct because in the passage, Twain predicts it will take 25 years for women to get the right to vote. He spoke in 1901, and the amendment came into force in 1920, five to six years earlier than Twain predicted. Choice (A) is not supported by the passage. Choice (B) is contradicted by the amendment. The amendment states that the government will enforce this new right (Choice D).

6. **D. U.S involvement in the war was a failure.** Choice (D) is correct because the United States did not prevent Vietnam from becoming Communist. Therefore, Choices (B) and (C) are incorrect. The United States fought in Vietnam because they believed Choice (A) to be true, but it's not a conclusion that can be drawn from the information.

7. **D. The photographs provided undisputable proof of the presence of the missiles in Cuba.** Choice (D) is correct because the photo provides clear proof that confirmed the rumors. Choices (A) and (B) are incorrect because photos are not needed to reach these conclusions. Choice (C) is incorrect because the confrontation, not the photos, convinced Cuba to remove the missiles.

8. **C. a series of social media posts saying that the army is secretly getting ready to take over Washington, D.C.** Of all the choices, only Choice (C) is deliberately false or misleading, thus falling into the danger Madison warned of. The remaining choices are about topics that are routinely or recently reported on and are not false or misleading.

9. **C. Germany's willingness to widen the war showed it was becoming increasingly desperate.** Choice (C) is correct because Germany felt it needed to increase submarine warfare, which risked drawing the United States into the war. Involving Mexico would counter the United States. This increased willingness to take risks suggests Germany was becoming more desperate. Therefore, Choices (A) and (B) are incorrect. Choice (D) is incorrect because the telegram shows U.S. involvement was concerning enough that it needed to be countered by involving Mexico in the war.

10. **A. President Clinton's decision not to attack Al-Qaeda directly after the attack was a mistake.** Only Choice (A) expresses an opinion. The other choices are facts.

11. **B. Order the State Department to increase scrutiny of visa applications.** According to the information, an executive order can be used to direct federal resources in certain ways, so Choice (B) is correct. Choices (A) and (D) are not mentioned in the information as ways that the president can use executive orders. In fact, the power to declare war belongs to Congress (Choice C). Choice (D) is incorrect because in the United States, no person is above the law.

12. **B. President Trump issued more executive orders per year than the other three presidents in the table.** Choice (B) is correct because the table shows that President Trump issued 55 executive orders, which is more than the three previous presidents. Therefore, Choice (D) Is incorrect. There is not enough data about one-term presidents to support Choice (A). Choice (C) may be true but cannot be concluded from the table because it does not break out the orders by first or second term.

13. **B. 41.** To determine the average number of orders issued per year, add the averages for each president and divide by 4: (38 + 36 + 35 + 55)/4 = 41. Therefore, Choice (B) is correct. Choice A is the median number of orders the presidents issued, and so is incorrect. (The median is the value in the middle when you arrange the values from smallest to largest.) Choice (C) is the average number of orders issued by the four presidents over their terms. Choice (D) is the total number of orders issued by all four presidents rounded to the nearest integer.

REMEMBER

You are allowed to use the on-screen calculator or your own TI-30XS MultiView calculator (only at a test center) on questions such as this one. The calculator is available on the social studies and science tests, not just the math.

14. **A. William J. Clinton.** The data shows that William J. Clinton (Choice A) issued more executive orders, 305, than the other three presidents. Therefore, the other choices are incorrect. Note that while Donald J. Trump issued the highest average number of orders per year, he still issued fewer executive orders than Clinton.

15. **B. Seema attends weekly prayers at her local mosque.** All the choices except Choice (B) are political rights, so this choice is correct.

TIP

On questions such as this one, the process of elimination can help you. If you eliminate all the choices that are political rights (Choices A, C, and D), that leaves only Choice B, which is correct. Even if you can only eliminate two of the choices, that improves your chances to fifty-fifty.

16. **D. Soldiers should have a say in choosing their elected officials.** Only Choice (D) gives a reason why 18-year-olds should vote. Choice (A) is incorrect because women were not discriminated against in this situation. The information says that women could vote at an earlier age than men. Choice (B) is not relevant to this situation. Choice (C) may be true but is not relevant.

17. **D. Voting patterns show that the United States is very divided politically.** Choice (D) is correct because the pattern shows that southern states as well as predominantly agricultural states are red, and more urban and industrial states are blue. In addition, only a few states are purple, which shows that most states are aligned with one party. While one hopes that Americans are interested in the future of the country (Choice A), this statement cannot be concluded from the map. Choice (B) is contradicted by the map. Some people may believe that Choice (C) is true, but it cannot be concluded from the map. In addition, in the U.S. system, there is no requirement that voters remain loyal to a party, though they have the right to do so.

18. **1B, 2A. equal, enforces.** Under the Constitution, the three branches are equal and use a system of "balance of powers" to prevent one branch from becoming too powerful. Therefore, the answer to Item (1) is equal. The role of the executive branch is to implement, or enforce, the laws passed by Congress (Item 2).

19. **1B, 2B. enacts, judicial.** The role of the legislative branch is to pass, or enact (Item 1), new laws. The judicial branch (Item 2) interprets the laws and ensures that they are being applied properly.

20. **D. The association is working to stop the management's illegal actions.** Choice (D) best summarizes the purpose of the letter, so it is correct. Choice (A) is one of the ways the association is fighting management but is only a detail that supports the main idea. Choice (B) is partially true — the apartments are being renovated into luxury apartments. The letter does not say they are unsafe. Choice (C) is only a detail about the association.

21. **B. to add urgency to her message.** Information about the problems former tenants experience will encourage current tenants to take the matter seriously, so Choice (B) is correct. Choice (A) is not consistent with the purpose of the letter. The letter is directed to tenants, not management, so Choices (C) and (D) are incorrect.

22. **C. the right to petition for redress of grievances.** The association is a group of neighbors advocating for their rights, so the answer is Choice (C). Therefore, the other choices are incorrect.

23. **A. freedom of speech and press.** By publishing newsletters and a website, the association is exercising its rights to free speech and press, so Choice (A) is correct. Therefore, the other choices are incorrect.

24. **A. Set up a picket line on the sidewalk in front of the building.** Choice (A) is another kind of protected free speech. (The picketers do, however, need to stay on public sidewalks and not walk on the association's property.) The other choices are not examples of protected free speech.

25. **A. The management already converted two other affordable buildings to luxury apartments.** Choice (A) offers further evidence to expose management's plans, and so would strengthen the argument. Choice (B) might encourage wealthy tenants to move to the building but doesn't strengthen the letter's argument. Choices (C) and (D) are not relevant to the letter, so these ideas should not be included.

26. **A. It will become easier for differently abled people to find federal jobs.** Choice (A) is correct because the order increases accessibility for differently abled people. Choice (B) is incorrect because the order only applies to the federal government. Choice (C) is contradicted by the information. The order should increase opportunities for the linguistically diverse, so Choice (D) is incorrect.

27. **C. continuity of government.** Choice (C) is correct because having a defined line of presidential succession is part of planning for continuity of government in case of an emergency. The other principles do not make sense.

28. **C. a peaceful transition of power.** The photo shows the first meeting between the two candidates after the election, which makes this meeting part of a peaceful transition of power. Election debates (Choice A) take place before the election, not after. The inauguration ceremony (Choice B) takes place in January. The victory celebration (Choice D) happens election night or soon after, and the winning candidate attends their own celebration.

29. **C. checks.** The system in which each branch has powers to counter, or "check," the power of others is called the system of checks and balances.

30. **C. Congress can override a veto.** Choice (C) is correct because Congress can override a president's veto with a two-thirds majority. Choice (A) is a power of Congress. Choices (B) and (D) are checks on the power of Congress.

31. **B. The House Oversight Committee, which reviews presidential actions.** The House Oversight Committee (Choice B) is the only choice that scrutinizes the president and so is correct. Choices (A) and (C) are leaders of the House. Their primary roles are to lead this co-equal branch but are not checks themselves. Choice (D) provides oversight of members of the House.

TIP

Don't be deceived by Choices B (House Oversight Committee) and D (House Ethics Committee)! When two choices are very similar, one can be right or both will be wrong. You can easily eliminate Choice D, since the House Ethics Committee does not scrutinize another branch of government. Choices A (Speaker of the House) and C (House Minority Leader) are also very similar. Both are leaders of one part of the legislative branch of government. Since you already know Choice B scrutinizes another branch of government, you can easily eliminate Choices A and C, too.

32. **C. to prevent one part of government from becoming too powerful.** Choice (C) is correct because the system limits each branch's powers. Choice (A) is only partially correct, so it cannot be the answer. Choice (A) is a good example of why it's helpful to read all the answer choices before you select an answer; this can help you to avoid quickly selecting a choice that is only partially correct. Choices (B) and (D) are not relevant to the separation of powers.

REMEMBER

Partially true answer choices are never correct! Always read all the answer choices to avoid selecting a partially true choice too hastily.

33. **D. They are both limitations on the power of the federal government.** Choice (D) is correct because they define and limit the powers of the government. Choice (A) is incorrect because both of them are in the Constitution. Choice (B) is incorrect because freedom of religion is only in the Bill of Rights. Choice (C) is contradicted by the information

34. **B. federalism.** The cartoon shows tension between the colonies acting together and keeping their freedom and autonomy. This is the same issue addressed by federalism, which clearly defines state and federal powers. Therefore, Choice (B) is correct. The remaining choices are not relevant to the cartoon.

35. **B. We must, indeed, all hang together *or*, most assuredly, we shall all hang separately.** Choice (B), attributed to Benjamin Franklin, echoes the same sentiment as the cartoon — encouraging European people of North America to band together against a common enemy. Therefore, the other choices are incorrect.

36. **C. 10.** The longest period in the stated range without an increase was between 1997 and 2007, or 10 years (Choice C). Therefore, Choice (A) is incorrect. Choice (B) covers the second-longest period, 1981–1990, or 9 years. Choice (D) covers the period from 2009–2021 but is not in the range specified (1981–2008) in the question. This is a good illustration of why it's important to read and understand the question.

37. **C. 2008.** The biggest increase was $0.80, which happened in 2008 (Choice C). The increase in 1997 was $0.40 (Choice A). The increase in 2007 was $0.70 (Choice B). The increase in 2009 was $0.60 (Choice D). As of the writing of this test, the minimum wage has not gone up.

REMEMBER

Keep in mind that you can use the on-screen calculator or your own TI-30XS calculator (only when testing at a test center) for questions such as this one.

38. **C. $7.25.** According to the information, workers are entitled to at least the federal minimum wage, so Choice (C) is correct. Therefore, the other choices are incorrect. Choice (A) is the difference between the two wages. Choice (B) is the state minimum wage. Choice (D) is the minimum wage in some jurisdictions, and a proposed new federal minimum wage. Let's hope everyone gets this raise!

Charts, graphs, and tables come up on three of the four GED tests: Science, Social Studies, and Math. If questions 36 to 38 are hard for you, review the information on charts, tables, and graphs in Chapter 10.

TIP

39. **B. They were based on mortgages issued to people with poor credit.** Choice (B) is stated directly in the passage. The remaining choices by themselves are not enough to cause a problem.

40. **D. declining sales.** Companies would likely see sales decline during a recession, so Choice (D) is correct. The remaining choices are effects on consumers.

41. **B. an online ad provider that controls most Internet advertising.** Choice (B) is the only choice that meets the definition of a monopoly — a company controlling an excessive part of a market or product. Choice (A) is incorrect because it is a utility and so is exempt from the laws against monopolies. Choice (C) is incorrect because even though that network is top-rated, there are many other networks available over the air and on cable. Choice (D) is incorrect because the laws don't apply to the toll road as it's not owned by a private company but by the public.

42. **B. a free market.** The information states that the law of supply and demand explains the operation of prices in free markets. Therefore, Choice (B) is correct. Choices (A) and (C) are conditions that determine how the law of supply and demand works. The law will work in any kind of economy as long as it is a free market, so Choice (D) is incorrect.

43. **B. warning about the expansion of Communism.** Choice (B) is correct because Churchill repeatedly names places where Communist influence is expanding. While the war had recently ended, the tone is not celebratory, so Choice (A) is incorrect. Churchill mentions Greece only as a minor exception to what is happening to democracy in the rest of Europe, so Choice (C) is incorrect. Choice (D) is incorrect because Churchill was already a former prime minister when he gave the speech.

44. **A. Churchill respects Stalin as an ally but fears his present intentions.** It's clear from the information that though Churchill acknowledges Stalin as an ally, he distrusts Stalin's current actions in Europe, so Choice (A) is correct. For this reason, Choices (C) and (D) are incorrect. Choice (B) is contradicted by the information.

45. **B. Poland.** According to Churchill, of these countries, only Poland (Choice B) has fallen to Communist control so far (though Czechoslovakia will later fall under Soviet domination). Therefore, the other choices are incorrect.

46. **B. Europe has been divided into one area with democratic governments and another under Communist dictatorships.** It's clear that Churchill believes that the new Communist governments are dictatorships, so Choice (B) is correct. Choice (A) confuses the literal with the figurative meaning of the phrase and so is incorrect. Choice (C) is incorrect because the countries remain intact, just their governments have changed. Choice (D) is contradicted by the information.

With long passages like this one, it may help to read the questions before you read the passage, in order to save time. Also remember to use the scroll bar or tabs to view the entire text. The answer you're looking for may be on the next screen!

TIP

47. **D. Africa.** Of the top countries for refugees mentioned in the information, seven are in Africa. Therefore, Choice (D) is correct, and the other choices are incorrect.

48. **A. The number of refugees worldwide has grown to an all-time high.** Choice (A) is directly stated in the passage and so is correct. Choice (B) is contradicted by the information; most refugees are fleeing violence or war. Choice (C) is also contradicted by the information; most refugees live in difficult circumstances. Choice (D) is incorrect because refugees flee to another country and internally displaced people flee within their own countries.

49. **A. It provides an underpinning for Western democracy today.** Choice (A) is correct because Western democracy traces its origins to Athens. Choice (B) is incorrect because Athens was a direct democracy. Choices (C) and (D) are contradicted by the information.

50. **B. Mineral wealth gives this country strategic and economic importance.** Choice (B) is correct because all of these resources are important to the global economy. The other choices are not supported by the information.

Answer Key

1.	B	18.	1B, 2A	35.	B
2.	C	19.	1B, 2B	36.	C
3.	B	20.	D	37.	C
4.	D	21.	B	38.	C
5.	C	22.	C	39.	B
6.	D	23.	A	40.	D
7.	D	24.	A	41.	B
8.	C	25.	A	42.	B
9.	C	26.	A	43.	B
10.	A	27.	C	44.	A
11.	B	28.	C	45.	B
12.	B	29.	C	46.	B
13.	B	30.	C	47.	D
14.	A	31.	B	48.	A
15.	B	32.	C	49.	A
16.	D	33.	D	50.	B
17.	D	34.	B		

Chapter **23**

Practice Test 1: Science

The Science test consists of multiple-choice, fill-in-the-blank, drop-down, and drag-and-drop questions intended to measure your understanding of general concepts in science. The questions are based on short passages that may include a graph, chart, or figure. Study the information given and then answer the question(s). Refer to the passage as often as necessary when answering the questions, but remember that you have a time limit, and you should try to spend as little time on any item as you can and still get the correct answer.

You have 90 minutes to complete this section of the GED test. The answers and explanations to this test's questions are in Chapter 24. Go through the explanations to all the questions, even for the ones you answered correctly. The explanations are a good review of the techniques I discuss throughout the book.

Remember, you are allowed to use a calculator on the GED Science test. For this test it's OK to use the calculator on your phone, but at some point, you'll want to get used to the TI-30XS MultiView calculator that is used on the test.

REMEMBER

On the real GED, you'll take the test on a computer. Instead of marking your answers on an answer sheet, like you do for the practice tests in this book, you'll use the keyboard and the mouse to indicate your answers. I formatted the questions and answer choices in this book to make them appear as similar as possible to what you'll see on the computer screen, but I had to retain some A, B, C, and D choices and provide an answer sheet for marking your answers. When you're ready for the included online practice test, you'll be able to see and try the actual question types as they appear on the test.

Use the timer on your phone to keep track of time. If you run out of time, mark the last question you answered. Then answer the rest of the questions. This will help you figure out how much more quickly you will have to work to complete the entire test in the time allowed.

Answer Sheet for Practice Test 1, Science

1. _____

2. _____

3. _____

4. _____

5. _____

6. _____

7. _____

8. _____

9. _____

10. _____

11. _____

12. _____

13. _____

14. _____

15. _____

16. _____

17. _____

18. _____

19. _____

20. _____

21. _____

22. _____

23. _____

24. _____

25. _____

26. _____

27. _____

28. _____

29. _____

30. _____

31. _____

32. _____

33. _____

34. _____

35. _____

36. _____

37. _____

38. _____

39. _____

40. _____

41. _____

42. _____

43. _____

44. _____

45. _____

46. _____

47. _____

48. _____

49. _____

50. _____

Science Test

TIME: 90 minutes

QUESTIONS: 50

DIRECTIONS: Read each question carefully and mark your answer on the answer sheet provided.

1. Pollination occurs when pollen grains move from the male part of a flower to the female part of another flower of the same species. Pollination is necessary for plants to reproduce and to produce fruit or seeds. Some plants self-pollinate, or the pollen moves through the air. Others require pollination by another organism that transfers the pollen. Bees are the most widely known pollinators. Many food crops are dependent on pollination by bees or other pollinators.

   Which of the following would be the most likely result of the bee population suddenly collapsing?

   (A) More plants would self-pollinate.

   (B) More plants would use air to pollinate.

   (C) Food production would drop.

   (D) Honey prices would go down.

   Questions 2–4 refer to the following information.

   Two parents have the following genotypes for eye color.

   The parent with the Bb genotype has brown eyes. The parent with the bb genotype has blue eyes.

   A Punnett square for eye color

2. Which allele is dominant for eye color?

   (A) green

   (B) brown

   (C) blue

   (D) hazel

3. What are the odds that the parents will have a child with brown eyes?

   (A) 1:4

   (B) 2:4

   (C) 3:4

   (D) 4:4

4. Approximately 89 percent of people from a certain Baltic country have blue eyes. Which of the following statements best explains this data?

(A) The allele for blue eyes is dominant there.

(B) The allele for hazel eyes is uncommon in that country.

(C) Cold weather in Baltic countries influences eye color.

(D) The allele for blue eyes is very common there.

Questions 5–7 refer to the following table.

This table describes the reproduction of reptiles:

Reptile Reproduction

Type of Reproduction	Explanation	Example
Oviparous	Reproduce by laying eggs.	Snakes and lizards (leathery shells) Crocodiles (hard shells)
Ovoviviparous	Give birth to live young that hatch from eggs inside the mother. Offspring get most of their sustenance from the egg.	Rattlesnakes and boa constrictors
Viviparous	Give birth to live young.	Skinks (a type of lizard)

5. Which of the following reptiles lays eggs with hard shells?

(A) skinks

(B) crocodiles

(C) rattlesnakes

(D) grass snakes

6. Which of these animals is oviparous?

(A) chickens

(B) cats

(C) bats

(D) boa constructors

7. Females of certain species of rattlesnake have been observed to stay with their young in nests. These same poisonous reptiles also take turns guarding and defending their young. In Australia, scientists have observed egg-laying snakes caring for their young, too.

Which of these statements can be concluded from this information?

(A) Reptiles are not true social animals.

(B) Only ovoviviparous snakes care for their young.

(C) Viviparous reptiles have parental instincts.

(D) If you see a very young rattlesnake, a mature snake may be nearby.

8. The piping plover is a small shorebird that nests on beaches. This species is found primarily in wetlands in the Dakotas, the Great Lakes, and the Atlantic shore. In winter they migrate to the Gulf Coast but have also been seen further south. Scientists estimate that their population is 7,800 to 8,400 individuals. They are considered endangered in the Great Lakes region and threatened in the Atlantic shore region.

   Which of the following would help conserve the piping plover population?

   (A) Decrease the number of wetlands in the Dakotas.

   (B) Protect other animals living in the nesting habitats.

   (C) Hold a plover information day at the nesting sites.

   (D) Prevent people from going into piping plovers' nesting habitats.

   Questions 9 and 10 refer to the following information.

   Protozoa are single-cell organisms that are capable of movement. Two ways that they move are by using cilia and flagella. *Cilia* are short protrusions on the outside of the cell. The cilia beat together to move. A *flagella* is a single, tail-like protrusion that beats to move.

9. Write *cilia* or *flagella* to describe the illustration:

10. Write *cilia* or *flagella* to describe the illustration:

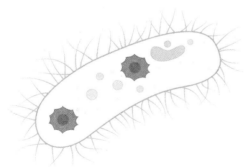

11. The lack of vitamin C can cause a disease called scurvy. Symptoms include tiredness, bone pain, skin problems, gum disease, and emotional changes. Scurvy was common on ships where sailors had little access to fresh food. Finally, in 1795, the British Navy realized that drinking lemon juice prevented scurvy. However, it was not until the 1930s that scientists discovered that a chemical, ascorbic acid, was the nutrient that prevented scurvy.

    Which of the following can be concluded from this information?

    (A) Correlation does not show cause.

    (B) Vitamin C is harmful because it's an acid.

    (C) Vitamin C is helpful so people should take doses many times the official RDA (recommended daily allowance).

    (D) The cause of scurvy is still unknown.

12. While weight loss is a billion-dollar industry, the way for healthy individuals to lose weight is no secret: using more calories than they consume.

Which is the most cost-effective way to use more calories?

(A) Buy a gym membership.

(B) Walk, run, and bike more.

(C) Order diet meals offered on TV.

(D) Eat candy as a reward for exercising.

13. Systems of the human body have specialized functions. These systems work together to accomplish specific tasks. For example, the skeletal system and the muscular system work together to move the body.

Which of these systems works with the respiratory system?

(A) the skeletal system

(B) the digestive system

(C) the circulatory system

(D) the immune system

14. HIV affects which of these body systems?

(A) the immune system

(B) the endocrine system

(C) the circulatory system

(D) the skeletal system

Questions 15 and 16 refer to the following information.

A parasite is an organism that takes nutrition from another organism, a host, while giving back nothing in return. A parasite can cause great harm to its host.

15. Which of these is a parasite?

(A) A lion's mane mushroom, which grows on tree stumps taking nutrients from the stumps.

(B) A truffle, which grows in the roots of a tree, taking sugar and giving nutrients to the tree.

(C) Wheat rust, a fungus that takes its nutrition from wheat plants and kills them.

(D) A chestnut tree, which is dying from chestnut blight fungus.

16. The fungus *Septobasidium* forms an unusual relationship with certain insects that feed on the bark of trees. When the fungus settles on an insect, the insect attaches itself permanently to the tree and begins drinking sap. The fungus then extracts nutrients from the insect without killing it.

Which of the following is or are parasites?

(A) the fungus

(B) the insect

(C) the fungus and the tree

(D) the fungus and the insect

Questions 17–19 refer to the following passage and illustration.

Students in a life science class are studying the effects of fertilizer. They plant two bean plants in flowerpots. They add a well-known garden fertilizer to one of the flowerpots. They give the plants the same amount of water and sunlight each day. They measure the plants each week and graph the results.

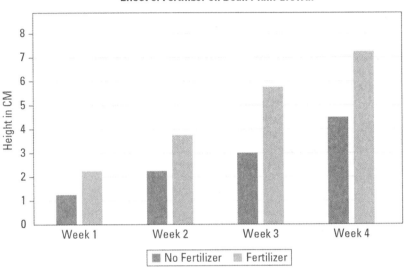

Effect of Fertilizer on Bean Plant Growth

17. Which statement can be concluded from the data in the table?

    (A) Fertilizer has a positive effect on plant growth.

    (B) Fertilizer will not work without water and sunlight.

    (C) Fertilizer has no effect on plant growth.

    (D) Fertilizer has a negative effect on plant growth.

18. What are the dependent and independent variables in this experiment?

    (A) independent — fertilizer, water, sunlight; dependent — plant height

    (B) independent — plant height; dependent — fertilizer

    (C) independent — fertilizer; dependent — water and sunlight

    (D) independent — fertilizer; dependent — plant height

19. Imagine that after measuring the plants in Week 4, one of the students notices that the plant without fertilizer doesn't receive full sunlight in the afternoon after school lets out. In the late afternoon, a shadow from a tree outside falls on only that plant. The class is going to repeat the experiment. What should the students do differently?

    (A) Rotate the flowerpots 180 degrees every day.

    (B) Increase the amount of water given to the plant without fertilizer.

    (C) Place both plants in places where light will not be blocked and switch the plants' positions once daily.

    (D) Place the plants in a window that is covered by a translucent shade to avoid drying out the plants from excessive sunlight.

20. A certain species of North American insect, the cicada, spend most of its life cycle as nymphs in small underground chambers. They only emerge once every 13 or 17 years. When cicadas emerge, their high-pitched sound announces their short return to the surface.

What advantage does this life cycle give cicadas?

(A) They can avoid predators.

(B) Their underground chambers aerate the soil.

(C) Their high-pitched sound can attract predators.

(D) They can live with their mates in the underground chambers.

21. Milk sickness was the cause of numerous deaths among settlers in the American Midwest. People became sick and died after drinking milk, but no one knew the cause. Anna Pierce Hobbs Bigsby, a respected local medical expert, believed a poisonous plant was responsible because the sickness never happened in winter months. Finally, an elderly Shawnee woman told her that the cause was a certain plant, white snakeroot. When cows ate that plant, the poison would enter their milk. Bigsby tested this hypothesis with a calf and found a correlation between cows consuming the plant and animals dying from drinking their milk. She tried to share her findings with people but her warnings were not taken seriously.

Which of these is the most likely reason people did not take Bigsby's warning seriously?

(A) At the time, people did not believe that certain plants were poisonous.

(B) Bigsby did not use good research methods.

(C) At the time, most of the medical community was not willing to pay attention to a woman.

(D) People disliked Bigsby.

Questions 22–24 refer to the following passage and image.

Water has some unusual properties. For example, as a solid, ice, it floats in liquid water. With most other substances, solid matter will sink when it is placed in liquid matter.

22. Which of the following is the most logical explanation of this characteristic of ice?

   (A) Ice is denser than liquid water.
   (B) Liquid water is denser than ice.
   (C) Water and ice have the same density.
   (D) Ice floats because it's lighter than air.

23. Which statement is also related to this property of water?

   (A) Lakes and ponds freeze from top to bottom.
   (B) Lakes and ponds freeze from bottom to top.
   (C) Freezing rain can coat sidewalks with ice.
   (D) Freezing fog can cause frost to form on bushes and trees.

24. The mass of 4 cubic centimeters of distilled water is 4 grams.

   What is the density of distilled water?

   (A) $1g/cm^3$
   (B) $2g/cm^3$
   (C) $4g/cm^3$
   (D) $16g/cm^3$

Questions 25–28 refer to the following text and graph.

The amount of a substance that can dissolve in a liquid changes according to the temperature of the liquid. The graph shows the solubility curves for four substances.

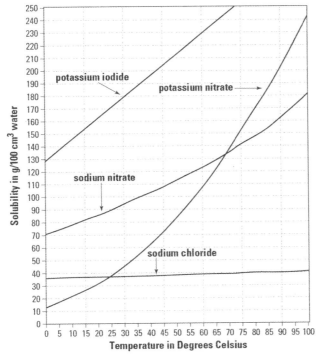

Solubility Curves

25. Which of the following can be inferred from the information in the graph?

(A) The solubility of all four substances goes up as temperature increases.

(B) The solubility of the four substances increases at the same rate.

(C) Temperature does not affect solubility.

(D) After 100° C, solubility will continue to increase.

26. At what temperature is the solubility of potassium nitrate and sodium nitrate the same?

(A) 25° C

(B) 45° C

(C) 70° C

(D) 75° C

27. Which substance's solubility increases the least as the temperature rises?

(A) potassium iodide

(B) sodium nitrate

(C) potassium nitrate

(D) sodium chloride

28. How much sodium chloride is dissolved at 60° C?

(A) 40 g

(B) 110 g

(C) 125 g

(D) 230 g

Questions 29–31 refer to the following passage.

The element carbon is the common element of all known life forms. It's very abundant in the universe — fourth, after hydrogen, helium, and oxygen. About 18.5 percent of the human body is carbon. Carbon atoms usually appear in a number of *allotropes,* which are arrangements of the atoms. Three allotropes found in nature are amorphous carbon (found in charcoal and soot), graphite, and diamonds. Each allotrope has different physical traits. In graphite, carbon atoms are arranged in two-dimensional sheets in hexagonal rings. In diamonds, carbon atoms are arranged in three-dimensional rings. In amorphous carbon, atoms are not in a particular arrangement. Diamonds and graphite have very different physical characteristics. For example, diamonds are one of the hardest substances in existence, and graphite is very soft and slippery. In fact, graphite makes a good lubricant; it is very useful in lubricating locks instead of oil. Graphite can also conduct electricity, whereas diamonds are a poor conductor. And diamonds are clear, whereas graphite is black. The clarity and crystalline structure of diamonds makes them useful in jewelry. That's why diamonds can be cut into shapes that sparkle with reflected light. Other allotropes, such as fullerines, have been created in labs. Each fullerine has a unique arrangement of carbon atoms.

29. Which allotrope of carbon is shown in the illustration?

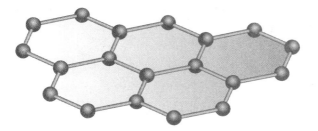

(A) diamond
(B) graphite
(C) fullerine
(D) amorphous carbon

30. According to information in the passage, which allotrope of carbon would be most useful in a cutting tool?

(A) diamond
(B) graphite
(C) fullerine
(D) amorphous carbon

31. Which characteristic of diamonds lets them be cut into shapes that sparkle?

(A) crystalline structure
(B) softness
(C) opaqueness
(D) slipperiness

32. Newton's first law says that an object at rest will stay at rest and an object in motion will stay in motion unless acted upon by another force.

Which of the following is an example of an object being acted on by another force?

(A) A baseball batter swings at a pitch and misses.
(B) A child rolls a bowling ball and it comes to a stop partway down the alley.
(C) An antiques dealer stores a valuable antique vase in a locked display cabinet.
(D) A meteor in space continues traveling in the same direction for millions of miles.

33. A simple machine changes the direction and/or strength of a force. Simple machines include a lever, a wheel and axle, a pulley, an inclined plane, a wedge, and a screw.

A hotel guest rolls a wheeled suitcase up a ramp into the hotel. Which simple machine are they using in addition to a wheel and axle?

(A) inclined plane
(B) wedge
(C) pulley
(D) lever

34. The pH scale measures how acidic or basic a substance is. The scale ranges from 0 to 14. A pH of 7 is neutral. A pH value higher than 7 is basic, and a pH lower than 7 is acidic. The pH scale is logarithmic. A substance with a pH of 5 is ten times more acidic than a substance with a pH of 6. Here are the pH values of some common substances:

- Bleach 12.5
- Ammonia 11
- Distilled water 7
- Milk 6.5
- Black coffee 5
- Vinegar 2.5

Which of the following is more acidic than black coffee?

(A) vinegar

(B) milk

(C) ammonia

(D) bleach

35. Ultraviolet (UV) light is a kind of non-visible light that has both beneficial and harmful effects for humans. About 10 percent of the Sun's electromagnetic output is UV. Most of the Sun's output, including UV, is absorbed or reflected back into space before it reaches Earth's surface. Only a small amount of UV reaches Earth's surface. UV is needed for the formation of vitamin D, a necessary nutrient, in humans and other vertebrates. However, excessive exposure to UV can lead to sunburn. While an occasional sunburn is simply a painful experience, repeated sunburns, especially for people with light skin, can lead to skin cancer later in life.

Which of these ideas supports the main idea of the information?

(A) Sunlight also contains infrared radiation.

(B) Without vitamin D, land vertebrates cannot absorb calcium needed for bone health.

(C) Visible light breaks down into colors from red to violet — the colors of the rainbow.

(D) If all the energy directed from the Sun to Earth reached the planet's surface, life on Earth would be impossible.

36. Mass is the measure of the amount of matter of an object. Weight is the measure of the pull of gravity on that object.

What happens to the weight and mass of a space probe when it leaves Earth and lands on the Moon? (Weight on the Moon is 16.5 percent of weight on Earth.)

(A) The weight is more, and the mass is less.

(B) The mass is more, and the weight is less.

(C) The weight is less, and the mass is the same.

(D) The mass and the weight remain constant.

Questions 37 and 38 refer to the following information and table.

Speed is the rate at which an object moves. A statistician gathered the top 5 average speeds in the Indianapolis 500 from recent years.

Top Average Speeds at the Indianapolis 500

Year	Average Speed (mph)
2021	190.69
2013	187.43
2014	186.56
1990	185.98
1991	176.46

37. What was the average speed for the 5 years in the table?

    (A) 185.42

    (B) 185.98

    (C) 186.56

    (D) 927.12

38. What was the median speed for those 5 years?

    (A) 185.42

    (B) 186.56

    (C) 187.43

    (D) 190.69

39. Heat is a form of energy. Heat can be transferred from object to object. Imagine you have been outdoors on a cold winter morning without gloves. Back inside, you get a cup of hot cocoa and wrap your fingers around it until they stop feeling cold.

    Which of the following can be inferred from this information?

    (A) Heat can be transferred, but not cold.

    (B) Heat and cold can be transferred.

    (C) Heat and cold counteract each other.

    (D) Blood circulation, not the cocoa, warmed the fingers.

40. Peter has recently moved to a new apartment on the fifth floor of a building. One night, he realizes that he can hear the music from the nightclub on the first floor perfectly in his bedroom. His bedroom is in the back of the apartment, and the nightclub is in the front of the building. He does not hear the music in any other part of his apartment, in the elevator, or on the stairs.

    Which of these statements explains why Peter can hear the music in his apartment?

    (A) Sound waves are traveling through the air into his apartment through the window.

    (B) Sound waves can travel through water.

    (C) Sound waves are traveling through the stairway to his apartment.

    (D) Sound waves can travel through solid materials.

41. Oceans absorb carbon dioxide in the air. As the amount of carbon dioxide in the atmosphere has increased, the amount of this gas dissolved in ocean waters has increased, too. In the ocean, carbon dioxide reacts to form carbonic acid.

What is a logical effect of this situation?

(A) The acidity of seawater will decline.

(B) The acidity of seawater will increase.

(C) The amount of carbon dioxide in the atmosphere will increase.

(D) The acidity of seawater will remain constant.

Questions 42 and 43 refer to the following passage and images.

The Kertid Crater is an enormous volcanic crater and lake in southern Iceland. Located in a region of frequent volcanic activity, the crater is about 3,000 years old. At first, scientists believed that, like two other craters in the region, a large volcanic explosion created this crater. However, geological evidence showed no evidence of an explosion. Scientists now believe that the crater formed after the eruption of the volcano. They believe that after the eruption, the cone of the volcano collapsed into the empty magma chamber.

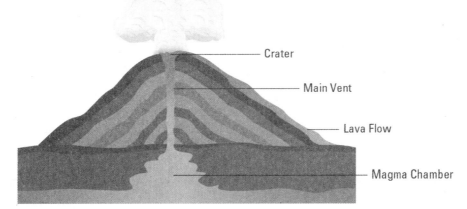

Main Parts of a Volcano

Source: Scoundrelgeo/Wikimedia Commons/CC BY-SA 4.0.

42. What was the scientists' first explanation of how the crater formed?

   (A) The volcano emptied in an eruption and then collapsed into the chamber below.

   (B) The volcano exploded and then collapsed into the crater.

   (C) A large volcanic explosion created the crater.

   (D) The eruption triggered an explosion that formed the crater.

43. Why did the scientists change their theory about the crater?

   (A) They couldn't find any evidence of an explosion.

   (B) Volcanoes only form craters when they explode.

   (C) Other craters nearby were formed by explosions.

   (D) Scientists concluded that explosions do not create craters.

Questions 44 and 45 reference the following passage and images.

The New Horizons probe is an interplanetary space probe designed to fly by and study the planet Jupiter, the dwarf planet Pluto, one of Pluto's moons, and other nearby bodies. When NASA launched it on January 19, 2006, it was the fastest object ever launched from Earth into space. At the time of the launch, Pluto, a much-beloved space object, was still considered a planet. It was downgraded to a dwarf planet later in 2006, but astronomers continue to disagree on this designation. The change in status apparently did not dissuade the probe from completing its mission. The trip to Pluto, the first of its kind, took about 9 years, and scientists were able to gather data about Pluto, its moon Charon, and other large objects in the vicinity. Apparently, this data did not help settle the controversy, as scientists continue to disagree about Pluto's status. The probe did provide important data about Pluto's atmosphere and allowed scientists to measure its size more accurately than ever before. After the Pluto flyby, the probe continued traveling, and is now heading toward the Sagittarius constellation. In 2021, it was still fully operational and was continuing to send back data about the outer reaches of the solar system. The probe is expected to continue traveling and leave the solar system.

Source: NASA

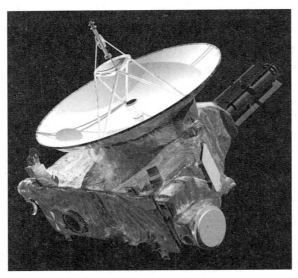

Source: NASA

44. Why is the New Horizons probe important?
   (A) With this probe, astronomers could study Pluto up close for the first time.
   (B) It provided data that proved Pluto was a planet.
   (C) It was the first probe to study Jupiter.
   (D) Its purpose was to restore Pluto's designation as a planet.

45. Which choice best describes the article's tone with regard to the decision to reclassify Pluto?
   (A) angry and upset
   (B) amused and disappointed
   (C) unemotional and matter-of-fact
   (D) scientific and technical

Questions 46–48 refer to the following passage.

The five Great Lakes — Lake Superior, Lake Huron, Lake Michigan, Lake Ontario, and Lake Erie — comprise one of the world's largest freshwater systems. According to U.S. government statistics, they contain 84 percent of North America's surface fresh water, and 12 percent of the world's fresh water. Millions of people depend on water from these lakes. In addition to consuming the water, people use this water for power generation and transportation. The levels of the lakes are carefully monitored by government bodies in the United States and Canada. Lake levels were unusually high in several recent years. In August 2020, Lake Michigan was 33 inches above its average long-term level. While that may not seem like much, water levels that high can cause damage to buildings, docks, harbors, beaches, and roads. By 2021, water levels had dropped, but were still 22 inches above average. The level dropped more in 2022 but was expected to rise again. While an abundant supply of fresh water is good, too much water is harmful, too. Scientists attribute the increase to climate change and warn that cities such as Milwaukee and Chicago will suffer long-term consequences if lake levels continue to rise.

46. What is the main idea of the passage?

    (A) Millions of people depend on the Great Lakes.

    (B) High water levels are causing problems in a valuable source of fresh water.

    (C) Rising lake levels ensure plenty of water for everyone.

    (D) In 2021, the level of Lake Michigan was at a record height.

47. Which of the following facts would strengthen the author's argument?

    (A) Marine life continues to flourish in the lakes.

    (B) Just a few years ago, Lake Michigan's level was at an historic low, and cities had to dredge harbors so ships could unload.

    (C) The high lake level has caused flooding because run-off from heavy storms has no place to go.

    (D) The high lake level ensures abundant supplies of water for millions of people who depend on it.

48. Which of the following can be concluded from the passage?

    (A) Governments need to take steps to manage high water levels in Lake Michigan.

    (B) Water levels will continue to drop from their high in 2020.

    (C) High water levels are a bigger concern than low water levels.

    (D) People who live along Lake Michigan do not need to worry about water security.

49. A scientist is studying the behavior of a large colony of bats that lives in an enormous cavern in Borneo. Scientific research has already determined that bats will not fly if the weather is rainy. The scientist wants to figure out if more bats will fly on dry nights after rainy weather than on dry nights following other dry nights. They plan on filming the bats each evening as they exit the cave to estimate the number of bats flying each night. They also believe that air temperature may affect how many bats fly, so they log the air temperature each day at the time the bats usually exit the cavern.

    How many independent variables does this experiment have? Write the number. [   ]

50. The gulf stream is a warm current in the Atlantic Ocean. It begins in the Gulf of Mexico and follows the eastern coast of the United States. It then heads toward Europe.

    Which of the following is a likely effect of the gulf stream?

    (A) It cools the east coast of the United States.

    (B) It helps ships sail more quickly from Europe to the United States.

    (C) It warms areas of Europe and the oceans nearby.

    (D) It helps planes to fly more quickly from the United States to Europe.

Chapter **24**

Answers for Practice Test 1, Science

n this chapter, I provide the answers and explanations to every question in the Science practice test in Chapter 23. If you just want a quick look at the answers, check out the abbreviated answer key at the end of this chapter. However, if you have the time, it's more useful for study purposes to read all the answer explanations carefully. Doing so will help you understand why some answers were correct and others not, especially when the choices were really close. It will also point you to areas where you may need to do more review. Remember, you learn as much from your errors as from the correct answers.

Go through the explanations to all the questions, even for the ones you answered correctly. The explanations offer a good review of the techniques I discuss throughout the book.

Answers and Explanations

1. **C. Food production would drop.** The result of a collapse of the bee population would be a drastic drop in food production (Choice C), because so many plants are dependent on pollination by bees. Choices (A) and (B) are contradicted by the information. Plants are dependent on pollinators to reproduce or produce fruit. Choice (D) does not make sense. Honey prices would go up and/or honey would entirely disappear as supplies were used up.

   TIP

   This question tests your understanding of cause-effect relationships. Cause-effect relationships appear frequently on the Science test as well as Social Studies and Language Arts. Understanding cause-effect relationships can help you raise your scores on all three tests!

2. **B. brown.** According to the information, the parent with brown eyes has one copy of a blue allele and one copy of a brown allele. Therefore, brown (Choice B) is dominant.

3. **B. 2:4.** The Punnett square shows that 2 of the 4 possible genotypes for children from these parents have at least one copy of the allele for brown eyes. Therefore, Choice (B) is correct.

4. **D. The allele for blue eyes is very common there.** Choice (D) is correct because for this regressive trait to be so common, many people would have to have this allele. Therefore, Choice (A) is incorrect. Choice (B) is not relevant. Choice (C) does not make sense.

5. **B. crocodiles.** Choice (B) is stated directly in the table. Skinks (Choice A) and rattlesnakes (Choice C) do not lay eggs. Grass snake eggs (Choice D), like other snakes' eggs, are leathery.

6. **A. chickens.** Chickens (Choice A) lay eggs, so are oviparous. Cats (Choice B) give birth to live young. Do not be confused by Choice (C), bats. Although bats fly, they are mammals and give birth to live young. Choice (D) is incorrect because boas are ovoviviparous and give birth to live young from eggs.

7. **D. If you see a very young rattlesnake, a mature snake may be nearby.** Choice (D) can be inferred from the information. Because female rattlesnakes care for their young, it's possible that a mature snake may be near a juvenile. Choice (A) cannot be concluded from the information. In fact, scientists are becoming more aware of social behavior among reptiles. Choice (B) is contradicted by the information. The Australian snake species is oviparous, so this choice cannot be true. Choice (C) cannot be concluded from the information, which is about ovoviviparous and oviparous snakes.

8. **D. Prevent people from going into piping plovers' nesting habitats.** Choice (D) is correct because this measure will ensure that nesting birds are not disturbed. Choice (A) will further reduce the population by reducing nesting sites. Choice (B) will result in an increase in predators, which will cause more reductions in the population. Choice (C) will likely increase traffic in nesting habitats and disturb the birds. Communities, however, do host information events away from the nesting sites, so people know to avoid the nesting areas. In 2019, a music festival in Chicago was cancelled because it was too near the nesting site of the first pair of piping plovers seen in Chicago for generations. Those birds got the rock star treatment!

9. **Flagella.** The long, tail-like structure is a flagella.

10. **Cilia.** The multiple, short protrusions are cilia.

11. **A. Correlation does not show cause.** Choice (A) is correct because starting in 1795, the navy officials knew that consuming lemon juice prevented scurvy, but scientists did not know the cause was a lack of ascorbic acid until the 1930s. Choices (B) and (D) are contradicted by the

information. Choice (C) cannot be concluded from the information, and most experts agree that taking such high doses is not necessary or advisable.

12. **B. Walk, run, and bike more.** Choice (B) will increase the calories you burn at little or no cost, so is a good way for healthy individuals to lose weight. Choice (A) may result in weight loss but is more expensive than Choice (B). In addition, buying a gym membership is no guarantee that people will use it. Choice (C) may reduce the calories people consume, but the question is about calories people use. Choice (D) may increase exercise, but the calories in the reward will counteract the calories burned while exercising.

13. **C. the circulatory system.** The respiratory system and the circulatory (Choice C) system work together to bring oxygen to the body and remove carbon dioxide.

14. **A. the immune system.** HIV affects the ability to defend itself against disease. Therefore, Choice (A) is correct.

15. **C. Wheat rust, a fungus that takes its nutrition from wheat plants and kills them.** Only Choice (C) describes a parasite. The rust takes nutrition from the plant but gives back nothing in return. The lion's mane mushroom (Choice A) is growing on a dead tree stump so is not a parasite. A truffle (Choice B) is not a parasite because it also contributes to the tree. In Choice (D), the chestnut tree is the host; the parasite is the fungus.

16. **D. the fungus and the insect.** Choice (D) is correct because the insect gets its nutrition from the tree, and the fungus gets its nutrition from the insect. If you selected Choices (A) or (B), keep in mind that these answers are only partially correct. This is a good illustration of why you should always read all the answer choices. Choice (C) is incorrect because the tree is the host.

17. **A. Fertilizer has a positive effect on plant growth.** The results show that for all 4 weeks, the plants with fertilizer were taller than the plants with no fertilizer. Therefore, Choice (A) is correct, and Choices (C) and (D) are incorrect. Choice (B) is true but is not a result of this particular experiment — a good reminder that you should avoid using background knowledge to answer items and only use information in the passage and/or illustration.

18. **D. independent — fertilizer; dependent — plant height.** Choice (D) is correct because the fertilizer is the variable that the researcher can control. The dependent variable is the result. Therefore, Choice (B) is incorrect. Choice (A) is incorrect because water and sunlight were not variables in this experiment. Choice (C) is incorrect because plant height, not water and sunlight, is the dependent variable.

The dependent variable is called that because its change is dependent on the changes to the independent variable(s).

19. **C. Place both plants in places where light will not be blocked and switch the plants' positions once daily.** The problem in this situation is that the two plants got different amounts of sunlight in the late afternoon. Only Choice (C) will ensure that the position of the plants will not affect the average amount of sunlight they receive during the experiment. Choice (A) would help the plants grow straighter but would not ensure that they get equal amounts of sunlight. Choice (B) would give one of the plants an extra advantage over the other one and make the results unreliable. Choice (D) would likely decrease the light available to both plants but would still not ensure that they both get the same amount of sunlight.

20. **A. They can avoid predators.** Choice (A) is correct because living underground for so long and emerging in such large numbers increases their survival rate. Choice (B) is not an advantage to cicadas. Choice (C) is a disadvantage to cicadas. Choice (D) cannot be concluded from the information.

21. **C. At the time, most of the medical community was not willing to pay attention to a woman.** Choice (C) is correct because at the time, most doctors were men, and people did not believe women made good doctors or scientists. Choice (A) is not supported by the information. People at the time knew that there were poisonous plants, but Bigsby couldn't figure out which one was responsible for milk sickness. Choice (B) is incorrect because Bigsby developed a hypothesis and tested it with the plant identified by the Shawnee woman. Choice (D) is contradicted by the information, which says that people respected her.

22. **B. Liquid water is denser than ice.** Ice is buoyant because its density is less than that of water, so Choice (B) is correct. Therefore, Choices (A) and (C) are incorrect. Choice (D) does not make sense. Ice is a solid, not a gas.

23. **A. Lakes and ponds freeze from top to bottom.** Because ice floats in water, lakes and ponds will freeze from top to bottom (Choice A). Therefore, Choice (B) is incorrect. Choices (C) and (D) are incorrect because they are not related to ice floating in water.

24. **A. 1g/cm³.** To calculate density, divide the mass by the volume in cubic centimeters (cm³): $4/4 = 1g/cm^3$ (Choice A). Choice (B) is the square root of 4. Choice (C) is the mass of the sample. Choice (D) is the square of the mass.

Keep in mind that for this question you don't need to use the on-screen calculator but it's available when you need it.

25. **A. The solubility of all four substances goes up as temperature increases.** The graph shows the solubility of all the substances increasing as the temperature rises, so Choice (A) is correct and Choice (C) is incorrect. The curves are different for each substance, so Choice (B) is incorrect. Choice (D) is not supported by the information in the graph. In fact, at 100° C, the water will start to boil, and as it converts to gas, the dissolved substances will precipitate.

26. **C. 70° C.** Choice (C) is correct. The curves for these two substances cross at approximately this point. Choice (A) is the point at which the curves for sodium chloride and potassium nitrate cross. The remaining choices are incorrect.

27. **D. sodium chloride.** The curve for sodium chloride rises the least, so Choice (D) is correct.

28. **A. 40 g.** The graph shows that at 60° C, 40 g of sodium chloride are dissolved, so Choice (A) is correct. The other choices show the amounts of the other substances dissolved at this temperature. Choice (B) is the amount of potassium nitrate dissolved, Choice (C) the amount of sodium nitrate, and Choice (D) the amount of potassium iodide.

Charts, graphs, and tables come up on three of the four GED tests: Science, Social Studies, and Math. If questions 25 to 28 are hard for you, review the information on charts, tables, and graphs in Chapter 10.

29. **B. graphite.** Choice (B) is correct because the passage says that in graphite, carbon is arranged in a hexagonal pattern in flat sheets. In amorphous carbon (Choice D), carbon atoms have no particular arrangement. The allotropes in the remaining choices have different arrangements.

30. **A. diamond.** According to the information, Choice (A), diamond, is one of the hardest substances in existence, so it would be useful in making a cutting tool. The passage does not give information about the hardness of fullerines (Choice C).

31. **A. crystalline structure.** Choice (A) is stated directly in the passage. The remaining choices are characteristics of graphite so are incorrect.

32. **B. A child rolls a bowling ball, and it comes to a stop part-way down the alley.** Choice (B) is correct because friction and gravity caused the ball to stop midway along the alley. An adult bowler would likely throw the ball hard enough to overcome friction and gravity. Choice (A) is incorrect because another force was not applied to the ball — the player made a strike. Choice (C) is not possible because the vase is safe from having a force applied to it while locked in the cabinet. Choice (D) is incorrect because the meteor is continuing to travel in space, where there is no friction or headwind to slow it.

33. **A. inclined plane.** Choice (A) is correct because a ramp is an inclined plane. A ramp directs horizontal force upwards. Therefore, the other choices are incorrect.

34. **A. vinegar.** Only vinegar is more acidic than black coffee, so Choice (A) is correct. The other options are less acidic than coffee or more basic.

35. **B. Without vitamin D, land vertebrates cannot absorb calcium needed for bone health.** Choice (B) is correct because this detail provides more information about the main benefit of UV to humans. Choices (A) and (C) are not relevant because they are about other kinds of light. Choice (D) adds a detail about light from the Sun, but it does not strengthen the main idea of the passage, which is about the benefits and harmful effects of UV light.

36. **C. The weight is less, and the mass is the same.** Choice (C) is correct because mass is the measure of matter, which remains the same. The probe's weight is 16.5 percent of what it was on Earth.

37. **A. 185.42.** Choice (A) is correct. You can try rounding the five speeds on this item, but since the answer choices are so close together, you are better off calculating the exact answer. Note that you can use a calculator on this question.

    To calculate the average speed, add the 5 values and divide by 5:

    190.69 + 187.43 + 186.56 + 185.98 + 176.46 = 927.12

    927.12 / 5 = 185.42

    Choice (B) was the average speed in 1990. Choice (C) is the median speed. Choice (D) is the sum of the 5 speeds in the table.

REMEMBER You are allowed to use the on-screen calculator or your own TI-30XS MultiView calculator (only at a test center) on questions such as this one. The calculator is available on the Social Studies and Science tests, not just the Math test.

38. **B. 186.56.** The median is the value in the middle when the values are ordered from largest to smallest. The values are already arranged in the table, so all you need to do is find the one in the middle. That one is the average speed in 2014, 186.56. Choice (B) is the average speed. Choice (C) is the average speed in 2013. Choice (D) is the average speed in 2021.

REMEMBER Mean, median, and mode are frequently tested on the GED, so it pays to know the difference. The mean is the average. To calculate the mean, you add all the values and divide by the number of values. The median is the value in the middle when the values are arranged in order. If there is an even number of values, average the two in the middle. Mode is the most common value. Mode is only relevant in large data sets and is not tested as frequently as *mean* and *median*.

39. **A. Heat can be transferred, but not cold.** Choice (A) is correct because heat is a form of energy that can move from object to object. Therefore, Choice (B) is incorrect. Choice (C) does not make sense. Choice (D) is only partially correct. While circulation of the blood brings warmth to different parts of the body, heat transferred from the cocoa also warmed the fingers.

40. **D. Sound waves can travel through solid materials.** Choice (D) is correct because sound waves can travel through solid materials. In all likelihood, the sounds are traveling through a beam in the wall that extends up from the first floor and the nightclub. Choice (A) is not correct because the nightclub is in the front of the building and the apartment is in the back. Soundwaves cannot exit the nightclub through the front of the building and enter a window at the back of the building. Choice (B) is true but does not explain why Peter can hear music in his bedroom. Choice (C) is not possible because he would hear the music in the stairway, and the information says that he does not.

41. **B. The acidity of seawater will increase.** The effect of increased carbonic acid in the ocean is that the ocean's acidity will increase, so Choice (B) is correct and Choices (A) and (D) are incorrect. Choice (C) does not make sense because burning fossil fuel is the cause of increased carbon dioxide gas in the atmosphere.

42. **C. A large volcanic explosion created the crater.** Choice (C) is stated directly in the information so is correct. Choice (A) is the scientists' revised, or second, theory. The other choices are not theories mentioned in the passage.

43. **A. They couldn't find any evidence of an explosion.** Choice (A) is stated directly in the information and so is correct. Choices (B) and (D) are contradicted by the information. Choice (C) supports the original theory, not the new one.

44. **A. With this probe, astronomers could study Pluto up close for the first time.** Choice (A) is stated directly in the information and so is correct. Choice (B) is contradicted by the information. Choice (C) is not supported by the information. In fact, at least 7 probes have been sent to Jupiter since 1973. Choice (D) is contradicted by the information. The probe was launched before Pluto's designation changed.

45. **B. amused and disappointed.** Words such as "much beloved," show that the author feels somewhat sad or disappointed about the change. In addition, ironic phrases, such as the decision did not "dissuade the probe from completing its mission," show an ironic but amused tone. Therefore, Choice (B) is correct. The other options do not describe the tone accurately.

46. **B. High water levels are causing problems in a valuable source of fresh water.** Choice (B) is correct because the passage focuses on both the importance of the lake system and the challenges posed by high water levels. The other choices are all true or mentioned in the passage but are not the main idea. Choice (A) is not the main idea. Choice (C) only states one part of the main idea. Choice (D) is a detail in the passage that supports the main idea.

47. **C. The high lake level has caused flooding because run-off from heavy storms has no place to go.** Choice (C) is another issue caused by high water levels so would strengthen the author's argument. The remaining choices would weaken the argument so are incorrect.

TIP

To determine which of the facts strengthen an argument, keep in mind the main idea of the reading. The answer will always relate to the main idea of the passage. In this case, you determined the main idea in the previous item. Your answer to that question can help you with this one.

48. **A. Governments need to take steps to manage high water levels in Lake Michigan.** Given the threat high water levels pose to so many people, Choice (A) is a logical conclusion. There is no evidence in the passage to support Choices (B) or (C). Choice (D) is contradicted by information in the passage.

49. **two.** The answer is two. The two independent variables are weather (dry or rainy) and temperature. If you thought that the answer was one (number of bats), then you mistook the dependent variable (number of bats) for an independent variable.

TIP

On questions like this one, you can answer *two* or 2. Both will be scored correctly. If you misspell a word, a reader will check it to see if it is close enough to count. But if you type the wrong number, it will be marked incorrect.

50. **C. It warms areas of Europe and the oceans nearby.** Choice (C) is the only choice that makes sense. The warm water from the gulf stream would likely raise temperatures in those locations. Therefore, Choice (A) is incorrect. Choice (B) is incorrect because the gulf stream would help ships sail from the United States to Europe, not the other way around. Choice (D) confuses the jet stream (a current in the air) with the gulf stream (a current in the water). The jet stream, which also flows from the United States to Europe, helps planes fly faster in that direction than on the return trip.

Answer Key

1.	C	18.	D	35.	B
2.	B	19.	C	36.	C
3.	B	20.	A	37.	A
4.	D	21.	C	38.	B
5.	B	22.	B	39.	A
6.	A	23.	A	40.	D
7.	D	24.	A	41.	B
8.	D	25.	A	42.	C
9.	Flagella	26.	C	43.	A
10.	Cilia	27.	D	44.	A
11.	A	28.	A	45.	B
12.	B	29.	B	46.	B
13.	C	30.	A	47.	C
14.	A	31.	A	48.	A
15.	C	32.	B	49.	2/two
16.	D	33.	A	50.	C
17.	A	34.	A		

Chapter 25

Practice Test 1: Mathematical Reasoning

The Mathematical Reasoning test consists of a series of questions intended to measure general mathematics skills and problem-solving ability. The questions are based on short readings that may include a graph, chart, or figure.

You have 115 minutes to complete this section. The answers and explanations to this section's questions are in Chapter 26. Go through the explanations to all the questions, even for the ones you answered correctly. The explanations are a good review of the mathematical techniques I discuss throughout the book.

The GED formula sheet is on the page before the first test question. Only some of the questions require you to use a formula, and you may not need all the formulas given. If you are familiar with the formulas and understand how to use them, you'll save some time on the test; you can then use that time for review or for harder items that give you trouble.

TIP

If you have time before the test, memorize the most commonly tested formulas: area of a square or rectangle, area of a circle, circumference, and the Pythagorean Theorem. Items using these formulas usually appear on the GED test.

On the real test, you will be able to use the online whiteboard (or an erasable tablet, if you test at a test center). For now, have a few pieces of scratch paper ready to calculate, write down formulas, or draw simple sketches to help you visualize a question. And remember to use your calculator when you think it can help you work more quickly and accurately. For these questions, you can use any calculator, including the one on your phone, though using a real TI-30XS MultiView calculator is the best preparation for the real test. Use the timer on your phone to keep track of time. If you run out of time, mark the last question that you answered. Then answer the remaining questions. This will give you an idea of how much faster you should work to answer all the questions on the real test.

REMEMBER

On the real GED, you'll be answering on a computer. Instead of marking your answers on a separate answer sheet, like you do for the practice test sections in this book, you'll see clickable ovals and fill-in-the-blank text boxes. You'll be able to click with your mouse and drag and drop items where indicated. The questions and answer choices in this book are formatted to appear as similar as possible to what you'll see on the actual test, but I had to retain some A, B, C, and D choices for marking your answers, and I provide an answer sheet for you to do so. When you're ready for the included online practice test, you will be able to see and try the actual question types as they appear on the test.

Answer Sheet for Practice Test 1, Mathematical Reasoning

1. _____

2. _____

3. _____

4. _____

5. _____

6. _____

7. _____

8. _____

9. _____

10. _____

11. _____

12. _____

13. _____

14. _____

15. _____

16. _____

17. _____

18. _____

19. _____

20. _____

21. _____

22. _____

23. _____

24. _____

25. _____

26. _____

27. _____

28. _____

29. _____

30. _____

31. _____

32. _____

33. _____

34. _____

35. _____

36. _____

37. _____

38. _____

39. _____

40. _____

41. _____

42. _____

43. _____

44. _____

45. _____

46. _____

47. _____

48. _____

49. _____

50. _____

Mathematics Formula Explanations

This displays formulas relating to geometric measurement and certain algebra concepts and is available on the GED® test — Mathematical Reasoning.

Area of a:

square	$A = s^2$
rectangle	$A = lw$
parallelogram	$A = bh$
triangle	$A = \frac{1}{2} bh$
trapezoid	$A = \frac{1}{2} h(b_1 + b_2)$
circle	$A = \pi r^2$

Perimeter of a:

square	$P = 4s$
rectangle	$P = 2l + 2w$
triangle	$P = s_1 + s_2 + s_3$
Circumference of a circle	$C = 2\pi r$ OR $C = \pi d; \pi \approx 3.14$

Surface area and volume of a:

rectangular prism	$SA = 2lw + 2lh + 2wh$	$V = lwh$
right prism	$SA = ph + 2B$	$V = Bh$
cylinder	$SA = 2\pi rh + 2\pi r^2$	$V = \pi r^2 h$
pyramid	$SA = \frac{1}{2} ps + B$	$V = \frac{1}{3} Bh$
cone	$SA = \pi rs + \pi r^2$	$V = \frac{1}{3} \pi r^2 h$
sphere	$SA = 4\pi r^2$	$V = \frac{4}{3} \pi r^3$

(p = perimeter of base with area B; $\pi \approx 3.14$)

Data

mean	mean is equal to the total of the values of a data set, divided by the number of elements in the data set
median	median is the middle value in an odd number of ordered values of a data set, or the mean of the two middle values in an even number of ordered values in a data set

Algebra

slope of a line	$m = \dfrac{y_2 - y_1}{x_2 - x_1}$
slope-intercept form of the equation of a line	$y = mx + b$
point-slope form of the equation of a line	$y - y_1 = m(x - x_1)$
standard form of a quadratic equation	$y = ax^2 + bx + c$
quadratic formula	$x = \dfrac{-b \pm \sqrt{b^2 - 4ac}}{2a}$
Pythagorean theorem	$a^2 + b^2 = c^2$
simple interest	$I = Prt$
	(I = interest, P = principal, r = rate, t = time)
distance formula	$d = rt$
total cost	total cost = (number of units) x (price per unit)

Æ Symbol Tool Explanation

The GED® test on computer contains a tool known as the "Æ Symbol Tool." Use this guide to learn about entering special mathematical symbols into fill-in-the-blank item types.

Symbol	Explanation	Symbol	Explanation	Symbol	Explanation
π	pi	|	absolute value	—	minus or negative
f	function	×	multiplication	(	open or left parenthesis
≥	greater than or equal to	÷	division	)	close or right parenthesis
≤	less than or equal to	±	positive or negative	>	greater than
≠	not equal to	∞	infinity	<	less than
2	2 exponent ("squared")	√	square root	=	equals
3	3 exponent ("cubed")	+	plus or positive		

TIME: 115 minutes

QUESTIONS: 50

DIRECTIONS: Find the answer to each question. Mark your answers on the answer sheet provided.

1. Jacob Smith searched for his name online to see how many results would come up. The search produced 354,000,000 results (and in under half a second, too!). If Jacob wrote this total as 3.54×10^x, the value of x would be ⬚.

2. You are one of 300 people who enter a lottery to get tickets to see your favorite recording artist. Tickets are numbered from 1 to 300. The lottery officials select every 15th person to get a ticket, starting with ticket number 8. Which of the following lottery numbers will also get a ticket?

   (A) 18

   (B) 88

   (C) 98

   (D) 108

3. $a = b^2 - (3 + 2c)$. Find a if $b = -3$, $c = -2$

   (A) −10

   (B) −9

   (C) 8

   (D) 10

4. Mercedes and Chen gather strawberries to make jam for the upcoming fall and winter. They gather A LOT of strawberries, enough to make 255 ounces of jam. They have an assortment of 3-, 6-, 12- and 24-ounce jars to put the jam in. Which combination of jars would contain all the jam that they made?

   (A) 15 3-oz. jars and 18 12-oz. jars

   (B) 7 6-oz. jars and 9 24-oz. jars

   (C) 13 3-oz. jars and 36 6-oz. jars

   (D) 13 18-oz. jars and 4 24-oz. jars

5. The local donut shop charges $0.89 for a single donut, $4.99 for a half-dozen donuts, and $9.49 for a dozen donuts. If you need to buy 36 donuts, how much would you save if you bought 3 dozen donuts as opposed to 36 individual donuts, before sales tax?

6. Jennie sees a new blouse at the store with a price tag of $20. When she goes to pay for it, she sees that the final cost after the tax is added is $21.20. What is the tax rate?

   (A) 1.2%

   (B) 5%

   (C) 6%

   (D) 12%

7. Caleb's normal commute to work takes about half an hour when he's driving in his car at an average rate of 40 mph. If he decided to take part in Bike-to-Work Day, how long would it take him to get to work if he averages 16 mph riding his bike?

   (A) 1 hour, 15 minutes

   (B) 1 hour, 25 minutes

   (C) 1 hour, 40 minutes

   (D) 2 hours, 30 minutes

8. The following line intercepts the y-axis at 4 and the x-axis at 5. What is the slope of the line?

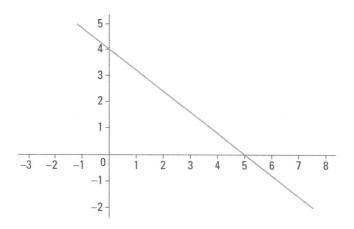

(A) 4/5

(B) −5/4

(C) −4/5

(D) 5/4

9. John's local pizza shop offers the following sizes of pizzas:

- **12-inch round pizza: $12.99**
- **14-inch round pizza: $15.99**
- **10 × 16-inch rectangular pizza: $17.99**

Toppings cost $1 each. Drinks are sold for $2, $2.50, and $3 for S, M, and L, respectively.

If John has $20 to spend, which of the following orders can he NOT place? (Assume there is no tax or tip on the order.)

(A) a rectangular cheese pizza with a small drink

(B) a 14-inch pepperoni pizza with a medium drink

(C) a 12-inch green pepper, onion, and mushroom pizza with a large drink

(D) a 14-inch pineapple and ham pizza with a medium drink

10. Anthony gets paid $12 per hour to work at the local snack bar. If he works over 40 hours in a particular week, he gets paid 50% more per hour for those additional hours.

Suppose Anthony works 50 hours in one week. How much will he get paid for that week?

(A) $180

(B) $480

(C) $600

(D) $660

11. What is the least common multiple of 24 and 32?

(A) 8

(B) 96

(C) 128

(D) 192

Questions 12-13 refer to the following image.

Average Daily Internet Usage (in hours) vs. Age Group

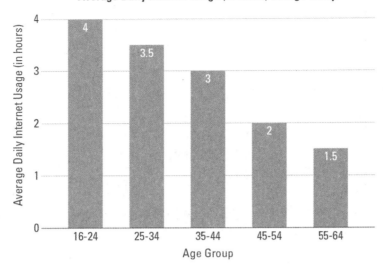

12. How many hours would you expect a 30-year-old to be online in the course of a 3-day weekend?

    (A) 7
    (B) 9
    (C) 10.5
    (D) 12

13. Between which two age groups was there the greatest difference in average daily Internet usage?

    (A) 16–24 and 25–34
    (B) 25–34 and 35–44
    (C) 35–44 and 45–54
    (D) 45–54 and 55–64

14. The cylinder in the figure shown here is inscribed in the square prism. They both have a height of 12 inches. The cylinder has a radius of 5 inches. What is the difference in volume between the prism and the cylinder?

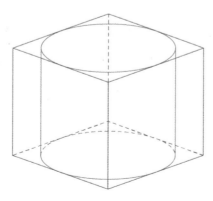

(A) 257.5 cubic inches

(B) 942.5 cubic inches

(C) 1,200 cubic inches

(D) 2,142.5 cubic inches

15. Elena's 6 quiz scores in her dental hygiene class were as follows:

84, 77, 98, 86, 95, 76

What is Elena's mean (average) score?

(A) 77

(B) 85

(C) 86

(D) 103.2

16. Mario is making pasta sauce for dinner. The family recipe includes the following ingredients:

- $\frac{3}{4}$ **pound of ground beef**

- **1 can of crushed tomatoes**

- $\frac{1}{2}$ **cup chopped onion**

- $1\frac{1}{2}$ **tsp dried basil**

Mario decides to double the recipe because he is cooking for a big family gathering. Which of the following portions is the *incorrect* amount for the new proportions?

(A) 1.5 pounds ground beef

(B) 2 cans crushed tomatoes

(C) .25 chopped onions

(D) 3 tsps dried basil

17. Nedra has to walk from one location in a park to another spot. If she stays on paved paths, she will walk 2 blocks due south, then 3 blocks due east, and then another 2 blocks due south. If she had instead just walked a straight path from one spot to the other, how long a distance would that be? Assume that the blocks are squares.

(A) 3 blocks

(B) 4 blocks

(C) 5 blocks

(D) 7 blocks

18. In a standard deck of 52 playing cards, four of them are aces. If you draw eight cards from the deck and none of them are aces, what is the probability that the ninth card you draw is an ace?

(A) 1:44

(B) 1:13

(C) 1:11

(D) 1:9

Object	Volume (in decibels)
Library	40
Electric Toothbrush	50
Freeway Traffic	70
Cicadas	80
Tractor	90
Snowmobile	100
Ambulance	120
Firecracker	150
Rifle	160

19. If your alarm clock goes off at 75 decibels, what fraction of the items are louder than your alarm clock?

   (A) 2/9

   (B) 1/3

   (C) 75/160

   (D) 2/3

20. Cicadas are insects that appear every few years. They are known for their high-pitched singing. If cicadas were 50% more decibels than they currently are, they would be as loud as what object?

   (A) an ambulance

   (B) a rifle

   (C) a library

   (D) an electric toothbrush

21. Consider the equation for the volume of a sphere: $V = \frac{4}{3}\pi r^3$. If you have two spheres and one of them has a radius that is triple the radius of the other sphere, how much greater is the volume of that first sphere?

   (A) 3 times as large

   (B) 9 times as large

   (C) 12 times as large

   (D) 27 times as large

22. During their family reunion, 36 kids from the Johnson family go to the local water park to cool off. While there, they can go on the water slides, the lazy river, both, or neither. If 10 kids do both rides, 25 kids only do the lazy river, and 4 kids don't do either ride, how many kids ride just the water slides?

   (A) 7

   (B) 17

   (C) 21

   (D) 32

23. Jessie is training for a local triathlon. She wants to be able to finish it in 3 hours. If she does the swim portion in 45 minutes, the running portion in an hour, and the biking portion in 1.2 hours, how will she finish relative to her goal?

(A) She will fail to reach her goal by 3 minutes.

(B) She will reach her goal exactly on time.

(C) She will reach her goal with 3 minutes to spare.

(D) She will fail to reach her goal by 5 minutes.

24. Mary has a picture that is 24 inches across by 36 inches tall that she wants to hang on a wall that is 10 feet across by 8 feet tall. If she wants the top of the picture to be two feet from the ceiling of the room, and the hooks to hang it are six inches down from the top of the picture, how far down from the ceiling will she have to place the nails to hang the picture?

(A) 24 inches

(B) 30 inches

(C) 36 inches

(D) 42 inches

25. Mr. and Mrs. Noronhas are putting 2-foot-square pavers into a rectangular pathway in their front yard. If the pathway is 4 feet wide and 30 feet long, how many pavers will they need?

(A) 8.5

(B) 30

(C) 60

(D) 80

26. During Darnell's time at the local community college, the enrollment had the following numbers.

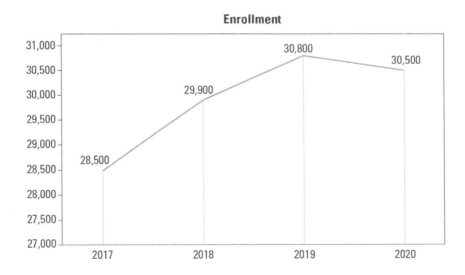

Enrollment

What was the percent increase in enrollment at the college from the time Darnell entered the school in 2017 to the time he left in 2020?

(A) 0.07%

(B) 4.9%

(C) 7.0%

(D) 8.1%

27. Kelly is trying to walk an average of 10,000 steps a day. The first three days, she walked 8,523, 11,378, and 7,906 steps. How many steps must Kelly walk on the fourth day to be on pace for her daily average?

(A) 2,193 steps

(B) 9,269 steps

(C) 10,000 steps

(D) 12,193 steps

28. Stefan has to fill four 10-gallon water jugs before the team practice. If the outdoor faucet has a flow rate of 11 to 12 gallons per minute, how long will it take Stefan to fill all four jugs?

(A) under 2 minutes

(B) between 2 and 3 minutes

(C) between 3 and 4 minutes

(D) over 4 minutes

29. Which of the following is in the shape of a rectangle?

(A) a can of cranberry sauce

(B) the label from a can of cranberry sauce

(C) an ice cream cone

(D) the paper wrapping from an ice cream cone

30. Sam likes to track how much mileage she gets on a tank of gas. She sees that for the current tank of gas, she drove 288 miles so far. Her gas gauge says she has used up $\frac{3}{4}$ of her 16-gallon tank. How many more miles can she expect to drive before she runs out of gas?

(A) 12

(B) 24

(C) 96

(D) 384

Questions 31 and 32 refer to the following information.

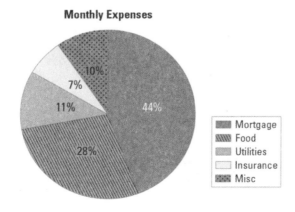

Monthly Expenses

31. Makayla has broken down her monthly expenses as shown in the figure.

Which of the following statements about her monthly expenses is true?

(A) She spends more on insurance than on utilities.

(B) She spends over a quarter of her money on things other than the mortgage and food.

(C) After the mortgage, the most she spends is on utilities.

(D) Her miscellaneous expenses are a fourth of what she spends on food.

32. Suppose Makayla's monthly budget is $3,500. If she decides to rent instead of paying a mortgage, and her rent is $1,175 a month and utilities are $350 a month, how much could she save each month by renting instead of owning?

33. What is the area of the following triangle?

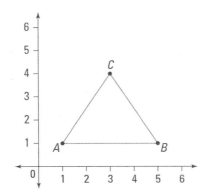

(A) 3.5

(B) 6

(C) 12

(D) 24

34. Brianna and Rachael both like to travel, but Brianna likes to fly while Rachael prefers to take the train.

When Brianna flies, the plane averages 300 mph, but it takes Brianna half an hour to get to the airport, another 2 hours to get through security and wait to board the plane, and then an additional hour after the plane lands to get her luggage, leave the airport, and get to her destination.

For Rachael, it also takes half an hour to get to the train station, but she only has to get there 30 minutes early to check in, and it only takes her 45 minutes from the time the train arrives at the station to get to her destination. However, the train only averages 125 mph.

If they both were to leave at the same time, for what travel distance would Rachael arrive at her destination first?

(A) 300 miles

(B) 400 miles

(C) 500 miles

(D) 600 miles

35. You live in a 1-bedroom apartment with the dimensions shown in the preceding illustration.

If you want to carpet part of your apartment, which of these scenarios can you do based on the following pricing?

Room Size	Materials	With Installation
10' × 10'	$200 – $700	$350 – $1,100
10' × 12'	$240 – $840	$420 – $1,320
12' × 12'	$290 – $1,000	$500 – $1,600
15' × 15'	$450 – $1,575	$800 – $2,500
One Large Room	$800 – $2,800	$1,400 – $4,400

(A) Install carpeting in the bedroom for $400.

(B) Install carpeting in the living room for $400.

(C) Buy materials for the living room for $275.

(D) Buy materials for both the bedroom and the living room for $640.

36. If you wanted to tile the kitchen, how much would you save in material costs by going with a ceramic tile as opposed to a marble tile?

MATERIAL	AVERAGE COST PER SQ. FT.
Ceramic	$4.60/Sq. Ft.
Porcelain	$5.05/Sq. Ft.
Marble	$6.20/Sq. Ft.
Limestone	$6.20/Sq. Ft.

37. What is the value of y_2 for point A if A has coordinates $(-3, y_1)$, A is on a line with point B $(3, -1)$, and the line containing A and B has a slope of $\frac{5}{2}$?

   (A) −16

   (B) −14

   (C) 14

   (D) 16

38. If a square has an area of 36 square inches, what is its perimeter?

   (A) 6

   (B) 12

   (C) 24

   (D) 36

39. What is the area of the following trapezoid?

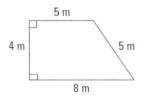

   (A) 20

   (B) 26

   (C) 32

   (D) 40

40. A standard basketball rim has a diameter of 18 inches. To the nearest tenth of an inch, what is the circumference of a standard basketball rim?

   (A) 28.3

   (B) 56.5

   (C) 113.1

   (D) 254.5

41. Which of the following figures is closest in area to the area of a circle with a radius of 5?

   (A) a square with sides of 9

   (B) a triangle with a base of 10 and a height of 15

   (C) a parallelogram with a base of 10 and a height of 15

   (D) a rectangle with sides of 8 and 10

42. Multiply $(2x - y) \times (2x - y)$.

   (A) $4x^2 - 4xy - y^2$

   (B) $4x - 2y$

   (C) $4x^2 - 4xy + y^2$

   (D) $2x^2 - y^2$

43. You have a jar full of nickels, dimes, and quarters. You count them and find you have *a* nickels, *b* dimes, and *c* quarters. Which expression represents the number of cents represented by the coins in your collection?

(A) $(a + b + c)(5 + 10 + 25)$

(B) $25a + 10b + 5c$

(C) $5a + 10b + 25c$

(D) $(5a)(10b)(25c)$

44. Subtract $\dfrac{x}{x-3} - \dfrac{2}{3x}$.

(A) $\dfrac{x-2}{-2x-3}$

(B) $\dfrac{2x}{3x(x-3)}$

(C) $\dfrac{3x^2 - 2x - 6}{3x(x-3)}$

(D) $\dfrac{3x^2 - 2x + 6}{3x(x-3)}$

45. Caroline uses the expression $10b + 20d$ to represent the money she makes from working *b* hours babysitting and *d* hours dog-sitting each week.

If she babysat for 15 hours and dog-sat for 8 hours last week, how much did Caroline earn?

(A) $230

(B) $310

(C) $380

(D) $460

46. The following table and graph list the number of U.S. athletes and medals won by U.S. athletes in 11 recent Summer Olympics.

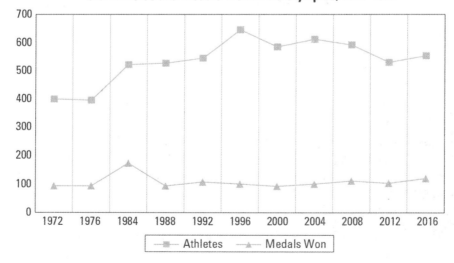

U.S. Athletes and Medals Won in the Olympics, 1972–2016

U.S. Athletes and Medals Won in the Olympics, 1972–2016

Year	U.S. Athletes	Medals Won
1972	400	94
1976	396	94
1984	522	174
1988	527	94
1992	545	108
1996	646	101
2000	586	93
2004	613	101
2008	593	112
2012	530	104
2016	554	121

In one of these years, the American athletes did not compete against any of the Soviet bloc countries because the Soviet Union and 14 other countries boycotted the games. During this year, the ratio of athletes to medals won was lower than any other year.

Which year was it?

(A) 1972

(B) 1984

(C) 1996

(D) 2012

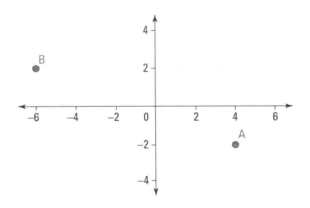

47. Find the distance from A to B to the nearest tenth.

48. When you solve the following system of linear equations,

$3x - 4y = 10$

$5x + 6y = 4$

What value do you get for *x*?

(A) −2

(B) −1

(C) 1

(D) 2

49. Annalucia opens an account with $1,200 that earns 4% in simple interest each year. How much in total will she have in her account (including interest) after 5 years?

(A) $240

(B) $1224

(C) $1440

(D) $4800

50. The following table lists the average length of a game in the four major sports leagues.

League	Average Length of Game
MLB (baseball)	3 hours, 8 minutes
NBA (basketball)	2 hours, 11 minutes
NFL (football)	3 hours, 12 minutes
NHL (hockey)	2 hours, 20 minutes

Tommy records a game from each of the four leagues. He is going to be on a train for 150 minutes and wants to watch a game to pass the time. Which games could he watch in their entirety while on the train?

(A) baseball or football

(B) football or hockey

(C) basketball or hockey

(D) baseball or basketball

Chapter **26**

Answers for Practice Test 1, Mathematical Reasoning

This chapter provides you with answers and explanations for the Mathematical Reasoning practice test in Chapter 25. The answers tell you whether you answered the questions right or wrong, but the explanations are even more important. They explain why your answers were right or wrong and give you some hints about the areas that were tested. Reading the explanations and checking the areas where your answers were incorrect will help you identify where you should spend more time preparing for the test.

Answers and Explanations

1. **8.** To write in exponential notation, you move the decimal point to the left until there is only one number in front of it. Each move to the left represents one power of 10. So, for 354,000,000, you have to move it 8 spots to the left until you have just 3.54 in front. Because you move it 8 spots, that 8 is the value of the exponent, as it represents 8 powers of 10.

2. **C. 98.** To calculate this answer, start at number 8 and then add 15 each time to find the next person to receive a lottery ticket. Of the numbers in the choices, only 98 (Choice C) comes up.

   8, 23, 38, 53, 68, 83, **98**, 113

   TIP

   Unless you can add quickly in your head, using the calculator is the fastest and most accurate way to answer this question. Input 8 and keep adding 15 until you find one of the answer choices. Another way to reach the solution is to subtract 8 from each answer choice and then divide by 15. The first choice to be evenly divisible by 15 is the answer.

3. **D. 10.** To solve this problem, simply substitute the values for b and c, and solve using the correct order of operations, paying attention to signed (positive and negative) numbers.

   $$(-3)^2 - (3 + 2 \times (-2)) = 9 - (3 - 4) = 9 - (-1) = 9 + 1 = 10$$

   So, Choice (D) is correct. Choice (A) made two errors with negative numbers. The square of a negative number is always positive. In addition, 1 was subtracted instead of added. Choice (B) also forgot that the square of a negative number is always positive. Choice (C) added −1 instead of subtracting it.

4. **C. 13 3-oz. jars and 36 6-oz. jars.** To answer this question, you need to calculate the amount of jam each combination of jars will hold. Choice (A) will hold more than 255 ounces, so it is incorrect: $15 \times 3 + 18 \times 12 = 45 + 216 = 261$ ounces.

   Choice (B) will also hold more than 255 ounces: $7 \times 6 + 9 \times 24 = 42 + 216 = 258$.

   Choice (C) results in exactly 255 ounces so is correct:

   $13 \times 3 + 36 \times 6 = 39 + 216 = 255$ ounces.

   Because only one choice is correct, you can simply double-check your calculation for Choice (C) and skip Choice (D), which will also hold more than 255 ounces: $13 \times 18 + 4 \times 24 = 234 + 96 = 330$.

   TIP

   On a question like this one, it's important to pay attention to order of operations. Remember to multiply from left to right and then add from left to right. Because you have to calculate the contents of each combination of jars, this question also will take a long time to answer. Therefore, it's one you might skip until later in the test.

5. **$3.57.** 3 dozen donuts would cost $3 \times \$9.49 = \$28.47$.

   36 individual donuts would cost $36 \times \$0.89 = \$32.04$.

   Therefore, the amount you would save would be $\$32.04 - \$28.47 = \$3.57$.

6. **C. 6%.** To find the tax rate, take the difference between the price paid ($21.20) and the price listed ($20): $\$21.20 - \$20 = \$1.20$. Take that result and divide it by the original price ($20). That percentage is the tax rate: $1.20 / 20 = 0.06 = 6\%$. So, Choice (C) is correct.

7. **A. 1 hour, 15 minutes.** If the normal commute takes half an hour at 40 mph, that means the commute is $0.5 \times 40 = 20$ miles. Thus, 20 miles at 16 mph = $20 \div 16 = 1.25$ hours, which is 1 hour and 15 minutes. (A quarter of an hour is 15 minutes.) Choice (B) is incorrect because it confuses .25 hours with 25 minutes. Choice (C) does not make sense. Choice (D) forgot to calculate the distance of Caleb's commute (20 miles) and used his driving speed (40 mph) instead: 40/16= 2.5.

8. **C. −4/5.** The slope of a line is equal to the change in the y coordinates divided by the change in the x coordinates. In this case, from intercept to intercept, the y coordinates went down 4, while the x coordinates went up 5, making the slope equal to −4/5.

9. **D. a 14-inch pineapple and ham pizza with a medium drink.** A good way to approach questions like this one is to look for choices that are likely to be too expensive and try those first. Start with the option that has the most expensive pizza selection: The rectangular cheese pizza with small drink (Choice A) costs $17.99 + $2 = $19.99. John can afford that one, so Choice (A) is not the answer. The next order most likely to be too expensive is Choice (D), a 14-inch pineapple and ham pizza with a medium drink. That order costs $15.99 + $2 + $2.50 = $20.49. That's more than $20, so Choice (D) is the answer. Plus, it has pineapple and ham on it, which is just wrong!

WARNING

Be careful with questions that use negative words such as *not*. Sometimes you may read too quickly and skip over the negative word in the question, Then, it's easy to select the first answer choice as correct. These kinds of questions show the value of reading the question carefully. This kind of question is not that common but can come up occasionally. When they do, the test makers usually, but not always, put the negative word in capital letters and/or boldface type.

10. **D. $660.** Choice (D) is correct because if he works 50 hours in one week, he gets paid $12 per hour for the first 40 hours and then he gets an additional 50% pay for the last 10 hours.

    $12 \times 40 = $480

    $12 \times 10 + $12 \times 10 \times .5 = $120 + $60 = $180

    $480 + $180 = $660

Choice (A) is the pay he will receive for the 10 hours over 40 hours. Choice (B) is his regular pay for working 40 hours in a week. Choice (C) is his pay for working 50 hours in a week without the extra pay for working more than 40 hours.

REMEMBER

Like question 4, this question requires correct order of operation: multiply from left to right and then add from left to right. If you use your calculator correctly, it will automatically use correct order of operation, which can be a big time saver. Just remember to input the whole expression. Try it now, and see for yourself!

11. **B. 96.** One way to find the least common multiple of two numbers is to just start listing the multiples of each number until you get one that is common to both.

Multiples of 24: 24, 48, 72, **96**, 120

Multiples of 32: 32, 64, **96**, 128

The first multiple that is common to both is 96 (Choice B). Choice (A) is a common factor to both, not a common multiple. Choice (C) is a multiple of only 32. Choice (D) is a common multiple of both but is not the least common multiple.

TIP

You can easily eliminate Choice (A) as incorrect because it is smaller than both 24 and 32, so cannot be a multiple of the numbers. This can help you if you run out of time and have to guess. Eliminating even one of the choices improves your odds of guessing correctly.

12. C. 10.5. According to the graph, people in the 25–34 age group average 3.5 hours of daily Internet usage. Therefore, over a 3-day weekend, you would expect a 30-year-old to average $3 \times 3.5 = 10.5$ hours (Choice C).

Choice (A) shows average usage for this age group over a two-day weekend. Choice (B) shows average usage for a 3-day weekend for a 35- to 44-year-old. Choice (D) shows average usage for a 16- to 24-year-old over the same time period.

13. C. 35–44 and 45–54. Choice (C) is correct because the difference between the 35–44 and 45–54 age groups is one hour of average daily Internet usage: $3 - 2 = 1$.

Every other pairing of age groups has a difference of 0.5 hour.

14. A. 257.5 cubic inches. The answer is Choice (A). To figure it out, use the formulas in the formula sheet to calculate the volume of the prism and the volume of the cylinder. Then subtract. Keep in mind that the radius of the circle (5 inches) means that each side of the base of the square prism measures 10 inches.

The volume of a prism is $V = l \times w \times h = 10 \times 10 \times 12 = 1{,}200$.

The volume of a cylinder is $V = \pi r^2 \times h = 5^2 \times 12 \times \pi = 942.47$, which rounds to 942.5.

So, the difference between the prism and the cylinder is $1{,}200 - 942.5 = 257.5$ (Choice A).

Choice (B) is the volume of the cylinder. Choice (C) is the volume of the prism. Choice (D) is the sum of the two volumes, not the difference.

TIP

If you don't know the meaning of the word *inscribed,* you can use the diagram to help you. It shows that the cylinder is inside the square prism. Diagrams can often help you figure out the meaning of unfamiliar words.

15. C. 86. The mean of the six scores is

$$\frac{84 + 77 + 98 + 86 + 95 + 76}{6} = \frac{516}{6} = 86$$

Therefore, Choice (C) is correct.

16. C. .25 chopped onions. Remember, on this item, you are looking for the answer choice that is incorrect. To figure out the answer, multiply all the ingredients by 2. To save time, compare each result to its answer choice. When you find the choice that is incorrect, you have found the answer.

$2 \times \frac{3}{4} = 1.5$ pounds ground beef (Choice A)

$2 \times 1 = 2$ cans crushed tomatoes (Choice B)

$2 \times \frac{1}{2} = 1$ cup chopped onions (Choice C)

Choice (C) incorrectly divides by 2 instead of multiplying, so it is the answer. You can stop calculating at this point and go on to the next item. For reference, here is the calculation for

Choice (D): $2 \times 1\frac{1}{2} = 2 \times \frac{3}{2} = 3$ tsp dried basil.

TIP

Did you select Choice A by mistake? Then maybe you didn't notice that you needed to find the *incorrect* choice. That's why it always pays to read the question carefully.

17. C. 5 blocks. To help you answer this question, make a drawing of the path Nedra follows.

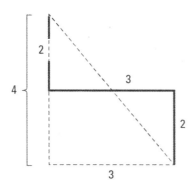

If Nedra were to walk directly from the starting point to the finishing point in a straight line, that would be equivalent to the hypotenuse of a right triangle with sides 3 and 4 (see diagram). Using the Pythagorean Theorem, which is on the formula sheet, the length of the hypotenuse would be

$3^2 + 4^2 = x^2$

$9 + 16 = x^2$

$25 = x^2$

$5 = x$

So, Choice (C) is correct. Choices (A) and (B) are the base and height of the triangle. Choice (D) is the number of blocks actually walked (2 + 3 + 2 = 7), not the length of the hypotenuse.

Using the erasable tablet or online whiteboard to make a diagram can help you with questions like this one.

TIP

18. C. 1:11. The chance of drawing an ace from a standard deck of playing cards is 4:52. If you remove 8 cards and none of them are aces, then the chance now becomes 4:44. That simplifies to 1:11 (Choice C). Choice (A) is the odds of drawing a certain ace, say the ace of hearts. Choice (B) is the odds of drawing one of the aces before 8 cards are removed. Choice (D) does not make sense.

19. D. 2/3. Of the 9 objects in the list, 6 have decibel levels higher than 75, so the fraction of items louder than 75 is 6/9, which simplifies to 2/3.

20. A. an ambulance. According to the table, cicadas have a decibel level of 80. 50% × 80 = 40. So if cicadas were 50% higher decibel level, their decibel level would be 80 + 40 = 120, which is the decibel level of an ambulance.

21. D. 27 times as large. Try this with actual numbers. If the original radius is 2, then the volume of the sphere is $V = \frac{4}{3}\pi 2^3 = \frac{4}{3}\pi \times 8 = \frac{32}{3}\pi$.

Now triple the radius so that it equals 6.

Now the volume of the sphere is $V = \frac{4}{3}\pi 6^3 = \frac{4}{3}\pi \times 216 = \frac{864}{3}\pi$.

And because 864 ÷ 32 = 27, that means the volume of the larger sphere is 27 times as large as the original sphere (Choice D).

If you selected Choice (A), you selected the difference between the two radii. Remember that it's always a good idea to test a formula with real numbers.

Note the nifty math shortcut: You don't need to divide the values by 3 or multiply by pi, because these operations are in both equations. You can compare the top numbers in the fractions directly. That helps avoid a lot of messy calculations. (Try it with your calculator.)

22. **A. 7.** The total is 36 kids in all. Four kids didn't go on any rides, so 32 kids went on rides. You know that 25 kids went on the lazy river. Ten of those kids also went on the water slides. With 32 kids going on rides, and 25 of them doing the lazy river, that leaves 7 who did just the water slides (32 − 25 = 7). Although 17 of the kids went on the water slides, 10 of them also went on the lazy river. So, the answer is Choice (A). Choice (B) is the total number of kids who went on the water slides. Choice (C) doesn't exclude the kids who didn't go on any rides. Choice (D) is the total number of kids who went on rides.

Many people find questions like this one hard to answer. If that's you, use the Flag feature to mark it for later. Or, simply guess and move on to the next question.

23. **C. She will reach her goal with 3 minutes to spare.** To answer this question, convert all the times to the same unit of measure, minutes. Then compare the sum of the actual times to her goal. The swim portion takes 45 minutes. The running portion takes one hour, which is 60 minutes. The biking portion takes 1.2 hours. To convert 1.2 hours to minutes, simply multiply 1.2 times 60, so 1.2 × 60 = 72 minutes. So, the total amount of time taken is 45 + 60 + 72 = 177 minutes. Because she wants to finish in 3 hours, and 3 hours is equivalent to 180 (3 × 60 = 180) minutes, she reaches her goal with 3 minutes to spare: 180 −177 = 3. So, Choice (C) is correct. Choice (A) incorrectly subtracts the goal from the actual time: 177 −180 = −3. Choice (D) uses 20 minutes instead of 0.2 hour to convert 1.2 hours into minutes.

24. **B. 30 inches.** There is a lot of extra information in this problem that you have to ignore in order to solve what is being asked. You are only interested in the location of the hooks and the distance from the top of the picture to the top of the wall.

If the top of the picture is two feet from the ceiling, that means the top of the picture is 24 inches from the ceiling. If the hooks to hang it are 6 inches below the top of the picture, that means the nails will have to be 24 + 6 = 30 inches from the top of the ceiling. So, Choice (B) is correct. Choice (A) does not account for the hooks. Choice (C) accounts for the hooks twice. Choice (D) does not make sense.

GED math questions sometimes include extra, unneeded information. One of your tasks as a test-taker is to eliminate the extra information. A good way to do this is to read the question before you read the information.

25. **B. 30.** To answer this question, determine the area of the pathway and the area of a single paver. Then divide the area of the pathway by the area of a paver. You can find the formula for area of a square or rectangle in the formula sheet. The total area of the pathway is 4 × 30 = 120 square feet. Each 2-foot-square paver has an area of 2 × 2 = 4 square feet. So, the total number of pavers needed will be 120 ÷ 4 = 30, or Choice (B). Choice (A) added the dimensions of the pathway and pavers, instead of multiplying them. Choice (C) divided the area of the pathway by the measure of one side of a paver (2) instead of the area of a paver. Choice (D) does not make sense.

26. **C. 7.0%.** When Darnell entered college in 2017, the enrollment was 28,500. When Darnell left the school in 2020, it was 30,500. Thus, the enrollment grew by 2,000 during that time, so the percent increase of enrollment was

$$\frac{2,000}{28,500} = .070 = 7.0\%$$

Therefore, Choice (C) is correct. Choice (A) doesn't move the decimal point two places to express the answer as a percent. Choice (B) is the percentage increase from 2017 to 2018. Choice (D) is the percentage increase from 2017 to 2019.

27. **D. 12,193 steps.** Kelly walked a total of 8,523 + 11,378 + 7,906 = 27,807 steps. If Kelly wants to average 10,000 steps a day, then after four days, she should have walked 40,000 steps. So, on the fourth day she needs to walk 40,000 − 27,807 = 12,193 steps, which means the answer is Choice (D).

28. **C. Between 3 and 4 minutes.** You can quickly figure out that Choice (C) is the likely answer using mental math. Because the faucet's flow rate is 11 to 12 gallons of water per minute, you know that it will take just under a minute to fill one of the jugs. So, it will take less than 4 minutes to fill all four jugs.

    You can check this answer by calculating. You know that four 10-gallon jugs hold a total of 40 gallons of water. If the flow rate is between 11 and 12 gallons per minute, then it will take anywhere from $\frac{40}{12} = 3.33$ minutes to $\frac{40}{11} = 3.64$ minutes.

29. **B. The label from a can of cranberry sauce.** A rectangle is a two-dimensional figure. Both the can of cranberry sauce (Choice A) and the ice cream cone (Choice C) are three-dimensional figures, so are incorrect. The paper wrapping from an ice cream cone (Choice D) is two-dimensional, but it forms a semi-circle when unwrapped and laid flat. Only Choice (D), the label on a cylinder (like a can of cranberry sauce), forms a rectangle when laid flat. And it can be the jellied or whole berry sauce — that doesn't matter. Just make sure you serve it with turkey at Thanksgiving!

30. **C. 96.** You can quickly figure out that the answer is Choice (C) using a simple shortcut. If Sam covered 288 miles using $\frac{3}{4}$ of a tank of gas, then simply divide 288 by 3 to find out how many miles she can cover on $\frac{1}{4}$ of a tank of gas: 288 ÷ 3 = 96.

    You can check this number by calculating. If 288 miles represents $\frac{3}{4}$ of her 16-gallon tank, then that means that she covers 288 miles using $\frac{3}{4} \times 16 = 12$ gallons, and so with each gallon, she can travel $\frac{288}{12} = 24$ miles. Because she has 4 gallons left in her tank — (16 − 12) = 4 — she can travel an additional 4 × 24 = 96 miles.

    Therefore, Choice (C) is correct. Choice (A) is the number of gallons she used so far. Choice (B) is the number of miles she gets per gallon. Choice (D) is the number of gallons she can get on a full tank of gas.

31. **B. She spends over a quarter of her money on things other than the mortgage and food.** You can use the process of elimination to answer a question like this one. Evaluate each answer choice one at a time, in order, until you find the answer. She spends 11% of her budget on utilities and only 7% on insurance, so Choice (A) is incorrect. Because she spends 44 + 28 = 72% on the mortgage and food, that means she spends 28% on things other than the mortgage and food, so Choice (B) is correct.

    You can stop with Choice (B) since you know that there is only one correct answer. For reference, here is why the other choices are incorrect. Choice (C) is incorrect because after the mortgage, the most she spends is on food, at 28%. Choice (D) is incorrect because miscellaneous expenses are 10%, which is more than one-third of what she spends on food, at 28%.

32. **$400.** With a monthly budget of $3,500, that means she spends $3,500 × 0.44 = $1,540 each month on the mortgage, and $3,500 × 0.11 = $385 on utilities. So, her total expenses for those two items are $1,540 + $385 = $1,925. If she rents, she will be paying $1,175 + $350 = $1,525 for those same expenses, so by renting, she will save $1,925 − $1,525 = $400 each month.

33. **B. 6.** The formula for area of a triangle is $A = \frac{1}{2}bh$. (You can find this formula on the GED Formula Sheet.) The base in this case is the distance from point A to point B, which is 4. The height is the distance from point C to the side connecting points A and B, which is 3. Thus, the area is $\frac{1}{2} \times 4 \times 3 = 6$.

Therefore, Choice (B) is correct. Choice (A) adds the base and height instead of multiplying them. Choice (C) omits multiplying by $\frac{1}{2}$. Choice (D) divides by $\frac{1}{2}$ instead of multiplying.

The calculator and the online whiteboard (or erasable tablet) can be very helpful on a multi-step question like this one.

Area comes up frequently on the GED Math test. Understanding how to use the formulas for the areas of the various shapes can help you score well on this test.

34. **A. 300 miles.** Brianna's total travel time can be defined by $\frac{x}{300} + 0.5 + 2 + 1$, where x is the number of miles of the trip, and 0.5, 2, and 1 represent the amount of time (in hours) it takes Brianna to get to the airport, wait for the flight to leave, and then get from the airport to her final destination.

Rachael's total travel time can be defined by $\frac{x}{125} + 0.5 + 0.5 + 0.75$, where x is the number of miles of the trip, and 0.5, 0.5, and 0.75 represent the amount of time (in hours) it takes Rachael to get to the train station, wait for the train to leave, and then get from the station to her final destination.

When you plug in 300 miles for x, Brianna's total travel time is

$\frac{300}{300} + 0.5 + 2 + 1 = 1 + 0.5 + 2 + 1 = 4.5$ hours.

When you plug in 300 miles for x, Rachael's total travel time is

$\frac{300}{125} + 0.5 + 0.5 + 0.75 = 2.4 + 0.5 + 0.5 + 0.75 = 4.15$

hours, which means that Rachael arrives first. Therefore, Choice (A) is correct. For all the other values listed, Rachael's total travel time is greater than Brianna's total travel time.

35. **D. Buy materials for both the bedroom and the living room for $640.** You can tackle this question by the process of elimination. Because you are trying to figure out which scenario you can afford, you should start with the choice that has the biggest budget, which is Choice (D).

Choice (D) is correct because the minimum cost for buying materials for a room similar in size to the bedroom and living room would be $240 + $290 = $530. If you have $640 for this project, then you should have enough.

The bedroom has an area of 11 × 11 = 121, which is greater than the room size of 10 × 12 = 120, so the minimum cost for installing carpeting will be more than $420, making Choice (A) incorrect.

The living room has an area of 12 × 13 = 156, which is greater than the room size 12 × 12 = 144, so the minimum cost for installing carpeting will be $500, which means that Choice (B) is incorrect.

The minimum cost for buying materials for a room the size of the living room is $290, so Choice (C) is incorrect.

36. $140.80. The area of the kitchen is $8 \times 11 = 88$ square feet.

By choosing ceramic tiling over marble tiling, you save $6.20 − $4.60 = $1.60 per square foot, which means you save $88 \times $1.60 = $140.80, overall.

37. A. −16. You can answer this question by plugging the values for the two points and the value of the slope into the equation for slope: $m = \frac{y_2 - y_1}{x_2 - x_1}$. (You can find the equation for slope on the GED Formula Sheet.) Doing so gives you $\frac{5}{2} = \frac{-1 - y_1}{3 - (-3)}$. The denominator simplifies to $\frac{5}{2} = \frac{-1 - y_1}{6}$. You can then cross-multiply and get $30 = 2(-1 - y_1)$.

You then divide both sides by 2 to get $15 = -1 - y_1$. Add 1 to both sides, $16 = -y_1$, and then be sure to divide both sides by −1 so that you get $-16 = y_1$. This means that Choice (A) is the answer. Choice (B) added −1 to both sides. Choice (C) added −1 to both sides and forgot to divide by −1. Choice (D) forgot to divide by −1.

38. C. 24. Because the area of a square is equal to the length of one side squared, a square with an area of 36 has sides of length 6; $\sqrt{36} = 6$.

The perimeter of a square is equal to 4 times the length of one side, so the perimeter is $4 \times 6 = 24$. Therefore, the answer is Choice (C). Choice (A) is the length of one side. Choice (B) is the length of two sides. Choice (D) is the area of the square.

39. B. 26. The area of a trapezoid is $A = \frac{1}{2}h(b_1 + b_2)$. (You can find this formula on the GED Formula Sheet.) It is important to remember that the height of a trapezoid is the length that is perpendicular to both bases, so in this example, the height is 4, meaning that the area is $A = \frac{1}{2} \times 4(5 + 8) = 2 \times 13 = 26$.

Therefore, the answer is Choice (B). This is a good question for using the calculator.

Another way you can look at this question is to treat the trapezoid as a combination of a rectangle and a right triangle. The dimensions for the right triangle would be the same height of 4, but with a base of 3, because the full base is 8, and 5 of that belongs to the rectangle. Given those measurements, you would calculate the total area as the area of the square plus the area of the triangle: $4 \times 5 + \frac{1}{2} \times 4 \times 3 = 20 + 6 = 26$.

40. B. 56.5. To calculate the circumference, use the formula in the GED Formula Sheet: $C = \pi d = 18\pi = 56.5$. So Choice (B) is correct. Choice (A) used the radius, 9, instead of the diameter. Choice (C) used the diameter instead of the radius, and also used the formula $2\pi r$. Choice (D) is the area of the interior of the hoop.

When you use your calculator, remember that pi is a constant key on the calculator. You don't have to key in 3.14. That can save time as well as a keystroking error.

REMEMBER

41. D. A rectangle with sides of 8 and 10. To answer this question, you need to calculate the area of the circle and the area of each of the figures in the choices and then compare them.

Start with the area of the circle. A circle with a radius of 5 has an area of $A = 5^2 \times \pi = 78.5$.

A square with sides of 9 has an area of $9^2 = 81$ (Choice A).

A triangle with a base of 10 and a height of 15 has an area of $A = \frac{1}{2}(10 \times 15) = 75$ (Choice B).

A parallelogram with a base of 10 and a height of 15 has an area of $A = 10 \times 15 = 150$ (Choice C).

A rectangle with sides of 8 and 10 has an area of $A = 8 \times 10 = 80$ (Choice D).

Thus, the closest is the rectangle, Choice (D): 80 − 78.5 = 1.5.

This question involves a lot of calculations with several different formulas, so this is a good question to flag for later in the test.

TIP

42. **C. $4x^2 − 4xy + y^2$.** Use the distributive property to solve this question:

$$(2x - y) \times (2x - y) = 2x \times (2x - y) - y \times (2x - y)$$

$$= 4x^2 - 2xy - 2xy + y^2$$

$$= 4x^2 - 4xy + y^2$$

Therefore, the answer is Choice (C).

Note that even if you can't do all the calculations, you can eliminate some of the choices as incorrect. You can quickly eliminate Choice (B) because it doesn't contain x^2. You can also eliminate Choice (D) because you know $2x \times 2x = 4x^2$. That leaves only two choices, which improves your chances if you want to guess.

TIP

43. **C. $5a + 10b + 25c$.** If you have a nickels, then the number of cents represented by them is $5a$. Similarly, if you have b dimes, then the number of cents represented by them is $10b$. And if you have c quarters, then the number of cents represented by them is $25c$.

Therefore, the expression that represents the value of all of the coins in the jar is $5a + 10b + 25c$, Choice (C).

44. **D. $\dfrac{3x^2 - 2x + 6}{3x(x-3)}$.** To combine these fractions, you have to write them both with a common denominator, which in this case is the product of the two individual denominators, $(x - 3) \times 3x$.

Thus, $\dfrac{x}{x-3} - \dfrac{2}{3x}$ becomes

$$= \frac{x(3x)}{(x-3)(3x)} - \frac{2(x-3)}{3x(x-3)}$$

$$= \frac{3x^2}{(x-3)(3x)} - \frac{2x-6}{3x(x-3)}$$

$$= \frac{3x^2 - 2x + 6}{(x-3)(3x)}$$

Therefore, the answer is Choice (D). Choice (A) doesn't have the correct common denominator. Choice (B) didn't change the numerator when changing the denominator. Choice (C) subtracted 6 instead of adding it.

Because question 44 has a lot of calculations, it's a good one to flag for later. If you run out of time and want to guess, you can improve your chances by eliminating some choices. Calculating the common denominator first lets you eliminate Choice (A). You can also eliminate Choice (B) because you know it didn't change the numerator when changing the denominator.

TIP

45. **B. $310.** If she babysat for 15 hours and dog-sat for 8 hours last week, then $b = 15$ and $d = 8$, and so her total earnings were $10 \times 15 + 20 \times 8 = 150 + 160 = 310$.

Therefore, Choice (B) is correct. Choice (A) calculates all her hours (8 + 15 = 23) at the hourly rate for babysitting ($10), and so is incorrect. Choice (C) mixes the values and calculates the hours for each task with the rate for the other task: $10 \times 8 + 20 \times 15 = 80 + 300 = 380$. Choice (D) calculates all 23 hours at the rate for dog-sitting: $23 \times 20 = 460$.

46. **B. 1984.** You can answer this question either by looking at the table and comparing the ratios for the four years, or by examining the graph and looking for which year had the smallest difference between the number of athletes and medals won. Also, keep in mind that although there are many years of data in the table and the graph, you only need to focus on the 4 years listed in the answer choices. That makes your job easier. In terms of ratios, the ratios for the 4 years are:

1972 = 400/94 = 4.3

1984 = 522/174 = 3.0

1996 = 646/101 = 6.4

2012 = 530/104 = 5.1

The lowest ratio is for 1984, which is Choice (B). You can confirm this by looking at the graph.

Questions about ratio come up frequently on the GED Math, Science, and Social Studies tests. Understanding how ratios work can help you on several tests.

TIP

47. **10.8.** You can think of the distance between two points as being the hypotenuse of a right triangle. Because this is the case, you can use the Pythagorean Theorem to answer the question. The right triangle connecting the points would have legs of 10 and 4. So the distance between the two points is $\sqrt{10^2 + 4^2} = \sqrt{100 + 16} = \sqrt{116} = 10.77$, which rounds to 10.8.

48. **D. 2.** To solve this linear system for x, you have to eliminate y by multiplying each equation by a number that allows you to combine them with each other and end up with just x's. Multiply the first equation by 6 and the second equation by 4.

$6(3x - 4y = 10) = 18x - 24y = 60$

$4(5x + 6y = 4) = 20x + 24y = 16$

Add the two equations, and you get $38x = 76$; $x = 2$.

49. **C. $1440.** To calculate the amount of interest, you use the formula $I = prt$, which is in the GED Formula Sheet. Thus, $I = 1200 \times .04 \times 5 = 240$. This represents the amount of interest earned over five years. To find out how much she will have in total in her account, you take the interest and add it to the original amount she used to open the account.

$1200 + $240 = $1440

Isn't that interesting?!

Choice (A) is only the interest she earned. Choice (B) adds only $24 in interest, not $240. Choice (D) multiplies her original deposit by 4.

50. **C. basketball or hockey.** You know that 150 minutes is equivalent to 2.5 hours. The only two sports whose games are within that allotted time are basketball (2 hours and 11 minutes) and hockey (2 hours and 20 minutes). If he tries to watch the other two sports, he will miss the end of the game!!

Answer Key

1.	8	18.	C	35.	D
2.	C	19.	D	36.	$140.80
3.	D	20.	A	37.	A
4.	C	21.	D	38.	C
5.	$3.57	22.	A	39.	B
6.	C	23.	C	40.	B
7.	A	24.	B	41.	D
8.	C	25.	B	42.	C
9.	D	26.	C	43.	C
10.	D	27.	D	44.	D
11.	B	28.	C	45.	B
12.	C	29.	B	46.	B
13.	C	30.	C	47.	10.8
14.	A	31.	B	48.	D
15.	C	32.	$400	49.	C
16.	C	33.	B	50.	C
17.	C	34.	A		

7

Getting More Test Practice: GED Practice Test 2

IN THIS PART . . .

Continue building your skills and your confidence with another full-length GED practice test.

Score your answers quickly and compare your results from this practice test with Practice Test 1.

Check out detailed answer explanations for every question and sample scoring criteria for the Extended Response.

Chapter **27**

Practice Test 2: Reasoning through Language Arts

Ready for more practice? You have 95 minutes to complete the question-and-answer section, followed by a ten-minute break, and then another 45 minutes to write the Extended Response (the essay). Remember, on the real GED test, you can't transfer unused time from one section to another. To keep track of time, use the timer on your mobile phone. If you run out of time, mark the last question you completed. Then finish the remaining questions. This will show you how much faster you need to work on the real GED to answer all the questions.

The answers and explanations to this test's questions are in Chapter 28. Review the explanations to all the questions, not just the ones you didn't get. Going over the answers is a good review technique.

REMEMBER

Practice tests work best when you take them under the same conditions as the real test. Unless you require accommodations, you'll be taking the GED test on a computer. You'll see all the questions on a computer screen and use a keyboard or mouse to indicate your answers. I formatted the questions and answer choices in this book to make them appear as similar as possible to the real GED test. I had to retain A, B, C, and D choices for marking your answers, and I provide an answer sheet for you to do so. Also, to make it simpler for you to time yourself, I present the questions for Reading Comprehension and Grammar and Language together in one section rather than separately (as on the real GED), with the Extended Response at the end of the test. If possible, write the essay on a computer (with spell-check, grammar-check, and autocorrect turned off) to simulate conditions on test day. Have a sheet of paper or two to use to jot down notes and organize your ideas. Otherwise, use the lined paper I provide for you.

Answer Sheet for Practice Test 2, Reasoning through Language Arts

1. _____

2. _____

3. _____

4. _____

5. _____

6. _____

7. _____

8. _____

9. _____

10. _____

11. _____

12. _____

13. _____

14. _____

15. _____

16. _____

17. _____

18. _____

19. _____

20. _____

21. _____

22. _____

23. _____

24. _____

25. _____

26. _____

27. _____

28. _____

29. _____

30. _____

31. _____

32. _____

33. _____

34. _____

35. _____

36. _____

37. _____

38. _____

39. _____

40. _____

41. _____

42. _____

43. _____

44. _____

45. _____

46. _____

47. _____

48. _____

49. _____

50. _____

DIRECTIONS: You may answer the questions in this section in any order. Mark your answers on the answer sheet provided.

Questions 1–10 refer to the following passage.

Select... ▾ the same. Many bottlers use the same municipal water that comes from your tap. They merely have Select... ▾ do some additional filtration to enhance the taste. Select... ▾ different. The mineral content of Select... ▾ from spring to spring, producing water with a unique taste. Other bottled waters Select... ▾ to the clean taste of water.

If you find mineral water whose taste you enjoy and don't mind the cost, enjoy. From our "Green" perspective, the plastic litter is a huge negative. Also, the effect on the environment of moving large quantities of potable water from one area to another make this an undesirable solution.

Many people enjoy Select... ▾ taste. So how can you get the same clean taste without the waste? The Select... ▾ expensive way is to use a jug with a charcoal filter cartridge. Filling that jug with clean tap water removes the chlorine and unpleasant tastes or odors. It also removes some of the lead found in the water pipes of older buildings. This is an Select... ▾ inexpensive choice. Certainly our morning coffee and tea tastes better for this filtration.

A more advanced and expensive counter-top system is a distillation pot. This system boils water, collects the steam, and condenses it into absolutely pure water. But not everyone likes the taste of totally mineral-free water, and the electricity costs add up.

There are also more extensive systems available. If you get tired of changing cartridges or storing the Select... ▾ can also have an under-the-counter system installed on your kitchen sink. In townhouses, you can add such a system on the main water pipe and provide the same filtration to the entire house. Some of these systems use carbon blocks and ceramic filters. The blocks are more effective than loose charcoal Select... ▾ of pesticides and other chemical contaminants. Ceramic filters remove cloudiness and micro-particles, spores, and other microscopic matter. They deliver excellent drinking water. In either case, there is little waste other than the filters.

1. Select... ▾ the same.

   (A) But not all brands of bottled water are

   (B) Not all brands of bottled water are

   (C) But, not all brands of bottled water are

   (D) Not all brands of bottled water is

2. They merely have Select... ▾ do some additional filtration to enhance the taste.

   (A) to remove the chlorine completely,

   (B) to remove the chlorine completely and

   (C) to complete the removal of the chlorine and

   (D) a removal of the chlorine and

3. [Select... ▾] different.

   (A) Bottled spring waters are

   (B) Bottled, spring waters are

   (C) Bottled spring waters were

   (D) Bottled spring waters is

4. The mineral content of [Select... ▾] from spring to spring, producing water with a unique taste.

   (A) water are different

   (B) water differ

   (C) waters differs

   (D) waters differ

5. Other bottled waters [Select... ▾] to the clean taste of water.

   (A) are carbonated, either naturally or artificially in the bottling process, carbonation can add

   (B) are carbonated naturally or artificially in the bottling process, carbonation can add

   (C) are carbonated. Either naturally or artificially in the bottling process. Carbonation can add

   (D) are carbonated, either naturally or artificially, in the bottling process. Carbonation can add

6. Many people enjoy [Select... ▾] taste.

   (A) there bottled water's

   (B) their bottled water's

   (C) they're bottled water's

   (D) their bottled waters

7. The [Select... ▾] expensive way is to use a jug with a charcoal filter cartridge.

   (A) less

   (B) least

   (C) lesser

   (D) lessor

8. This is an [Select... ▾] inexpensive choice.

   (A) effective, and

   (B) effective and

   (C) effective

   (D) effective; and

9. If you get tired of changing cartridges or storing the [Select... ▾] can also have an under-the-counter system installed on your kitchen sink.

   (A) plastic, jug in your fridge, you

   (B) plastic jug, in your fridge, you

   (C) plastic jug in your fridge you

   (D) plastic jug in your fridge, you

10. The blocks are more effective than loose charcoal [Select... ▾] of pesticides and other chemical contaminants.

   (A) filters also removing traces

   (B) filters. Also removing traces

   (C) filters; also removing traces

   (D) filters for removing traces

Questions 11–17 refer to the following business letter.

BEST Institute of Technology

75 Ingram Drive
Concord, MA 01742

To whom it may concern:

I am pleased to provide a strong, positive recommendation of Jane Fairfax of the Sheridan Square [Select... ▾]. The BEST Institute of Technology [Select... ▾] with the Sheridan Square ERC in recruiting candidates for our professional and technical training programs since April of last year.

[Select... ▾] Ms. Fairfax provided many important services to our programs. Her duties included:

- Setting up information presentations and job readiness seminars
- Distributing print materials
- Counseling applicants
- Arranging five graduation ceremonies at Sheridan Square ERC

Ms. Fairfax [Select... ▾] a strong advocate for our program, which has trained more than 250 adult learners during the past 18 months. The fact that Sheridan Square has become our primary source of referrals [Select... ▾] a tribute to Ms. Fairfax's efforts. She has [Select... ▾]. On a personal level, it has been a joy to work with Ms. Fairfax, and I wish her the very [Select... ▾].

Dale Worth, PhD, Executive Director

11. I am pleased to comment on the relationship of our organization to Jane Fairfax of the Sheridan Square [Select... ▾].

   (A) employment resource Center

   (B) Employment resource Center

   (C) Employment Resource Center

   (D) Employment resource center

12. The BEST Institute of Technology [Select... ▾] with the Sheridan Square ERC in recruiting candidates for our professional and technical training programs since April of last year.

   (A) has partnered

   (B) partnered

   (C) partners

   (D) is partnering

GO ON TO NEXT PAGE ➡

13. Select... ▼ Ms. Fairfax provided many important services to our programs.

   (A) In support, of the partnership,

   (B) In support of the partnership

   (C) In support of the partnership.

   (D) In support of the partnership,

14. Ms. Fairfax Select... ▼ a strong advocate for our program, which has trained more than 250 adult learners during the past 18 months.

   (A) has always been

   (B) always is being

   (C) had been always

   (D) have always been

15. The fact that Sheridan Square has become our primary source of referrals Select... ▼ a tribute to Ms. Fairfax's efforts.

   (A) are

   (B) is

   (C) were

   (D) was

16. She has Select... ▼ .

   (A) pursued her responsibilities with a high degree of professionalism

   (B) with a high degree of professionalism pursued her responsibilities

   (C) pursued with a high degree of professionalism her responsibilities

   (D) pursued with professionalism a high degree of responsibilities

17. On a personal level, it has been a joy to work with Ms. Fairfax, and I wish her the very Select... ▼ .

   (A) best in her future endeavors

   (B) best, in her future endeavors

   (C) best in her future, endeavors

   (D) best, in her future, endeavors

Questions 18–25 refer to the following excerpt adapted from Customer Service For Dummies, *by Karen Leland and Keith Bailey (Wiley).*

The Customer Care Coupon

A new copy shop Select... ▼ near our office. Modern and full of new, streamlined, state-of-the-art Select... ▼ store was just what I needed. Select... ▼ I waited 15 minutes to get served because of a shortage of trained staff. They bounced back by apologizing, explaining the situation, Select... ▼ a coupon that was worth 100 free copies. Okay, I thought, fair enough. They're new and getting their act together, so Select... ▼ big deal. A week later, I went back for a second time. Right away, I Select... ▼ it was a big mistake. I waited 20 minutes for service. Select... ▼ apologized, explained the situation, and gave me a coupon for 100 free copies. This time I was Select... ▼ little less understanding. Two weeks later, I went back and the same thing happened again. I didn't want another free coupon — they inconvenienced me just once too often. My opinion of their services was so soured that I began looking for another copy shop.

18. A new copy shop [Select... ▼] near our office.

   (A) recent opened

   (B) recently opened

   (C) opened recent

   (D) recently opening

19. Modern and full of new, streamlined, state-of-the-art [Select... ▼] store was just what I needed.

   (A) copiers. The

   (B) copiers, the

   (C) copiers; the

   (D) copiers and the

20. [Select... ▼] I waited 15 minutes to get served because of a shortage of trained staff.

   (A) Because to get served

   (B) When for the first time I went there,

   (C) To get served because

   (D) The first time I went there,

21. They bounced back by apologizing, explaining the situation, [Select... ▼] a coupon that was worth 100 free copies.

   (A) and given me

   (B) and giving myself

   (C) and giving me

   (D) and gave me

22. They're new and getting their act together, so [Select... ▼] big deal.

   (A) its no

   (B) it's no

   (C) it's know

   (D) its' no

23. Right away, I [Select... ▼] it was a big mistake.

   (A) known

   (B) news

   (C) new

   (D) knew

24. [Select... ▼] apologized, explained the situation, and gave me a coupon for 100 free copies.

   (A) But they

   (B) After they

   (C) They

   (D) When they

GO ON TO NEXT PAGE

25. This time I was [Select... ▾] little less understanding.

   (A) a

   (B) too

   (C) to

   (D) an

Questions 26–31 refer to this excerpt from The Prince, *by Niccolò Machiavelli (Project Gutenberg;* www. gutenberg.org) *and the following short passage about* The Art of War, *an ancient Chinese military textbook.*

The Prince

A prince ought to have no other aim or thought, nor select anything else for his study, than war and its rules and discipline; for this is the sole art that belongs to him who rules, and it is of such force that it not only upholds those who are born princes, but it often enables men to rise from a private station to that rank. And, on the contrary, it is seen that when princes have thought more of ease than of arms they have lost their states. And the first cause of your losing it is to neglect this art; and what enables you to acquire a state is to be master of the art. Francesco Sforza, through being martial, from a private person became Duke of Milan; and the sons, through avoiding the hardships and troubles of arms, from dukes became private persons. For among other evils which being unarmed brings you, it causes you to be despised, and this is one of those ignominies against which a prince ought to guard himself, as is shown later on. Because there is nothing proportionate between the armed and the unarmed; and it is not reasonable that he who is armed should yield obedience willingly to him who is unarmed, or that the unarmed man should be secure among armed servants. Because, there being in the one disdain and in the other suspicion, it is not possible for them to work well together. And therefore a prince who does not understand the art of war, over and above the other misfortunes already mentioned, cannot be respected by his soldiers, nor can he rely on them. He ought never, therefore, to have out of his thoughts this subject of war, and in peace he should addict himself more to its exercise than in war; this he can do in two ways, the one by action, the other by study.

On *The Art of War*

The Art of War is an ancient text by a revered Chinese general, Sun Tzu. This book is considered to be one of the most insightful books on war ever written. One of the most important factors that contributes to military success, according to Sun Tzu, is leadership. On leadership, Sun Tzu said, "The commander of an army stands for these virtues: wisdom, sincerity, benevolence, courage, and strictness." Some of these characteristics seem obvious, but others are contradictory. A military leader clearly needs wisdom. And a good military leader needs sincerity in order to win the trust of subordinates and troops. And, of course, courage is a necessity in war. But what about benevolence and strictness? Obviously, balance is needed. Strictness is necessary to maintain discipline and order. But at the same time, a good leader cannot be harsh, unjust, or arbitrary. A good leader needs to consider each situation and make decisions that are fair and generous when warranted.

26. According to *The Prince*, why should a prince concentrate on the study of war?

   (A) It is the knowledge that preserves their position.

   (B) It allows the prince to lead a more comfortable life.

   (C) Not being focused on war makes you more beloved by the people.

   (D) Peaceful men are respected by their soldiers.

27. According to *The Prince*, why should a prince master the study of war and be armed?

    (A) Having a large army ensures lots of jobs.

    (B) People are suspicious of princes with large armies.

    (C) Slaves fear soldiers.

    (D) The armed do not readily yield authority to the unarmed.

28. How does Machiavelli think the population will react to a prince who is unarmed?

    (A) They will follow him.

    (B) They will respect him.

    (C) They will fear him.

    (D) They will despise him.

29. Which of these phrases best describes Machiavelli's attitude to the study of the art of war?

    (A) Study infrequently.

    (B) In times of peace, prepare for war.

    (C) Avoid war to gain the respect of your people.

    (D) Warriors respect only warriors.

30. According to "On *The Art of War*," what would a good general do if he found out that one of his top subordinates might be too sick to fight?

    (A) Make him fight anyway, even though he might die.

    (B) Send the subordinate to a hospital far from the front.

    (C) Harshly punish the subordinate in front of everyone.

    (D) Ask the subordinate what he needs in order to return quickly.

31. Which of these statements would Machiavelli and Sun Tzu agree on?

    (A) A strong leader crushes all opposition and dissent.

    (B) To maintain power, leaders only need superior strength.

    (C) To maintain power, leaders must master the art of war.

    (D) A ruler can delegate military affairs to his generals.

Questions 32-36 refer to the following passage from The Adventures of Tom Sawyer, *by Mark Twain (Project Gutenberg;* www.gutenberg.org). *The speaker is Tom Sawyer's guardian, his Aunt Polly.*

"Hang the boy, can't I never learn anything? Ain't he played me tricks enough like that for me to be looking out for him by this time? But old fools is the biggest fools there is. Can't learn an old dog new tricks, as the saying is. But my goodness, he never plays them alike, two days, and how is a body to know what's coming? He 'pears to know just how long he can torment me before I get my dander up, and he knows if he can make out to put me off for a minute or make me laugh, it's all down again and I can't hit him a lick. I ain't doing my duty by that boy, and that's the Lord's truth, goodness knows. Spare the rod and spile the child, as the Good Book says. I'm a laying up sin and suffering for us both, I know. He's full of the Old Scratch, but laws-a-me! he's my own dead sister's boy, poor thing, and I ain't got the heart to lash him, somehow. Every time I let him off, my conscience does hurt me so, and every time I hit him my old heart most breaks. Well-a-well, man that is born of woman is of few days and full of trouble, as the Scripture says, and I reckon it's so. He'll play hookey this evening*, and I'll just be obleeged to make him work, tomorrow, to punish him. It's mighty hard to make him work

Saturdays, when all the boys is having holiday, but he hates work more than he hates anything else, and I've GOT to do some of my duty by him, or I'll be the ruination of the child."

*Southwestern for "afternoon"

32. Why did Mark Twain write this dialogue in such an ungrammatical manner?

   (A) He did not know any better.
   (B) He assumed his readers spoke in a "folksy" dialect.
   (C) He wanted to reflect the character of the speaker.
   (D) Everyone spoke like that back then.

33. Which of these statements does Aunt Polly use to support punishing Tom?

   (A) Man that is born of woman is of few days and full of trouble.
   (B) Spare the rod and spile the child.
   (C) Old fools is the biggest fools there is.
   (D) Can't learn an old dog new tricks.

34. Why does the speaker believe she is committing a sin?

   (A) She can't make Tom go to church.
   (B) She occasionally hits Tom.
   (C) She is not strict enough with Tom.
   (D) She makes Tom work on Saturdays.

35. What evidence is there in the text to support the idea that the speaker considers herself a good, God-fearing woman?

   (A) She makes references to religion.
   (B) She worries about making Tom work on Sundays.
   (C) She gets mad at Tom Sawyer for the tricks he pulls.
   (D) She wants Tom Sawyer to go to school every day.

36. What does Tom Sawyer hate the most?

   (A) work
   (B) painting fences
   (C) playing hookey
   (D) annoying his aunt

Questions 37 and 38 refer to the following excerpt from the Central Intelligence Agency Careers website (www.cia.gov).

Instilling Inclusive Work Practices

In our organization, we are working to ensure every officer's views are heard and that their ideas and skills are given due consideration. This enables us to fully leverage our talented and dedicated workforce.

The Agency has a variety of employee resource groups comprised of employees [Select... ▼] a common affinity (gender, sexual orientation, disability, ethnic, and racial backgrounds) and their allies. The employee resource groups make the organization stronger by:

- increasing cultural awareness,

- providing insight, practical solutions, and best practices, and

- promoting engagement and collaboration.

[Select... ▼] mentoring, coaching, training, and recognition for collaborative and inclusive behaviors foster employee engagement, professional development, and career advancement.

37. The Agency has a variety of employee resource groups comprised of employees [Select... ▼] a common affinity (gender, sexual orientation, disability, ethnic, and racial backgrounds) and their allies.

(A) whom share

(B) who share

(C) whom shares

(D) who shares

38. [Select... ▼] mentoring, coaching, training, and recognition for collaborative and inclusive behaviors foster employee engagement, professional development, and career advancement.

(A) In addition,

(B) However,

(C) In contrast,

(D) In other words,

Questions 39–44 refer to the following passage.

Facilities for Access to Creative Enterprise (FACE)

Originally founded in 1992 to train unemployed youth in small "hand skill" craft workshops, this project provides occupational and entrepreneurial skills as an alternative to scarce traditional manufacturing jobs. Beginning with glass engraving and sign writing, FACE now offers training in more than 200 hand skill occupations, including computer repair, antique restoration, clothing manufacturing, graphic design, masonry, sail making, locksmithing, watch and jewelry repair, and wood turning. Funded through the Youth Training Program, FACE provides 800 internships under the premise that if young people can't secure employment, they can develop skills to create their own businesses.

Based on its experience, FACE has developed a Certificate in Small Business and Enterprise Skills. The aim of the certificate is "to develop the skills of enterprise management across a range of occupational sectors, within small business and in general employment and which are applicable in a wide range of personal and social contexts outside work." Competencies include self-evaluation, decision making, initiative taking, resource and time management, opportunism and self-motivation, problem solving, and learning-to-learn skills, as well as communication and number skills vital to personal effectiveness.

39. What is the overall purpose of the FACE project?

(A) to provide manufacturing jobs

(B) to engrave glass and make signs

(C) to train jobless young people

(D) to offer a training certificate

40. Which of the following are examples of hand-skill craft occupations? Write the letters in the box.

┌─────────┐
│   │
└─────────┘

(A) computer repair

(B) jewelry repair

(C) sail making

(D) robotic assembly

41. How can young people best secure employment?

(A) by getting factory jobs

(B) by creating new enterprises of their own

(C) by learning to make furniture

(D) by obtaining a Certificate in Small Business

42. What is the difference between the training in hand-skill crafts and the Certificate in Small Business and Enterprise Skills?

(A) The training is on specific crafts, and the certificate develops general business and personal skills.

(B) The training focuses on job-search skills, and the certificate develops personal skills.

(C) The training develops personal skills through training in a craft, and the certificate recognizes academic achievement.

(D) The training is on traditional hand crafts, and the certificate is on high-tech skills.

43. Which competency is included in each part of the program? Write the letters in the appropriate boxes.

Hand-Craft Training	Certificate in Small Business Skills

(A) self-evaluation

(B) anger management

(C) graphic design

(D) mobile phone repair

44. What wording in the passage suggests that FACE does not expect its graduates to find work with large industrial employers after completing their training?

(A) develop occupational skills

(B) an alternative to scarce traditional manufacturing jobs

(C) competencies include self-evaluation and decision making

(D) in general employment

Questions 45–50 refer to the following business email message.

TO: James Tiberius, President, ABLE Books, Inc.

FROM: Akira Hudson, Director, New Book Development

RE: Survival Math Book Proposal

We meet mathematical problems every day in our lives. How we handle them makes the difference between winning and losing. Many of our decisions require knowledge of "survival mathematics," the skills and concepts that help us survive in an increasingly complex world. Many students drop high school mathematics as soon as they can. Few are willing or able to take in school the life skills courses that would help them later in life. As a result, they never learn some of the important math life skills. This book has a built-in target audience, the people who need "survival mathematics" to get ahead in this world.

The key life skills are the everyday arithmetic that helps one survive in the marketplace. We propose to help readers learn and practice the following skills:

- Different methods of earning a paycheck: A comparison of hourly wages, piecework, commission, and salary.

- Pay and deductions on pay slips: What comes off and why, and making sure your paycheck is correct.

- Budgeting: Making your money last from paycheck to paycheck, creating a household budget, and covering all your regular expenses.

- The deal: How to read ads. Just how good a deal is "the deal"? Do coupons really save money?

- Credit cards: How you pay, what you pay for, and the real cost of loyalty programs.

- Compound interest: The true cost of borrowing money. We show you how to compare interest rates on debt, ranging from bank loans to credit card debt, and how to work out just how expensive credit card debt is.

- Payday loans: Working out the true costs of these high-interest, short-term loans.

- Compound interest on savings: Earning money on money. We explain how you can reinvest to earn more, and the magic of time in accumulating wealth.

- Keeping more of what you earn: Some simple strategies to minimize taxes, from education and retirement savings to mortgage interest deductibility.

- Owning a car: Calculating the pros and cons. We compare used versus new, purchase versus lease, and examine the true cost of owning a car. Because a car is probably the second-biggest purchase most people will ever make, this is an important part of consumer knowledge. This unit is specially aimed at first-time car purchasers.

The application of basic arithmetic skills will help readers become better consumers and teach them how to deal with mathematical issues in everyday life.

45. Why does the writer of the email suggest that this new book is needed?

(A) Many students don't take enough math courses in high school.

(B) Many students want to take advanced math in college but lack the preparation.

(C) Many people make a lot of math mistakes in their checkbooks.

(D) Many people don't use coupons at the supermarket.

46. According to the email, what is the point of budgeting?

    (A) to minimize taxes

    (B) to avoid running out of money between paychecks

    (C) to set aside some savings from each paycheck

    (D) to allocate some money for donations to charity

47. What does *regular* mean in this excerpt from the passage?

    Budgeting: Making your money last from paycheck to paycheck; creating a household budget; covering all your regular expenses.

    (A) usual

    (B) special

    (C) extra

    (D) favorite

48. Why are car purchases considered important enough to be given a heading of their own?

    (A) Everyone needs a car.

    (B) Students in particular want to buy cars.

    (C) Car loans are more expensive than credit card debts.

    (D) Cars are among the largest purchases most people ever make.

49. Which of the following would be a good additional topic for the book? Write the letters in the correct box.

In the Book	Not in the Book

    (A) saving money by postponing routine maintenance on your car

    (B) saving money on major purchases by "shopping around"

    (C) taking full advantage of employer plans to save for retirement

    (D) reducing costs by canceling anti-virus software on your computer

50. What is the primary purpose of this email?

    (A) to convince people to study more math

    (B) to inform readers of ways to save money

    (C) to convince readers to buy the book

    (D) to convince the company to publish the book

    At this point, you may take a 10-minute break before beginning the Extended Response.

Extended Response

TIME: 45 minutes

YOUR ASSIGNMENT: The following articles present arguments from both supporters and critics of promoting higher education for all. In your response, analyze both positions presented in the two articles to determine which one is best supported. Use relevant and specific evidence from the articles to support your response. If possible, write your essay on a computer with spell-check, grammar-check, and autocorrect turned off. Otherwise, use the following sheets of lined paper to prepare your response. Spend up to 45 minutes in reading the passages and planning, writing, revising, and editing your response.

Article 1: Higher Education for More Americans

Earning a post-secondary degree or credential is no longer just a pathway to opportunity for a talented few; rather, it is a prerequisite for the growing jobs of the new economy. Throughout this decade, employment in jobs requiring education beyond a high school diploma will grow more rapidly than employment in jobs that do not: of the 30 fastest-growing professions, more than half require at least some post-secondary education. U.S. government statistics show that 35 percent of the job openings will require at least a bachelor's degree, and an additional 30 percent of the job openings will require some college or an associate's degree, leaving only 35 percent of job openings for individuals with a high school education or less. Clearly, more education opens more doors to employment.

More education also opens the door to greater income. Again, the data is clear. According to recent U.S. government statistics, recent college graduates earn, on average, $22,000 more than people with a high school education or the equivalent — an all-time high! The same holds for individuals with some college or with a professional credential or associate's degree. In fact, the data shows a steady correlation between more education and higher income.

Many critics rightly point out high levels of student debt, rising tuition costs, and abusive lending practices. All of these are undeniable and suggest that more work needs to be done to control costs and ensure that a college education pays off for everyone.

At least some studies also show a relationship between education and feelings of happiness or satisfaction with life. Although researchers stress that all people can find happiness and satisfaction with life, they also say survey data shows that 94 percent of people with a bachelor's degree or higher reported feeling happy or very happy with their lives, but only 89 percent of high school graduates felt the same way. They also said that people with at least a bachelor's degree were less likely to report negative emotions, such as worry, sadness, or depression, than people with less education.

Article 2: Higher Education Is Not for Everyone

Although some studies purport to show that higher education results in more opportunity and income, the actual situation is more complex. Even though it is true that many occupations that require higher education pay more, this is not true of all fields. In recent years, many high school graduates were induced to seek associate's or bachelor's degrees while taking on large amounts of student debt. However, when the students graduated, they found that the promised jobs were not available or that the pay was so low that they could not afford to pay back their loans. Right now, the average student with debt owes around $32,000; most owe between $25,000 and $50,000. The average student debt today is 20 percent higher than in 2004, outpacing inflation over that same period. Total student debt in the United States is at least $1.75 trillion dollars, which represents more than Americans owe on auto loans. Clearly all of this debt is a risk to the individuals and to the American economy, prompting the government to pause student debt repayment during the coronavirus pandemic. In addition, in 2022, the government cancelled nearly 6 billion dollars in student debt that was deemed to be fraudulent — most of it from one for-profit university.

At the same time, many good jobs are open to those who cannot afford college or are interested in other occupations. Numerous pathways to successful employment work well and do not require years of college or university education. Whether it is apprenticeships in trades, training through the military, or entrepreneurial initiative, these approaches work. One approach that has recently gained attention is the "coding bootcamp," a kind of intense training in creating computer code, which frequently results in well-paying jobs in the fast-growing field of technology.

And then there are the people who made it without even finishing high school. That list includes Dave Thomas, founder of Wendy's; John D. Rockefeller; and many others. A whole collection of wealthy entrepreneurs started with just a high school diploma, like Richard Branson of Virgin Records, Virgin Atlantic airline, and now Virgin Galactic, a private space travel venture. We also know of many successful entrepreneurs who dropped out of university to start businesses, from Steve Jobs to Bill Gates and Mark Zuckerberg. That does not mean degrees are useless; it does tell us that drive and ideas are more important than formal education.

Chapter 28

Answers for Practice Test 2, Reasoning through Language Arts

You've done the test. Now you need to check your answers. If you just want a quick look at what you got right or wrong, check out the abbreviated answer key with just the answers at the end of this chapter. The better approach is to read all the answers and explanations so that you find out the reasoning behind the answers. You can discover just as much from your errors as from understanding why the right answers are correct.

Answers and Explanations

1. **B. Not all brands of bottled water are.** Choice (B) is an effective introduction to the paragraph and introduces no errors. Although starting a sentence with *and* or *but* isn't a grammar error, it's confusing to start this article with *but.* Therefore, Choices (A) and (C) are incorrect. Choice (C) also contains an unnecessary comma. Choice (D) introduces a subject-verb agreement error.

2. **B. to remove the chlorine completely and.** Choice (B) joins the two phrases correctly with *and.* Choice (A) is incorrect because it creates a comma splice. The other two options do not make sense.

3. **A. Bottled spring waters are.** Only Choice (A) uses correct subject-verb agreement and avoids other errors. Choice (B) has an unneeded comma. There is no reason to use the past tense (Choice C). Choice (D) has incorrect subject-verb agreement.

4. **C. waters differs.** Only Choice (C) has correct subject-verb agreement. The subject of the sentence is *content,* which is singular and requires a singular verb. So the correct form of the verb is *differs.* Using the word *waters* instead of *water* as in Choice (B) has no effect on the sentence and introduces a subject-verb agreement error with *differ.* The other choices merely introduce new errors or offer no change.

5. **D. are carbonated, either naturally or artificially, in the bottling process. Carbonation can add.** Choice (D) is correct because inserting a period after *bottling process* creates two complete sentences. Choices (A) and (B) create comma splices. Choice (C) creates a fragment.

6. **B. their bottled water's.** In the case of *there/their/they're,* the correct choice is *their.* The word *there* refers to location, while *their* shows possession, and *they're* is the contraction of *they are.* Because the sentence is talking about someone's water, the possessive form is correct, which is Choice (B). Therefore, Choices (A) and (C) are incorrect. Choice (D) is incorrect because it omits a necessary apostrophe needed to show that the taste belongs to the water.

7. **B. least.** The expense of three or more things is being compared in this section of the passage, so the superlative *least* is the answer (Choice B). Therefore, Choices (A) and (C) are incorrect. Choice (D) is incorrect because *lessor* means "landlord." This is a good example of how an unusual homonym can cause confusion.

8. **B. effective and.** Choice (B) is correct because no punctuation is needed to join two adjectives (*effective* and *inexpensive*) with *and.* Therefore, Choices (A) and (D) are incorrect. It's possible to put two adjectives in a row without *and,* as in Choice (C), but a comma is needed between them, so that choice is incorrect.

9. **D. plastic jug in your fridge, you.** This item focuses on commas. Only Choice (D) uses a comma correctly to join a dependent clause to an independent clause. Choice (C) omits this necessary comma, while Choices (A) and (B) add unnecessary commas.

10. **D. filters for removing traces.** Choice (D) correctly joins the phrase beginning with *removing* to the main clause by adding the preposition *for.* Choice (A) doesn't make sense. Choices (B) and (C) create sentence fragments.

11. **C. Employment Resource Center.** In the letter, the Sheridan Square Employment Resource Center is a title; therefore, all words except prepositions and articles must be capitalized. The other choices, which do not capitalize all the necessary words, are therefore incorrect.

12. **A. has partnered.** You need the present perfect tense *has partnered* here rather than the simple past tense *partnered* because the action started in the past and is ongoing. Your clue to this tense is the phrase *since April of last year.* None of the other choices improve the sentence.

13. **D. In support of the partnership,** Choice (D) is correct because a comma is needed after this introductory phrase. Choices (B) and (C) are, therefore, incorrect. Choice (A) adds an extra comma.

14. **A. has always been.** The present perfect tense is required here because the action began in the past and is ongoing, and a singular verb, *has,* is required because the subject of the sentence, *Ms. Fairfax,* is singular. The tenses in Choices (B) and (C) do not make sense. Choice (D) is incorrect because the subject of the sentence is singular and *have* is plural.

15. **B. is.** The subject of the sentence is *fact,* which is singular, so a singular verb is required. This question shows that the subject of a verb is not always the noun closest to it. Choice (A), *are,* agrees with the plural word *referrals,* which is just before it but not the subject of the sentence. The past tense does not make sense in this sentence, so Choices (C) and (D) are incorrect.

16. **A. pursued her responsibilities with a high degree of professionalism.** Choice (A) is the most straightforward ordering of the words. The other choices are awkward. Choice (D) changes the meaning of the sentence and does not make sense.

On the Grammar and Language Component of the GED, answer choices that change the meaning of the sentence are almost always incorrect.

TIP

17. **A. best in her future endeavors.** No commas are needed in this expression, so Choice (A) is correct. All the other choices add unnecessary commas.

18. **B. recently opened.** In this sentence, the adverb *recently* is needed to modify the verb *opened,* so Choice (B) is correct. Therefore, Choices (A) and (C) are incorrect. Choice (D) is incorrect because changing *opened* to *opening* results in a sentence fragment, because *opening* is not a complete verb.

19. **B. copiers, the.** Choice (B) is correct because it creates one complete sentence. The remaining choices are incorrect because they create sentence fragments.

20. **D. The first time I went there,** Choice (D) is a transitional phrase that shows the relationship among the actions in the story. The remaining choices are awkward or ungrammatical.

21. **C. and giving me.** Choice (C) puts the verbs in correct parallel structure: *apologizing, explaining,* and *giving.* Maintaining parallel structure in sentences is important and is frequently tested on the GED. Choices (A) and (D) have faulty parallel structure. There is no reason to change *me* to *myself* (Choice B).

22. **B. it's no.** Choice (B) uses the correct word *no* and the correct contraction for *it is, it's.* Therefore, Choice (C), which uses the incorrect homonym, the verb *know,* is incorrect. There is no reason to change *it's* to the possessive word *its* (Choice A). There is no such word as *its',* so Choice (D) is incorrect.

23. **D. knew.** The past tense of the verb *know, knew* (Choice D), is needed here, not its past participle, *known* (Choice A), or its homonym, *new* (Choice C). Choice (B) makes no sense.

24. **C. They.** Choice (C) is correct because his sentence has three verbs (*apologized, explained, gave*) with the same subject, *they.* Adding *after* (Choice B) or *when* (Choice D) makes the whole sentence a dependent clause, which cannot stand alone. Adding *but* (Choice A) does not make sense.

25. **A. a.** Choice (A) is the correct word to use in this expression. The phrase *too little less understanding* creates an awkward sentence with too many words modifying *understanding*, so Choice (B) is incorrect. Choice (C) does not make sense, and there is no reason to use *an* (Choice D), which is only used before vowel sounds.

26. **A. It is the knowledge that preserves their position.** The text clearly states that princes lose their states when they neglect this art. Although Choice (B) may be true, it has nothing to do with the question. Choices (C) and (D) are the opposite of what the text states.

27. **D. The armed do not readily yield authority to the unarmed.** Although Choices (A), (B), and (C) are all possible, they don't answer the question. However, further into the text, Machiavelli states that it's unreasonable for the armed to yield power to the unarmed.

28. **D. They will despise him.** This answer is stated directly in the passage.

29. **B. In times of peace, prepare for war.** The last sentence of the text makes it clear that Choice (B) is the best answer. Although Choice (D) may be partially correct, it's not the whole answer. Choices (A) and (C) are contradicted by the text.

30. **D. Ask the subordinate what he needs in order to return quickly.** Only Choice (D) follows the advice of balancing benevolence and strictness. Choices (A) and (C) are excessively cruel. Choice (B) is excessively kind.

31. **C. To maintain power, leaders must master the art of war.** Both writers believe that military mastery is important to staying in power. Sun Tzu would disagree with Choices (A) and (B). Machiavelli would disagree with Choice (D).

32. **C. He wanted to reflect the character of the speaker.** The speaker in this case is Aunt Polly. She's a simple country woman with little education. This pattern of speech reflects that. Choices (A) and (B) are certainly wrong because Mark Twain was a talented and capable writer. Choice (D) is simply wrong.

33. **B. Spare the rod and spile the child.** This statement is the only one that supports punishing Tom. Choice (A) shows that Aunt Polly feels conflicted about how she should raise Tom. Choices (C) and (D) are not related to child-rearing.

34. **C. She is not strict enough with Tom.** The correct answer refers to the quote, "spare the rod and spoil the child." The speaker, Aunt Polly, goes on to say, "I'm a laying up sin." She is a good woman who wants to do the right thing. Not being strict enough with Tom goes against Biblical rules as she understands them.

35. **A. She makes references to religion.** The key evidence about the speaker's religiosity consists of her frequent references to the Bible, religion, sin, and so on. The remaining choices are mentioned in the passage but do not demonstrate that she is religious.

Finding evidence to support a statement comes up on the Language Arts, Social Studies, and Science sections of the GED. Mastering this skill can really pay off!

TIP

36. **A. work.** Aunt Polly says, "He hates work more than he hates anything else." Therefore, the other choices are incorrect. He likes playing hookey (Choice C), which means, "missing school without permission." Tom certainly annoys his aunt, but the passage makes no mention of his feelings about it, so Choice (D) is incorrect.

If you selected Choice (B), keep in mind that you need to answer based only on the information in the passage. While painting the fence is one of the most famous episodes in this book, it's not mentioned in the passage.

REMEMBER

37. **B. who share.** Choice (B) is correct because the subject pronoun *who,* not the object pronoun *whom,* is needed. The correct verb form is *share* because its subject, *who,* refers to a plural noun, *groups.* The other options use the wrong pronoun or have a subject–verb agreement error, or both.

38. **A. In addition,** Choice (A) is correct because the sentence adds an idea to the information that comes before it. Only this transitional phrase shows this relationship. Therefore, the remaining choices are incorrect.

39. **C. to train jobless young people.** The overall purpose of the FACE project is to train unemployed youth. Manufacturing jobs are in short supply, resulting in the need for entrepreneurial skills, so Choice (A) is incorrect. Glass engraving and sign writing (Choice B) are the first skills FACE began to teach. Choice (D) is a later offering of the program, not its main purpose.

40. **A, B, C.** These choices are all mentioned in the passage as hand-craft skills that participants can learn in the program. Robotic assembly (Choice D) is a high-tech computer-assisted approach to manufacturing, not a hand-craft skill, and is not mentioned in the passage.

TIP

An easy way to approach a drag-and-drop question such as this one is to consider each of the choices as a true-false statement. Select the choices that are true (Choices A, B, and C), and eliminate the ones that are false, in this case Choice (D).

41. **B. by creating new enterprises of their own.** The best way for youth to secure employment is to "create their own businesses," as the passage states. Jobs are being lost in traditional manufacturing, so Choice (A) is incorrect. Furniture making (Choice C) and obtaining a business certificate (Choice D) don't refer directly to securing employment.

42. **A. The training is on specific crafts, and the certificate develops general business and personal skills.** Only Choice (A) accurately states the purpose of each offering. The remaining choices partially state or misstate the purposes of the offerings.

43. **Hand-Craft Training: C. Certificate: A.** Anger management (Choice B) and mobile phone repair (Choice D) aren't mentioned in the passage.

44. **B. an alternative to scarce traditional manufacturing jobs.** Choice (B) is the most clear and direct statement in the text that the FACE program doesn't expect graduates to find traditional jobs in industry but instead is preparing them for some alternative form of employment. Choices (A) and (D) could apply to any form of employment, so they're wrong. Choice (C) mentions skills that are developed in the certificate but are not linked to a specific kind of employment.

45. **A. Many students don't take enough math courses in high school.** According to the introduction to the text, students both drop mathematics courses and are unwilling or unable to take life skills courses, so Choice (A) is correct. The other choices are not mentioned in the passage.

46. **B. to avoid running out of money between paychecks.** The item about budgets specifically mentions making the money last between paychecks, so Choice (B) is correct. Choices (C) and (D) are also reasons to budget but are not mentioned in the passage. Choice (A) is not a reason to budget.

REMEMBER

As shown in both Questions 45 and 46, it's important to remember that your answers need to be based on information in the passage and not on your own background knowledge.

47. **A. usual.** Only Choice (A) indicates a recurring expense. Choices (B) and (C) have the opposite meaning. Choice (D) does not make sense.

48. **D. Cars are among the largest purchases most people ever make.** As the proposal states, cars are the second-largest purchase most people will ever make. Although Choices (A) and (B) are partially correct, they don't answer the question. Choice (C) is not mentioned in the passage and is, in any event, not true.

49. **In the Book: B, C. Not in the Book: A, D.** The book focuses on ways to use math to make prudent decisions. Both Choices (B) and (C) are these kinds of decisions. While Choices (A) and (D) might save money, they can both result in harm in the future and so do not belong in the book.

50. **D. to convince the company to publish the book.** The letter gives reasons why this book is needed and is directed to the president of the company. Therefore, Choice (D) is correct. The letter is not directed to people outside the company, so the remaining choices are incorrect.

Sample Extended Response

Here's an example of an essay in response to the articles about higher education. Your essay will look different, but this example can help you compare your response to a well-structured essay. Your essay could raise many of the same points that this essay does, perhaps organized differently, but above all, it should be well organized with a clear introduction, conclusion, and supporting evidence.

Compare the following sample to the response you wrote, and then compare it to the criteria the GED Testing Service uses to evaluate your writing (see Chapter 8 for more details on the scoring criteria):

- » Creation of an argument and use of evidence
- » Development and organizational structure
- » Clarity and command of standard English conventions

Right now, I am working on getting my GED. While data that shows getting a GED results in more opportunities, the two articles show that there is disagreement about whether education beyond high school or GED is worth it. After examining the data in both articles, the first article makes the stronger case: higher education is worth it.

As clearly stated in the first article, the more education you have, the more money you are going to make. In fact, pay goes up steadily from some college to an associate's degree to a bachelor's degree and beyond. I have found this to be true among my family and friends, too. My husband's income increased after he got a certificate from our community college. In fact, his success motivated me to go on to get my GED.

Critics of higher education report that student debt has gone up and is at an all time crisis, and that many student loans were recently cancelled because they were fraudulent. It is unfortunate that this happened, but obviously, the general data still shows that income goes up with education. I think that people need to choose their schools and majors carefully. My husband got his certificate from our local community college at a very low cost. He had no debt at all. With a few more courses, he says he can get an associate's degree, which will qualify him for an even better job at the hospital where he works.

Critics say that you can get a good job, such as a computer coder, with only a short training course. This is true, too, but it's not for everyone. Coding jobs are tough and boring. And on these jobs, there is not much room for advancement. For some people this kind of job is OK, but other people have different goals. Personally, I want to get a job as child care worker. I can get a much better job in this field if I get a state certificate. And I can get an even better job with a bachelor's degree. I could even become a kindergarten teacher!

For me, I see a lot of advantages to getting more education. As the first article says, there are more job opportunities and higher pay for people with more education. People just need to be careful to choose their schools and future jobs carefully and avoid taking a lot of debt. In addition, there is no price on happiness—achieving my dream of being an early childhood educator is worth the cost of a few years of education.

Answer Key

1.	B	19.	B	37.	B
2.	B	20.	D	38.	A
3.	A	21.	C	39.	C
4.	C	22.	B	40.	A, B, C
5.	D	23.	D	41.	B
6.	B	24.	C	42.	A
7.	B	25.	A	43.	Hand-Craft Training: C. Certificate: A.
8.	B	26.	A		
9.	D	27.	D	44.	B
10.	D	28.	D	45.	A
11.	C	29.	B	46.	B
12.	A	30.	D	47.	A
13.	D	31.	C	48.	D
14.	A	32.	C	49.	In the Book: B, C. Not in the Book: A, D.
15.	B	33.	B		
16.	A	34.	C	50.	D
17.	A	35.	A		
18.	B	36.	A		

Chapter 29

Practice Test 2: Social Studies

'm a firm believer that practice makes better, if not perfect. So here's another Social Studies practice test. Give yourself 70 minutes to complete the 50 questions in this practice test to best simulate the real test-taking experience. Remember, on the real test you can use the on-screen calculator (or your own calculator if you take the test at a testing center). The answers and explanations to this test's questions are in Chapter 30.

REMEMBER

On the real GED, you'll take the test on a computer. Instead of marking your answers on an answer sheet, like you do for the practice tests in this book, you'll use the keyboard and mouse to indicate your answers. I formatted the questions and answer choices in this book to make them appear as similar as possible to what you'll see on the computer screen, but I had to retain some A, B, C, D choices for marking your answers, and I provide an answer sheet for you to do so.

You have 70 minutes to answer the 50 questions on this practice test. Use the timer on your phone to keep track of time. If you run out of time, mark the last question you answered. Then answer the rest of the questions. This will help you figure out how much more quickly you will have to work to complete the entire test in the time allotted.

Answer Sheet for Practice Test 2, Social Studies

1. _____

2. _____

3. _____

4. _____

5. _____

6. _____

7. _____

8. _____

9. _____

10. _____

11. _____

12. _____

13. _____

14. _____

15. _____

16. _____

17. _____

18. _____

19. _____

20. _____

21. _____

22. _____

23. _____

24. _____

25. _____

26. _____

27. _____

28. _____

29. _____

30. _____

31. _____

32. _____

33. _____

34. _____

35. _____

36. _____

37. _____

38. _____

39. _____

40. _____

41. _____

42. _____

43. _____

44. _____

45. _____

46. _____

47. _____

48. _____

49. _____

50. _____

TIME: 70 minutes

QUESTIONS: 50

DIRECTIONS: Mark your answers on the answer sheet provided.

Questions 1–4 refer to the following passage, which is excerpted from Cliffs Quick Review U.S. History I, *by P. Soifer and A. Hoffman (Wiley).*

The First Inhabitants of the Western Hemisphere

In telling the history of the United States and also of the nations of the Western Hemisphere in general, historians have wrestled with the problem of what to call the hemisphere's first inhabitants. Under the mistaken impression he had reached the "Indies," explorer Christopher Columbus called the people he met "Indians." This was an error in identification that has persisted for more than five hundred years, for the inhabitants of North and South America had no collective name by which they called themselves.

Historians, anthropologists, and political activists have offered various names, none fully satisfactory. Anthropologists have used "aborigine," but the term suggests a primitive level of existence inconsistent with the cultural level of many tribes. Another term, "Amerindian," which combines Columbus's error with the name of another Italian explorer, Amerigo Vespucci (whose name was the source of "America"), lacks any historical context. Since the 1960s, "Native American" has come into popular favor, though some activists prefer "American Indian." In the absence of a truly representative term, descriptive references such as "native peoples" or "indigenous peoples," though vague, avoid European influence. In recent years, some argument has developed over whether to refer to tribes in the singular or plural — Apache or Apaches — with supporters on both sides demanding political correctness.

1. Which name has been favored since 1960?

   (A) Amerindian

   (B) Native American

   (C) native peoples

   (D) indigenous peoples

2. Why did Columbus call the native inhabitants "Indians"?

   (A) They were in the Western Hemisphere.

   (B) He thought he'd reached the Indies.

   (C) North and South America had not been discovered.

   (D) They were the hemisphere's first inhabitants.

3. Who used the term *aborigine*, according to the passage?

   (A) historians

   (B) political activists

   (C) Columbus

   (D) anthropologists

4. How was America named?

   (A) after an Italian explorer

   (B) after its first inhabitants

   (C) after its discoverer

   (D) after Columbus

Questions 5–9 refer to the following passage, which is excerpted from Cliffs Quick Review U.S. History I, *by P. Soifer and A. Hoffman (Wiley).*

The Voyages of Christopher Columbus

Christopher Columbus, a Genoese sailor, believed that sailing west across the Atlantic Ocean was the shortest sea route to Asia. Ignorant of the fact that the Western Hemisphere lay between Europe and Asia and assuming the earth's circumference to be a third less than it actually is, he was convinced that Japan would appear on the horizon just three thousand miles to the west. Like other seafarers of his day, Columbus was untroubled by political allegiances; he was ready to sail for whatever country would pay for his voyage. Either because of his arrogance (he wanted ships and crews to be provided at no expense to himself) or ambition (he insisted on governing the lands he discovered), he found it difficult to find a patron. The Portuguese rejected his plan twice, and the rulers of England and France were not interested. With influential supporters at court, Columbus convinced King Ferdinand and Queen Isabella of Spain to partially underwrite his expedition. In 1492, Granada, the last Muslim stronghold on the Iberian Peninsula, had fallen to the forces of the Spanish monarchs. With the Reconquista complete and Spain a unified country, Ferdinand and Isabella could turn their attention to overseas exploration.

5. Why was Columbus's estimate of the time required to reach Japan wrong?

   (A) He thought Japan was much farther away.

   (B) He thought Japan was much closer.

   (C) He was just taking a blind guess.

   (D) He was using Vespucci's maps.

6. Why did the Spanish Crown sponsor Columbus's exploration?

   (A) The royals were competing with England for new colonies.

   (B) Queen Isabella admired Columbus.

   (C) The war with the Muslims was over, and they could focus on other things.

   (D) The Crown worried about French competition in the region.

7. Columbus sailed in what direction to reach Asia?

   (A) east

   (B) south

   (C) north

   (D) west

8. What about Columbus made finding sponsors for his voyage difficult?

   Write the correct letter(s) in the box. [_____]

   (A) He was arrogant.

   (B) His demands were out of line.

   (C) He was a shrewd politician.

   (D) He refused to learn Spanish.

9. How much funding did Columbus finally receive?

   (A) complete funding

   (B) partial funding

   (C) a small percentage

   (D) a commission on whatever he discovered

Questions 10–12 refer to the following graph.

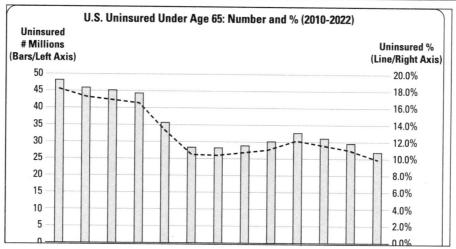

Source: U.S. Census Bureau / U.S. Department of Commerce / Public Domain

10. Among adults under age 65, what happened to the uninsured rate between 2013 and 2016?

(A) It decreased.

(B) It increased.

(C) It stayed the same.

(D) It showed no pattern.

11. In which year was the uninsured rate highest for adults under 65?

(A) 2010

(B) 2011

(C) 2012

(D) 2013

12. Which of the following statements best explains the change in the uninsured rate beginning in 2014?

(A) Americans' health improved.

(B) Healthcare costs declined significantly.

(C) The Affordable Care Act took effect.

(D) Unemployment increased.

Questions 13–15 refer to this graph.

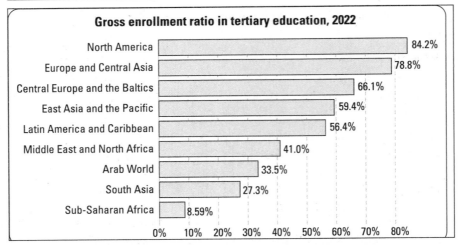

Gross enrollment ratio in tertiary education, 2022

North America — 84.2%
Europe and Central Asia — 78.8%
Central Europe and the Baltics — 66.1%
East Asia and the Pacific — 59.4%
Latin America and Caribbean — 56.4%
Middle East and North Africa — 41.0%
Arab World — 33.5%
South Asia — 27.3%
Sub-Saharan Africa — 8.59%

Total enrollment in post-secondary education, regardless of age, expressed as a percentage of the five-year age group following secondary school leaving.
Source: https://ourworldindata.org/grapher/gross-enrollment-ratio-in-tertiary-education

13. Which region of the world has the highest level of enrollment in higher education?

    (A) Latin America and the Caribbean

    (B) Europe and Central Asia

    (C) East Asia and the Pacific

    (D) North America

14. What is the difference between the enrollment ratios for Europe/Central Asia and East Asia/Pacific? [ ]

15. Which of these individuals would be considered a college student in the graph?

    (A) A woman who graduated from high school ten years ago and recently started college.

    (B) A nineteen-year-old who got her GED last month and started college right away.

    (C) A learner taking GED classes at a community center.

    (D) A teacher who graduated from college five years ago and recently started a master's degree.

Questions 16–20 refer to the following passage, which is excerpted from The Declaration of Independence, 1776.

Declaration of Independence

We hold these truths to be self-evident: that all men are created equal; that they are endowed by their Creator with certain inalienable rights; that among these are life, liberty, and the pursuit of happiness. That to secure these rights, governments are instituted among men, deriving their just powers from the consent of the governed; that whenever any form of government becomes destructive of these ends it is the right of the people to alter or to abolish it, and to institute a new government, laying its foundation on such principles, and organizing its powers in such form, as to them shall seem most likely to effect their safety and happiness. Prudence, indeed, will dictate that governments long established should not be changed for light and transient causes; and accordingly, all experience hath shown, that mankind are more disposed to suffer, while evils are sufferable, than to right themselves by abolishing the forms to which they are accustomed. But when a long train of abuses and usurpations, pursuing invariably the same object, evinces a design to reduce them under absolute despotism, it is their right, it is their duty, to throw off such government, and to provide new guards for their future security. Such has been the patient sufferance of these colonies; and such is now the necessity which constrains them to alter their former system of government. The history of the present king of Great Britain is a history of repeated injuries and usurpations, all having in direct object the establishment of an absolute tyranny over these states. To prove this, let facts be submitted to a candid world.

16. What truths were self-evident?

   (A) that all men are not created equal

   (B) that men don't have rights

   (C) that men are suffering

   (D) that men have certain rights

17. From where do governments get their power?

   (A) from the people

   (B) from the Creator

   (C) among men

   (D) from a new foundation

18. According to the Declaration of Independence, the people should overthrow their government when it does which of the following?

   Write the letter(s). [_____]

   (A) when government prevents abuse

   (B) when government abuses and usurps people's rights

   (C) when government resorts to absolute despotism

   (D) when government increases taxes

19. How does the Declaration of Independence describe the king of Great Britain?

   (A) He caused injuries.

   (B) He was a kindly ruler.

   (C) He was an absolute tyrant.

   (D) He was a friend of the people.

20. Why should a new government be instituted in this case, according to the passage?

   (A) There were light and transient reasons.

   (B) It was long established.

   (C) The people were suffering.

   (D) They needed to abolish the accustomed forms.

"DUE PROCESS OF LAW."

Source: The Library of Congress/Public Domain.

21. What is the social issue being depicted in this editorial cartoon?

    (A) The legal system has sentenced innocent people to death.

    (B) The legal system is biased.

    (C) The legal system is slow and has many obstacles.

    (D) The legal system is expensive.

22. What does the building at the top of the hill represent?

    (A) a courthouse

    (B) the Capitol Building

    (C) the White House

    (D) the National Archives Building

23. Which of the following statements is closest in meaning to the main idea of the cartoon?

    (A) The administration of justice is the firmest pillar of government (George Washington).

    (B) Justice is blind (legal saying).

    (C) I think the first duty of society is justice (Alexander Hamilton).

    (D) Justice delayed is justice denied (legal saying).

Resistance to Slavery

Resistance to slavery took several forms. Slaves would pretend to be ill, refuse to work, do their jobs poorly, destroy farm equipment, set fire to buildings, and steal food. These were all individual acts rather than part of an organized plan for revolt, but the objective was to upset the routine of the plantation in any way possible. On some plantations, slaves could bring grievances about harsh treatment from an overseer to their master and hope that he would intercede on their behalf. Although many slaves tried to run away, few succeeded for more than a few days, and they often returned on their own. Such escapes were more a protest — a demonstration that it could be done — than a dash for freedom. As advertisements in southern newspapers seeking the return of runaway slaves made clear, the goal of most runaways was to find their wives or children who had been sold to another planter. The fabled Underground Railroad, a series of safe houses for runaways organized by abolitionists and run by former slaves like Harriet Tubman, actually helped only about a thousand slaves reach the North.

24. Why did enslaved people refuse to work?

   (A) They were ill.

   (B) They did their jobs poorly.

   (C) They destroyed farm equipment.

   (D) They were resisting enslavement.

25. According to the text, the Underground Railroad helped only about 1,000 enslaved people escape. Why is the Underground Railroad still considered "fabled"?

   (A) It offered hope of permanent escape to all enslaved people.

   (B) It was the most successful option for escaping slavery.

   (C) It supported rebellions of enslaved people.

   (D) It is only a story or fable.

26. Who organized the Underground Railroad?

   (A) Harriet Tubman

   (B) railroad companies

   (C) abolitionists

   (D) runaways

Questions 27–30 refer to the following report.

Weather Report

Good morning and welcome to America's weather on WAWT, the voice of the world in the ear of the nation. Today is going to be hot. That's H-O-T, and we all know what that means. The big "P" is coming back for a visit. We are going to have pollution today for sure. With our record heat today on each coast, there is a problem. If you think that it's hot here, it's even hotter up higher. And that means unhealthy air leading to unhealthy people. I can hear the coughs and sneezes coast to coast. I think I hear a whole series of gasps from our nation's capital, good ol' Washington, D.C., and it's not Congress that is producing all that hot air. And out in western California, it's just as bad. Just the other day, I looked up "poor air quality" in the dictionary, and it said "see California." Lots of luck breathing out there.

This morning, once again, there's a layer of hot air just above ground level. That's where we live — ground level. This air acts like a closed gate, and it keeps the surface air from going up and mixing.

Of course, we are all going to drive our cars all day in heavy traffic, and some of us will go to work in factories. And, surprise — by afternoon, all those pollutants from the cars mix with the emissions from the factories and get trapped by the layer of hot air, and at ground level the heat and sunlight convert them to smog. Unhealthy air is here again. Tomorrow and every day after, we'll probably have more of the same until we learn to take care of our environment.

Well, I'll see you tomorrow, if the air's not too thick to see through.

27. When is the worst time for pollution?

(A) in the morning

(B) in the afternoon

(C) late at night

(D) before breakfast

28. Which of the following is a source of pollution?

(A) record heat

(B) air rising from ground level

(C) automobile exhaust

(D) warmer air aloft

29. According to the report, what is worsening the pollution?

Write the letter(s) of the appropriate factors. [   ]

(A) hot air aloft trapping emissions

(B) record heat and sunlight

(C) Congress

(D) California

30. What is the best way to prevent pollution?

(A) Change the temperature.

(B) Reduce emissions.

(C) Get rid of the hot air layer.

(D) Prevent air from rising.

Questions 31–33 refer to the following passage.

The End of the Soviet Union

The repudiation of the Brezhnev Doctrine, which had sanctioned the intervention of the Soviet Union in other Communist countries, marked the beginning of the collapse of the Soviet Union. The Soviet Union's defeat in the war in Afghanistan made Soviet leaders realize that the Doctrine was not sustainable. However, this left the other Communist states free to pursue their own political reforms, because they no longer had to fear reprisals from Moscow. Soon, various Communist countries, as well as several Soviet republics, began to move toward reform or independence. Inside the Soviet Union, new policies of Mikhail Gorbachev, perestroika and glasnost, opened new fissures in Soviet society and government. Eventually, the Communist governments in Eastern Europe collapsed. The Berlin Wall fell in November, 1989, and a divided Germany reunited. Finally, the Soviet Union broke up. An agreement among the leaders of the Soviet republics, held in Almaty, Kazakhstan, on December 21, 1991, formalized the end of the Soviet Union. Gorbachev resigned on December 25, 1991. The republics that had comprised the Soviet Union became sovereign states. The Soviet Union had ended.

31. Which of the following started the process that led to the collapse of the Soviet Union?

   (A) repudiation of the Brezhnev Doctrine

   (B) fall of the Berlin Wall

   (C) perestroika and glasnost

   (D) independence of the former Soviet republics

32. Put the events in chronological order. Write the letters in order. [   ]

   (A) The Berlin Wall fell.

   (B) The Brezhnev Doctrine was repudiated.

   (C) Gorbachev resigned.

   (D) Leaders of the Soviet republics formalized the end of the Soviet Union.

33. What happened to the republics of the Soviet Union?

   (A) They remained Communist.

   (B) They joined the Russian Federation.

   (C) They joined together in a new country.

   (D) They became sovereign states.

Questions 34–38 refer to the following passage, which is excerpted from Cliffs Quick Review U.S. History I, *by P. Soifer and A. Hoffman (Wiley)*

The Panic of 1873

During his second term, President Grant was still unable to curb the graft in his administration, Secretary of War William Belknap was impeached by the House, and he resigned in disgrace for taking bribes from dishonest Indian agents. The president's personal secretary was involved with the Whiskey Ring, a group of distillers who evaded paying internal revenue taxes. A much more pressing concern though was the state of the economy.

In 1873, over-speculation in railroad stocks led to a major economic panic. The failure of Jay Cooke's investment bank was followed by the collapse of the stock market and the bankruptcy of thousands of businesses; crop prices plummeted and unemployment soared. Much of the problem was related to the use of greenbacks for currency. Hard-money advocates insisted that paper money had to be backed by gold to curb inflation and level price fluctuations, but farmers and manufacturers, who needed easy credit, wanted even more greenbacks put in circulation, a policy that Grant ultimately opposed. He recommended and the Congress enacted legislation in 1875 providing for the redemption of greenbacks in gold. Because the Treasury needed time to build up its gold reserves, redemption did not go into effect for another four years, by which time the longest depression in American history had come to an end.

34. According to the passage, which of the following was a problem President Grant had in his second term in office?

   (A) corruption

   (B) whiskey

   (C) tax debts

   (D) personal bankruptcy

35. What type of money was used for investment at this time?

   (A) British pounds

   (B) silver

   (C) gold

   (D) greenbacks

36. What was the cause of the Panic of 1873?

    (A) crop failures

    (B) bankruptcy

    (C) over-speculation

    (D) tax evasion

37. What followed the failure of Jay Cooke's bank?

    (A) collapse of the stock market

    (B) increase in market value

    (C) business profitability

    (D) rising crop prices

38. How did Congress end the depression?

    (A) It provided easy credit.

    (B) It leveled prices.

    (C) It built up gold reserves.

    (D) It hoarded greenbacks.

Questions 39–41 refer to the following figure.

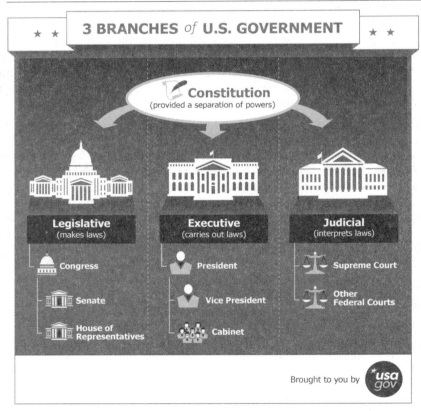

Source: USA.gov

39. Which branch of government includes the cabinet? ☐

40. The legislative branch is composed of which two bodies? Write the letters. ☐

    (A) House of Representatives

    (B) Supreme Court

    (C) vice president

    (D) Senate

41. What is the purpose of having three branches of government? ☐

Questions 42 and 43 refer to the following graph.

Women Serving in the U.S. House

Legend: —— Democrats ------ Republicans

42. The 19th Amendment to the Constitution, which gave all American women the right to vote, was passed in 1920, during the 66th Congress. Which of the following explains the presence of women serving in Congress prior to then? Choose the letter or letters. ☐

    (A) There was no federal law against women serving in Congress.

    (B) People began to ignore the laws that stopped women from voting.

    (C) Some states already allowed women to vote.

    (D) Women began to organize to vote long before they were able to vote.

43. Which party has had a higher proportion of women in Congress in recent years? ☐

Questions 44 and 45 refer to the following passage.

The 19th Amendment to the Constitution says, "The right of citizens of the United States to vote shall not be denied or abridged by the United States or by any State on account of sex. Congress shall have power to enforce this article by appropriate legislation." The amendment was approved by the House in May 1919 and by the Senate in June 1919. It was ratified by 36 of the 48 states, the number needed to approve it, by August 18, 1920. However, several states refused to ratify it, and the last of the 48 states to ratify it did so only in 1984.

44. Which of the following can be concluded about the 19th Amendment?

    (A) It had strong, widespread support.

    (B) It was not considered important.

    (C) It was controversial.

    (D) It was considered unnecessary in states where women could already vote.

45. Why does the 19th Amendment give Congress the right to pass laws to enforce it?

    (A) Congress needed to be forced to implement the amendment.

    (B) The amendment was not clear.

    (C) States or local governments might continue to prevent women from voting.

    (D) To prevent the amendment from being repealed.

46. Under the Constitution of the United States, some powers belong to the federal government and some powers belong to the states. Which of the following is a power that belongs to <u>state</u> governments?

    (A) to declare war

    (B) to print money

    (C) to make treaties

    (D) to provide education

47. Under the Constitution of the United States, some powers belong to the federal government and some powers belong to the states. Which of the following is a power that belongs to the <u>federal</u> government?

    (A) to create an army

    (B) to set up local governments

    (C) to issue driver's licenses

    (D) to implement assistance programs

Questions 48–50 refer to the following information.

Each branch of the federal government has powers that limit the powers of other branches. Write the letter of the power next to the branch of government.

    (A) Can declare a law unconstitutional

    (B) Can veto legislation

    (C) Can override a veto

48. Executive branch [   ]

49. Legislative branch [   ]

50. Judicial branch [   ]

Chapter **30**

Answers for Practice Test 2, Social Studies

This chapter has the answers and explanations for the Social Studies practice test in Chapter 29. I provide detailed answer explanations to help you review areas where you may need to do more work. Reading the explanations, even for the questions you got right, will help you understand how these question-and-answer items are set up. If you're short on time and just want to check your answers, you can skip directly to the abbreviated answer key at the end of the chapter.

Answers and Explanations

1. **B. Native American.** In the 1960s, after much debate, *Native American* was chosen as the name for the indigenous peoples. Other terms, such as *Indian, Amerindian,* and *indigenous peoples,* were discarded.

2. **B. He thought he'd reached the Indies.** Columbus thought he had reached the Indies when he landed in North America, so he called the natives "Indians." The other choices — the natives being in the Western Hemisphere (Choice A), the fact that the Americas hadn't been discovered yet (Choice C), or the natives being the hemisphere's first inhabitants (Choice D) — just don't make sense.

3. **D. anthropologists.** This information is stated directly in the passage. Therefore, the other choices are incorrect.

4. **A. after an Italian explorer.** According to the passage, America was named after Italian explorer Amerigo Vespucci. Therefore, Choices (B) and (D) are incorrect. Choice (C) is incorrect because the European explorers who first reached the Americas did not "discover" it. These lands were already inhabited by millions of native peoples.

5. **B. He thought Japan was much closer.** Columbus thought the earth's circumference was a third less than it really was. As a result, he thought Japan was much closer than it turned out to be. Therefore, the other choices are incorrect.

6. **C. The war with the Muslims was over, and they could focus on other things.** The passage states directly that Spain had been at war, trying to recapture the Iberian Peninsula from Muslim conquerors. That done, the king and queen now had time and resources to focus on other activities. Nothing in the passage indicates that the Spanish Crown was worried about competition from other countries (Choices A and D). Choice (B) may have been true but is not supported by information in the passage.

7. **D. west.** According to the passage, Columbus sailed west to cross the Atlantic Ocean in search of Asia. Therefore, the other choices are incorrect.

8. **A, B. He was arrogant; His demands were out of line.** Columbus was regarded as arrogant. He demanded that the patrons cover all costs and award him the governorship of whatever colonies he established. Nothing in the text talks about learning Spanish (Choice D), and Columbus's behavior is certainly not that of a shrewd politician (Choice C).

 On a drag-and-drop question such as this one, think of the choices as a series of true/false statements. Select the choices that are true, in this case Choices (A) and (B), as your answers.

TIP

9. **B. partial funding.** According to the passage, Columbus convinced the rulers to partially fund the voyage. The remaining choices are not supported by the passage.

10. **A. It decreased.** The bars on the graph show a clear, consistent decrease for the years between 2013 and 2016.

 Charts, graphs, and tables come up on three of the four GED tsts: science, social studies, and math. If items 10-12 are hard for you, review the information on charts, tables, and graphs in Chapter 10.

TIP

11. **A. 2010.** The tallest bar on the graph is for this age group is in 2010.

12. **C. The Affordable Care Act took effect.** Only Choice (C) provides a logical explanation for the decrease: The ACA made insurance easier to obtain, which led to the decline among uninsured. Choice (A) would not affect insurance coverage. Choice (B) does not make sense because Medicare begins at age 65 and the table is about Americans ages 19 to 64. Choice (D) would likely result in an increase in uninsured individuals because many Americans get their healthcare insurance from their workplaces.

13. **D. North America.** The longest bar on the bar chart corresponds to North America, so Choice (D) is correct.

14. **19.4%.** The difference between the two ratios is 78.8 − 59.4 = 19.4. This question is an example of when the calculator can help you.

15. **B. A nineteen-year-old who got her GED last month and started college right away.** The data in the graph is for college students who graduated from high school in the last five years. The only person who qualifies is the teenager in Choice (B). The others graduated from high school too long ago (Choices A and D) or have not graduated yet (Choice C).

TIP

The answer to a question can be in any part of the graph, including the title, the labels, or, as in this question, the explanatory text at the bottom.

16. **D. that men have certain rights.** The passage lists two self-evident truths: that all men are created equal and that the Creator endowed men with certain rights. (*Self-evident* means "evident without need of explanation or proof.")

17. **A. from the people.** According to the passage, governments were to get their power from the people. Getting power from the Creator (Choice B), among men (Choice C), and from a new foundation (Choice D) are incorrect answers, according to the passage.

18. **B, C. when government abuses and usurps people's rights; when government resorts to absolute despotism.** These two choices are correct. Choice (A) is not a reason to overthrow a government. Choice (D) doesn't qualify as "destructive" enough to warrant revolution.

19. **C. He was an absolute tyrant.** George III had become an absolute tyrant. He was neither a kindly ruler (Choice B) nor a friend of the people (Choice D). Causing injuries (Choice A) isn't the best choice because, although it is partially true, the text clearly goes further to paint the picture of King George as a tyrant.

20. **C. The people were suffering.** The people were suffering because of the evils of the old government, which was the main reason why they sought a new government. The other choices may have some truth to them, but they aren't the main reasons, according to the passage.

21. **C. The legal system is slow and has many obstacles.** The female figure representing justice is riding a snail on a path strewn with rocks and boulders. This indicates that the legal system is slow and full of obstacles. The other choices may be true but are not related to the main idea of this cartoon.

22. **A. a courthouse.** The only building in the answer choices that is related to the legal system is a courthouse, so Choice (A) is correct.

23. **D. Justice delayed is justice denied (legal saying).** This common saying is closest in meaning to the cartoon and so is correct. Choice (B) is tempting because the image that represents justice is wearing a blindfold, which suggests that the legal system is impartial. However, that is not the main idea of this cartoon.

24. **D. They were resisting enslavement.** Refusing to work was a way that enslaved people showed resistance to enslavement. Illness (Choice A), by itself, was not a way to resist enslavement, though feigning illness was a way to avoid work. Therefore, this choice is not correct. Poorly done jobs (Choice B) and destroyed equipment (Choice C) were other ways they showed resistance.

25. **A. It offered hope of permanent escape to all enslaved people.** The Underground Railroad actually succeeded in getting enslaved people to Canada, a permanent safe haven, and a new life. The text doesn't support the idea that it was the most successful escape method (Choice B) nor that it supported rebellions (Choice C). And there's no question that it actually existed (Choice D).

26. **C. abolitionists.** The Underground Railroad was organized by abolitionists. Other possible players, such as Harriet Tubman and runaways, may have been involved, but, according to the passage, they weren't the organizers. The Underground Railroad was metaphorical, so Choice (B) is incorrect.

27. **B. in the afternoon.** Pollution tends to be at its worst in the afternoon when exhausts and emissions are trapped. According to the passage, other times of day don't have as much pollution.

28. **C. automobile exhaust.** Of the factors in the choices, only automobile exhaust is a source of pollution. Record heat (Choice A) and warmer air aloft (Choice D) are factors that make the pollution worse, but they aren't sources of the pollution. Choice (B), air rising from ground level, would disperse pollution at ground level.

29. **A, B. hot air aloft trapping emissions; record heat and sunlight.** According to the passage, the emissions are made worse by the effect of hot air trapping the air pollution close to the ground (Choice A) and heat and sunlight converting the emissions to smog (Choice B). Although Congress (Choice C) may be a source of hot air, it plays no role in this case. And California (Choice D) is just there to trip you up because it's mentioned in the passage as a place with poor air quality.

30. **B. Reduce emissions.** Pollution can best be prevented by reducing emissions. The other choices (changing the temperature, eliminating the hot air layer, and preventing air from rising) may contribute, but they aren't the best answers.

31. **A. repudiation of the Brezhnev Doctrine.** The process of dissolution began when the Soviet Union stopped controlling its satellites directly. This started reform or independence movements, which spread into the Soviet Union itself. The other events are related to the collapse of the Soviet Union, but none of them started the movement toward dissolution.

32. **The correct order is B, A, D, C. The Brezhnev Doctrine was repudiated; The Berlin Wall fell; Leaders of the Soviet republics formalized the end of the Soviet Union; Gorbachev resigned.** Although other events happened in between, this is the order of the events in the question.

33. **D. They became sovereign states.** The former Soviet republics became sovereign states. The other choices are not supported by information in the passage.

34. **A. corruption.** The main problems President Grant faced involved graft in his administration, which meant that members of his administration faced all sorts of problems and left their jobs under pressure. The other answers are incorrect, based on the passage.

35. **D. greenbacks.** Greenbacks — not British pounds, gold, or silver — were used as a source of investment capital.

36. **C. over-speculation.** Over-speculation (Choice C) in railroad stocks led to the Panic of 1873. The factors in the other choices, such as crop failures (Choice A), bankruptcy (Choice B), and tax evasion (Choice D), may have also occurred, but they didn't directly cause the Panic of 1873.

37. **A. collapse of the stock market.** The failure of Cooke's bank was followed by a collapse of the stock market. The other choices are the opposite of what happened, according to the passage.

38. **C. It built up gold reserves.** The main way Congress ended the depression was to build up its gold reserves to be used to redeem greenbacks (Choice C). Credit (Choice A), prices (Choice B), and greenbacks (Choice D) didn't have as much to do with the end of the depression.

39. **executive.** The graphic shows the cabinet under the executive branch. The role of the cabinet members is to lead various government departments and agencies. Members of the cabinet also advise the president.

On a fill-in-the-blank question such as this one, you must spell the answer correctly to receive credit.

REMEMBER

40. **A, D. House of Representatives; Senate.** These two bodies together form the U.S. Congress. The Supreme Court (Choice B) is in the judicial branch. The vice president (Choice C) is in the executive branch and is also president of the Senate. However, this does not make this official one of the two legislative bodies in Congress.

41. **to provide a separation of powers.** The purpose of the three branches is to provide checks and balances through the separation of powers.

42. **A, C. There was no federal law against women serving in Congress; Some states already allowed women to vote.** Choice (A) is correct because there was no federal law that barred women from serving in Congress. Choice (C) is correct because at the time of the amendment, women could vote in Wyoming, Utah, Colorado, Idaho, Washington, California, Oregon, Montana, Arizona, Kansas, Alaska, Illinois, North Dakota, Indiana, Nebraska, Michigan, Arkansas, New York, South Dakota, and Oklahoma. There is no support in the passage for Choice (B). Choice (D) would not explain the presence of women in Congress before the passage of the amendment.

43. **Democratic Party.** Starting from approximately the 102nd Congress, there has been a higher proportion of women in Congress from the Democratic Party than from the Republican Party. The line for the Democratic Party is consistently higher than the line for the Republican Party in this part of the graph.

44. **C. It was controversial.** While the rapid passage might suggest the 19th Amendment had strong support, the fact that only 36 states ratified it showed that Americans were not of one mind about the amendment at the time of its passage. In fact, passage of the amendment was a hard-won battle over many years.

45. **C. States or local governments might continue to prevent women from voting.** Because the law was controversial, the government needed the power to enforce it, especially in places where equal voting rights were controversial. The remaining choices do not make sense.

46. **D. to provide education.** Providing education (Choice D) is a power reserved by the states. The federal government has the power to declare war (Choice A), to print money (Choice B), and to make treaties (Choice C).

47. **A. to create an army.** Only the federal government can raise an army (Choice A). The powers in the other choices are reserved by the states.

48. **B. Can veto legislation.** The executive branch (the president) can veto bills made by the legislative branch if they do not agree that the bill should become a law.

49. **C. Can override a veto.** The legislative branch can override a president's veto with a two-thirds majority in both the House and the Senate. This way, a bill can become law over the president's objection.

50. **A. Can declare a law unconstitutional.** The courts can declare a law (or a provision of a law) unconstitutional if they believe it does not follow the Constitution. A majority of the judges on the Supreme Court must agree in order to declare a law unconstitutional. Usually, this number is five.

Answer Key

1.	B	19.	C	37.	A
2.	B	20.	C	38.	C
3.	D	21.	C	39.	executive
4.	A	22.	A	40.	A, D
5.	B	23.	D	41.	to provide a separation of powers
6.	C	24.	D	42.	A, C
7.	D	25.	A	43.	Democratic Party
8.	A, B	26.	C	44.	C
9.	B	27.	B	45.	C
10.	A	28.	C	46.	D
11.	A	29.	A, B	47.	A
12.	C	30.	B	48.	B
13.	D	31.	A	49.	C
14.	19.4%	32.	B, A, D, C	50.	A
15.	B	33.	D		
16.	D	34.	A		
17.	A	35.	D		
18.	B, C	36.	C		

Chapter 31

Practice Test 2: Science

The Science test includes multiple-choice, fill-in-the-blank, drop-down, and drag-and-drop questions. They measure your reading comprehension of passages and visuals. You have 90 minutes to complete all 50 questions in this practice test. Do the easiest questions first and remember to use process of elimination on multiple-choice questions if you can't find the answer.

Don't forget, you are allowed to use a calculator on the GED Science test.

The answers and explanations for this practice test are in Chapter 32. Be sure to review the explanations for all the questions, even for the ones you got right. The explanations are a good review of the techniques that I discuss throughout the book.

REMEMBER

On the real GED, you'll take the test on a computer. Instead of marking your answers on an answer sheet, like you do for the practice tests in this book, you'll use the keyboard and mouse to indicate your answers. I formatted the questions and answer choices in this book to make them appear as similar as possible to what you'll see on the computer screen, but I had to retain some A, B, C, D choices for marking your answers, and I provide an answer sheet for you to do so.

You have 90 minutes to answer the 50 questions on this practice test. Use the timer on your phone to keep track of time. If you run out of time, mark the last question you answered. Then answer the rest of the questions. This will help you figure out how much more quickly you will have to work to complete the entire test in the time allotted.

Answer Sheet for Practice Test 2, Science

1. _____

2. _____

3. _____

4. _____

5. _____

6. _____

7. _____

8. _____

9. _____

10. _____

11. _____

12. _____

13. _____

14. _____

15. _____

16. _____

17. _____

18. _____

19. _____

20. _____

21. _____

22. _____

23. _____

24. _____

25. _____

26. _____

27. _____

28. _____

29. _____

30. _____

31. _____

32. _____

33. _____

34. _____

35. _____

36. _____

37. _____

38. _____

39. _____

40. _____

41. _____

42. _____

43. _____

44. _____

45. _____

46. _____

47. _____

48. _____

49. _____

50. _____

Questions 1 and 2 refer to the following passage.

We have many perennial plants in our gardens. Plants such as roses and irises grow and flower year after year. They become dormant through the winter and then come back to life in the spring. Tulips are beautiful flowers that are among the earliest to come up every spring. They are fragile in appearance but manage to survive the uncertain weather of spring, and then bloom in a rainbow of colors. Tulips have a distinctive fragrance.

Tulips grow from bulbs. As the plant grows in summer, it develops two bulbs that store moisture and food. When the weather turns, the plant becomes dormant. The roots and leaves dry out and fall off, but the bulbs develop a tough outer skin to protect themselves. However, the bulbs do not reliably regrow. Depending on conditions, the bulbs may regrow or simply remain in the ground. Conversely, bulbs may remain in the ground for several years and then suddenly regrow. Gardeners report that sometimes old tulip beds that were replanted with grass or other plants have tulips emerge unexpectedly years later. Tulips really depend on cultivation by humans to survive. This is why most gardeners say that tulips act more like annuals than perennials. The only way to ensure that you have tulips in the spring is to plant new bulbs in the fall. The bulbs develop roots in early fall, and then foliage and blossoms emerge in spring.

1. Write *annual* or *perennial* on the correct line. Though considered a/an [   ], the tulip acts more like a/an [   ].

2. What is the life cycle of a tulip? Write the letters in the correct order. [   ]

   (A) The plant becomes dormant.

   (B) A gardener plants a tulip bulb in fall.

   (C) The tulip grows and blossoms once.

   (D) The plant develops two new bulbs.

   (E) The bulb grows roots.

Question 3 refers to the following passage.

Cells are the basic unit of all living things in the universe. Not only are flowers, weeds, and trees composed of cells, but you, your dog, and all other living things are also composed of cells. However, cells are different from organism to organism. That is why some plants produce roses and others produce dandelions and why some cells are in people and others in fish.

3. Which of the following is supported by information in the passage?

   (A) Some organisms are unicellular.

   (B) Cells contain genetic information.

   (C) Cells are differentiated.

   (D) Cells can reproduce.

Questions 4 and 5 refer to the following passage from the Surgeon General's Report on Active Living (www.surgeongeneral.gov).

Engaging in regular physical activity is one of the most important things that people of all ages can do to improve their health. Physical activity strengthens bones and muscles, reduces stress and depression, and makes it easier to maintain a healthy body weight or to reduce weight if overweight or obese. Even people who do not lose weight get substantial benefits from regular physical activity, including lower rates of high blood pressure, diabetes, and cancer. Healthy physical activity includes aerobic activity, muscle-strengthening activities, and activities to increase balance and flexibility. As described by the Physical Activity Guidelines for Americans, adults should engage in at least 150 minutes of moderate-intensity activity each week, and children and teenagers should engage in at least one hour of activity each day.

4. According to the passage, how much time should be spent on exercise?

    (A) 2 hours per week for adults and 1 hour per week for children

    (B) 120 minutes per week for adults and 150 minutes per week for children

    (C) 180 minutes per week for adults and 60 minutes per week for children

    (D) 2½ hours per week for adults and 1 hour per day for children

5. Based on the information in the passage, which two of the following statements are true? Write the letters. [＿＿＿＿] [＿＿＿＿]

    (A) Exercise can lower the blood pressure of people suffering from high blood pressure.

    (B) Exercise provides psychological benefits as well as physical ones.

    (C) Elderly people will derive little benefit from exercise.

    (D) People who have achieved their ideal weight no longer need to exercise daily.

Questions 6 and 7 refer to the following passage.

Have you ever wondered how a rocket ship moves? Perhaps you have seen science-fiction movies in which a captain uses a blast of the rocket engines to save the ship and its crew from crashing into the surface of a distant planet.

Usually, a fuel, such as the gasoline in a car, needs an oxidizer, such as the oxygen in the air, to create combustion, which powers the engine. In space, there is no air and, thus, no oxidizer. The rocket ship, having a clever design, carries its own oxidizer. The fuel used may be a liquid or a solid, but the rocket ship always has fuel and an oxidizer to mix together. When the two are mixed and combustion takes place, a rapid expansion is directed out the back of the engine. The force pushing backward moves the rocket ship forward. In space, with no air, the rocket ship experiences no resistance to the movement. The rocket ship moves forward, avoids the crash, or does whatever the crew wants it to do.

6. Why is the rocket engine the perfect propulsion method for space travel?

    (A) It extracts the oxygen from space for combustion.

    (B) It can operate without an external oxidizer.

    (C) It carries a lot of fuel.

    (D) It produces a forward thrust.

7. Fuel on a rocket ship may be in the form of [＿＿＿＿].

Questions 8–15 refer to the following passage.

Where Does All the Garbage Go?

When we finish using something, we throw it away, but where is "away"? In our modern cities, "away" is frequently an unsightly landfill site, full of all those things that we no longer want. A modern American city generates solid waste at an alarming rate. In a recent year, New York City produced 14,000 tons of trash every day. On average, an American produces nearly five pounds of solid waste per day. In spite of all the efforts to increase recycling, we go on our merry way producing garbage without thinking about where it goes.

In any landfill, gone is not forgotten by nature. By compacting the garbage to reduce its volume, we slow the rate of decomposition, which makes our garbage last longer. In a modern landfill, the process produces a garbage lasagna. There's a layer of compacted garbage covered by a layer of dirt, covered by a layer of compacted garbage, and so on. By saving space for more garbage, we cut off the air and water that bacteria need to decompose the garbage and, thus, preserve it for future generations. If you could dig far enough, you might still be able to read 40-year-old newspapers. The paper may be preserved, but the news is history.

One of the answers to this problem is recycling. Any object that can be reused in one form or another is an object that shouldn't be found in a landfill. Most of us gladly recycle our paper, which saves energy and resources. Recycled paper can be used again and even turned into other products. Old, recycled paper is not as valuable as hidden treasure, but when the cost of landfills and the environmental impact of producing more and more paper are considered, it can be a bargain. If plastic shopping bags can be recycled into a cloth-like substance that can be used to make reusable shopping bags, maybe American ingenuity can find ways to reduce all that garbage being stored in landfills before the landfills overtake the space for cities.

8. Why are the disposal methods used in modern landfills as much a part of the problem as a part of the solution?

   (A) They look very ugly.
   (B) They take up a lot of valuable land.
   (C) The bacteria that aid decomposition do not thrive.
   (D) Newspapers are readable after 50 years.

9. Why is recycling paper important?

   (A) Recycling increases the greenhouse effect.
   (B) Recycling reduces the need for new landfill sites.
   (C) Paper is not biodegradable.
   (D) Recycling increases logging.

10. Why is solid waste compacted in a modern landfill?

   (A) to reduce the odor
   (B) to help the bacteria decompose the waste
   (C) to make the landfill look better
   (D) to reduce the amount of space it occupies

11. What is the modern landfill compared to?

(A) an efficient way of ridding cities of solid waste

(B) a garbage lasagna

(C) a place for bacteria to decompose solid waste

(D) a huge compost bin

12. Why is it important for cities to establish recycling programs?

(A) Recycling makes people feel good about their garbage.

(B) Recycling centers are more attractive than landfills.

(C) Recycling lets someone else look after your problem.

(D) Recycling is more sustainable than using landfills.

13. What can individual Americans do to reduce the amount of waste that is going into landfills?

(A) Eat less.

(B) Reuse and recycle as much as possible.

(C) Stop using paper.

(D) Import more nitrogen.

14. What is the role of bacteria in a landfill?

(A) They help get rid of rodents.

(B) They prepare the garbage for recycling.

(C) They are part of the inorganic cycle.

(D) They help decompose waste.

15. If municipalities lose money recycling paper, why do they continue?

(A) The politicians don't know that they are losing money.

(B) Municipalities don't have to make money.

(C) The public likes to recycle paper.

(D) The cost is less than acquiring more landfill sites.

Question 16 refers to the following passage based on information on the NASA website (www.nasa.gov).

The seasons on Earth are caused by the tilt of the Earth as it rotates on its axis and revolves around the Sun. The 23.5-degree tilt of the Earth's axis results in changes of the angle of incident sunlight. A common misconception is that the seasons are caused by the distance between the Earth and Sun. In fact, summer in the Northern Hemisphere occurs at aphelion, the farthest distance between the Earth and Sun, and follows summer solstice when incident sunlight is most concentrated along the Tropic of Cancer, 23 degrees 26 minutes 22 seconds.

16. The point at which the Earth and Sun are farthest apart is called the

(A) solstice.

(B) aphelion.

(C) axis.

(D) Tropic of Cancer.

Questions 17 and 18 refer to the following passage.

Airbags

All new cars are equipped with airbags. In a crash, the airbags quickly deploy, protecting the driver and front-seat passenger by inflating to prevent them from moving around and being injured by the steering wheel or front dash. When used together with seatbelts, airbags save lives. A person in the front seat of a modern car equipped with airbags who also wears a seat-belt stands a much better chance of surviving a crash than an unbelted person. The two safety devices work together to save lives but must be used properly. For example, an infant car seat should be placed in the back seat. The success of front-seat airbags has prompted other airbags to be added to cars. Some cars now boast side airbags in case of a side-impact accident and knee airbags to prevent injury to lower extremities in a frontal collision. Some new cars now have five or more airbags installed.

17. In a front-end collision, the front-seat [_____] protect the driver from injury.

18. Where is the safest place for an infant in a car seat in a car equipped with airbags?

(A) in the right rear passenger seat

(B) in the front passenger seat

(C) in the left rear passenger seat

(D) in the middle rear passenger seat

Questions 19 and 20 refer to the following diagram, which is excerpted from The Sciences: An Integrated Approach, *3rd Edition, by James Trefil and Robert M. Hazen (Wiley).*

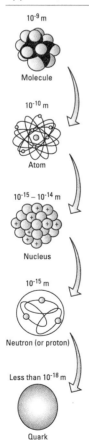

10^{-9} m

Molecule

10^{-10} m

Atom

$10^{-15} - 10^{-14}$ m

Nucleus

10^{-15} m

Neutron (or proton)

Less than 10^{-18} m

Quark

19. According to this diagram, what is the building block upon which the other particles are made?

(A) atom

(B) molecule

(C) neutron

(D) quark

20. According to this diagram, how many times larger is a molecule than a quark?

(A) 100

(B) 1,000

(C) 1,000,000

(D) 1,000,000,000

21. The seat you are sitting on seems solid, but in reality, it is composed of atoms. Each of the atoms is composed of a nucleus, which is composed of neutrons and protons, but much of the space occupied by an atom is just empty space. This means that the chair you are sitting on is mostly empty space. It follows that when you stand on the floor of a building, you are ultimately being supported by [ ].

Question 22 refers to the following passage from the U.S. Department of Energy/Pacific Northwest National Laboratory website (www.pnnl.gov/science/highlights/highlight.asp?id=4386).

Proteins found in nature form the molecular machines that make life possible. Peptoids are highly stable, protein-like molecules developed by scientists to mimic natural proteins. They are cheap, versatile, and customizable and can be designed to have specific forms and functions. Molecular self-assembly is key in biology to building well-defined protein materials. The researchers were able to achieve a controllable self-assembly of peptoids on a flat surface by manipulating molecular-level interactions through advanced chemistry and microscopy techniques.

22. How have scientists been able to mimic natural proteins?

(A) They have built molecular machines.

(B) They have developed peptoids.

(C) They have assembled cheap, versatile chemical elements.

(D) They have cloned molecular interactions.

Questions 23 and 24 refer to the following passage.

The Surface of the Moon

The Moon, a hostile, barren landscape, has no atmosphere, great variance in temperature, and only 17 percent of Earth's gravity. On the surface, astronauts found boulders as large as houses in huge fields of dust and rock. Although the astronauts and scientists had maps and photos of the Moon's surface, the astronauts were not 100 percent sure of what they would encounter until they landed. The astronauts survived, thanks in part to careful planning and extensive training for the mission. Part of their preparation included training in northern Iceland, where the geography was thought to resemble the Moon's. Thirty-two astronauts trained in Iceland, including 9 of the 12 astronauts who walked on the Moon.

23. Which of the following is another detail that would support the idea that landing on the Moon was dangerous?

    (A) Solar radiation is much stronger on the Moon than on Earth.

    (B) The Moon only receives light from the Sun on one side.

    (C) The Moon rotates on its axis.

    (D) The same side of the Moon always faces Earth.

24. Why did astronauts train in Iceland?

    (A) The low temperatures resembled those of the Moon.

    (B) The land resembled the Moon in certain ways.

    (C) Iceland has huge boulders.

    (D) Iceland's small population made it safe to make a test landing there.

Questions 25 and 26 refer to the following passage.

Pushing Aside the Water

If you fill a glass right to the brim with water, you have to drink it at its present temperature. If you decide that you want to add ice, the water spills over the brim. The ice has displaced an amount of water equal to the volume of the ice.

When you lower yourself into a luxurious bubble bath in your tub, the water rises. If you could measure the volume of that rise, you could figure out the volume of your body. Because you would displace a volume of water in the tub equal to the volume of your body, the new combined volume of you plus the water, minus the original volume of the water, equals the volume of your body. Next time you sink slowly into that hot bathwater, make sure that you leave room for the water to rise, or make sure that you are prepared to mop the floor.

25. When you sink into a tub of water, you displace

    (A) your weight in water.

    (B) your weight plus the weight of the water left in the tub.

    (C) the volume of your body plus the volume of the bubbles.

    (D) a volume equal to the volume of your body.

26. If you wanted to find the volume of a small, irregularly shaped rock, how could you do it?

    (A) Immerse the rock in a pre-measured volume of water and measure the increase.

    (B) Measure the rock and calculate the volume.

    (C) Determine the rock's mass and calculate the volume.

    (D) Put the rock in a bubble bath.

Questions 27–29 refer to the following passage.

Newton's First Law of Motion

In 1687, Isaac Newton proposed three laws of motion. These laws are not the types of laws that we are familiar with; they are statements of a truth in the field of physics. Newton's first law of motion states that a body at rest prefers to remain at rest, and a body in motion prefers to stay in motion unless acted upon by an external force. One example you may be familiar with is the game of billiards. Each of the balls will remain in its position unless hit by the cue ball. Once hit, the ball will continue to roll until the friction of the table's surface or an external force stops it. Inertia is the tendency of any object to maintain a uniform motion or remain at rest.

27. If your car becomes stuck in a snowbank, what must you do to free it?

(A) Apply a force downward to increase the traction of the wheels.

(B) Leave it at rest until it wants to move.

(C) Apply a force in the direction you want it to move.

(D) Sit on the hood to increase the weight on the front tires.

28. Which of the following is a result of inertia?

(A) A skateboard hits a large crack in the sidewalk, and the skateboarder flies off their skateboard.

(B) A baseball player swings at a pitch and hits a grand-slam home run.

(C) A golfer tees off and makes a hole in one.

(D) A volleyball player returns a serve.

29. When you are driving at a steady speed on the highway, it takes great effort to stop suddenly because

(A) the weight of the car is too light.

(B) it takes too much power to start driving again.

(C) brakes have an unlimited stopping potential.

(D) your car tends to continue at the same rate.

Question 30 refers to the following passage.

Newton's Second Law of Motion

Newton's second law of motion states that when a body changes its velocity because an external force is applied to it, that change in velocity is directly proportional to the force and inversely proportional to the mass of the body. That is, the faster you want to stop your car, the harder you must brake. The brakes apply an external force that reduces the velocity of the car. The faster you want to accelerate the car, the more force you must apply. Increasing the horsepower of an engine allows it to apply greater force in accelerating. That is why drag-racing cars seem to be all engine.

30. If you want a car that accelerates quickly, which attributes give you the best acceleration?

(A) light weight and two doors

(B) automatic transmission

(C) automatic transmission and two doors

(D) light weight and high horsepower

Question 31 refers to the following passage.

Newton's Third Law of Motion

Newton's third law of motion states that for every action there is an equal and opposite reaction. If you stand on the floor, gravity pulls your body down with a certain force. The floor must exert an equal and opposite force upward on your feet, or you would fall through the floor.

31. A boxer is punching a punching bag. What is the punching bag doing to the boxer?

(A) bouncing away from the boxer

(B) reacting with a force equal and opposite to the force of their punch

(C) swinging back an angle perpendicular to that of the punch

(D) swinging back with a force greater than that of the punch

Questions 32–34 refer to the following passage.

Why Don't Polar Bears Freeze?

Watching a polar bear lumber through the frigid Arctic wilderness, you may wonder why it doesn't freeze. If you were there, you would likely freeze. In fact, you may feel cold just looking at photographs of polar bears.

So why don't polar bears freeze? Polar bears have black skin. Because black absorbs light energy, this means that, in effect, polar bears have a huge solar heat collector covering their bodies. Covering this black skin are hollow hairs. These hairs are clear but look white. Because these hairs are clear, they allow sunlight to reach the skin, where it is absorbed, while also acting as insulation.

32. The most important element in retaining the polar bear's body heat is its [   ].

33. What is the polar bear's solar heat collector?

(A) caves

(B) ice

(C) its furry coat

(D) its skin

34. Which of these additional details is relevant to the passage?

(A) Arctic explorers wear bright colors (usually red) for safety reasons.

(B) The polar bear's white appearance provides it with effective camouflage.

(C) A layer of fat under the bear's skin provides additional insulation.

(D) Polar bears' habitat is shrinking because of global warming.

Questions 35 and 36 refer to the following diagram, which is excerpted from James Trefil and Robert M. Hazen., 2000/John Wiley & Sons.

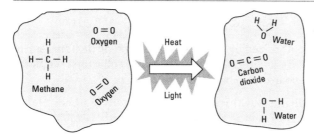

35. When methane (natural gas) burns, it produces light, heat, carbon dioxide, and water. Why would natural gas be a good choice for keeping your house warm in winter?

   (A) The chemical reaction produces carbon dioxide.

   (B) The chemical reaction produces light.

   (C) The chemical reaction produces water.

   (D) The chemical reaction produces heat.

36. If firefighters were faced with a methane fire, what would they want to eliminate to put out the fire?

   (A) light

   (B) nitrogen

   (C) carbon dioxide

   (D) oxygen

Questions 37 and 38 refer to the following passage.

DNA Testing

DNA has become part of everyone's vocabulary, and several crime shows on television use it as a key plot element. DNA has put criminals in jail and freed the innocent. It is used as proof in trials and is an important dramatic tool on many television dramas and talk shows. Because a child inherits the DNA of their parents, DNA testing can be used to prove paternity and maternity. Nowadays, many people use DNA tests to find out more information about their ancestry and ethnic heritage.

37. Paternity tests compare DNA to determine whether an individual is a child's [   ].

38. Because every person's DNA is unique (except for identical twins), it is a highly reliable forensic tool. Which of these forensic tools is also unique to all individuals?

   (A) blood type

   (B) shoe prints

   (C) fingerprints

   (D) sketch artist renderings

Questions 39–44 refer to the following passage. Some information in the passage is adapted from the NASA website (www.nasa.gov).

Space Stuff

Each space flight carries items authorized by NASA, but the quirky little items astronauts have carried onboard their spacecraft frequently catch the interest of collectors. Auction sales have been brisk for material carried aboard various space flights.

On the second crewed Mercury flight, Gus Grissom carried two rolls of dimes. He was planning to give these to the children of his friends after he returned to Earth. If you carried two rolls of dimes worth ten dollars around Earth, they would still add up to ten dollars. When Gus Grissom returned to Earth, however, these dimes became space mementos, each worth many times its face value. Though seemingly innocuous, sometimes unauthorized objects cause hazards. A sandwich smuggled aboard a NASA Gemini flight created crumbs that floated around the inside of the space capsule. That event triggered a Congressional hearing.

Although NASA has authorized astronauts to carry small personal items into space, it does not allow astronauts to sell these items as souvenirs. Nevertheless, many items have found their way to market. The astronauts who flew on Apollo 15 were disciplined for selling stamped envelopes they had carried with them to the moon.

As you might expect, living in space is very different from living on Earth. In space, astronauts' bodies change. Because they spend a lot of time in a weightless environment, their leg muscles and lower backs begin to lose strength. Their bones also begin to get thin. The heart and blood change, too. When we stand up on Earth, blood goes to our legs. Without gravity, the blood moves to the upper body and head. When the astronauts return to Earth, they often look puffy and feel weak. Thus, Grissom's dimes became an even bigger hazard. In fact, an incident with the spacecraft's hatch made Grissom's return to Earth more challenging. A later investigation examined whether the added weight of the dimes had contributed to the difficulties.

39. On which crewed Mercury mission did Gus Grissom carry rolls of dimes?
    (A) first
    (B) second
    (C) third
    (D) fourth

40. What is the most likely reason the sandwich crumbs posed a safety hazard?
    (A) They could get into the spacecraft's gauges and switches.
    (B) They could attract insects and pests.
    (C) They could trigger a Congressional hearing.
    (D) They could block the spacecraft's windshield.

41. Which of the following is a safety hazard posed by Grissom's dimes?
    (A) They could become radioactive because of increased radiation in space.
    (B) They could damage his space suit.
    (C) They could become the subject of an investigation.
    (D) They could weigh him down after returning to earth.

42. What might be a helpful piece of exercise equipment onboard the International Space Station?
    (A) a trampoline
    (B) a hot tub
    (C) a jump rope
    (D) a treadmill

43. Which of the following is a reason that astronauts would have trouble walking upon their return to Earth?
    (A) They are no longer used to Earth's gravity.
    (B) Their bones begin to get thin.
    (C) They have gained weight.
    (D) They are happy to be back on Earth.

44. Why were the Apollo 15 astronauts punished?
    (A) The souvenirs were fake.
    (B) The souvenirs caused an accident in space.
    (C) Astronauts are not allowed to profit by selling souvenirs from space.
    (D) Astronauts are not allowed to bring personal items into space.

Questions 45 and 46 refer to the following passage.

Work

When we think of work, we think of people sitting at desks operating computers or building homes or making some other effort to earn money. When a physicist thinks of work, they probably think of a formula — force exerted over a distance. If you don't expend any energy — resulting in a force of zero — or if your force produces no movement, then no work has been done. If you pick up your gigantic super-ordinary two-pound hamburger and lift it to your mouth to take a bite, you do work. If you want to resist temptation and just stare at your hamburger, you do no work. If your friend gets tired of you playing around and lifts your hamburger to feed you, you still do no work, but your friend does. In scientific terms, two elements are necessary for work to be done: A force must be exerted, and the object to which the force has been exerted must move.

45. If the formula for work is Work = Force × Distance, how much more work would you do in pushing a 40-pound box 3 feet instead of 2 feet?

(A) half as much

(B) three times as much

(C) a third as much

(D) one-and-one-half times as much

46. Although you may see that you do work in climbing a flight of stairs, why do you also do work when you descend a flight of stairs?

(A) It is hard to descend stairs.

(B) You have traveled a distance down the stairs.

(C) You feel tired after descending stairs.

(D) You have exerted a force over a distance.

Questions 47 and 48 refer to the following figure and passages, which are excerpted from C. Lon Enloe., 2000/John Wiley & Sons.

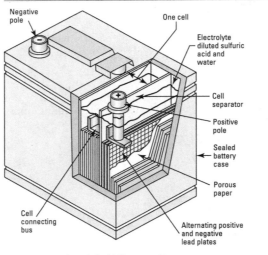

Lead-Acid Storage Battery

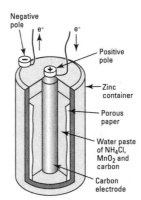

Dry-Cell Battery

The Lead-Acid Storage Battery

One battery you rely on is the 12-volt lead-acid storage battery used in gas-powered cars and trucks. This battery is composed of six separate cells, each developing about 2 volts. By connecting the six cells in series, the overall voltage becomes the sum, or 12 volts.

The Dry-Cell Battery

The traditional dry-cell or flashlight battery is a zinc-carbon battery. It derives its name from the fact that the liquid portion has been replaced by a moist paste of ammonium chloride, manganese dioxide, and carbon. These components are the anode portion of the cell, and the zinc container serves as the cathode.

47. If you wanted a 48-volt lead-acid battery, how many cells would it need?

    (A) 24

    (B) 26

    (C) 28

    (D) 36

48. What replaces the liquid-acid portion of the lead-acid battery in a dry-cell battery?

    (A) a moist paste

    (B) a powder

    (C) dry acid

    (D) carbon and zinc

Questions 49 and 50 refer to the following passage.

The Cell and Heredity

Each cell in a living organism consists of a membrane surrounding a cytoplasm. The cytoplasm is like jelly and has a nucleus in its center. Chromosomes are part of the nucleus. They are important because they store DNA. Most DNA molecules are made up of two strands that are coiled around each other in a double helix formation. The strands are made up of four chemical bases: adenine, guanine, cytosine, and thymine. DNA carries the genetic code that is the basis of heredity.

49. What determines what traits that you inherit from your parents?

    (A) the cell

    (B) the atom

    (C) the nucleus

    (D) DNA

50. What makes up the DNA molecule?

    (A) membrane

    (B) cytoplasm

    (C) jelly

    (D) four chemical bases

Chapter 32

Answers for Practice Test 2, Science

n this chapter, you find the answers and explanations for the Science practice test in Chapter 31. Review the answer explanation for all the questions, even for the ones you got right, and keep track of areas where you need some additional studying. If you just want a quick look at the answers, check out the abbreviated answer key at the end of this chapter. After you review your answers and finish any additional studying, you are ready for the online practice test.

Answers and Explanations

1. **perennial, annual.** These answers are correct because even though plants develop new bulbs, they do not reliably regrow. The plants depend on humans to cultivate them.

2. **B, E, C, D, A.** This order correctly restates the life cycle, the description of which is spread throughout the passage.

TIP

The GED science test often includes readings on various cycles in nature, such as the water cycle, the rock cycle, and the carbon cycle. Frequently, a drag-and-drop question like this one will test your understanding of the order of the cycle. Notice here that the first stage of the cycle, planting a bulb in fall, is mentioned at the end of the passage. Read the passage carefully to ensure you put the stages in the correct order — they may not come up in the correct order in the passage.

3. **C. Cells are differentiated.** Although all of the choices are true, only Choice (C) is supported by information in the passage.

4. **D. 2½ hours per week for adults and 1 hour per day for children.** The passage states that adults should exercise for 150 minutes (2½ hours) per week, and children should exercise for 60 minutes (1 hour) daily. This item is a good example of why you should pay attention to how numbers are labeled — in this case, hours or minutes.

5. **A, B.** According to the passage, exercise can lower the blood pressure of people suffering from high blood pressure, and exercise provides psychological benefits as well as physical ones. The other choices are contradicted by the information in the passage.

TIP

On a drag-and-drop question such as this one, think of the answer choices as a series of true/false statements. Select the choices that are true. In this case, Choices (A) and (B) are your answers.

6. **B. It can operate without an external oxidizer.** In space, there's no oxidizer to take part in the chemical reaction needed for combustion. A rocket ship carries its own oxidizer and, thus, can travel through airless space (which doesn't contain oxygen). Because the passage specifically discusses oxidizers, Choice (B) is the best answer.

7. **a liquid or a solid.** The passage states in the second paragraph that "the fuel used may be a liquid or a solid."

TIP

This question shows the importance of giving a complete answer. Both "solid" and "liquid" are correct, but neither one is the complete answer: "a solid or a liquid." There is no partial credit on the GED, so make sure your fill-in responses are complete.

8. **C. The bacteria that aid decomposition do not thrive.** The passage states that with the methodology used for burying solid waste in a modern landfill, the bacteria needed for decomposition can't do their work. The reason for using landfills is that they require less space — not that they promote decomposition. Thus, the landfill and the processes used within it are as much a part of the problem as they are a part of the solution. The other choices may be partially correct, but the key point in the text concerns the decomposition of wastes.

9. **B. Recycling reduces the need for new landfill sites.** Recycling newspapers, or many other items that would go to the landfill, reduces the need for new landfill sites.

10. **D. to reduce the amount of space it occupies.** Solid waste is compacted to reduce the amount of space it occupies, which also happens to make the landfill last longer. The waste is compacted in spite of the fact that doing so slows down decomposition and lengthens the life of the garbage.

11. **B. a garbage lasagna.** A modern landfill is compared to garbage lasagna because it's made up of alternating layers of compacted garbage and dirt. This method prevents timely decomposition.

12. **D. Recycling is more sustainable than using landfills.** Landfills are costly and allow solid waste to accumulate without decomposing. Recycling will solve this and other issues associated with landfills. Therefore, Choice (D) is correct.

13. **B. Reuse and recycle as much as possible.** As long as you dispose of waste by taking it to the curb or the dump, there will be an excess amount of waste being disposed of. Every piece of waste that you can reuse or recycle lives on to be useful again and, thus, eliminates some of the waste in America.

14. **D. They help decompose waste.** The passage states that bacteria decompose waste. Therefore, Choice (B) is incorrect. Choice (A) is not discussed in the passage. Decomposition is part of the organic cycle, so Choice (C) is incorrect.

15. **D. The cost is less than acquiring more landfill sites.** Landfill sites are more expensive to acquire than the cost of recycling. In most cities, people hope to find new uses for recycled materials, which could increase the value of garbage.

16. **B. aphelion.** The passage states, "summer in the Northern Hemisphere occurs at aphelion, the farthest distance between the Earth and Sun. . ."

TIP

Even though this is a dense paragraph, you don't have to spend a lot of time reading it as long as you read the question first. You just need to scan quickly for the definition given in the question.

17. **airbags.** The purpose of the airbags, according to the passage, is to absorb some of the forces in a front-end crash and prevent injury to the occupants.

TIP

On a fill-in item, such as this one, clues in the sentence can help you find the answer. In this case, the verb "protect" indicates that the answer is plural: "airbags." However, you don't need to worry about whether you write air bags or airbags. Both responses will be accepted as correct.

18. **D. in the middle rear passenger seat.** According to the passage, the infant car seat should be placed in the rear seat. You can infer that the safest place in the rear seat would be in the middle seat, in case of a side collision.

19. **D. quark.** The diagram (going from bottom to top) indicates the process of building up a molecule. The quark is the smallest particle, and the molecule is the largest. Sometimes you have to read a diagram in an unfamiliar way to answer the question.

20. **D. 1,000,000,000.** According to the diagram, a quark is 10^{-18} meters across and a molecule is 10^{-9} meters across. The molecule would be $10^{-9} / 10^{-18} = 1 / 10^{-9}$ or 1,000,000,000 times the size of a quark.

A number with a negative exponent, like 10^{-9}, equals 1/10 to the positive power of the negative exponent (for example, $10^{-9} = 1/10^9$).

REMEMBER

You can use the on-screen calculator on the GED science test, or you can bring your own TI-30XS MultiView calculator if you test at a testing center. Scientific notation is one of the functions available on the calculator. Make sure you know how to use this handy tool before test day!

21. **atoms.** The passage states that everything is composed of atoms. As a result, the floor must be composed of atoms.

22. **B. They have developed peptoids.** This is another dense science reading where you need to read carefully and pay attention to the answer choices. Many of the incorrect answers use language from the passage; however similar the words may be, the other choices don't answer the question. According to the second sentence of the passage, the only correct answer is Choice (B).

23. **A. Solar radiation is much stronger on the Moon than on Earth.** Only this statement presents a hazard to astronauts or their vehicle.

24. **B. The land resembled the Moon in certain ways.** This information is stated directly in the passage. The other choices are not supported by information in the passage.

25. **D. a volume equal to the volume of your body.** The passage tells you that you would displace a volume equal to your own volume.

26. **A. Immerse the rock in a pre-measured volume of water and measure the increase.** An object displaces a volume of water equal to its volume. Thus, putting an irregularly shaped object in a pre-measured volume of water is one way to measure the volume of that object. The other methods would not work. Choice (C) would only work if you knew the density of the rock, which you do not. Though bubble baths are mentioned in the passage, Choice (D) would not help you determine the volume of the rock.

27. **C. Apply a force in the direction you want it to move.** According to Newton, a force must be applied to move an object at rest. Newton, who never drove a car, said that you have to apply an external force on the object at rest (the car in this question) in the direction you want it to move. If you want your car to move deeper into the snow, you push it down. If you have a crane or a helicopter, which the passage doesn't mention, you apply a force upward to lift it out of the snow. Choice (C) is the best answer.

28. **A. A skateboard hits a large crack in the sidewalk, and the skateboarder flies off their skateboard.** Choice (A) is correct because when the skateboard hits a crack, the skateboarder flies off the skateboard in the same direction they were traveling in. All the other choices are examples of a body being acted upon by another force, either changing the velocity and/or direction, or putting it in motion.

29. **D. your car tends to continue at the same rate.** When driving at a uniform rate of speed, the car resists changes in speed. The car wants to continue to travel at the same speed. To change that speed suddenly, you must apply great effort to your brakes. While the weight, or mass, of the car plays a role in changing speed, that is only a partial answer.

30. **D. light weight and high horsepower.** Newton's second law of motion states that when a body changes its velocity because an external force is applied to it, that change in velocity is directly proportional to the force and inversely proportional to the mass of the body. If you decrease the weight of the body and increase the size of the external force, the acceleration increases.

TIP

Did you select Choice (A)? If so, you may have been working too quickly. Only the first part of the choice is correct; having two doors is not relevant. Always read all the choices completely before you select your response.

31. **B. reacting with a force equal and opposite to the force of their punch.** Newton's third law of motion states that for every action there's an equal and opposite reaction. If the boxer is exerting a force on the punching bag, the bag is exerting an equal and opposite force on the boxer.

32. **hair** or **fur.** The passage states that the hair acts as insulation, retaining the polar bear's body heat.

33. **D. its skin.** The passage states that the polar bear's dark skin collects heat from the sun.

34. **C. A layer of fat under the bear's skin provides additional insulation.** The passage is primarily about how polar bears stay warm and avoid freezing. Only Choice (C) supports this main idea. The other choices are not relevant.

35. **D. The chemical reaction produces heat.** In cold weather, you need a source of heat to warm your house, and methane produces heat in the chemical reaction. The other answers are incorrect.

36. **D. oxygen.** Methane requires oxygen to produce light and heat. If there's no oxygen, the methane can't burn.

37. **father, mother,** or **parent.** A paternity or maternity test can determine whether an individual is the biological parent of another person.

38. **C. fingerprints.** Identical twins have the same DNA but different fingerprints, so fingerprints are unique to all individuals. Blood type (Choice A), shoe prints (Choice B), and artist sketches (Choice D) aren't as reliable as fingerprints.

39. **B. second.** According to the passage, Grissom carried the dimes on the second crewed Mercury voyage.

40. **A. They could get into the spacecraft's gauges and switches.** The crumbs could float anywhere in the weightless environment and cause problems with the gauges and switches, which would affect safety. The other choices do not make sense.

41. **D. They could weigh him down after returning to Earth.** Of the choices, only this one is a likely safety hazard, and so is the answer.

42. **D. a treadmill.** Because the astronauts lose muscle mass in their legs, having a treadmill onboard would help them exercise their lower extremities. NASA's treadmills are especially designed for use in space. They include special bungee ropes to hold the astronauts to the machine. Astronauts report that it's a fun, bouncy way to exercise. None of the other choices would work in space. A hot tub (Choice B) does not provide exercise.

43. **A. They are no longer used to Earth's gravity.** Only this choice explains why the astronauts would have trouble walking. The other choices do not make sense.

44. **C. Astronauts are not allowed to profit by selling souvenirs from space.** According to the passage, NASA forbids the sale of items carried into space. Therefore, Choice (C) is correct. The souvenirs were authentic space items, so Choice (A) is incorrect. Choice (B) is not supported by information in the passage. Choice (D) is contradicted by the passage; NASA can authorize astronauts to bring personal items with them. However, the astronauts are not allowed to sell them.

45. **D. One-and-one-half times as much.** Because the force remains constant, the work done is proportional to the distance traveled, which means you would do 3/2 or $1\frac{1}{2}$ times as much work.

Questions on the GED Science test such as this one may ask you to apply a scientific formula. But relax — you are never expected to know or memorize the formula; it's always given to you. You just have to know how to apply it.

46. **D. You have exerted a force over a distance.** Walking down the stairs, you have to exert a force over a distance (the definition of work in physics). In real life, it seems easier to walk down a flight of stairs than to walk up it, but, in both cases, work is being done.

47. **A. 24.** If you want a 48-volt lead-acid battery, and each cell produces 2 volts, you need 24 cells $(48 \div 2 = 24)$.

48. **A. a moist paste.** The moist paste replaces the acid in the battery.

49. **D. DNA.** DNA stores the genetic code, which determines heredity, and you get your DNA from your parents.

50. **D. four chemical bases.** According to the passage, DNA is a double helix molecule made up of adenine, guanine, cytosine, and thymine, which are all chemical bases.

Answer Key

1.	perennial, annual	18.	D	35.	D
2.	B, E, C, D, A	19.	D	36.	D
3.	C	20.	D	37.	father, mother, or **parent**
4.	D	21.	atoms	38.	C
5.	A, B	22.	B	39.	B
6.	B	23.	A	40.	A
7.	a liquid or a solid	24.	B	41.	D
8.	C	25.	D	42.	D
9.	B	26.	A	43.	A
10.	D	27.	C	44.	C
11.	B	28.	A	45.	D
12.	D	29.	D	46.	D
13.	B	30.	D	47.	A
14.	D	31.	B	48.	A
15.	D	32.	**hair** or **fur**	49.	D
16.	B	33.	D	50.	D
17.	airbag	34.	C		

Chapter 33

Practice Test 2: Mathematical Reasoning

I n 115 minutes, you have to solve a series of questions involving general mathematical skills and problem solving. These questions may be based on short passages, graphs, charts, or figures. You must do the first five questions without a calculator, but after that, you can use a calculator for the rest of the test. For now, the calculator on your phone is fine, but eventually you will want to become familiar with the TI-30XS MultiView calculator that you will use during the real test. You will also have an online whiteboard or an erasable tablet (only at a test center) to help you visualize problems, jot down equations, or write notes. For now, have a couple of sheets of scratch paper handy.

You also have at your fingertips a list of formulas to help you with some of the questions. Remember that the calculator and list of formulas aren't a magic solution. You have to know how to use them. The GED formula sheet is on the page before the first test question. Only some of the questions require you to use a formula, and you may not need all the formulas given.

TIP

If you have time before the test, memorize the most commonly tested formulas: area of a square or rectangle, area and circumference of a circle, and the Pythagorean Theorem. Questions using these formulas appear frequently on the GED test.

REMEMBER

On the real GED, you'll take the test on a computer, where you use the mouse and the keyboard to indicate your answers. The questions and answer choices are formatted in this book to make them appear as similar as possible to what you'll see on the computer screen, but I had to retain some A, B, C, and D choices and provide an answer sheet for you to mark your answers. When you're ready for the included online practice test, you will be able to see and try the actual question types as they appear on the test.

Use the timer on your phone to keep track of time. If you run out of time, mark the last question you answered. Then answer the rest of the questions. This will help you figure out how much more quickly you have to work to complete the entire test in the time allowed.

Answer Sheet for Practice Test 2, Mathematical Reasoning

1. _____

2. _____

3. _____

4. _____

5. _____

6. _____

7. _____

8. _____

9. _____

10. _____

11. _____

12. _____

13. _____

14. _____

15. _____

16. _____

17. _____

18. _____

19. _____

20. _____

21. _____

22. _____

23. _____

24. _____

25. _____

26. _____

27. _____

28. _____

29. _____

30. _____

31. _____

32. _____

33. _____

34. _____

35. _____

36. _____

37. _____

38. _____

39. _____

40. _____

41. _____

42. _____

43. _____

44. _____

45. _____

46. _____

47. _____

48. _____

49. _____

50. _____

Mathematics Formula Explanations

This displays formulas relating to geometric measurement and certain algebra concepts and is available on the GED® test — Mathematical Reasoning.

Area of a:

square	$A = s^2$
rectangle	$A = lw$
parallelogram	$A = bh$
triangle	$A = \frac{1}{2} bh$
trapezoid	$A = \frac{1}{2} h(b_1 + b_2)$
circle	$A = \pi r^2$

Perimeter of a:

square	$P = 4s$
rectangle	$P = 2l + 2w$
triangle	$P = s_1 + s_2 + s_3$
Circumference of a circle	$C = 2\pi r$ OR $C = \pi d$; $\pi \approx 3.14$

Surface area and volume of a:

rectangular prism	$SA = 2lw + 2lh + 2wh$	$V = lwh$
right prism	$SA = ph + 2B$	$V = Bh$
cylinder	$SA = 2\pi rh + 2\pi r^2$	$V = \pi r^2 h$
pyramid	$SA = \frac{1}{2} ps + B$	$V = \frac{1}{3} Bh$
cone	$SA = \pi rs + \pi r^2$	$V = \frac{1}{3} \pi r^2 h$
sphere	$SA = 4\pi r^2$	$V = \frac{4}{3} \pi r^3$

(p = perimeter of base with area B; $\pi \approx 3.14$)

Data

mean	mean is equal to the total of the values of a data set, divided by the number of elements in the data set
median	median is the middle value in an odd number of ordered values of a data set, or the mean of the two middle values in an even number of ordered values in a data set

Algebra

slope of a line	$m = \frac{y_2 - y_1}{x_2 - x_1}$
slope-intercept form of the equation of a line	$y = mx + b$
point-slope form of the equation of a line	$y - y_1 = m(x - x_1)$
standard form of a quadratic equation	$y = ax^2 + bx + c$
quadratic formula	$x = \frac{-b \pm \sqrt{b^2 - 4ac}}{2a}$
Pythagorean theorem	$a^2 + b^2 = c^2$
simple interest	$I = Prt$
	(I = interest, P = principal, r = rate, t = time)
distance formula	$d = rt$
total cost	total cost = (number of units) x (price per unit)

Æ Symbol Tool Explanation

The GED® test on computer contains a tool known as the "Æ Symbol Tool." Use this guide to learn about entering special mathematical symbols into fill-in-the-blank item types.

Symbol	Explanation	Symbol	Explanation	Symbol	Explanation
π	pi	|	absolute value	—	minus or negative
f	function	$\times$	multiplication	(	open or left parenthesis
$\geq$	greater than or equal to	$\div$	division	)	close or right parenthesis
$\leq$	less than or equal to	$\pm$	positive or negative	$>$	greater than
$\neq$	not equal to	∞	infinity	$<$	less than
2	2 exponent ("squared")	$\sqrt{}$	square root	=	equals
3	3 exponent ("cubed")	+	plus or positive		

1. Yvonne is studying a map. Her destination is 4 miles due north of her current location, but to avoid a small lake, the road goes 3 miles due west to an intersection and then goes northeast to her destination. Approximately how much extra must she drive because of the way the road goes?

   (A) 4 miles

   (B) 5 miles

   (C) 7 miles

   (D) 8 miles

2. After asking for directions to a restaurant, Sarah was told it was 1,000 yards ahead, but her car's odometer reads distances in miles and tenths of miles. How many miles (to the nearest tenth) does she have to drive to find the restaurant? (There are 1,760 yards in a mile.) You may use numbers, a decimal point (.), and/or a negative sign (−) in your answer. [＿＿＿] miles

3. Arthur is making a circular wall hanging, using small pieces of cloth glued onto a backing that is attached to a frame. If he wants a wall hanging that is 7 feet 8 inches across, including a 2-inch fringe all around the backing, how many square feet of backing does he need to cover, rounded to one decimal place?

   (A) 42.2

   (B) 43.0

   (C) 45.7

   (D) 46.1

4. The vertices of a triangle are A(−6,4), B(−8,−6), and C(8,7). Mark the vertices on the coordinate plane. What is the longest side of the triangle? [＿＿＿]

Question 5 refers to the following graph.

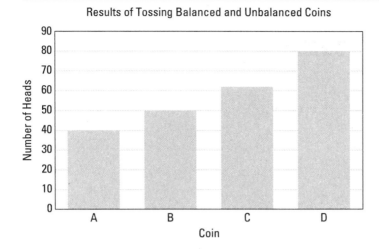

Results of Tossing Balanced and Unbalanced Coins

5. As an experiment, students in a statistics class toss four coins 100 times each and chart the results. Three coins are not fairly balanced. From the chart, which coin is closest to being fairly balanced?

(A) coin A

(B) coin B

(C) coin C

(D) coin D

6. Donna is a very dedicated runner. To improve her breathing, she has started inhaling for two steps and then exhaling for two steps. Her average step is 27 inches long. How many times does she inhale in 1,000 yards of her daily 1-mile run?

(A) 111

(B) 333

(C) 589

(D) 5,332

7. Sam and Arnold were eating ice-cream cones. Arnold wondered what volume of ice cream his cone would hold if filled to the top. Sam measured the cone and found it to be 2½ inches across the top and 5½ inches high. The cone would hold ⬚ cubic inches of ice cream, rounded to one decimal place, if it were filled to the top. You may use numbers, a decimal point (.), and/ or a negative sign (−) in your answer.

Question 8 refers to the following table.

Room Level Dimensions

Room	Measurement (In Feet)
Dining room	10×8
Living room	20×13
Kitchen	14×8
Solarium	19×8
Bedroom	14×13
Office	12×8

8. Singh has bought a new condo and wants to carpet the living room, dining room, and bedroom. A nearby store has carpet that he likes for $35.00 per square yard plus free installation. How much will the new carpet cost without tax? You may use numbers, a decimal point (.), and/or a negative sign (−) in your answer. ☐

Questions 9 and 10 refer to the following information.

Carlos wants to buy a used car. He has been told that a car loses 4.3 cents from its book value for every mile over 100,000 that it has traveled. He sees just the car he wants, but it has 137,046 miles on the odometer. The book value of the car is $13,500.

9. Which is the best estimate of the realistic value of the car to the nearest $10, according to the information Carlos was told?

(A) $10,910

(B) $11,000

(C) $12,020

(D) $14,980

10. According to the information Carlos was told, the realistic actual value of the car to the nearest dollar is ☐ .

11. Elena wants to paint a mural on the wall of her house. The wall is 9 feet high and 17 feet long. To plan the mural, she draws a scale drawing of the area for the mural on a piece of paper 11 inches long. How high, in inches, should the drawing be to maintain scale?

(A) 6.2

(B) 5.8

(C) 8.5

(D) 9.0

12. If the slope of a line is 0.75, and $y_2 = 36$, $y_1 = 24$, and $x_1 = 12$, what is the value of x_2?

(A) 28

(B) 14

(C) –14

(D) –28

Questions 13 and 14 refer to the following table.

Literacy Rates in Selected Countries

Country	Literacy Rate (%)
China	90.9
Cuba	99.8
Ethiopia	35.9
Haiti	54.8
India	61.0
Israel	97.1
Russia	99.4
South Africa	82.4
United States	99.0

13. If the literacy rates of China, the United States, and Russia were compared, the highest literacy rate would be how many times larger than the lowest?

(A) 1.0

(B) 1.1

(C) 1.2

(D) 1.3

14. How many countries have a literacy rate higher than the United States?

(A) 1

(B) 2

(C) 3

(D) 4

15. The dimensions of a cube are 7 inches on all sides. Which expression shows the volume of the cube?

(A) 7^1

(B) 7^2

(C) 7^3

(D) 3^7

Peter's grades are 81, 76, 92, 87, 79, and 83.

16. To renew his scholarship, Peter's average grade must be above the average grade for the school, which is 82. By how many points is he above or below that standard?

    (A) 2

    (B) 1

    (C) −1

    (D) −2

17. If Peter's goal is to get an average grade of 90 percent, by how many total points is he failing to achieve his goal?

    (A) 42

    (B) 43

    (C) 44

    (D) 45

18. Workers at Olga's Cookie Shop store molasses in a cylindrical tank that measures 4.8 feet tall and 2.1 feet in diameter. How many cubic feet of molasses can workers store in the tank? You may use numbers, a decimal point (.), and/or a negative sign (−) in your answer. [   ]

19. Amy's son received $1,574 in gifts when he graduated from middle school. If she lets her son spend $74, and she invests the rest of the money in a certificate of deposit paying 1.4 percent simple interest for the four years until he starts college, how much money will be in the certificate of deposit? You may use numbers, a decimal point (.), and/or a negative sign (−) in your answer. [   ]

20. Consider the equation $E = mc^2$. If the value of m triples and the value of c remains constant, the effect on E would be how many times larger?

    (A) the same

    (B) 3 times larger

    (C) 9 times larger

    (D) 27 times larger

21. Tyrone recently got permission to telework from home, so he is setting up his home office. He wants to put a chair mat under his desk. In front of the chair mat, he wants to put a small area rug. According to their labels, the chair mat measures 36 inches by 48 inches, and the rug measures 3 feet by 4 feet. How much total surface area will be covered by the chair mat and the rug in square feet?

    (A) 12

    (B) 24

    (C) 1,728

    (D) 3,456

22. Vladimir wants to install a small cylindrical water tank to store rain water for his garden. He wants a tank with a 6-foot diameter. He can buy a tank that is 4 feet tall or 6 feet tall. How many more cubic feet of water can the larger tank hold?

    (A) 57

    (B) 113

    (C) 170

    (D) 283

23. Forty tenth-grade social studies students are on a field trip, but many of the students don't feel well. Ten students are healthy, but each of the remaining 30 has a sore throat, a cold, or both. If 15 students have sore throats and 25 have colds, how many students have both?

    (A) 25

    (B) 20

    (C) 15

    (D) 10

24. Graph the point $(-3,4)$ on the coordinate plane.

25. A local hospital offers a 4-week parenting course for new parents. The cost is $40 per person, but 75% of the cost is paid for by a government grant. The hospital absorbs the rest of the cost, so the classes are free to the parents. If 11 parents take the course this month, how much will the hospital absorb? $[_____] You may use numbers, a decimal point (.), and/or a negative sign (−) in your answer.

26. Jerry has started a business selling computers. He can buy a good used computer for $299 and sell it for $449. The only question he has is whether he will make money. If his overhead (rent, light, heating, and cooling) amounts to $48 per unit and his taxes amount to $2 per unit, how many computers will he have to sell to make $700 profit per week?

    (A) 6

    (B) 7

    (C) 8

    (D) 9

27. Jerry also repairs customers' computers. The minimum charge is $45 for one hour. Each additional hour is $30. This week, he repaired 3 computers in under an hour. It took him 3 hours to repair a fourth computer. How much did he make this week repairing computers? [   ] You may use numbers, a decimal point (.), and/or a negative sign (−) in your answer.

Questions 28 and 29 refer to this table.

Top Installed Geothermal-Electric Capacity, by Country, in 2019

Country	Installed Capacity (Gigawatts)
United States	3.7
Indonesia	2.1
Philippines	1.9
Turkey	1.5
New Zealand	1.0

28. Which country has the highest installed geothermal-electric capacity?

(A) Indonesia

(B) Philippines

(C) Turkey

(D) New Zealand

29. Iceland has an installed geothermal-electric capacity of 0.8 gigawatt. What is the difference between Iceland's installed capacity and the next highest on the list?

(A) 0.2 gigawatt

(B) 0.7 gigawatt

(C) 1.3 gigawatts

(D) 2.9 gigawatts

30. Elayne wants to buy a new fuel-efficient car. She notices that a new car is advertised as getting 100 miles per gallon in city driving and 70 miles per gallon on the highway. After a week of record keeping, she produces the following table for her old car.

Day	City Driving (Miles)	Highway Driving (Miles)
Monday	30	5
Tuesday	35	25
Wednesday	25	10
Thursday	30	20
Friday	20	5
Saturday	5	70
Sunday	5	75

If Elayne's old car gets 18 miles per gallon in the city and 12 miles per gallon on the highway, and gas costs $2.70 a gallon, how much would she save in a week by buying this new fuel-efficient car?

(A) $12.15

(B) $22.50

(C) $47.25

(D) $57.60

Question 31 refers to the following table.

Interest Rates Offered by Different Car Dealerships

Dealer	Interest Rate Offered
A	Prime + 2%
B	7.5%
C	1/2 of prime + 5%
D	Prime + 20% of prime for administrative costs

31. Donald is looking for a new car, but each dealership offers him a different interest rate. If the prime lending rate is 6 percent, which dealer is offering Donald the best terms to finance his car?

    (A) Dealer A

    (B) Dealer B

    (C) Dealer C

    (D) Dealer D

32. Henry wanted to find out how many people watched *Four's a Mob*, the newest sitcom, this week. He did a survey of 12 of his friends and found that 9 of them had seen the last episode. What percentage of his friends watched the sitcom this week? You may use numbers, a decimal point (.), and/or a negative sign (−) in your answer. ☐

33. The Corner Bookstore is going to mail 3 GED books to an adult school. The books are 1¾ inches thick. How deep should the box be in order to hold all the books with room for ¼ inch of packing material above and below the books?

    (A) 2 inches

    (B) 2¼ inches

    (C) 5¼ inches

    (D) 5¾ inches

34. In September, Ken and Ben decided to lose some weight by the following July. They figured that by supporting each other, eating a balanced diet with reduced calories, and exercising, they could lose 0.5 pound per week. If Ken and Ben stick to their plans, approximately how much weight could they each lose between the beginning of September and the end of June, assuming there are about 4 weeks in a month?

(A) 20 pounds

(B) 30 pounds

(C) 36 pounds

(D) 48 pounds

35. Mary and Samantha are planning a 900-mile trip. Mary says that she can drive at an average speed of 45 miles per hour. Samantha says that she will fly, but it takes her 45 minutes to get to the airport and 1 hour and 15 minutes to get from the airport to her destination after she lands. If she has to be at the airport 3 hours before takeoff and the airplane travels an average of 300 miles per hour, how many hours longer is Mary's travel time compared to Samantha's (not counting time for rest or sleeping)?

(A) 8

(B) 9

(C) 12

(D) 16

Question 36 refers to the following information and graph.

The Queenly Hat Company of Lansing, Michigan, produces designer hats for women who feel that a hat completes an outfit. Their sales vary from quarter to quarter and region to region. The following chart reflects their sales for one year.

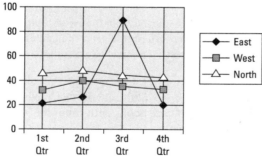

36. Of the three regions, which regions and in which quarter are sales figures approximately in the ratio of 2:1?

(A) east and west in 2nd quarter

(B) west and north in 3rd quarter

(C) east and north in 3rd quarter

(D) west and east in 1st quarter

Questions 37 and 38 refer to the following table.

Life Expectancy in the United States, by Current Age

Age (In Years)	Males	Females
10	66.6	71.5
20	56.9	61.6
30	47.7	52.0
40	38.6	42.5
50	29.7	33.2
60	21.6	24.6
70	14.93	16.54

37. Trent and Tina are unidentical twin brother and sister. From the data presented in the table, which of these possible predictions is most likely if they are currently 30 years old?

(A) Trent will likely live longer than his sister Tina.

(B) Tina will likely live longer than her brother Trent.

(C) They are identical twins and so will likely live to the same age.

(D) The average life expectancy for Tina is 47.7 years.

38. On average, what age will a 20-year-old female reach?

(A) 56.9

(B) 61.6

(C) 76.9

(D) 81.6

39. The cost of a finished item of a certain product is equal to 2 times the production cost, plus 120 percent of the overhead costs at the retail level, plus profit. If three stores, A, B, and C, each sell the product, and Store B has a 50-percent raise in rent, how will this affect the selling price for the item?

(A) The selling price will go down.

(B) The selling price will remain the same.

(C) The selling price will go up.

(D) Customers can get a discount with a coupon.

40. Sol wants to write the population of the United States in scientific notation for a project he is working on. If the population of the United States is estimated at 328,000,000 and he writes it out as 3.28×10^x, the value for x is [_____].

41. Harry and Karry are preparing for the big race. They have been keeping track of their times in the following table.

Comparative Times

Harry's Times (In Seconds)	Karry's Times (In Seconds)
15.6	15.9
14.9	16.1
16.0	15.8
15.8	16.2
16.1	14.8

What conclusion can you reach from comparing their mean times?

(A) Karry is slightly faster.

(B) Harry is slightly slower.

(C) They are about even.

(D) Karry has a higher average time.

42. The total floor area of Maria's new apartment is 1,400 square feet. If the ceilings are 9 feet high and her air system withdraws and replaces 63 cubic feet of air each minute, how long, in minutes, does it take to withdraw and replace all the air in her apartment?

(A) 180

(B) 200

(C) 220

(D) 240

43. Peter is emptying his swimming pool. He can pump 9 cubic feet of water per minute. If his pool measures 45 feet by 12 feet with an average depth of 4 feet, when will his pool be empty if he starts pumping at noon on Tuesday?

(A) 4 a.m. on Wednesday

(B) 6 p.m. on Tuesday

(C) 2 p.m. on Tuesday

(D) 4 p.m. on Tuesday

44. Mohammed works in sales. He has earned an average of $420 per week for the last four weeks. If he earned $480 the first week, $400 the third week, and $550 the final week, how much did he earn the second week of the month?

(A) $190

(B) $250

(C) $280

(D) $340

45. Georgia took her children shopping for school clothes. She started shopping with a $500 gift card and a credit card in her purse. When she returned home after shopping, $126 remained on the gift card and she had $83 in credit card receipts. How much did she spend shopping? You may use numbers, a decimal point (.), and/or a negative sign (−) in your answer. [   ]

46. If you cut almost all the way around the top and bottom of an empty vegetable can and then open it flat along the seam, what shape would you end up with?

   (A) two circles

   (B) a rectangle with a circle on each side

   (C) a rectangle

   (D) a rectangle with a circle on each end

47. Sonya's car uses gasoline in direct proportion to her speed. If she increases her average speed by 10 miles per hour to save time, the consequence is that

   (A) she would save money.

   (B) she would spend more money on fuel.

   (C) she would spend the same amount as before.

   (D) she would use up her savings paying speeding tickets.

48. If a circle is drawn with its center at the origin and a diameter of 8 units, where will the circumference intersect the negative y-axis? Circle this point on the graph.

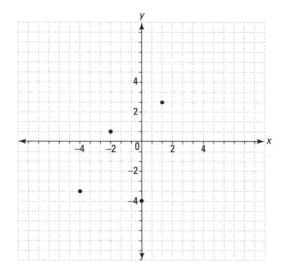

49. A fuel gauge reads 1/8 full. If the fuel tank holds 24 gallons, how many gallons of fuel will fill it?

   (A) 3

   (B) 19

   (C) 21

   (D) 24

50. As part of a mathematics test, Ying was given the following equations to solve:

   $4x + 2y = 20$

   $2x + 6y = 35$

   What is the value of y?

   (A) 4

   (B) 5

   (C) 6

   (D) 7

Chapter 34

Answers for Practice Test 2, Mathematical Reasoning

This chapter gives you the answers and explanations for the Mathematical Reasoning practice test in Chapter 33. The first question you may ask yourself is why you should bother with the explanations if you got the answers right. The simple answer is: The explanation walks you through the steps you follow to answer the question. This reinforces your understanding in preparation for the real test. If you made an error, the explanation can save you from a lot of frustration. By following the steps, you can discover why and where you went wrong and figure out a way not to repeat the error on similar questions on the real test. After you finish reviewing your answers, you may want to review relevant chapters in this book. Then, when you are ready, you can take the full-length online practice test.

Answers and Explanations

1. **A. 4 miles.** This problem is a test of your knowledge of how to use the Pythagorean Theorem. Sketch out a map for this question: Her destination is 4 miles due north of her current location. To get to her destination she has to drive due west and then northeast. Due north and due west are at right angles. So Yvonne's journey is a right triangle, with the last part being the hypotenuse. Pythagoras (the guy who, as you may expect, is credited with discovering the Pythagorean Theorem) said that the square of the hypotenuse of a right triangle is equal to the sum of the squares of the other two sides $\left(a^2 + b^2 = c^2\right)$. Thus, the square of the last leg of Yvonne's journey equals $16 + 9 = 25$. The square root of 25 is 5. However, the question asks how much farther Yvonne must travel: She ended up driving $5 + 3 = 8$ miles but was originally only 4 miles from her destination. Therefore, she traveled $8 - 4 = 4$ miles extra.

REMEMBER

You can save time on test day by memorizing a few commonly tested formulas, such as the Pythagorean Theorem. But you don't have to depend on your memory either. If you forget or get flustered, just click the Formula Sheet button and refresh your memory.

2. **0.6.** To convert yards into miles, you have to divide the number of yards you want to convert into miles by 1,760 (because 1 mile equals 1,760 yards). One thousand yards is about 0.57 mile $\left(1,000 / 1,760 = 0.568181818\right)$. Odometers usually read to one decimal point, so Sarah should drive about 0.6 mile, rounded up because the second decimal place is larger than 5, which would be just past the restaurant.

3. **A. 42.2.** The wall hanging has a diameter of 7 feet 8 inches, and it has a 2-inch fringe all the way around it. To calculate the diameter that will be covered by the backing, you have to subtract the width of the fringe (which you get by multiplying 2 inches by 2 because the fringe adds 2 inches to both sides of the circle): 7 feet 8 inches $- 4$ inches $= 7$ feet 4 inches.

   Because the units must be the same to calculate the area, you need to convert the diameter into inches: 7 feet 4 inches $= 7 \times 12 + 4 = 88$ inches. The diameter is twice the radius, so the radius of the backing is $88 / 2 = 44$ inches.

   Now you can use the formula for the area of a circle given on the formula page, $A = \pi r^2$, where π is approximately 3.14. Thus, the area is $3.14 \times 44 \times 44 = 6,079.04$ square inches.

   Because the question asks for an answer in square feet, you have to convert square inches to square feet by dividing by 144 $\left(12 \text{ inches} = 1 \text{ foot}; 12^2 = 144\right)$: $6,079.04 / 144 = 42.215555$ or 42.2, rounded to one decimal place.

TIP

The calculator can really help you on an item with many complicated calculations like this one. On the calculator you can use the pi key or simply key in 3.14.

4. **BC.** Calculating the length of each side requires many steps. Luckily, all you have to do is mark the vertices on the coordinate plane and then determine the longest side.

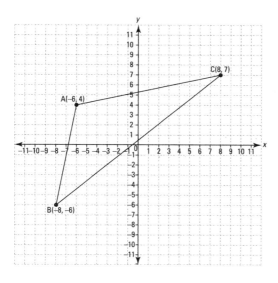

From the drawing, you can determine that the longest side is *BC*.

5. **B. coin B.** This question asks you to draw an inference from a graph. Looking carefully at the graph, Coin B in the first set comes closest to 50 percent, which is the theoretical chance of a heads or tails landing when the coin is balanced.

6. **B. 333.** Here, you're asked to solve a problem using basic operations. If Donna inhales for two steps and exhales for two steps, and each step is 27 inches long, then she inhales once for each 108 inches she covers: $27 \times 4 = 108$. In 1,000 yards (which equal 36,000 inches because there are 36 inches in a yard), she takes $36,000 / 108 = 333.3$ breaths, which rounds to 333.

7. **9.** The shape of an ice-cream cone is a cone, and the formula for determining the volume of a cone is $\frac{1}{3} \times \pi \times \text{radius}^2 \times \text{height}$, where π is approximately equal to 3.14. (This formula appears on the formula sheet.)

To make the calculations simpler using the calculator, change the fractions to decimals:

$2\frac{1}{2} = 2.5, 5\frac{1}{2} = 5.5$, and $\frac{1}{3} = 0.3333333$

Now you have to insert the values from the question into the formula (remember that you find the radius by dividing the diameter by 2): Volume $= 0.3333333 \times 3.14 \times (2.5 / 2)^2 \times 5.5 = 8.9947896$, or 9.0 cubic inches, rounded to one decimal place.

8. **$2,030.** In this question, you're given more information than you need. You're given the dimensions of every room in the condo, but Singh doesn't want to carpet all of them. Because you can use the calculator in this part of the test, you can calculate an accurate answer. The first thing to do is to calculate the area of each of the rooms Singh wants to carpet with the formula for area: *Area = length × width*. (This formula is in the formula sheet.)

Substituting the numbers from the table for each room, here are the areas you come up with:

Living room: $20 \times 13 = 260$

Dining room: $10 \times 8 = 80$

Bedroom: $14 \times 13 = 182$

Next, add the areas of the three rooms: $260 + 180 + 82 = 522$.

Because the lengths and widths are in feet, the answer is in square feet, but the cost of the carpet is in square yards. To convert square feet into square yards, you divide by 9: $522 / 9 = 58$, which is the area in square yards.

The carpet costs \$35.00 a square yard, so you have to multiply the total area Singh wants to carpet by the cost per square yard: $58 \times \$35.00 = \$2,030$.

9. **C. \$12,020.** If you want to use approximate values in this problem, you can say that the car depreciates about 4 cents, or \$0.04, a mile over 100,000 miles. This car is about 37,000 miles over that milestone, which means it's depreciated about $\$0.04 \times 37,000 = \$1,480$. You can then subtract this value from the book value: $\$13,500 - \$1,480 = \$12,020$.

10. **\$11,907.** Using the same calculation you use in Question 9 but with exact values, you get $13,500 - (0.043 \times 37,046) = 11,907.02$ or \$11,907, when rounded to the nearest dollar.

11. **B. 5.8.** This problem tests your skills in geometry and involves similarity of geometrical figures. To draw a scale drawing, the lengths and widths must be reduced in the same ratio. Use a simple proportion. With x as the drawing height, 11 as the drawing length, 9 as the actual height, and 17 as the actual length, you can write $\frac{x}{11} = \frac{9}{17}$.

    By cross-multiplying, you get $17x = 9(11)$. This simplifies to 5.8 when rounded.

12. **A. 28.** This question tests your skills in algebra by asking you to evaluate a term in an equation. The equation for the slope, m, of a line is $m = \frac{y_2 - y_1}{x_2 - x_1}$

    Substituting the values into the equation, you get $0.75 = \frac{36 - 24}{x_2 - 12}$

    Then, because 0.75 is the same as 3/4, you can say the following: $\frac{3}{4} = \frac{12}{x_2 - 12}$

    Cross-multiplying, you get the following: $x_2 = \frac{84}{3} = 28$

13. **B. 1.1.** From the table, you can see that of the three countries, the highest literacy rate is Russia at 99.4 percent, and the lowest is China at 90.9 percent.

    If you divide the literacy rate for Russia by that for China, you get $99.4 / 90.9 = 1.093509351$ or 1.1, rounded to one decimal place, which is Choice (B).

14. **B. 2.** According to the table, the literacy rate of the United States is 99.0. Only two countries have literacy rates higher than that, Russia (99.4) and Cuba (99.8). As you examine these statistics, keep in mind that literacy is difficult to measure and other sources might calculate them differently.

15. **C. 7^3.** The volume of a cube is determined by the formula length $\times$ width $\times$ height. For this cube, the formula becomes $7 \times 7 \times 7$, which can be simplified to 7^3 (pronounced "seven cubed").

16. **B. 1.** Peter's average grade is $(81 + 76 + 92 + 87 + 79 + 83) / 6 = 83$. Because Peter's average grade is 83, it is one point higher than the school's, so the answer is Choice (B), 1.

17. **A. 42.** This question is a test of your skills in data analysis. You already determined that his average grade is 83. He's failing to meet his goal by 7 percent. Each percent is equivalent to one point per subject, or $7 \times 6 = 42$ points.

18. **16.6.** This question tests your skills in measurement involving volume of a cylinder. The volume of a cylinder is calculated using the formula, $V_{\text{cylinder}} = \pi \times \text{radius}^2 \times \text{height}$. Substitute the numbers from the question into the formula:

    $$\text{Volume of cylinder} = 3.14 \times \left(2.\frac{1}{2}\right)^2 \times 4.8 = 16.61688 \text{ or } 16.6$$

19. **$1,584.** Using the formula for simple interest given on the formula sheet, you can calculate the simple interest over 4 years and then add the principal amount. The principal amount is $1,500 because she lets her son spend $74 of the money right away. The total interest for 4 years, using the formula, would be $1,500 \times 0.014 \times 4 = \$84$. The interest added to the principal would total $1,584 ($1,500 + \$84 = \$1,584$).

20. **B. 3 times larger.** This question tests your knowledge of equations by asking you to analyze how a change in one quantity in an exponential equation, $E = mc^2$, results in a change in another quantity. The variation between E and m in this function is linear and direct, which means that whatever happens to m also happens to E. If m is 3 times larger, so is E.

21. **B. 24.** This question tests your ability to figure out the areas of two different objects and combine them. The answer should be expressed in square feet, but the dimensions of the chair mat are in inches. When you convert the dimensions of the chair mat into feet, you quickly realize that the rug and the chair mat are the same size: 36 inches by 48 inches = 3 feet by 4 feet. Then, calculating the dimensions of the two is easy: $2(3 \times 4) = 24$. Choice A is the area of only one of the items. Choice (C) is the area of one of the items in square inches. Choice (D) is the area of both items expressed in square inches.

REMEMBER

Always make sure that you express the answer in the unit of measure that the question specifies. In this case, the unit of measure is square feet.

22. **A. 57.** Using the formula for the volume of a cylinder, you can figure out the volume of each tank and then subtract the volume of the smaller tank from the volume of the larger tank. The volume of the smaller tank is $\pi \times 3^2 \times 4 = 113.04$. The volume of the larger tank is $\pi \times 3^2 \times 6 = 169.56$. Rounding to the nearest cubic foot and then subtracting the volume of the smaller tank from that of the larger tank, you get $170 - 113 = 57$.

23. **D. 10.** This question tests your knowledge of equations. Create an equation in which x is the number of people with both a sore throat and a cold. Thus $(15 - x)$ is the number of students with a sore throat only and $(25 - x)$ is the number of students with a cold only. The total number of students with a sore throat only, with a cold only, and with both is equal to 30. So $(15 - x) + (25 - x) + x = 30$. Solve for x: $x = 10$.

24. **(−3,4).**

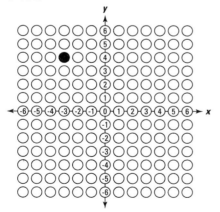

25. **110.** This question tests your knowledge of math basics. This item is a good one to calculate quickly using mental math. You know that the grant will cover 75% of the cost of the course, so the hospital will absorb 25%, which is one-fourth. The course costs $40 per person, and one-fourth of $40 is $10. The information says that 11 parents will take the course, so the total amount that the hospital will absorb is 10×11, or $110.

26. **B. 7.** To calculate the total cost of the computer, you have to add the purchase cost plus the overhead $(299 + 48 + 2 = 349)$. Because each computer costs Jerry \$349 and he sells it for \$449, he has a net profit of \$100 $(\$449 - \$349 = \$100)$ per computer.

    To calculate the number of computers Jerry would have to sell to make \$700 a week, divide the amount of profit he wants to make (\$700) by the profit on each computer (\$100): $\frac{700}{100} = 7$.

27. **\$240.** The minimum charge for repairing a computer is \$45 and each additional hour costs \$30. Jerry repaired 4 computers and had 2 additional hours. You can solve this problem by writing the equation 4(\$45) + 2(\$30) = \$240.

28. **A. Indonesia.** The country with the largest installed capacity is Indonesia, with 2.1 gigawatts. The remaining countries have smaller installed capacities.

29. **A. 0.2 gigawatt.** The next country in the list is New Zealand, with an installed capacity of 1.0. The difference between the two countries' installed capacity is $1.0 - 0.8 = 0.2$.

30. **D. \$57.60.** You can answer this question by figuring out the costs of the old car per week and the costs of the new car per week, by dividing the miles driven by the mileage and multiplying by the cost per gallon. For example, that week, Elayne drove 150 miles in the city, so she spent 150 miles / 18 mpg × \$2.70 = \$22.50 on gas for her old car. You can make a chart like this one:

Day	City Driving	Cost for Old Car	Cost for New Car	Highway Driving	Cost for Old Car	Cost for New Car
Monday	30			5		
Tuesday	35			25		
Wednesday	25			10		
Thursday	30			20		
Friday	20			5		
Saturday	5			70		
Sunday	5			75		
TOTAL	150	\$22.50	\$4.05	210	\$47.25	\$8.10

The savings are the difference between the old car's costs and the new car's costs:

$(\$22.50 + \$47.25) - (\$4.05 + \$8.10) = \$57.60$

Because item 30 requires a lot of calculations, it might be one to flag and return to later to avoid spending too much time on it.

TIP

31. D. Dealer D. This question tests your ability to use number operations. If you adapt the table, it looks like this:

	Interest Rate Offered	Equivalent Rate
A	Prime + 2%	$8\% \left(6\% + 2\%\right)$
B	7.5%	7.5%
C	1/2 of prime + 5%	$8\% \left(\left[\frac{1}{2} \text{ of } 6\%\right] + 5\% = 3\% + 5\%\right)$
D	Prime + 20% of prime for administrative costs	$7.2\% \left(6\% + \left[20\% \text{ of } 6\%\right] = 6\% + 1.2\%\right)$

Dealer D is offering the best terms for financing the car.

32. 75%. The question tells you that 9 of 12 people that Harry asked had watched the sitcom. Therefore, to calculate, divide 9 by 12: $9 \div 12 = 0.75$. Then, convert that number to a percentage by moving the decimal point two places to the right and adding a percentage sign: 75%. Always be careful to include the correct numbers and symbols when answering questions like this one.

33. D. 5¾ inches. You can solve the problem by multiplying fractions, but for this problem, it's probably easier to convert the fractions to decimals ($1\frac{3}{4} = 1.75$) and use your calculator. To do this, multiply the dimension of the books by 3 and multiply the dimension of the packaging by two, and add the two numbers: $\left(1.75 \times 3\right) + 2(0.25) = 5.75$.

34. A. 20 pounds. This question tests your skills in using estimation to solve a problem involving number operations. If there are about 40 weeks in the 10 months from September to June, then each of them could lose about 20 pounds $\left(40 \times 0.5\right)$.

35. C. 12. This question tests your skills in measurement to solve a problem involving uniform rates. If Mary can drive at an average speed of 45 miles per hour, it will take her $900 / 45 = 20$ hours to drive the 900 miles. Samantha, on the other hand, will travel at 300 miles per hour on a plane for a flying time of $900 / 300 = 3$ hours, but she will add $45 + 75$ (1 hour and 15 minutes is 75 minutes) $+ 180$ (that's 3 hours in minutes) $= 300$ minutes, which is 5 hours (300/60). Her total trip would be 3 hours $+$ 5 hours $= 8$ hours in duration, or 12 hours shorter than Mary's trip, not counting time for breaks or sleep.

36. C. east and north in 3rd quarter. Looking at the graph, in the third quarter, the east plant region seems to have sold twice (ratio of 2:1) as many hats as the north plant region.

37. B. Tina will likely live longer than her brother Trent. This question tests your ability to interpret data presented in a table. The table shows that for people age 30, women will live longer than men, which is Choice (B). Choice (C) is not possible because the question states that they are unidentical twins. Choice (D) gives Trent's life expectancy and so is incorrect.

Read the answers as carefully as you read the questions. Women may have a greater life expectancy, but that doesn't necessarily mean that they age better or worse than men. That's a topic for another question.

38. D. 81.6. This question asks you to find the age that a 20-year-old woman will live to on average. Given that the table shows life expectancy for 20-year-old females to be 61.6 years, the average woman will live to be $20 + 61.6 = 81.6$ years old. Choices (A) and (B) show the number of years a male and female would have to live at age 20. Choice (C) gives the age a male of 20 would likely live to. Always read each question carefully to make sure you answer that question, and not a different one.

39. **C. The selling price will go up.** This question tests your skills in analysis by asking you to explain how a change in one quantity affects another quantity. The price of the article is set by a linear function involving the overhead (the costs of doing business that don't change with how many products you sell — things like rent, utility bills, salaries, and so on), the cost of acquiring the item, and the profit. If any of these numbers go up, the selling price goes up, too, which is why the correct answer is Choice (C).

40. **8.** This question tests your skills in number operations by asking you to write a large number in scientific notation. To write 328,000,000 in scientific notation starting with 3.28×10, you count the number of places to the left that the decimal point needs to move. That number is 8: 3.28×10^8.

41. **D. Karry has a higher average time.** This question tests your skills in statistics by asking you to compare averages. Harry's average time is $(15.6 + 14.9 + 16.0 + 15.8 + 16.1)/5 = 15.68$. Karry's average time is $(15.9 + 16.1 + 15.8 + 16.2 + 14.8)/5 = 15.76$. Karry has a higher average time (which means that Harry is slightly faster).

Choices (A) and (B) are essentially the same. Since multiple-choice items can have only one answer, these choices can easily be eliminated as incorrect.

TIP 42. **B. 200.** This question tests your skills in measurement by asking you to solve a problem involving volume. If the total floor area is 1,400 square feet and the ceilings are 9 feet high, the volume of the apartment is $1,400 \times 9 = 12,600$ cubic feet. If the air system can replace 63 cubic feet per minute, it requires $12,600/63 = 200$ minutes to withdraw and replace all the air, which is Choice (B). The other answer choices are wrong, but Choices (A) and (C) are close enough that if you tried to do the question using approximations, you might select the wrong answer choice.

When some of the answer choices are close in value, it's usually a good idea to do the calculations instead of estimating.

TIP 43. **D. 4 p.m. on Tuesday.** This question tests your skills in measurement and geometry. You have to solve a problem involving uniform rates. Peter's swimming pool holds $45 \times 12 \times 4 = 2,160$ cubic feet of water. He can pump 9 cubic feet per minute. It would take him $2,160/9 = 240$ minutes to empty the pool. To get from hours to minutes, divide by 60 (because every hour has 60 minutes). So it would take Peter $240/60 = 4$ hours to empty his pool. If he started pumping at noon on Tuesday, Peter would finish four hours later, which is at 4 p.m. on Tuesday.

44. **B. $250.** This question tests your skills in algebra by asking you to use an average number to calculate a missing value. If Mohammed earned an average of $420 for four weeks, he earned a total of $420 \times 4 = \$1,680$ for the four-week period. In the other three weeks, he earned $\$480 + \$400 + \$550 = \$1,430$. In the missing week, he earned $\$1,680 - \$1,430 = \$250$.

45. **$457.** This question tests your skills in number operations. Georgia spent $\$500 - \$126 = \$374$ using the gift card, plus $83.00 in credit card purchases, so she spent $\$374.00 + \$83.00 = \$457.00$.

46. **B. a rectangle with a circle on each side.** This question tests your skills in geometry and spatial visualization. If you cut open and almost remove the ends of the can, open the can along the seam, and then lay it flat, you'd have a rectangle and two circles, one on each side of the rectangle. Questions of this type require the use of imagination. Imagine opening a can, cutting the seam, and making it lay flat.

47. **B. she would spend more money on fuel.** This question tests your skills by asking you to read carefully to answer a question. If Sonya's car uses gasoline in direct proportion to her speed, then the faster she goes, the more gas she uses. The more gas she uses, the more it costs her to drive, which is an economic consequence — so she would spend more money on fuel.

48. $(0,-4)$. If the center is at the origin and the diameter (which is twice the radius) is 8 units, the circle will intersect each of the axes (that's the plural of axis) at a distance of 4 units from the center. Therefore, it intersects the negative y-axis at $(0,-4)$.

49. **C. 21.** If the gauge reads 1/8 full, it has $24/8 = 3$ gallons of fuel left in it. Because it holds 24 gallons, it needs $24 - 3 = 21$ gallons to fill it.

TIP

Did you select Choices (A) or (D)? This shows the value of reading the item carefully and answering with the exact information requested, the amount needed to fill the tank. In this case, Choice (A) is the amount of fuel already in the tank. Choice (D) is the total capacity of the tank. To determine the amount needed to fill the tank, you need to subtract 3 from 24: 24 - 3 = 21.

50. **B. 5.** To solve these equations, you need to subtract one from the other and end up with just the y's. To get rid of one of the variables using this method, you need to have the same coefficient in front of the variable that you're planning to eliminate. (The coefficient is a fancy word for the number in front of a variable. In the expression $4x$, the coefficient is 4.) You can multiply each term of an equation by a number and still maintain the equation. Here's how:

Multiply the second equation by 2 and leave the first equation as it is:

$$(4x + 2y = 20) = 4x + 2y = 20$$
$$2(2x + 6y = 35) = 4x + 12y = 70$$

Subtract, and you get $10y = 50; y = 5$.

Note that you can also multiply the second equation by -2 and add the two equations together. Either way gets you the same answer.

Answer Key

1.	A	18.	16.6	35.	C
2.	0.6	19.	$1,584	36.	C
3.	A	20.	B	37.	B
4.	*BC*	21.	B	38.	D
5.	B	22.	A	39.	C
6.	B	23.	D	40.	8
7.	9	24.	(−3,4)	41.	D
8.	$2,030	25.	110	42.	B
9.	C	26.	B	43.	D
10.	$11,907	27.	$240	44.	B
11.	B	28.	A	45.	$457
12.	A	29.	A	46.	B
13.	B	30.	D	47.	B
14.	B	31.	D	48.	(0,−4)
15.	C	32.	75%	49.	C
16.	B	33.	D	50.	B
17.	A	34.	A		

8

The Part of Tens

IN THIS PART . . .

Check out ten tips for preparing for the GED test in the weeks, days, and hours leading up to the test.

Plan your path to surviving on the day of the test and maximizing your scores.

Discover all the things you can do with your GED diploma after you pass all the sections of the GED test, including much more than using it as decoration in your home or workplace.

Chapter **35**

Ten Surefire Ways to Prepare for the GED Test

O f course you want to do well on the GED test — otherwise, you wouldn't be reading this book. But you also know that your time is limited, so this chapter gives you ten ideas and tips for preparing for the test, from selecting the right test-taking time to working through practice tests and getting familiar with the computer format, so you can do your very best on test day.

These tips are all part of preparing for the big day. You want to be able to arrive at the test site with the least amount of worry and stress. Removing as many sources of stress as possible before that day will make everything go more smoothly.

Strategizing Your Test Preparation

You can take all the tests in one day if you want. If you do so in a testing center, you will only have 10 minutes between each test, and you will be at the test center for over 7 hours. Most people spread the tests over several days, weeks, or even months, and schedule them as they feel ready.

To get started on the right foot, I recommend that you begin with the subject matter where you feel you are strongest. For many test-takers, that test is Science. Science has the highest passing rates of all the tests. Many test-takers finish with Math or Reading and Language Arts in order to have more time to prepare for those sometimes daunting tests.

TIP

Use the charts in Chapter 4 to devise your plan of attack. They will help you determine your strengths and areas for improvement, figure out the best order to take the tests, and determine how much preparation you need for each test. The GED Testing Service's GED & Me app also contains a tool to help you plan your preparation.

Deciding Where You Will Test

An important decision you need to make is whether to take the test at home or at a testing center. Although testing at home is convenient, your home has to meet a number of requirements. At the same time, when you test at home, you have to use the on-screen calculator and whiteboard. If you want to use the erasable whiteboard and your own TI-30XS MultiView calculator, you have to test at a testing center. Many test-takers find having those tools helpful, especially for the writing and math tests.

Remember, you can take some of the tests at home and others at a testing center. For example, you might take the Math test at a testing center so that you can bring your hand-held calculator, and take the others at home. Requirements for testing in person vary by state. You can find information for your state at www.ged.com/policies/. A few states do not offer the online test, and fees and other requirements vary by state. You can find information about online testing in your state at www.ged.com/state-information-online-testing/. For complete criteria on selecting where to test, see Chapter 1.

REMEMBER

To take the GED test, you need an acceptable picture ID. Because what's acceptable may vary from state to state, check with your local testing center (or check the information you receive when you register). The picture ID required is usually a driver's license, state ID card, passport, or other government-issued ID (including a *matricula consular* issued by a Mexican consulate in the United States). At any rate, it's usually something common and easy to get — if you plan ahead! If you already have an ID, check the expiration date to make sure it will be valid the day you take the test.

Setting a Time and a Place to Study

Whether you study on your own, with a group, or with an instructor, find a regular place to study and set up a study schedule. If possible, set up an area on a desk or table in your home and keep all your study materials there. That way, you don't have to hunt for them every time you want to study. If you can't do that, keep all your study materials together in a box or bag. If you decide to study at the public library, you might invest in an inexpensive backpack to store and carry your materials.

Next, make a schedule. Keep your work schedule and other responsibilities in mind. The best time for you to study may be early in the morning or at night after your kids go to bed. Whatever you decide, stick to your schedule as if your grade depends on it (and, by the way, it does!).

Getting Familiar with the Computer, Calculator, and Formula Sheet

On the real GED test, you'll be typing on a keyboard, using a mouse to select or drag items, and reading and digesting information on the screen. You'll also be using an on-screen or real scientific calculator. The day of the test isn't the time to get familiar with these tools. Be sure to get familiar with them before the test. You can get started by reading the information in the Appendix. If you don't have a computer, most public libraries offer computer access. Also consider taking a basic keyboarding class or computer literacy class at a local library, adult education center, or community center. These classes are usually free, and they're useful if you're a novice.

Make sure that you're familiar with the layout of the screens on the test. Luckily, the screen layout is the same whether you test at home or at a testing center. (Check out Chapter 2 for information on the screen layout of each test.) Then use the free, quarter-length test at www.ged.com/study/free_online_ged_test/. Finally, the GED Ready Practice Test will let you know for sure whether you have the computer skills you need to succeed.

Get familiar with the TI-30XS MultiView calculator, too — the hand-held or on-screen version, whichever one you will be using. It's a scientific calculator with a lot of functions, not all of which you will use on the test. The GED Testing Service's website, ged.com, has a number of calculator resources, including a reference sheet that shows you all the features you need to know, a tutorial that walks you through using the calculator, and an actual on-screen calculator emulator you can practice with. If you test at a testing center, you can use the on-screen version or bring your own TI-30XS MultiView calculator. If you test at home, you have to use the on-screen version. Prepare with the calculator you will actually use — the on-screen or the real one. You don't want to be fumbling on test day.

The Math section has a formula sheet that can help you a lot. As you get familiar with the computer, find out the location of the formula sheet. You can reference the formula sheet at any time during the test, which can help you avoid depending on your memory on test day. Nevertheless, you may want to memorize a few easy and commonly used formulas, too, such as the area of a rectangle.

Taking Practice Tests

Taking practice tests before you take the actual test will help you get familiar with the test format, the types of questions you'll be asked, and what subject areas you may need to work on. Take as many practice tests as you can before test day, starting with the practice tests that come with this book. Take them under the same conditions as the actual test (and be sure to practice with the time limits, too).

You can find two complete practice tests for each section of the GED in this book (check out Parts 6 and 7), as well as a complete online test (see the Introduction for instructions on how to access the online test bank). Still want more practice? The GED Testing Service also provides some free, quarter-length practice tests at www.ged.com/study/free_online_ged_test/. Before you schedule your test, you should definitely take the GED Ready Practice Test at www.ged.com/study/ged_ready/. It will tell you whether you are ready to test or you need more preparation. It will give you an estimated score and a rating of red (not likely to pass), yellow (too close to call), and green (likely to pass), along with detailed feedback on skills to review.

Studying Subject-Matter Books

If you've taken all the practice tests in this book and reviewed the answer explanations (see Parts 6 and 7) and completed the online practice test, you may have identified key areas for improvement. Although those practice tests can't help you predict your score on the real GED test, they can help prepare you for the actual test and give you a general idea of your strengths and areas for improvement. If you didn't get at least 70 percent correct on any of the practice tests in this book, then you need to work on your test-taking skills and the subject matter.

TIP

To brush up on test content, visit your local bookstore or library (so you don't end up spending all your hard-earned money) for the many *For Dummies* books that are meant just for students. For example, consider the following fun, interesting, and easy-to-read books (all published by Wiley) that can either improve your skills or simply make you more familiar with certain subjects:

>> *Algebra I For Dummies,* 2nd Edition, by Mary Jane Sterling

>> *Biology For Dummies,* 3rd Edition, by René Fester Kratz

>> *The Civil War For Dummies,* by Keith D. Dickson

>> *Congress For Dummies,* by David Silverberg

>> *English Grammar For Dummies,* 3rd Edition, by Geraldine Woods

>> *Everyday Math For Dummies,* by Charles Seiter

>> *Geometry For Dummies,* 3rd Edition, by Mark Ryan

>> *Politics For Dummies,* 3rd Edition, by Ann M. DeLaney

>> *U.S. History For Dummies,* 4th Edition, by Steve Wiegand

To find other helpful *For Dummies* books, check out www.dummies.com.

TIP

In many ways, the GED is primarily a reading test. Strong reading skills will help you raise your score, so consider ramping up your reading. Choose content you will enjoy and that is related to the test. Try reading a few short stories or even a novel of interest to you. Read as many nonfiction articles in magazines, newspapers, or online as you can. Try to vary the content of your reading. Choose articles on current events, history, politics, and science.

Enrolling in a GED Test Preparation Class

If you like to interact with other people and prefer a teacher to guide you through your preparation, consider taking a *GED test preparation class* — a class designed to prepare you to take and pass the GED test. Costs for these classes vary widely, and many are offered free of charge. Consider whether you learn better on your own or in a group, and whether you have the time to take a class, and make your decision accordingly.

TIP

To find a class in your location, create an account at the GED Testing Service website, ged.com. It will help you find adult education programs in your area where you can prepare for free. You can also ask around. Talk to people you know who have taken the GED test or people at your local GED testing center. You may also be able to take online courses (where you do your assignments on your own and contact your instructor via the internet), which may be a good choice for you.

You may also find that some subject areas, like math, require more help. Many people take a class for math and for writing and prepare for the other tests on their own.

After deciding on a few potential classes, visit the class or instructor if possible. Make sure that their teaching style matches your learning style. The preparation class will be a big investment of your time, so shop around wisely.

TIP

After finding a preparation class, consider joining or forming a study group with other GED test-takers. You can help each other study and ask each other questions about different aspects of the test. Be wary before committing to a group, though: If the other group members' idea of studying is to party for three hours to get ready for five minutes of study, and you want to study for three hours and then spend five minutes on social activity, you won't be happy. Talk to the other members of the study group and find out what their goals are for the group. If you can find a suitable group, make a commitment and enjoy your new friends.

Preparing for the Test in Your Mind

To make yourself less anxious about the GED test, visualize yourself taking the test on test day. In your mind, see yourself enter the room, sit down at the computer, and reach out to the keyboard. Go through this routine in your mind until it begins to feel familiar. Then see yourself starting the test and scrolling through questions (questions that are likely familiar to you because you've taken many practice tests). See yourself noting the easy questions and beginning to answer them. By repeating this visual sequence over and over again in your mind, you help make it familiar — and what's familiar isn't nearly as stressful as what's unfamiliar. (This process, by the way, is called *visualization* and really works at putting your mind at ease for the test.) And if you are taking the test at home, you can set up your test area and practice this routine for real!

Getting Good Rest the Week before the Test

As part of your plan for preparation, include some social time, some down time, and plenty of rest time because everyone performs better when well rested. In fact, your memory and ability to solve problems improve remarkably when you're properly rested.

REMEMBER

Whatever you do, don't panic about your upcoming test and stay up all night (or every night for a week) right before the test. Last-minute cramming rarely works. Instead, plan your last week before the test so that you get plenty of sleep and are mentally and physically prepared for the test.

Setting Up Your Test Area or Getting to the Test Site

On certain days and occasions, you just don't want to be late, get lost, or have a problem. These days include your wedding day, an important interview, and the day you take the GED test. So be prepared whether you are taking the test at home or at a test center.

If you are taking the test at home, both your computer and the room you test in have to meet special requirements. Don't leave this to the last minute. Check the latest requirements on the ged.com website and the email you receive when you sign up for the test. The week before the test, make sure you can meet all the requirements. Check again the night before the test, too. You can view all the requirements at www.ged.com/take-the-ged-test-online/.

TIP

If you take the GED at home, you need to work in a private room with no interruptions. If you have roommates, make arrangements well before test day. If you have children, ask another person to keep an eye on them during the test so that you don't have any interruptions!

TIP

No matter where you test — at home or at a testing center — arrange your work area. Make sure that your chair is at a comfortable height, arrange the keyboard and mouse, and adjust the height and angle of the screen. If you are left-handed, you may need to move the mouse to the left of the keyboard. Make sure you allow time to do this before your test starts! If you test at home, the only drink you are allowed to have is water in a clear container, so prepare that if you think you will get thirsty. Just save your fancy-colored goblets for the victory celebration after you pass the test!

If you are going to a testing center to take the test, make sure you are prepared. Make sure you plan a route to the testing site from your home or job or wherever you'll be commuting from. Map it out and practice getting to the test center. Prepare everything you will need, including your ID, your TI-30XS MultiView calculator, and your glasses if you need them for the test. If you're driving to the test center, make sure that you know where to park. Arrive early enough so that you can be sure to find a spot. Remember, you can't leave your car in the middle of the street if you expect to drive it home, too!

TIP

Leave extra time for surprises. You never know when your street could be declared the site for an elephant crossing or when a herd of oxen decides to meander across your road. The crowd, oxen, and elephants could make you late for the tests unless you allow yourself some extra time.

Chapter **36**

Ten Tips for Surviving Test Day

Besides all those hours of studying, to succeed on the GED test, you also need to know what to do on the day of the test and how to stay focused through each test section. In this chapter, I give you ten quick and easy ways to help you survive the GED test.

Wear Comfortable Clothes

Consider the following situation. You're about to sit in front of a computer screen for at least 70 minutes (both the Mathematical Reasoning and Reasoning through Language Arts tests are longer). You'll be sitting on what will probably be an uncomfortable chair. The room may be too warm or too cold.

Choosing from the following answers, what's the appropriate dress for the GED test?

(A) formal dress because this is an important occasion

(B) a parka over a bathing suit because one can never predict the weather

(C) something very comfortable so that you can concentrate on the test

(D) your best clothes because you need to impress others

If you picked Choice (C), you have the right idea. Dress comfortably and in layers. All your concentration should be on the test, not on your clothes, not on the people around you, and not on the conditions in the room.

TIP

It pays to have everything organized the night before — your ID, your clothes, the directions to the test center, your TI-30XS MultiView calculator, a nutritious snack to eat before the test or during a break, your glasses (if you wear them), and so on. If you test at home, you can prepare the room, too. You don't want to be rushing on the day of the test.

Arrive at the Test Site Early

Consider the following two characters, Paula Prepared and Peter Procrastinator. Both have prepared to take the test, but they have their own personalities and individual quirks. On test day:

>> Peter drives up to the test center 5 minutes before the test and feels nothing but panic. He can't find legal parking and enters the test center just in time to begin the test. He's so distracted that he takes 15 minutes to calm down.

>> Paula arrives 40 minutes early. She has time to get a drink of water, use the restroom, and relax before the test. Sitting calmly at the computer, Paula gets comfortable, arranges the keyboard and mouse, and begins the test in a relaxed manner.

Who would you rather be?

Here's something else to consider: If you're late to the test site, you may not be allowed to enter, you'll likely have to reschedule the test for another time, and you'll probably have to pay again for the test. Who needs all this grief? All you have to do to prevent this tragedy is to arrive early for the test, which, contrary to popular belief, isn't as difficult as it may seem. You can plan ahead by checking out some route maps to the test site on the internet. If you decide to drive yourself, check the availability of parking and even practice your route to the test site. Do your research, leave extra time for unforeseen situations, and arrive early and ready for the test.

It pays to be early if you test at home, too. You can check in up to 30 minutes before the time of your test. After you check in, you will join a queue for the first available proctor.

Keep Conversations Light and Short

A little bit of stress is normal when you walk into a test. So the last thing you want to do is increase your stress level by getting into a conversation and losing your focus.

Although it may seem antisocial, keep conversations to a minimum just before the test. If someone wants to exchange pleasantries about the weather, go ahead. If they want to arrange to go for coffee after the test, plan away. If they want to get into a serious conversation about how hard the test is, get away as fast as you can. Don't let anyone at the testing center stress you out. Pretend you only speak Klingon, go to the restroom, or start coughing. Nobody wants to start up a conversation with a Klingon-speaking, contagious person with a weak bladder. Or you may want to try some more plausible excuses, but whatever you do, escape!

Arrange Your Work Area

You're going to be sitting in front of a computer screen for at least 70 minutes. Before starting the test, be sure to adjust the screen, the keyboard, the mouse, and the chair to comfortable positions. If you're left-handed, you may need to rearrange your keyboard and mouse. If you notice any problems, let someone know right away. There is one adjustment you can't make until the test starts: enlarging the size of the font. That can help some people a lot!

Relax and Breathe

Feeling a bit of stress before taking the GED test is normal. Psychologists even say that a little bit of stress can help you function better. But it's a balancing act; you don't want to become so stressed that you can't think.

Here are some techniques that may help you relax before you take the GED test, or anytime you're feeling a bit stressed:

>> **Think positively.** Instead of listing all the negative things that may happen, think about the positive things that can come out of this situation. You *can* pass the GED test. You *can* go on to college. You *can* get a great job. You *can* receive a surprise inheritance — well, maybe that's going too far. Don't be greedy. Just be positive!

>> **Breathe deeply.** The first thing to remember during a stressful situation is to breathe. The second thing is to breathe deeply. Follow these steps:

- **Find your diaphragm.**

  No, not a *diagram* — although you could use a diagram to find your diaphragm. Your *diaphragm* is that flat muscle under your ribcage that fills your lungs with air. It's above your navel.

- **Breathe in and make your diaphragm rise as much as you can.**

- **Exhale slowly.**

- **Repeat, making your diaphragm rise higher each time.**

After you see how this process relaxes you, try it just before each test section.

>> **Count backward from ten (in your head).** You can do this before any test, not just the math one. Start to count backward from ten with no thoughts in your mind. If a thought, even a teeny one, enters your mind, you have to start over. See how many times it takes to count from ten to one without a single thought entering your mind.

Don't do this *during* the test, only *before* to help relax you. This exercise could eat up precious time if you tried it during one of the tests.

>> **Clench and unclench your fists.** This simple relaxation technique involves your hands and reminds you to relax:

- **Sit with your hands in front of you.**

- **Inhale deeply as you slowly clench your fists.**

- **After your fists are clenched, slowly exhale as you unclench them.**

You may have to repeat this process several times before you begin to feel relaxed.

>> **Envision a relaxing scene.** Look at a blank wall and envision a favorite relaxing scene. Try to see a point beyond the horizon. As you do, feel your eyes relax. Let your eyes relax until the feeling spreads to every part of your body. Enjoy the feeling long enough to let go of all the stress that has built up. When you're calm and full of energy, return to the test.

Stay Focused on the Task at Hand

An archer who wants to hit the bull's-eye keeps all their mental faculties focused on the goal at hand. Nobody ever hit the center of the target daydreaming about their next social gathering. For this reason, put your mind on a leash; don't let it wander during the test. You want your mind sharp, keen, and focused before and during the test, so concentrate on the task at hand — doing your best and passing the GED test.

Look at Only Your Test

If there were a Biggest Mistake Award for test-takers, it'd go to someone who looks at their neighbor's computer screen during the test. This action is called cheating and is a very serious matter. Not only will you be asked to leave the testing center, but you may have to wait for several months to a year before you're allowed to schedule another test. So keep your eyes on your own test. More than likely, your neighbor will have a different test anyway.

If you take the test at home, follow all the instructions carefully. In particular, make sure that preparation materials are put away and small electronics are out of reach.

Start with the Easy Questions

As you work through the questions, answer the easy ones first. Then you'll be ready to tackle the other questions in a relaxed, confident mood. Flag answers that you're unsure about and skip questions that are hard or time-consuming. Then use the Review Screen to return to these questions when you're ready to tackle them.

Write Clearly and Carefully

Following a few tips can help you write a passing essay. First, gather ideas using the on-screen whiteboard or the erasable tablet provided at the testing center. Your responses will be evaluated on clarity, so organize your ideas before you write. As you write, use complete sentences, but don't worry too much about small mistakes. Review your spelling and grammar after you finish writing. And, finally, stay on topic; anything else will count against you.

Do Your Best, No Matter What

Not everyone passes the GED test the first time. If you've taken the test before, don't automatically think you're a failure — instead, see the situation as a learning experience. Use your last test as motivation to figure out areas for improvement. Whether you're taking the test for the first time or the third, focus on doing your best on this test. Keep reminding yourself that you have prepared and are ready!

TIP

After the test, give yourself a small reward. Whether it's an ice-cream cone, a run in the park, or dinner with a loved one, do something nice for yourself. You deserve it! Remember to thank all the people who supported you along the way, too.

Appendix

Practicing Basic Computer Skills for the GED Test

Whether you take the GED test at home or at a testing center, you will take the test on a computer. You use the mouse to select the correct answer, you use the keyboard to type up your Extended Response essays, and you use the calculator and built-in formula sheet on-screen for the math and some science and social studies questions. Best of all, you get your results and a detailed breakdown of how you did within hours of completing the test.

Don't worry: Even if you're not familiar with using a computer, the test doesn't require you to be either an expert typist or an expert computer user. The GED Testing Service assures that even amateur users of computers won't be at any disadvantage in taking the test. However, it's to your advantage to practice your computer skills before test day so your unfamiliarity with the keyboard or mouse doesn't slow you down or frazzle you.

In this appendix, I walk you through the basic computer skills you need to know to take the computerized GED test. That includes using the mouse to click on the appropriate answer choice, to drag and drop items, or to manipulate text; getting familiar with the layout of the keyboard and some special keys you may need for typing in the basic word processor included on the test; and figuring out how to use the calculator, formulas menu, and symbols menu on-screen in the Mathematical Reasoning and Science test sections.

If you're unsure about how to do any of these skills, my advice is to practice, practice, practice. Working with the online practice tests in this book, or any word processor, will allow you to practice these skills. If you don't have a computer, check your local library, community college, adult education center, or community center. These places often have computers available for public use, free of charge. They may even offer basic instruction. And if you find you need more computer keyboard practice, install one of the free or inexpensive typing tutors on your computer.

TIP

The GED Testing Service (ged.com) offers a free quarter-length test, which isn't scored, at https://ged.com/study/free_online_ged_test/. When you feel ready for the actual GED test, you can take the GED Ready Official Practice Test for a fee. It's required if you want to take the online test at home and recommended for everyone else. It allows you to practice doing an online test under conditions similar to what you'll experience when taking the real test. It's worthwhile just to get familiar with the computer format alone.

Using a Mouse

The mouse skills you need to know when taking the GED test on a computer are pretty basic, and, no, they don't include figuring out how to put a tiny piece of cheese in a mousetrap without getting snapped yourself! I cover the basics of using a *computer* mouse in the following sections.

Making selections

The most basic skill for using a computer mouse is just knowing how to select the correct answer. On the GED test, you do so in one of two ways: point and click or drag and drop.

Point and click

In Figure A-1, you have a traditional multiple-choice question with four possible answers. To select an answer in this situation, you simply need to click on the correct choice. That means you need to move the mouse cursor (the pointer) over the spot for the correct answer and then click the left mouse button. If you change your mind, simply click on another answer choice to override your first selection. You can click on the different answer choices as often as you want; just make sure the one you want is selected before you move on to the next question.

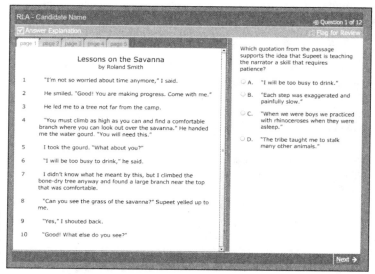

FIGURE A-1:
Standard split-screen multiple-choice item.

© 2014 GED Testing Service LLC

Math and science hot-spot questions also require you to use your mouse to select an answer. In these questions, the computer screen has a series of virtual "hot spots" or areas representing the correct answer. When you click on one of these hot spots with your mouse, it registers your answer. The remainder of the screen is wrong, so be sure of your answer when you click. In the example hot-spot question in Figure A-2, you simply click above the number on the plot line for the point to appear. Hot-spot items are not on every test, so don't worry about these items too much.

Drag and drop

When you encounter a question that tells you to "drag and drop," you simply pick up an object with your mouse (by clicking on the object and holding the left mouse button down), drag it to where you want it, and then drop it (release the mouse button) in that new location. See Figure A-3 for the drag-and-drop feature that the GED test employs.

Moving around the page

The sample screen in Figure A-4 includes several tabs at the top of the text side of the screen. These tabs indicate that the text you're expected to read covers more than one screen page. Recognizing these tabs and what they represent is important because you need to read all the material before you answer the question.

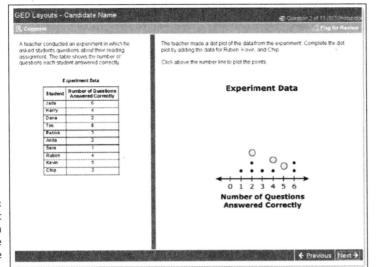

FIGURE A-2:
Hot-spot
item with
virtual live
spots on the
diagram.

© 2014 GED Testing Service LLC

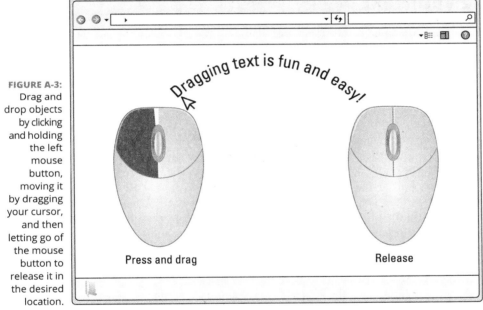

FIGURE A-3:
Drag and
drop objects
by clicking
and holding
the left
mouse
button,
moving it
by dragging
your cursor,
and then
letting go of
the mouse
button to
release it in
the desired
location.

© John Wiley & Sons, Inc.

The second thing to note in Figure A-4 is a scroll bar on the right edge. It's the bar that runs up and down the right-hand side, with an arrow on either end and a darker section somewhere along its length. That bar tells you that you need to scroll up or down for more text (where there isn't enough content to create a new page or tab). To use your mouse to move the scroll bar up and down and make the screen move so you can see the additional text, simply click on the top or bottom of the bar. Alternatively, you can drag the light portion of the bar up or down for the same effect or use the scroll wheel on your mouse. When you're finished with the item, click on the Previous or Next buttons on the bottom right of the screen to go to a new or previous question.

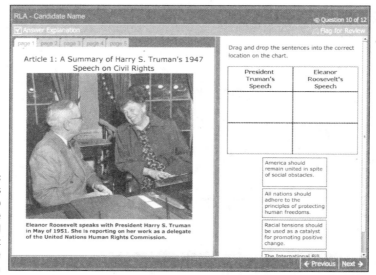

page 1 | page 2 | page 3 | page 4 | page 5

Article 1: A Summary of Harry S. Truman's 1947 Speech on Civil Rights

Eleanor Roosevelt speaks with President Harry S. Truman in May of 1951. She is reporting on her work as a delegate of the United Nations Human Rights Commission.

Drag and drop the sentences into the correct location on the chart.

President Truman's Speech	Eleanor Roosevelt's Speech

America should remain united in spite of social obstacles.

All nations should adhere to the principles of protecting human freedoms.

Racial tensions should be used as a catalyst for promoting positive change.

The International Bill

← Previous | Next →

FIGURE A-4:
The tabs at the top left of the screen tell you that there's more text to read.

© 2014 GED Testing Service LLC

Editing your text

Another important skill to be comfortable with using on the computer is the cut-and-paste or copy-and-paste functions. Cutting or copying and pasting means you can move some text to another position on your page by highlighting it with your mouse. *Cutting* means deleting it from the original position, while *copying* means exactly that: You leave the text in its original location as well as insert a copy into a new location. That can come in handy when you're writing an Extended Response on the GED test.

To cut or copy and paste, move the cursor to the beginning of the text you want, click on it with the left mouse button, and then continue holding down the button as you drag the mouse across the text to highlight the entire portion you want to copy or cut. Then click on the highlighted text with the right mouse button and select *cut,* which means delete, or *copy.* Holding the right mouse button down, you can move the text in its entirety to a new position. When the text is where you want it, simply release the mouse button. For you expert word processors, you can also use the customary keyboard shortcuts. You highlight the text you want and then use the keyboard to activate the function: press Ctrl + C for copy, Ctrl + X to cut, or move the cursor to a new location and press Ctrl + V to paste.

You also need to be familiar with the concept of *redo* and *undo* while you're writing and editing text. If you've used a word processor before, you know that those two little curved arrows at the top of the screen allow you to reverse an action. Those arrows are the Redo and Undo buttons. You have the option to use these buttons on the Extended Response sections and on the fill-in questions on the test.

Using the calculator

When you need a calculator to answer questions on the Mathematical Reasoning, Science, and Social Studies tests, a digital image of a calculator appears on-screen, or you can bring a hand-held TI-30XS MultiView Scientific Calculator if you test at a testing center. When the on-screen calculator is available, you will see a calculator button in the upper-left corner of your screen. You interact with the on-screen calculator the same way you would with one in your hand. The only difference is that you push the buttons with the mouse by moving the cursor over the appropriate buttons and then clicking. If you're unsure how to use that calculator, the test offers a cheat sheet with instructions. However, to save yourself precious time while taking the exam, get some practice beforehand; the test uses a Texas Instrument 30XS calculator (see Figure A-5). You can try out the on-screen calculator by logging into your account on ged.com. If you can afford it, you can buy the real thing for less than $20.

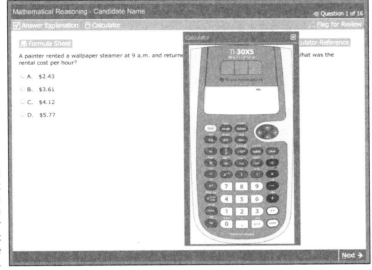

FIGURE A-5:
The GED test provides an on-screen calculator for most work in the Math test.

Finding math formulas and symbols

In the Mathematical Reasoning, Science, and Social Studies tests, you use formulas, and some questions require special symbols or signs. Don't worry — you don't need to memorize pages of formulas; the computerized GED test provides all the formulas you need in a handy, easy-to-access window (see Figure A-6). To access them, click the Formula Sheet button in the upper-left corner of your screen.

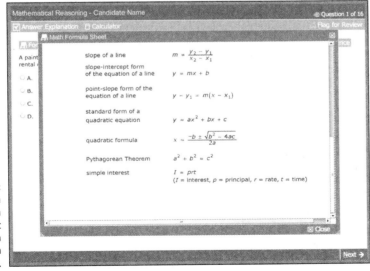

FIGURE A-6:
Clicking on the Formula Sheet button makes them appear.

You can also find the special symbols that aren't shown on your keyboard in the Symbols window by clicking the Symbol button at the top of the screen (as you can see in Figure A-7), clicking the symbol you want, and then clicking the Insert button.

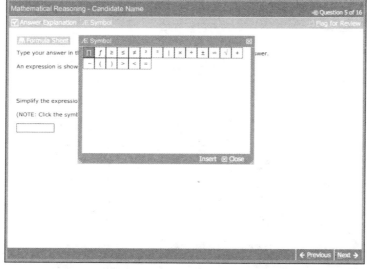

FIGURE A-7: Click on Symbol to make the symbols appear. Then select the symbol and click Insert.

Practicing Your Typing on a Keyboard

If you're more at home with a tablet or a mobile phone or you still remember (or use) your old typewriter fondly, you'll want to sit down at a computer and practice typing on a keyboard before you take the GED test. You don't need to become a typing master; as long as you can type with reasonable speed, you'll be fine. The only time you need to do more than simply click with the mouse is on the Extended Response and fill-in questions, when you have to write either a short essay or a few words or numbers.

Not being able to type may slow you down, so you should at least have a familiarity of where individual letters, punctuation, and numbers are located on the keyboard. For an example of a standard computer keyboard, check out Figure A-8. (*Note:* Standard North American keyboards aren't standard everywhere. If you learned to use a keyboard in a different language, practice with this form of keyboard before doing the test. Doing so will help you avoid typos and wasting time searching for letters, symbols, and punctuation that may not be in the accustomed locations.) Two keys you also need to know are the Enter key and the Shift key. The Enter key, identified with the word *Enter* or a hooked arrow, starts a new paragraph or line of text. The Shift key is identified with the word *Shift* or sometimes just an up arrow. You hold it down when you want to insert a capital letter, and you use it to access the symbols found with numbers on the keyboard. So, for example, pressing Shift + 5 produces the percent sign. Pressing Shift + 1 gives you the exclamation mark. The Shift key also accesses various punctuation marks, the plus sign, and the dollar sign. (The multiplication sign is in the Symbols window.)

FIGURE A-8:
Standard
North
American
keyboard,
like what
you'll see
on the
computerized
GED test.

© John Wiley & Sons, Inc.

Reading and writing on a computer screen is very different from reading and writing on paper. Studies have shown that people tend not to read as deeply when reading from a screen and aren't able to organize their thoughts as easily when writing on-screen. However, you'll have an erasable tablet and/or an online whiteboard to jot down and organize ideas for your essay. Practice reading and writing on-screen before you take the GED test, especially if you're not accustomed to working that way. It, too, is a skill that improves with practice.

Index

L

labels, on graphs, photos, diagrams and maps, 165, 166, 167

language, improving, 70–71

legal documents, 68

legends, on graphs and maps, 166

Leland, Karen (author)

Customer Service For Dummies, 344–346

letters, 68

life science, on Science test, 11, 159

line graphs, 165

literary passages, 68–69

literature, in RLA test, 10

London, Jack (author)

In a Far Country, 237–238

A Look Back...The Black Dispatches: Intelligence During the Civil War, 138–139

M

Machiavelli, Niccolò (author)

The Prince, 346–347

Madison, James (president), 137–138

managing your time, 129–130, 171, 211

manuals, 68

maps, 122–123

math formulas, 451–452

math symbols, 451–452

Math Word Problems For Dummies (Sterling), 203

Mathematical Reasoning test

about, 12, 46–48, 199, 213

answers to practice questions, 224–228

drag-and-drop questions, 12

drop-down questions, 12

example questions, 47–48, 206–209

fill-in-the-blank questions, 12, 33–34, 208

Flag for Review button, 35

format, 201

formula sheet, 210–211

multiple-choice questions, 12, 32–33, 206–208

practice questions, 214–223

practice test 1, 309–336

practice test 2, 409–434

question types, 205–211

questions, 31–35

skills, 199–201

solving strategies, 205–211

special features of, 209–211

time management for, 211

tips for, 201–203

measurement, 200

mechanics, in Reasoning Through Language (RLA) test, 64–65

Miles, Jonathan (author)

Physical Science: What the Technology Professional Needs to Know, 400–401

mouse

clicking and dragging with, 19–20

using, 447–452

multiple passage sets, Reasoning Through Language Arts (RLA) test, 78–79

multiple-choice questions

about, 19–20

choosing answers from, 125–127

Mathematical Reasoning test, 12, 32–33, 206–208

Reasoning Through Language Arts (RLA) test, 21–23, 38–39

Science test, 30, 167–168

Social Studies test, 10, 27–28, 125–127

traditional, 76–77

N

NASA, 170, 176–177, 178, 186–187, 392, 398–399

NASA's Earth Observatory (website), 181, 183–184

NASA's Glenn Research Center (website), 174, 178, 179

NASA's Jet Propulsion Laboratory (website), 177

NASA's Science (website), 177, 183, 184

National Oceanic and Atmospheric Administration (website), 181–182

National Science Foundation (website), 183

navigating pages with a mouse, 448–450

19th Amendment, of U.S. Constitution, 259

nonfiction passages, 68

nonfiction prose, 68

number operations, 200

number sense, 200

O

Occupational Safety & Health Administration (website), 181, 187

official, 56

on time, being, 55

online calculator, 438–439

studying subject-matter books, 439–440

subject-matter books, studying, 439–440

success, on Extended Response, 103–104

surface area, formulas for, 311, 411

Surgeon General's Report on Active Living, 390

Sutz, Richard (author)

Speed Reading For Dummies, 69

Swanson, Stephen (author)

Physical Science: What the Technology Professional Needs to Know, 400–401

synthesis questions, in Reasoning Through Language Arts (RLA) test, 67

T

tables, 123–124, 165

tabs, 22–23

Technical Stuff icon, 2

Technical Support (website), 3

test day, tips for, 443–446

test-taking strategies, 57–59

text

editing with a mouse, 450

questions about, 121–125

text passages, 67, 122, 164

textbook selections, 68

thinking positive, 445

time

for each GED test section, 57

using wisely, 57–58

time management

arriving early, 444

for Mathematical Reasoning test, 211

for Science test, 171

for Social Studies test, 129–130

Tip icon, 2

titles, on graphs, diagrams and maps, 165, 166

topics

practicing writing on, 104

Science test, 158–160

total cost formula, 311, 411

traditional multiple-choice questions, 76–77

transition sentence, 106

trapezoid, area of, 311, 411

Trefil, James (author)

The Sciences: An Integrated Approach, 3rd Edition, 393–394, 397–398

triangle, area and perimeter of, 311, 411

Tubman, Harriet, 138–139

Twain, Mark (author)

The Adventures of Tom Sawyer, 347–348

"Votes for Women" speech, 259

U

U.S. Constitution, 259, 262

U.S. Department of Energy/Pacific Northwest National Laboratory, 394

U.S. Department of Labor (website), 181

U.S. founding documents, in RLA test, 10

U.S. History For Dummies (Wiegand), 128, 133–134, 137, 139–141, 142–143, 145–146, 440

U.S. Surgeon General (website), 176

usage, in Reasoning Through Language Arts (RLA) test, 65–66

V

vertical axis, on graphs, 165

visual materials, questions about, 121–125, 164–167

visualization, 441

volume, formulas for, 311, 411

"Votes for Women" speech (Twain), 259

W

Waldinger, Robert (professor), 233–234

Warning! icon, 2

The Wealth of Nations (Smith), 141–142

websites

Australian War Memorial, 146–147

Cheat Sheet, 3

CIA (Central Intelligence Agency), 138, 348–349

EPA (Environmental Protection Agency), 175, 176, 180, 182–183, 184–185, 191–192

Federal Government Jobs, 168

free sample tests, 71–72

GED Testing Service, 8, 15, 51–52

NASA, 170, 176–177, 178, 186–187, 392, 398–399

NASA's Earth Observatory, 181, 183–184

NASA's Glenn Research Center, 174, 178, 179

NASA's Jet Propulsion Laboratory, 177

NASA's Science, 177, 183, 184

National Oceanic and Atmospheric Administration, 181–182

National Science Foundation, 183

Occupational Safety & Health Administration, 181, 187

practice tests, 51–52

Project Gutenberg, 347–348

Science test resources, 161

special accommodations, 14

Surgeon General, 390

Technical Support, 3

U.S. Department of Energy/Pacific Northwest National Laboratory, 394

About the Author

For over 30 years, Tim Collins, PhD, has specialized in materials development for the GED, and his books and media publications have helped countless learners pass this life-changing test.

Altogether, he has worked in the field of education for over 40 years, and he has taught learners of all ages and backgrounds from early childhood to adult. He began his career as a high school teacher in Morocco, where, as part of a school-wide improvement program, he helped his school reduce the number of dropouts while aiding school-leavers to pass the required graduation test. As a result of this community-wide effort, the graduation rate increased from one of the lowest in the country to one of the highest. Since then, he has taught young children in Spain; university students in China, Spain, and the United States; and adult learners in the United States. Beginning in 1987, he began to specialize in materials development and worked for several major educational publishers.

Tim knows the challenges of pursuing education as an adult. While working full time, he completed his PhD at the University of Texas at Austin. After that, he worked as a professor at a major U.S. college of education for 15 years, where he helped prepare teachers to meet the challenges of today's elementary, middle school, and high school classrooms. Tim currently manages international education programs in 11 countries in West and Central Africa while continuing to develop materials that give adult learners the skills they need to succeed.

Dedication

This book is dedicated to adult learners everywhere. *You can do it!*

Author's Acknowledgments

Many people played key roles in the development of this newest edition, which has been thoroughly updated to reflect the latest changes to the GED test. I owe a debt of gratitude to several people at Wiley, including Victoria Anllo, Tim Gallan, Chrissy Guthrie, Marylouise Wiack, Kristie Pyles, and Elizabeth Stilwell. The eagle eye of copy editor Marylouise Wiack made every page better. I'd also like to thank my agent, Grace Freedson, for her constant support. This book is inspired by the life and work of Malcolm Knowles and by adult educator par excellence Julia Child. Finally, no acknowledgement would be complete without thanking Mary Jane Maples, who got me started in educational publishing so many years ago.

Publisher's Acknowledgments

Acquisitions Editor: Elizabeth Stilwell

Development Editor: Christina Guthrie

Copy Editor: Marylouise Wiack

Managing Editor: Kristie Pyles

Production Editor: Tamilmani Varadharaj

Cover Image: © fizkes/Shutterstock